THE WORLD OF INDICA

CW00544127

The twenty-first century has seen a f _____ ... ...
use of quantitative knowledge for governing social life after its explosion in the 1980s. Indicators and rankings play an increasing role in
the way governmental and non-governmental organizations distribute
attention, make decisions and allocate scarce resources. Quantitative
knowledge promises to be more objective and straightforward as well as
more transparent and open for public debate than qualitative knowledge,
thus producing more democratic decision-making. However, we know
little about the social processes through which this knowledge is constituted nor its effects. Understanding how such numeric knowledge is produced and used is increasingly important as proliferating technologies of
quantification alter modes of knowing in subtle and often unrecognized
ways. This book explores the implications of the global multiplication
of indicators as a specific technology of numeric knowledge production
used in governance.

RICHARD ROTTENBURG holds a Chair in Anthropology at Martin
Luther University of Halle-Wittenberg, Germany. His research focuses
on the anthropology of law, organization, science and technology
(LOST).

SALLY ENGLE MERRY is Silver Professor of Anthropology at New York
University and a Faculty Director of the Center for Human Rights and
Global Justice at the New York University School of Law.

SUNG-JOON PARK is a lecturer at the Institute for Anthropology of
Leipzig University.

JOHANNA MUGLER is a lecturer at the Institute for Social Anthropology
at the University of Bern.

CAMBRIDGE STUDIES IN LAW AND SOCIETY

Cambridge Studies in Law and Society aims to publish the best scholarly work on legal discourse and practice in its social and institutional contexts, combining theoretical insights and empirical research.

The fields that it covers are: studies of law in action; the sociology of law; the anthropology of law; cultural studies of law, including the role of legal discourses in social formations; law and economics; law and politics; and studies of governance. The books consider all forms of legal discourse across societies, rather than being limited to lawyers' discourses alone.

The series editors come from a range of disciplines: academic law; socio-legal studies; sociology; and anthropology. All have been actively involved in teaching and writing about law in context.

Series editors

Chris Arup *Monash University, Victoria*

Sally Engle Merry *New York University*

Susan Silbey *Massachusetts Institute of Technology*

A list of books in the series can be found at the back of this book.

THE WORLD OF INDICATORS

The Making of Governmental Knowledge through Quantification

Edited by

Richard Rottenburg,
Sally E. Merry,
Sung-Joon Park
and
Johanna Mugler

CAMBRIDGE
UNIVERSITY PRESS

CAMBRIDGE
UNIVERSITY PRESS

University Printing House, Cambridge CB2 8BS, United Kingdom

Cambridge University Press is part of the University of Cambridge.

It furthers the University's mission by disseminating knowledge in the pursuit of education, learning and research at the highest international levels of excellence.

www.cambridge.org
Information on this title: www.cambridge.org/9781107086227

© Cambridge University Press 2015

This publication is in copyright. Subject to statutory exception and to the provisions of relevant collective licensing agreements, no reproduction of any part may take place without the written permission of Cambridge University Press.

First published 2015

Printed in the United States of America by Sheridan Books, Inc.

A catalogue record for this publication is available from the British Library

Library of Congress Cataloguing in Publication data
The world of indicators : the making of governmental knowledge through quantification / edited by Richard Rottenburg, Sally E. Merry, Sung-Joon Park and Johanna Mugler.
   pages   cm
Includes index.
ISBN 978-1-107-08622-7 (hardback) – ISBN 978-1-107-45083-7 (paperback)
1. Social indicators.   2. Economic indicators.   3. Social policy.   4. Social planning – Statistical methods.   5. Public administration – Statistical methods.
I. Rottenburg, Richard, editor.
HN25.W66   2015
306 – dc23   2015021713

ISBN 978-1-107-08622-7 Hardback
ISBN 978-1-107-45083-7 Paperback

Cambridge University Press has no responsibility for the persistence or accuracy of URLs for external or third-party internet websites referred to in this publication, and does not guarantee that any content on such websites is, or will remain, accurate or appropriate.

CONTENTS

FIGURES

TABLES

ABBREVIATIONS

ABS	Asset-Backed Security
ALMA	African Leaders Malaria Alliance
CCVI	climate change vulnerability indicator
CDS	Credit Default Swap
CHMT	Council Health Management Team
CIF	Climate Investment Funds
DEB	double-entry book-keeping
DLA	Department of Land Affairs (South Africa)
GDP	Gross Domestic Product
GFATM	Global Fund to Fight AIDS, Tuberculosis and Malaria
HDI	Human Development Index
HIS	health information system
ICT	information and communication technology
IIF	Institute of International Finance
IMD	International Institute for Management Development
IPCC	Intergovernmental Panel on Climate Change
IPSA	Independent Parliamentary Standards Authority (UK)
ITN	insecticide-treated net
LIC	low-income country
LOLF	Loi organique relative aux lois de finances (Constitutional Bylaw on Budget Acts)
LVI	Livelihood Vulnerability Index
M&E	monitoring and evaluation
MBS	Mortgage-Backed Security
MDG	Millennium Development Goal
MEP	Monitoring and Evaluation Plan (Tanzania)
MERG	Monitoring and Evaluation Reference Group
MFI	microfinance institution
MIV	microfinance investment vehicle
MIX	Microfinance Information Exchange
MoH	Ministry of Health
NDPP	National Director of Public Prosecution (South Africa)
NGO	non-governmental organization
NMCP	National Malaria Control Programme

NPA	National Prosecuting Authority (South Africa)
NPM	New Public Management
NSI	national statistical institute
OMC	Open Method of Coordination
ONS	Office for National Statistics (UK)
PAT	Positive Accounting Theory
PEPFAR	US President's Emergency Program for AIDS Relief
PFMA	Public Finance Management Act 1999 (South Africa)
PMI	Presidential Malaria Initiative (Tanzania)
PPCR	Pilot Program for Climate Resilience
RBM	Roll Back Malaria
RDT	rapid diagnostic test
SPTF	Social Performance Task Force
TA	Transparency Agenda
TASO	The AIDS Support Organization
USN	US News and World Report
WEF	World Economic Forum

CONTRIBUTORS

William Davies is Senior Lecturer at Goldsmiths, University of London. He is author of *The Limits of Neoliberalism: Authority, Sovereignty and the Logic of Competition* (2014) and *The Happiness Industry: How Government and Big Business Sold Us Wellbeing* (2015).

Alain Desrosières (1940–2013) A former student of the Ecole Polytechnique in France, he was a statistician at the Institut National de la Statistique et des Etudes Economiques (INSEE) and a sociologist and historian of science at the Ecole des Hautes Etudes en Sciences Sociales (EHESS) (Paris), well known for his work in the history of statistics. He is the author of *The Politics of Large Numbers: A History of Statistical Reasoning* (1998) and other important works published in French such as *Les catégories socio-professionnelles* (with Laurent Thévenot, 2002) and *Prouver et Gouverner, Une analyse politique des statistiques publiques* (2014).

Wendy Espeland is Professor of Sociology at Northwestern University. She received her B.S. degree from Arizona State University and her Ph.D from the University of Chicago. Her current research investigates quantification as a complex social process that changes how we understand the world and how, and to whom, we cede authority. She is completing a book with Michael Sauder entitled, *Fear of Falling: How Media Rankings Changed Legal Education in America*, which analyses the effects of media rankings on higher education. She has recently published articles about quantification in the *European Journal of Sociology*, *American Sociological Review*, *American Journal of Sociology* and the *Annual Review of Law and Social Science*. She has received fellowships from the Russell Sage Foundation, Radcliffe Institute for Advanced Study and Wissenschaftskolleg zu Berlin.

Dennis Eucker is a political scientist working on adaptation to climate change, disaster risk management and sustainable development. His dissertation dealt with the relation between poverty and vulnerability to climate change in the Mekong River Delta in Vietnam. Currently he works as research coordinator and integrated expert at Catholic University of Mozambique.

Andrew Farlow is Senior Research Fellow at the Oxford Martin School of the University of Oxford, and at the Department of Zoology of the University of Oxford. After studying economics at Gonville and Caius College, Cambridge, and at Oxford, he now works on a variety of interdisciplinary projects in the areas of financial instability and global health. He has provided advice to a wide range of organizations including the World Health Organization, the Bill and Melinda Gates Foundation, UK Department for International Development and Médecins-Sans-Frontières. His most recent book *Crash and Beyond: Causes and Consequences of the Global Financial Crisis* was published in 2013.

Hannah Förster is an economist and received her Ph.D during her work at the Potsdam Institute for Climate Impact Research. During her Ph.D studies she was involved in agent-based economic modelling. As a Postdoctoral fellow she dedicated her time to studies concerning climate impacts and adaptation. During that time she became interested in the energy issue. She thus moved on to work as a senior researcher at the energy and climate division at Öko-Institut e.V. There, apart from economic analyses, she deals to a large extent with European climate policy, greenhouse gas projections, and the measuring of progress of renewable energies.

Rene Gerrets is Assistant Professor of Anthropology at the University of Amsterdam. Building on his doctoral thesis entitled 'Globalizing International Health: The Cultural Politics of "Partnership" in Tanzanian Malaria Control', which explored the rise of partnership as a dominant ideology and organizational form in the field of international health, Gerrets' ongoing research uses malaria as a lens for exploring how performance-based assessment is shaping contemporary health governance in East African settings. Anchored in Tanzania, a second line of research examines how biomedical institutions established during the colonial era generate memory through the material traces they left behind.

Barbara Grimpe received a Ph.D in Sociology from the University of Constance, Germany, based on a multi-sited ethnography of public debt management with UNCTAD in Geneva/Switzerland, as well as Argentina, Indonesia and Burkina Faso. Since then she has worked on interdisciplinary projects conducting empirical research on trust in microfinance (University of Zurich) and responsible innovation (University of Oxford). Selected publication: B. Grimpe, M. Hartswood and M. Jirotka, 'Towards a Closer Dialogue Between Policy and Practice: Responsible Design in HCI', *Proceedings of the SIGCHI Conference on Human Factors in Computing Systems* (2014) 2965–74.

Sally Engle Merry is Silver Professor of Anthropology at New York University and a faculty director of the Center for Human Rights and Global Justice at the New York University School of Law. Her recent books include *Colonizing Hawai'i: The Cultural Power of Law* (2000), which received the 2001 J. Willard Hurst Prize from the Law and Society Association; *Human Rights and Gender Violence: Translating International Law into Local Justice* (2006); *The Practice of Human Rights: Tracking Law between the Local and the Global* (co-edited with Mark Goodale, Cambridge University Press, 2007); and *Gender Violence: A Cultural Perspective* (2009). She has authored or edited five other books, most recently *Governance by Indicators* (2012), and published over 100 articles and reviews. In 2007, she received the Kalven Prize of the Law and Society Association, an award that recognizes a significant body of scholarship in the field. In 2010, she was awarded the J.I. Staley Prize from the School of Advanced Research for *Human Rights and Gender Violence*, an award 'for a book that exemplifies outstanding scholarship and writing in anthropology'. In 2013, she received the honorary degree of Doctor of Law, *honoris causa* from McGill University, Montreal.

Johanna Mugler is a Social Anthropologist. She is an assistant professor at the chair for Political and Legal Anthropology at the Department of Social Anthropology at the University of Bern, Switzerland and member of the International Max Planck Research School on Retaliation, Mediation and Punishment at the Max Planck Institute for Social Anthropology in Halle, Germany. Johanna earned her postgraduate degrees at the Ludwig-Maximilian University in Munich and at the University of Cape Town. She did her Ph.D at the Martin Luther University Halle-Wittenberg with a doctoral thesis entitled *By Their Own Account: An Ethnography of (Quantitative) Accountability and* *the National Prosecuting Authority in South Africa* (submitted August 2014, defence eminent). Currently she is conducting field research in London, Paris and Switzerland for her post-doctoral work in which she explores the fiscal accountabilities of global taxpayers and the emergence of new international business taxation norms and standards.

Boris Orlowsky obtained his Ph.D from the Potsdam Institute for Climate Impact Research. He continued his career as a Post-doctoral fellow and Senior Scientist at ETH Zurich, working on climate extremes and their socio-economic impacts. He is currently at Helvetas Swiss Intercooperation, where he applies climate science in the field of development cooperation.

Sung-Joon Park is Lecturer at the Institute for Anthropology of Leipzig University. He has been a doctoral student at the Department for Anthropology of the University of Halle and the Max Planck Institute for Social Anthropology in Halle. He received his Ph.D from the University of Halle with a thesis entitled *Pharmaceutical Government: An Ethnography of Stock-Outs and the Institutionalization of Antiretroviral Therapy in Uganda.* His research focuses on biomedicine and science in Uganda and the larger African context. His recent publications include *Travelling Models in African Conflict Management: Translating Technologies of Social Ordering* (co-edited with Andrea Behrends and Richard Rottenburg, 2014).

Theodore M. Porter is Professor of History at the University of California, Los Angeles. His books include *Trust in Numbers: The Pursuit of Objectivity in Science and Public Life* (1995) and *Karl Pearson: The Scientific Life in a Statistical Age* (2006). At this moment he is perhaps not so far from finishing *The Unknown History of Human Heredity*, a book that will emphasize the key role of insane asylums and the data they collected in the history of eugenics and human genetics. His chapter for this volume links to a long-term interest in the political economy of numbers and the contradictions of quantification.

Richard Rottenburg holds a chair in anthropology at the University of Halle and is Heuss-Professor at the New School for Social Research in New York for the academic year 2014/15. He directs a research group focusing on the anthropology of law, organization, science and technology (LOST Research Group). He has written numerous journal articles, books and edited volumes on economic anthropology, networks of formal organizations, the making of objectivity, biomedicine and governmentality, the making of anthropology, and on theorizing translation, experimentalization, quantification and governance. At the heart of his current work, inspired by renditions of pragmatist social theory, are the emergence of material-semantic orderings and their institutionalization created in and through contingent ordering practices. The main objects of these inquiries are evidentiary practices (mainly experiments, test, measurements) and multilayered infrastructures, which can solidify and circulate evidence to confirm and to critique juridico-political assemblages.

Evelyn Ruppert is a Professor and Director of Research in the Department of Sociology at Goldsmiths, University of London. She was previously a Senior Research Fellow at the Centre for Research on Socio-cultural Change (CRESC) and co-convened a research theme entitled 'The Social Life of Methods'. She is currently Principal Investigator of an ESRC funded project, 'Socialising Big Data' (2013–14) and an ERC funded Consolidator Grant project, 'Peopling Europe: How Data Make a People' (ARITHMUS, 2014–19). She is also Founding and Editor-in-Chief of a new SAGE open access journal, *Big Data and Society: Critical Interdisciplinary Inquiries*, launched in June 2014.

Till Sterzel studied geography, meteorology and geoinformatics. His research focuses on the interlinkage of cities, urbanization and climate change, and on implications of global environmental change for violent conflict. He works as a scientific consultant for climate-babel, which he co-founded. Climate-babel is a network of scientists providing services around climate change research and training for practice and practitioners. Till's ongoing Ph.D thesis at the University of Potsdam and the Potsdam-Institute for Climate Impact Research develops and applies a method for globally systematizing socio-ecological vulnerabilities to global environmental change phenomena.

Anja Weber is currently writing her Ph.D at the Humboldt University in Berlin, dealing with local perceptions of the international climate change discourse. She first studied social and cultural anthropology and worked in the field of development cooperation in Vietnam, focusing on analysis of climate change impacts and adaptation strategies for local development planning.

Olaf Zenker is Junior Professor at the Institute of Social and Cultural Anthropology, Freie Universität Berlin. Previously, he was Ambizione Research Fellow (SNSF) at the Institute of Social Anthropology, University of Bern. Holding master degrees in social anthropology (LSE) and linguistics and literature (University of Hamburg), he received his Ph.D from the Martin Luther University in Halle, where he was a doctoral student and post-doctoral fellow at the Max Planck Institute for Social Anthropology. Focusing on South Africa and Northern Ireland, his research has dealt with issues of statehood, the rule of law, modernity, conflict and identity formations, sociolinguistics and anthropological epistemologies. His recent co-edited and authored books include: *Transition and Justice: Negotiating the Terms of New Beginnings in Africa* (2015); *Irish/ness is All Around Us: Language Revivalism and the Culture of Ethnic Identity in Northern Ireland* (2013); and *Beyond Writing Culture: Current Intersections of Epistemologies and Representational Practices* (2010).

CHAPTER ONE

A WORLD OF INDICATORS: THE MAKING OF GOVERNMENTAL KNOWLEDGE THROUGH QUANTIFICATION

Richard Rottenburg and Sally Engle Merry

INTRODUCTION

Why another contribution to metrology?

There is something new about the use of quantitative knowledge for governing social life in the twenty-first century.[1] In the words of Alain Desrosières in this volume, 'the recent extension of the use of [such] indicators by New Public Management raises new questions and introduces a discontinuity in the longstanding traditional usage of statistics by governments, which dates back to the eighteenth century'.

From the United Nations' efforts to improve the statistical capacity of resource-poor countries to local school districts' penchant for measuring children's achievements in order to evaluate teachers, governance increasingly requires numerical data. Quantitative evidence is seen as essential for developing reasonable policy at local, national and international levels. The promise of evidence-based policy-making is that it is not only more objective and less prone to misuse, but also more transparent, more democratic, and more open to public debate than decisions taken by politicians and business leaders with reference to qualitative forms of knowing. Yet, the creation of these systems is rarely

---

[1] This volume goes back to a workshop held in October 2011 in Halle, Germany, at the Max Planck Institute for Social Anthropology. The conference was titled 'A World of Indicators: Knowledge Technologies of Regulation, Domination, Experimentation and Critique in an Interconnected World' and was organized by Johanna Mugler and Sung-Joon Park of the LOST-Group situated at Halle University and directed by Richard Rottenburg. Most authors of this volume participated at the workshop. Amy Field Craven substantially improved the clarity and accessibility of arguments by editing the chapters in this volume written by authors whose native language is not English.

transparent or public. The rapid development and proliferation of more and more sophisticated measurement and quantification systems pose crucial questions about how knowledge produced by measurement and quantification influences the ways we set the norms we wish to follow, the technologies and instruments we regard as indispensable for organising collective life, and the role numeric representation should play in contemporary world orders (Rottenburg 2000; Espeland and Stevens 2008; Heintz 2010; Merry 2011).

The broad field of numeric representation – here used synonymously with quantification and with measurement as the translation of (assumed) realities into numbers – includes various elementary forms of counting and measuring along with several increasingly sophisticated forms of aggregating numbers. As a study in metrology, this book focuses on the making and use of indicators as one of these forms. The word 'index' is often used for aggregated indicators but also frequently synonymously with 'indicator' and hence refers to the same type of numeric representation. Indicators and indexes used in governance are a particular form of quantification that focuses primarily on finding an answer to policy questions such as: 'Is our intervention making an impact? Is this the impact we want?'. Our book thus explores the implications of the global proliferation of the indicator as a specific technology of numeric knowledge production relevant to governance. It includes theoretical discussions of the nature and historical formation of quantification and the link of indicators to neoliberalism, as well as case studies of processes of commensuration, quantification and indicator creation in the fields of global finance and local microfinance, public health, malaria control, criminal justice, public statistics, climate change, political accountability and access to land. The collection interrogates processes through which numeric data is generated, analysed and shaped into quantitative summary representations of otherwise hidden realities by means of indicators.

Understanding how such numeric knowledge is produced and used is increasingly important, as proliferating technologies of quantification alter modes of knowing in intricate ways that mostly go unobserved. As global interconnections increase, the demand for readily comparable and accessible knowledge escalates. While it remains difficult and problematic to provide adequate knowledge of social, economic, cultural and political variation across the world, simplified, quantitative knowledge promises a solution to the need to know about the world and offers a guide to action under conditions of rapid globalization and high uncertainty. A corporation that wishes to build a factory in another country, a university that seeks to plant a centre in another country, a retailer that tries to develop a new market, or a non-governmental organization (NGO) that advocates for children's rights, all face the challenge of understanding new social and cultural spaces. Comparative knowledge of all relevant sites is essential yet hard to acquire. Simple, readily comparable quantitative propositions and various forms of aggregated numeric representations facilitate the ability of organizations and individuals to navigate complex and disorienting situations.

Parallel to the increase of global interconnections, a world-wide enforcement of neoliberal forms of governance has been taking place since the 1980s, and more forcefully since the end of the Cold War and the disaggregation of the Soviet empire. This induced an explosion of calculative practices and forms geared towards the control of cost efficiency and the economic viability of accountable units – an operation which, as the chapters of this book show, is less straightforward than it sometimes seems. This proliferation of calculative practices caused an increase in the development and use of quantification, primarily in the form of indicators and rankings that are intended to ensure that the most economical solutions have been chosen and that they are permanently in control, even in spaces where the conventional demand-and-supply mechanism does not work or is not supposed to work. The new importance quantification and mainly indicators gained in the 1980s was part of a radical redefinition of the relations between democracy and market that implied a shift in the definitions of liberty and governance. This process continues to evolve and has gained new momentum since the beginning of the twenty-first century.

However, we still know relatively little about the social processes through which this knowledge is constituted or the kinds of effects it has. Even as it grows in significance with the move toward evidence-based governance, our understanding of the social formation of quantitative knowledge and its contribution to governance is limited. There are clearly practices of falsifying data, of gaming indicators, and of presenting deliberately misleading information through statistics, but these are not the central concern of this book. The goal of this collection is to consider the production of numeric knowledge as such with the assumption that it constitutes a practice that cuts across most domains of social life. What are the particularities, opportunities and constraints of this form of knowledge? How is it limited or enhanced by

3

the availability of what kinds of data or the use of what kinds of expertise? Are there systemic inequalities and misrecognitions in the production of global quantitative knowledge? The book focuses on how the processes of quantification, even as they seek to generate reliable information, nevertheless encode particular cultural understandings, political interests and ontologies. What to quantify, how to name it, how to make diverse phenomena commensurable, how to aggregate elementary data, and how to present the results to various publics depend on practices and forms of knowing that are embedded in institutions of power and professional education. The production of indicators depends not only on expert opinion or on the relevant epistemic community but also on administrative infrastructures that collect and process data and on the larger institutional setup of which they are part. Successful indicators, i.e. indicators that are widely used and have important impacts, are typically backed by powerful institutionalized organizations (in the sense of Meyer and Rowan 1977) and present knowledge that conforms to prevailing ideas about the world, often based on previously established templates and models of information gathering and presentation. How exactly this is done, and within what institutional frameworks and which structures of power and expertise, are pathways which remain largely unexamined.

Quantification privileges the perspectives of those with infrastructural, financial and professional resources and experience in the production of large-scale numeric knowledge over those who do not have these resources. However, there is also an old and close link between statistics and reform. Statistics are central to industrial capitalist states' efforts to design support structures that counteract and neutralize those market mechanisms that systemically exclude people designated as temporarily or permanently unnecessary in the labour force (Hacking 1990; Desrosières 1998: chapters 5 and 6). Currently, grassroots and advocacy groups and other non-state actors try to employ the high credibility of numeric evidence to promote alternative understandings of dominant institutions (Hetherington 2011; Bruno et al. 2014). Indicators have become powerful advocacy tools. They are invaluable for drawing attention to problems such as poverty, disease, low access to infrastructure, violence against women globally or discrimination against racial minorities in court processes. Statistical data is an effective way of making the problems of vulnerable populations visible and in need of redress. Moreover, quantitative data is critically important in exposing corruption and abuse of power. While the making of numeric evidence still presupposes substantial calculative resources, this knowledge technology increasingly can be harnessed in many ways.

The book examines indicators as a globally circulating knowledge technology that can be used to quantify, compare and rank virtually any complex field of human affairs. However, definitions of what to quantify and which methodological approaches should be used to capture different facets of public life through indicators are far from self-evident. Intense negotiations and contestations occur about these issues, but these seldom appear in public discourse. Instead indicators are typically presented as taken-for-granted facts. Yet, indicators are not neutral representations of the world, but novel epistemic objects of regulation, domination, experimentation and critique. They mainly appear in the domains of law, economics, health-care, education, and throughout state administration.

By following the scientific and political construction of indicators as they propagate and stabilize specific ideas and models of social and economic change, the book examines the production of indicators and the authority they convey. It explores the varieties in scope, sophistication, flexibility, accuracy, costs and payoff in the use of indicators. It examines their logics and assumptions as well as their circulation as a means of organizing and shaping or challenging modern institutions and social life. This includes examining the effects of differences in narrative, visual or numerical presentations of knowledge. This analysis raises questions about the nature of the publics or the organizational audiences that are imagined when different data representation schemes are selected.

Analysing the politics of quantification and particularly the rise of indicators in global governance exposes subtle transformations in contemporary processes of globalization. These transformations reveal important characteristics of the contemporary entanglements of science and politics that affect forms of public life. At the core of this entanglement is an emerging controversy about the kind of evidentiary practices that are accepted as accurate and reliable to inform public reasoning and political decision-making (see Alain Desrosières, Chapter 13). The workings of 'mechanical objectivity' as examined by Theodore Porter (1995) and of 'meta-codes' as analysed by Richard Rottenburg (2009a; orig. 2002) have, during the last fifty years or so, infiltrated many domains of life up to a point where they start to become increasingly controversial. The perhaps most prominent domain where the increasing importance of indicators became contentious and scandalized is finance and banking after the dramatic crisis of 2008 (see Andrew Farlow, Chapter 9).

SOME CONTEXT FOR QUANTIFICATION

Particularly since the seminal contributions to metrology by Alain Desrosières, Ian Hacking and Theodore Porter (frequently quoted in this introduction), it is generally accepted that capitalist economies, democratic politics and modern societies are inconceivable without numeric representation in the running of affairs. Statistics and accounting have emerged as key forms of knowledge production and technologies of governance of industrialized states; probability theory, random sampling, market ideology and the democratic welfare state have co-evolved around the notion that independent agents choose freely and yet – in aggregate – predictably (see also Krüger, Daston and Heidelberger 1987). Since the 1980s the use of numeric representations has spread into broader social spheres, due mainly to neoliberal reforms and marketization processes such as performance-related funding of public service providers, privatization of public infrastructures, the spread of so-called New Public Management (NPM) and benchmarking. Trends of 'responsibilization' (such as Corporate Social Responsibility), 'projectification', 'NGO-ization', 'certification' and 'multistakeholder governance' (Bruno and Didier 2013) are related phenomena that partly result from neoliberal structural changes of capitalism and to some extent critically react to them. These transformations have vast implications not only for relations between state, economy and civil society, but also for relations between wealthy and poor countries around the globe.

From its beginnings, modernity had an affinity between governance and evidence accessible to the public, as Foucault's work demonstrates (Foucault 1966). This evidence tended to be numeric because of emerging understandings of objectivity and easy accessibility for the public. Questions like where to build a road, a railway, a school, a hospital, a waste disposal site, or how and for what ends to use taxes invited answers based on numeric evidence. Neoliberal governance, as we have known it since the 1980s, maintains this frame, but turns it toward different questions and answers. The creation of numeric evidence has migrated from the realm of government of the state to that of independent agents (corporations, civil society organizations, NGOs, international organizations and social activists). The latter produce their own quantifications as they compete for resources (in performance-related funding, for example). Thus, numeric evidence becomes linked to the idioms of subsidiarity, self-monitoring, self-auditing and responsibility. Situated within a discourse of increased civic freedom, control has partly become a matter of self-control and was interpreted as a shift away from petrified and unjust old structures of domination that privileged only a few, towards more democracy, freedom to choose, participation and transparency. The relations between democracy, freedom and market were fundamentally redesigned.

Numeric representation in governance, first of all, consists of methodologies to achieve two main political purposes: (1) to simplify complexity in order to come to a conclusion and be able to act collectively or in the name of a collective, and, in doing so, (2) to demonstrate adherence to public responsibility and absence of personal or group bias. Political decisions often imply the distribution of public money and affect access to public services. Therefore they must claim – and if necessary prove – to be rational and just, and must therefore be achieved transparently, based on evidence that, again, must be produced through established procedures and standards, which always imply the use of technical expertise. Political decisions also often refer to future developments which are hard to anticipate, let alone anticipate in sufficient detail, and yet political programmes are evaluated for their competence and responsibility to prevent potential damage. In this context, numeric representation as a form of exploration and data mining, guided by theoretically informed models for how to translate uncertainty into risk, plays a crucial role.

Quantification is fundamentally about creating units that can be counted and described numerically with the aim of putting them in some order. The practice of ordering is useful for predicting developments and for designing interventions based on an appropriate understanding of the inherent logic of this order. This implies the redefinition of existing classifications or the creation of new ones (in terms of ordering things in social space, such as gender-disaggregated labour statistics) and often the redefinition of existing or the creation of new time units (ordering things in time, such as in the application of performance indicators with regard to the phases of a project).

Through measurement the world becomes knowable without distracting details, neatly compartmentalized and ordered, and knowable at a distance. Things that at first appeared incommensurable can be made commensurable. Through numeric representation, one always

7

loses some aspects of the reality in question but gains others that were invisible before quantification. Numeric representation lends itself to the generation of comparisons and rankings of known phenomena, but also to the re-arrangement of data collected for some other purposes into endless new alternative configurations that enable the detection of previously unseen interconnections. Established forms are mostly simple, unambiguous and easy to understand, or at least they appear to be. In fact, they may be too naively presumed by some publics to be clear and easy to understand. Once quantifications are well established in public debates, they tend to hide the theoretical and normative assumptions inscribed in them and the complexities, messiness and contingencies that went into their making. While this observation can partly be *deduced* from the very nature and purpose of quantification as a mode of doing objectivity and 'thin description', and can partly be *induced* from empirical examinations of what 'counts' as strong evidence in public debates, it is rarely true for those who make indicators or closely work with them (see e.g., Sung-Joon Park, Chapter 8). Some of the more recent quantifications that are becoming established and gaining importance in political debate are indexes of rather complex and vast phenomena, such as the HDI (Human Development Index, UNDP), the HPI (Human Poverty Index, UNDP), RoLI (Rule of Law Index, World Justice Project), or the GII (Gender Inequality Index, UNDP).

One particularly important form of quantification in the neoliberal context is the design of experiments aimed at identifying the factors that affect a certain situation or development. Here, quantification is not about ordering things in social space and time per se, but instead about identifying correlations, such as those discovered through randomized trials in development economics. It aims above all to prove the existence of a correlation statistically and is achieved through projects that test the assumptions upon which they were designed in the first place. Hence, these projects are defined and run as experiments to test an intervention and, at the same time, to collect data on the impact the intervention has. Interventions as controlled experiments for the purpose of generating numeric data start from a known and given state of affairs considered to be problematic, and proceed towards the identification of unknown correlations, as in epidemiology. The HIV/AIDS pandemic, for example, became the prototype for a specific way of measuring. At first only the symptoms were known, but statistical analyses later exposed the correlations. This helped to set medical research on the causes of the symptoms in the right direction so that the causes could then be identified in the lab. When a potential treatment was identified in the lab, further testing and treatment became synonymous. Finally, a specific protocol, in which the intervention became part of the trial, was accepted as the norm in many fields outside the HIV crisis (Rottenburg 2009b) and currently is part of the attempts to curb the Ebola crisis of 2014 in Sierra Leone, Liberia and Guinea.

In another version of quantification as trial, one starts from knowing the end and to some extent also the causes of a problem, but not the means to achieve the end, such as poverty alleviation. Here large intervention programmes are divided into single projects that are monitored in terms of cost development, effectiveness, unintended consequences, and milestones structured around achievement indicators, all orchestrated by the 'Logical Framework Approach'. The 'MIT Poverty Action Lab' illustrates this approach well.[2] Normally it follows a distinct pattern. At the beginning, there are two statistically equivalent groups. One group receives, for example, a water purification system and the other does not. Certain observed differences can be attributed to the presence or absence of the water purification programme. In other words, experimentality has replaced older forms of modern, melioristic interventions. Statistics is at the heart of this type of procedure.

A crucial difference between large-scale state interventions typically understood to be the hallmark of modernity and newer neoliberal experiments to design evidence-based melioristic interventions is the way they conceive of time. Heroic interventions of modernity, based on the narrative of progress, describe the future as something that can be known and shaped in such a way that it will be an improvement on the present. For most current neoliberal interventions, however, the future is unknown and risky. Accordingly, interventions only envisage the next step beyond what they have done, rather than a long trajectory of improvement.

However, there are other forms of quantification that remained at least partly unaffected by the spread of experimentality and the postmodern caution about the future. Relatively open explorations are often run by centralized, permanent infrastructures established for a particular problem. They collect heterogeneous sets of data, aggregate and correlate them and design new quantifications of diverse

[2] See www.povertyactionlab.org.

complexities in the frame of permanent projects with open questions. The US National Oceanic and Atmospheric Administration is one of many examples; the European Epidemic Intelligence Information System for Sexually Transmitted Infections (EPIS STI) is another one.[3]

Non-experimental, decentralized, non-hierarchical and participative explorations are increasingly facilitated by the rapid development of the Internet and the increasing speed and capacity of computing as a numeric infrastructure. Web 2.0 platforms, often aiming at lay mass participation, generate a new type of information gathering based on quantification through rigid forms of standardization for the purpose of crowdsourcing. The platform 'Geocommons'[4] is one successful example of this new type of measurement, and the 'Extreme Citizen Science Blog'[5] another one. While these new forms of lay expertise in processes of quantification are partly an expression of an increasing scepticism towards the type of institutionalized expertise implied in political decision-making, at the same time, they strongly reinforce the power of measurement and massively contribute to its spread into all sectors of life. They also reinforce the ideology that the market-type aggregations of individual choices to establish the common good and even the general will (in the emphatic sense of Rousseau's *volonté general*) can function as a democratic control mechanism for genuine political forms of decision-making. However, crowdsourcing is not necessarily more accurate or reliable than other, politically controlled forms of measurement and it is not necessarily more participative or even emancipatory. If, for instance, the American application for smartphones called 'Yelp' assists people in finding a restaurant that best corresponds with their location, taste and pocket, this might be a useful extension of a market mechanism. Yet, with another American application called 'Sketch Factor', a new quality of quantification emerges.[6] 'Sketch Factor' aims to offer people in urban spaces information about secure and insecure routes in terms of crime rates and other forms of 'sketchiness' without relying on official statistics generated by the institutions in charge. In most cities 'Sketch Factor' primarily generates the information solely from the users of the app by crowdsourcing. Similar to the logics of rumour, this information brings to life what it pretends to depict and shapes political life as if it was a market space. 'Sketch Factor' does what

[3] See http://ecdc.europa.eu/en/activities/surveillance/sti/Pages/epis_sti.aspx.
[4] See http://geocommons.com.   [5] See http://uclexcites.wordpress.com.
[6] See www.sketchfactor.com.

neoliberal ideology promises: to generate participation and even control over government institutions run by mechanisms inspired by market logics.[7]

In sum, numeric representations of various forms have become the
most robust mode of making objective arguments in public life. This
is mostly because quantification best translates the political into the
neutral and technical and offers the most effective meta-code for understanding across social, cultural and disciplinary boundaries. In this book
we examine technologies of quantification in the making of governmental knowledge in globalized contexts through a series of case studies
and theoretical papers.

TECHNOLOGIES OF QUANTIFICATION IN THE MAKING OF GOVERNMENTAL KNOWLEDGE

Despite the fact that they are designed to produce scientific objectivity,
forms of quantification never simply reflect the world. Instead, they are
the product of a series of interpretive decisions about what to quantify,
how to categorize, and how to label it. The more diverse and less countable the phenomenon being quantified, the more difficult and weighty
these decisions are. Some indicators are more accurate in representing
a phenomenon than others, but interpretation underlies all quantification systems. If the goal is to quantify the rule of law, for example, there
are clearly significant challenges in defining what that is, finding criteria
that describe it, and matching existing data to those criteria. It is likely
that those developing the measure will base their conception of the rule
of law on principles familiar to them from their own nomos-sphere.
They are also likely to rely on the experiences and quantifications of
previous teams of 'experts' who have worked on defining the rule of law.
Moreover, the quantification process will be constrained by the kinds of
data and the resources that are available, which in turn is the product
of what states and private organizations have decided to quantify and

---

[7] Under the larger theme widely debated as 'smart policing' it is mainly police departments who try
to improve law enforcement by various attempts to integrate more and more, and more sophisticated data analysis systems for better monitoring, prevention and police intervention. These
systems are necessarily based on highly standardized numeric information with all its implications debated in this volume; see e.g., the cooperation between Palantir (a private software
company) and the Los Angeles Police Department, available at www.palantir.com/solutions/
law-enforcement. The illustration on the cover of this book critically exposes what the communication of certain numeric representations and their visualizations bring about in terms of
civic ordering.

to invest in converting into numeric representations. What becomes quantified is often the product of what seems to be a problem. The very act of numeric representation encodes particular concerns and puts constraints on the kinds of information that are available. While certain problems and hidden connections are made visible through refined modes of quantification, others remain hidden or even become invisibilized.

The essence of quantification systems is commensuration and comparison. To gather data, it is essential to make things commensurable: to decide on a principle of similarity so that things can be grouped together, counted and calculated. Only when that is established can data be transformed into information, and in a further step, information transformed into knowledge. There are three logical steps in the making of useful data, although in practice they do not necessarily occur in logical sequence but through iterative processes that can start at any point or can take several steps at the same time.

(1) Create equivalences across different cases. In a logically first step, an object of analysis and some equivalence has to be created across all the individual instances this object can adopt. This requires finding a commonality among individual instances, a shared trait, and ignoring differences. For example, if the researcher wants to compare rates of domestic violence in different societies, it is necessary to establish equivalence across a wide range of forms of conflict within domestic situations that could include insults, humiliation, slicing car tyres, attacking pets and children, intimidation, blows, coercion, injuries, and withholding financial support, to name a few examples. These are very different actions with differing meanings within a relationship and quite different experiences, but it is necessary to see them all as manifestations of the same thing, as somehow equivalent, in order to count, measure, quantify and further calculate with them. It is essential to construct a way to make distinct individual acts equivalent as instances of one thing, in this case: of domestic violence.

Alain Desrosières (1998: 10–11) describes the process as one that 'allows a large number of events to be recorded and summarised according to standard norms'. These spaces of equivalence, he argues, normally are practical before they become cognitive so that we are dealing with a fundamentally pragmatic process. Random, unpredictable, individual behaviour is converted into patterns and averages and becomes regular and predictable through the statistical summary of these acts. Once this construction is accepted, as in the case of the idea of the 'average man', it becomes a real thing, and in this sense we are dealing with a fundamentally performative practice that still has enormous predictive power (Osborne and Rose 2003).

(2) *Develop categories*. In a logically second step, categories have to be defined and organized into a system of classifications, i.e. into a taxonomy, so that all things belong in one or the other class which ideally are mutually exclusive and encompassing. The creation of categories implies the drawing of boundaries and is about the general in the particular or, in other words, about the question of how to move from the individual case to the general through the construction of consistent equivalence classes. At the same time the creation of categories is part of the ancient debate about the controversial divide between realism and nominalism. However, the important question for numeric representation in governance is not whether classification is a form of realism, assuming that the classes are an expression of the order of nature, or whether classification is a form of nominalism, contending that its classes are constructions. This dichotomy rather seems misguided and certainly misguides the issue at hand. The claim of realism is not simply a weakness to be overcome by following the constructivist line, but it is rather a juridico-political necessity that is here to stay as long as proofs of accountability and hence 'the pursuit of objectivity in science and public life' (the subtitle of Theodore Porter's 1995 book) are considered reasonable endeavours.

For example, domestic violence can be categorized using distinct legal categories such as rape, assault, harassment, threats; or it can be divided into categories of more or less severe violence, drawing boundaries along a continuum. Both of these categorizations make it possible to designate an action as either one category or another, and both have their essential value in discovering different dimensions of one and the same problem. While it is vital to be aware of the multiple possible ways to classify and count domestic violence and of the unavoidable arbitrariness in privileging one or the other, there are immensely negative consequences to abandoning the search for a mode of dealing with domestic violence that is valid and legitimate for all human communities. Classifications normally begin by using available local categories of distinction, but over time and in order to facilitate classification of wider fields, sometimes including the entire globe, they strive for more generic categories. For example, Bowker and Star (1999) describe how the international system of classifying causes of death moved from local conceptions of disease to more generic terms that were able to cross national boundaries.

Classifications also reflect the kinds of interests and concerns given in a society, while at the same time they shape these interests and concerns. For example, when Fiji presented its country report to the committee that monitors the women's convention, CEDAW (Convention on the Elimination of All Forms of Discrimination Against Women), its data was disaggregated by ethnicity between Fijians and Indians but not by gender. In Fijian society, the ethnic divide is politically and socially very significant, eclipsing the importance of gender in public debate. The choice of categories thus reflected this social landscape. However, as categories often change for reasons other than following changes in the social landscape, their new format will itself have an impact on the social landscape. The causation is bidirectional and thus the one cannot be deduced from the other.

The creation of categories for the purpose of statistics and governance is, after all, an arena of significant interpretive work, shaped by pre-existing categories, theoretical concerns and practical purposes. Debates recur in the history of statistical classifications about 'a sacrifice of inessential perceptions; the choice of pertinent variables; how to construct classes of equivalence; and last, the historicity of discontinuities' (Desrosières 1998: 239). Taxonomies inevitably bring things together that do not necessarily occur together and attach a common label to them, thus constituting a single category. Moreover, each category has to be applicable in all situations in which the taxonomy is meant to order things in a meaningful way. In the field of governmental knowledge in a globally interconnected world, this means primarily that categories have to work in as many locations and countries across the globe as possible. In order to understand how categories are formed, it is essential to examine the process of their creation, i.e. the practices, templates, actors and networks that together constitute the expertise to draw up comparative categories.

(3) *Code individual phenomena into categories*. In a logically third step, the individual phenomena of concern need to be coded into the categories created in steps one and two. The encoding process refers to the decision to attribute an individual case to a particular class. This decision is again quintessentially interpretive work that has to ignore or downplay certain aspects of the case and highlight others. Here cultural, social, political and technical dimensions play important roles that are

quite independent of the object to be encoded. In the end it appears that objectively given things are simply sorted out and quantified, while in fact these things only appear as objectively given and only become real as a result of having been encoded. Over time and with use, they become more established and accepted. As Alain Desrosières puts it, collective objects or aggregates of individuals thus can come to 'hold', to be accepted as real, at least for a while. He explained, 'When the actors can rely on objects thus constructed, and these objects resist the tests intended to destroy them, aggregates do exist – at least during the period and in the domain in which these practices and tests succeed' (1998: 101). In other words, if these aggregates work in an institutionalized practice, they will be accepted as real. It is their institutionalization that makes them real.

Perhaps the most important part of this stabilization through institutionalization is the increasingly dense, encompassing and complex web of cross-references between numeric forms of world-making. While one particular form of quantification might try to be as cautious and differentiated as possible towards one issue, it unavoidably cross-references several other issues by using the most simple and undifferentiated key figures and indicators (Rottenburg 2009a: 181 ff.).

In sum, this vast web of numeric representations which stabilize each other is characterized by a specific superficiality in comparison to the depth of narrative representations of reality. However, as the authors of this volume argue, most explicitly Wendy Espeland (Chapter 3) and Evelyn Ruppert (Chapter 6), numeric representations presuppose narrative forms of knowing and generate new narratives to make sense of them, since numbers, after all, do not speak for themselves. In his article, 'Thin Description' (2012), Theodore Porter compellingly demonstrates that quantifications as 'thinning practices' do not (in what others have qualified as the enormously destructive historical processes of modernization, rationalization and bureaucratization) systematically supplant deeper, narrative forms of knowing, which he calls 'thickening practices'. He rather claims that the two practices are suited to diverse circumstances (2012: 222) and evolve in the dynamic relationships between localizing and universalizing tendencies (2012: 220).

The three delineated steps in the making of useful data by classification of things in order to facilitate commensuration and comparison are, as we have shown, unavoidably interpretive processes. They are driven not only by the things to be classified, but also by what people want to know, by historically established classifications that appear as 'natural', by theoretical assumptions subject to critical reflection and by practical considerations of what is affordable, possible and what works technically.

For example, a group of activists working to develop a global survey of violence against women would want as inclusive and full a conception of violence as possible. They would be anxious to avoid non-disclosure, or situations in which women would fail to report violence. They would design a survey instrument to ask questions about how often women experienced violence in several ways and think about how to make the interview situation safe and private. UN statisticians working on the problem would have a different concern. They would want guidelines for national statistical offices that encourage states to do such surveys on their own. Thus, the goal would be to make a survey that was simple and short and would not be offensive or disturbing to the officials representing states. When, again, criminal justice organizations carry out surveys of domestic violence globally, they would count whether the victims called the police and whether they thought police did a good job. As in this example, any data collection process must also inevitably consider what can be quantified at what price. More elaborate and careful surveys, such as the first example of measuring violence against women, inevitably cost more. Using pre-existing administrative data, collected for other purposes, is usually less expensive (Merry and Coutin 2014). In their analysis of the international system of recording causes of death, Bowker and Star (1999: 102–6) make a similar point. They draw attention to the fact that often the number of categories cannot be too numerous for purposes of encoding and analysis or because they need to fit on a form that has to be well-arranged for those who have to work with it. The chapters of this volume show nicely that classifications for the purpose of quantification in the context of socio-political ordering often are primarily a technical and practical problem, solved pragmatically by practitioners and experts rather than theoreticians.

Clearly, the processes which undergird comparisons – those of building comparability of data and measurable categories – are political and social processes shaped not only by given and unchallenged assumptions and taken-for-granted taxonomies, but also by infrastructures and institutional arrangements, expertise, critical reflection, intentions, interests and resources. To understand quantification, it is necessary to look at the relevant processes of interpretation and categorization and ask questions such as: Who is doing the interpretation and classification? What are their convictions and what are their interests? Who is consulted? Who sits around the planning table? Who can speak with authority? Those with authority are typically those with experience and expertise. Such social factors influence how equivalence and classification are established.

Global surveys carry the additional burden of developing categories that can travel across various borders – infrastructural, legal, political, social, cultural borders – while remaining commensurable. This creates a paradox: the survey categories need to be translated into local terms in order to quantify local ideas and behaviour accurately, but need to retain their trans-local meanings in order to make comparisons possible across these borders. The categories must refer to the same thing wherever they are used even though the underlying phenomenon being quantified manifests itself differently in different places.

This tension has been explored by Richard Rottenburg in his analysis of processes of translation and code switching in the field of development projects (2009a). Like in any other professional field of public concern, technologies of inscription produce the facts of this domain conceived as a global organizational network (Rottenburg 2009a: 177–200). Development work, like most practices facilitated by trans-local or global networks, is seen to take place in a 'trading zone'. Inside this interstitial space a generic language or 'meta-code' is being developed by the actors that is capable of crossing boundaries and is juxtaposed to a 'cultural code', a language imagined as the province of particular socio-cultural groups. The technical language of the meta-code assumes that reality can be represented without distortion and that it can exist alongside distinct cultural codes. The meta-code is of course also situated but is pragmatically treated as universal in order to make communication in heterogeneous trading zones possible and hence allow development projects to happen (Rottenburg 2012). It is the language in which the certified, institutionalized 'reality' is being expressed; in Alain Desrosière's words, it is the language in which the spaces of equivalence are made possible, and in Theodore Porter's framework it is the realm where mechanical objectivity is allowed to operate undisturbed. There is constant switching between the codes as the various parties negotiate using the meta-code while attributing differences to the cultural code. Sally Engle Merry found a similar pattern in UN discussions about gender (another heterogeneous trading zone) in which participants assumed a universal understanding of gender identities while relegating differences to the domain of culture (Merry 2006).

Richard Rottenburg argues that the actors of a 'technical game', that part of negotiations in heterogeneous trading zones that relies on representations with universal claims, have to assume that their meta-code (their mechanical objectivity) is outside political, social and cultural frames of reference and simply founded in reality. This assumption – and this is the key point – is unavoidable for negotiations in any trading zone in order to deal with each other at all; it is the elementary way to make equivalences where there is diversity and incommensurability. Yet at the same time, the actors involved in heterogeneous trading zones normally have no difficulty in conceding, when outside the trading zone, that the value of the meta-code is limited to the zone. Attempts to finally eradicate the incoherence of a universalist claim that at the same time is not really universal but only of limited validity, is something for ambitious theories but not for people that make things 'hold together', to use the wording suggested by Alain Desrosières (1998: 9).

In a similar way, global systems of quantification assert meta-codes that claim universality even though they are products of distinct and situated negotiations, mostly embedded in national histories and loaded with a significant level of contingency. Numeric meta-codes circulate globally as technically neutral and universal technologies without reference to their situated origins. Yet, on their journeys they are ultimately translated into local situations at the moment of quantification. Here important questions of commensuration arise. The difficulty of translating categories across various boundaries – infrastructural, legal, political, social and cultural – is a core issue in this collection.

INDICATORS AS A SPECIFIC TECHNOLOGY OF QUANTIFICATION

What exactly is a quantitative indicator? It can be a simple measurement such as the Mid-Upper Arm Circumference (MUAC), a quick way to determine whether or not a child is malnourished by using a simple coloured plastic strip to measure the circumference of its arm. The circumference can be interpreted as an indicator of malnutrition by comparing the measurement to a table with the standard distribution supplying the critical values that distinguish between well nourished, poorly nourished and undernourished children. An indicator can be a particular mathematical aggregation of a few measurements, as most readers will probably know from the other end of nourishment-related problems. Obesity cannot be determined just by measuring weight; it must also be related to height, age and sex. The calculation known as BMI, body-mass-index is mass (kg) divided by the square of the height (m) while the result has then to be related to a table with the standard distribution and values distinguishing the range of normality and abnormality. The indicators and indexes discussed in this book are the product of far more complicated calculations, but the logic is the same. The Human Development Index (HDI), for instance, is an aggregation (geometrical mean) of three other indicators: (1) Life Expectancy Index (LEI); (2) Education Index (EI); and (3) Income Index (II). The calculation of the HDI hence is this:

$$HDI = \sqrt[3]{LEI \cdot EI \cdot II}$$

The implied Education Index (EI) again is a particular aggregation of Mean Years of Schooling Index (MYSI), and Expected Years of Schooling Index (EYSI). One of the more popular indicators is, of course, Gross Domestic Product (GDP) which unsurprisingly is suspected to be a poor measure of the wealth generated by a nation within a year and therefore the cause of ongoing controversies (see Alain Desrosières, Chapter 13; on the history of economic quantifications see Porter 1995: 49–72; on the invention of GDP see Speich 2013).

THEORETICAL FRAMINGS FOR QUANTIFICATION PRACTICES IN GOVERNANCE

Over the last three decades, scholars of the history and philosophy of science and technology have examined the implications of numbers and calculative practices for the construction of knowledge. Research on the history of statistics and statistical reasoning highlights how this form of knowledge provides new ways of understanding that are premised on notions of scientific objectivity (Hacking 1975; 1990; Porter 1986; 1995; Daston 1988; Desrosières 1998). These scholars argue that reliance on numerical information is a relatively modern development, dating from perhaps the seventeenth or eighteenth century. As Hacking (1990) shows, statistics were fundamental to the rise of the modern nation state and its practices of governance in the

nineteenth century. His study of the role of numbers in state formation highlights the importance of technologies such as cost-benefit
analysis in managing decisions in industrializing states. Studies on the
history of ideals of scientific objectivity and related practices in the mid-
nineteenth century and on the increasing importance of mechanical
objectivity in public, political and bureaucratic life in the early twentieth century contribute to our understanding of how numbers acquire
the connotation of providing impartial and objective knowledge
(Daston 1988; Porter 1995).

This work is complemented by research on accounting and auditing that reveals the growing importance of numbers and calculations in
everyday life. Much of this work on accounting is theoretically informed
by Michel Foucault's power/ knowledge/ discipline framework, which
highlights the power inherent in the way any knowledge is constructed,
including the knowledge which positions itself as critique. Developing
Foucault's idea of governmentality, scholars argue that accounting is
not a purely technical and neutral practice but should be perceived as a
'social and institutional practice' that fosters forms of disciplinary power
(Miller, Hopper and Laughlin 1991; Hopwood and Miller 1994; Mennicken and Vollmer 2007; Espeland and Vannebo 2007). Peter Miller
(2001) argues that such calculative practices are fundamental to forms
of governance. Social studies of accounting and auditing argue that
we are now living in an 'audit culture' or facing an 'audit explosion',
as these calculative practices have come to typify modern society and
reach into white-collar and professional worlds such as university teaching or public management (Power 1997; Strathern 2000). The drive to
increase accountability leads to stricter practices of auditing in order
to certify governing practices as valid and effective. Poovey's work on
book-keeping (1998) argued that this technology created the modern
'fact', while Carruthers and Espeland (1991) examined the rhetorical
side of book-keeping, focusing on the legitimating role of accounts. This
literature raises concerns that the increasing importance of quantitative
evidence leads to a situation in which only those operations which are
counted and can be counted, count at all, and that qualitative and more
complex operations will receive less and less attention (see for instance,
Espeland and Sauder 2007; 2014).

Analyses of standardization and scientific rationalization practices in
science and technology studies provide another valuable framework for
considering the role of numeric representation in governance. Technologies of quantification and formal representation (mathematical

formulae and models, charts, graphic depictions) are indispensable in creating standards in processes of modern rationalization (Berg 1997; Bowker and Star 1999; see also from organization theory Brunsson and Jacobsson 2000). This body of literature demonstrates how scientific knowledge is produced through a deeply social process requiring networks of supporters and technologies that are gradually accepted as providing truthful information (Bloor 1976; Shapin and Schaffer 1985; Bijker, Hughes and Pinch 1987; Rottenburg 2009a). These studies stress that the meaning, purpose and intended and unintended effects of techno-scientific representations of reality, e.g. numbers, as results of complex protocols differ distinctively between different social domains. They call for more careful empirical analysis of the proliferation of numbers and calculative practices in social life (Callon, Millo and Muniesa 2007; MacKenzie, Muniesa and Siu 2007).

Despite the transformative influence of numbers in all domains of social life, dominant interpretations in the field of quantification are mainly provided by economists and psychologists, who have a long history of grappling with the issues outlined here, though in a less reflective manner and more oriented towards finding better indicators. What is new, perhaps since the 1980s and with remarkable acceleration since the beginning of the twenty-first century, is the transfer of these technologies of knowledge production by quantification into the fields of governance and law on the global stage. A differentiated and in-depth social scientific understanding of the use of numbers and calculative practices in these social fields is essential. There is already a growing body of scholarship interrogating the global expansion of quantification and indicators in governance. However, there is relatively little from an ethnographic perspective starting from the shop floor, so to speak, and employing a theoretical frame largely inspired by the Foucauldian tradition.

This collection is unique in its use of ethnographic and historical approaches to understanding the nature of indicators and their significance in global governance. The book seeks to strengthen the social scientific understanding of numerical representations, and in particular, to explore indicators as a knowledge technology of regulation, experimentation and critique by moving beyond the analysis of indicators as tools of domination. In addition to serving as technologies of control and discipline, indicators also provide everyday guidance under conditions of uncertainty and insecurity of contemporary life worlds, as well as a resource for less powerful actors to make problems visible and politically salient. Non-state actors use indicators to hold governmental organizations accountable and to articulate claims to justice and access to resources. The collection shows how indicators produce novel epistemic objects and thereby constitute an important epistemological transformation in contemporary processes of accountability in globalization.

THE CHAPTERS

The chapters in this book show that indicators can be found in almost any domain of public life today. In governance, in the fields of law, human rights, welfare, health, economics and academia indicators have emerged as a dominant mode of simplifying and apprehending complex problems by producing measurable entities, which can be compared, ranked and monitored.

The volume starts off with Theodore Porter's chapter. He offers a historical contextualization of indicators and opens up an ironic parenthesis that reaches out to Alain Desrosières' chapter on retroaction that concludes the volume. The ten chapters in between are held together by this parenthesis.

Porter demonstrates that indicators originally were mainly intended for presentation to the public, which was encouraged to use them to judge how well they were governed. The beauty of a single number was the simplicity of reasoning it allowed citizens who could not be assumed to have much sense of nuance. The appeal to a public sphere later encouraged state agencies to move a step further and rely on numerical indicators even as evidence of the rationality and fair-mindedness of their own decisions as well. During the twentieth century, these public uses were increasingly interwoven with a new administrative technology – today often called 'neoliberal governance' – designed to reconcile decentralized action (subsidiarity, self-responsibility) with centralized assessment (standardization to facilitate exchange and valuation in vast spaces and to make long distance control something the actors aim to achieve by pursuing their interests). This new administrative technology is always subject to a trade-off between two opposing ideals: on the one hand, the rigidity in commensuration, classification and standardization set by centres of calculation in order to make things comparable and quantifiable when in fact they are rather heterogeneous and non-quantifiable entities; and, on the other hand, the demand for decentralized translations of these abstract classifications to make them relevant or in any other sense usable for a particular site to particular actors. Porter ironically speaks of 'deceits' inevitably resulting out of the contradictions between the rigidities of trans-local standardizations and the infidelities of their local translations.

Porter concludes that the fine line between rigidity and deceit has become one of the characteristic features of the modern age, which is older than neoliberalism – still conceding that neoliberalism added momentum to this feature, as Alain Desrosières insists in the final chapter to the volume. The ten ethnographic chapters of this volume that are held together by the parenthesis set by Porter and Desrosières examine this dilemma of quantification in great detail, and with a sharp focus on the crafting and communicating of, and living with, indicators in the fields of global finance and local microfinance, public health, malaria control, criminal justice, public statistics, climate change, political accountability and access to land.

The chapters by Wendy Espeland, Johanna Mugler, Evelyn Ruppert and Olaf Zenker analyse indicators in the context of increasing demands for accountability and as part of a global trend to render accountability and regulation in quantitative terms. On the one hand, accountability measured by indicators is supposed to make it easier for outsiders to understand, monitor and evaluate the actions of politicians, state actors and national or transnational organizations. Among other things, indicators have the task to make ordinary citizens feel that they can trust politicians, state bureaucrats and experts like medical health professionals, lawyers or economists. The public communication of simplified and easily accessible numerical information is supposed to generate confidence amongst lay people and proof that it makes sense to give their votes and tax money to those largely invisible actors behind institutional walls. Indicators are there to verify that it is safe to put one's lives and hopes into the hands of the state apparatus. On the other hand, quantitative forms of accountability devices assist people with political and/or extensive economic power, who have been given the task of working in the interest of a specific or wider public, to make decisions in an increasingly fast and uncertain working environment. These chapters want to know how exactly this works.

Espeland's work describes the widely published *US News and World Report* (*USN*) law school rankings, which exemplify the powerful and influential impact indicators can have. The law school rankings are tightly coupled to the status of law schools and therefore determine students' school admission preferences, their willingness to accept high tuition fees, or their chances in the labour market. As a result of the power these rankings gained in this organizational field, Espeland shows that law schools felt forced to change their admission practices, enrolment policies and allocation of funds, and they began to game the numbers. Her chapter in this volume goes further, examining people's reaction to being measured. It examines the reception process and the narratives indicators evoke. She shows how law school leaders talk back to rankings, how they put back what numbers have removed, simplified or misrepresented. In other words, she examines how they resist what she calls the 'disciplinary power' of rankings. Espeland argues that exploring the stories numbers elicit helps us to understand how people who are governed by numbers make sense of them and that this perspective is crucial for widening our understanding of the meaning and power of indicators.

Mugler's chapter is also concerned with how people, in her case study South African prosecutors, cope with the 'disciplinary power' of indicators and rankings. She shows that the widespread social scientific worry that quantitative forms of accountability will supersede or replace more qualitative forms of account giving is not characteristic of the National Prosecuting Authority (NPA) in South Africa. Here, she argues, the power of 'numbers' is counteracted by prosecutors' alternative expressions of accountability like professionalism, ethics, responsibility and liability. It is also challenged by the numerical competence of managerial prosecutors who are much more aware of the constructedness, reactivity, and yet usefulness of quantifications than critics are often willing to acknowledge about professionals. Mugler argues that because the NPA performance information is only partly made public and mostly used for internal management purposes and the loose coupling of resources and quantitative knowledge, the anxiety and stress that indicators elicit in other professional settings are absent among the South African prosecutors.

Ruppert and Zenker, like Mugler, both describe examples from national governments and state institutions and look at quantitative accountability not from the perspective of professionals but from the perspective of the people who are supposed to benefit from accountability. These are settings where citizens or service consumers often do not have an accessible alternative. They are unable to use a different social welfare office, prosecutor or land claims court when indicators tell them that their office, prosecutor or court's performance is unacceptable.

Ruppert points out that more public information does not inevitably come with more accountability. Her study on the British Transparency Agenda (TA) argues that transparency through indicators does not necessarily lead to more informed citizens and more accountable state employees, if information – huge amounts of information – is simply placed on the Internet. Rather, as she points out, transparency indicators, like any other object, have to be enacted and only thereby bring a transparent state into being. She argues that while the TA purports to wrest knowledge from experts and put it into the hands of a data-aware public, specific kinds of 'technical capital' (skills, resources, knowledge) are required to make sense of these newly accessible but enormous bodies of data. The function of this provision of data might not only be to reveal the workings of the state, but also, depending on the selected metrics, to hide aspects of its workings. Ideas like transparency, accountability and social and historical justice are normative concepts, which lose their value in enabling a democratic discourse if they are completely replaced by numbers. On the other hand, numbers are essential to promoting democratic discourse.

Zenker explores this paradox in his study of the social life of settlement statistics in the ongoing land restitution process in South Africa. He shows how settlement statistics have been transformed in a short period of time into widely accepted indicators of state performance. While acknowledging the broadly aired criticisms of indicators, he also points to the capacity of numerical representations and simplifications to enable public debates and make hidden injustices (for example, the worrying deficiencies in the organization of land restitution) visible and open to processing. He shows how the indicators assist actors in this field to switch codes between claim-specific settings and the national arena of land reform. This power to make visible is of special relevance in a context like the new South Africa, where the needs and demands of the majority of the population were ignored for decades and where the state was unaccountable to this majority. This issue of how quantitative accountability interacts with, competes with or supersedes other previously existing understandings of accountability constitutes a general theme for all of the authors as they interrogate the social lives of indicators. The authors offer new lenses with which to explore the purpose, meaning, efficacy and power of indicators.

The chapters by Sung-Joon Park and Rene Gerrets examine the global proliferation of indicators in the domain of biomedicine and ask how the production of quantitative knowledge affects the provision

25

of health-care. The growing importance of indicators seems to fit neatly into a more general expansion of the paradigm of evidence-based medicine throughout the world. As the authors suggest, indicators are pivotal for understanding the frequently discussed transformation of international health to global health. As they describe, indicators underpin the emergence of new regimes of global health governance where a huge amount of donor money flows to countries of the Global South. Concomitantly, the number of health projects has been rising, which in turn leads to a remarkable expansion of indicators to measure programmatic outputs and inputs in these projects. These indicators include a broad range of social, statistical, bureaucratic, economic and logistic information, which constitutes a health apparatus that spans the globe.

The proliferation of indicators in the field of global health renews hopes into a better future, as Gerrets describes for malaria interventions in Tanzania, and as Park for the scaling-up of free access to antiretroviral therapy in Uganda. Yet, expectations of indicators, for example that they can eradicate malaria or halt the HIV epidemic, ignore the long and complex history of donor-driven public health experimentations in sub-Saharan African countries in which humanitarian initiatives to save lives and improve people's living conditions often undermined and weakened existing public health systems, as various scholars have critically pointed out (Turshen 1999; Prince and Marsland 2014).

Against this background, Gerrets and Park take the absence of reliable infrastructures to supply test kits, lab equipment, medicines and other health commodities as a point of departure in examining the enactment of various types of indicators in rural and urban health facilities in Tanzania and Uganda. Both authors contrast the proliferation of indicators with the occurrence of drug stock-outs, which are common for both settings, but have dramatic consequences, particularly in the domain of HIV treatment.

Gerrets' contribution probes the ways malaria is categorized, counted, measured and turned into data, when treatment and diagnosis are decoupled in Tanzanian health facilities because anti-malarial drugs are most of the time out of stock. He argues that these contextual constraints lead to a variety of practices of diagnosing and recording of malaria, all of which bring different objects into being. The biomedical definition of malaria, underwriting current efforts to base malaria interventions on accurate monitoring and evaluation (M&E) assessments, obscures and conflates how malaria is enacted in the Tanzanian health settings. In this mix of contextual constraints and waves of public health reforms, the term malaria denotes many things which all differ ontologically but are counted as one single disease.

Park's chapter focuses on HIV treatment in Uganda. In contrast to the malaria interventions described by Gerrets, donor aid for mass HIV treatment programmes is usually considered to be adequate. Antiretroviral therapy, unlike other types of medication, demands more strictly a regular and permanent supply of antiretrovirals to maintain HIV as a chronic condition. However, as Park describes, the emerging global health infrastructures are characterized by fragmentation, which, together with a shortfall of donor aid, produce a massive shortage of antiretrovirals, leading to the rationing of these life-saving medicines. The chapter approaches the rationing of antiretrovirals through the concept of hope to pay attention to the manifold improvisations of therapy enabling hospitals to maintain a minimum level of care. Resonating with Espeland's contribution, the hopes expressed in the improvisation of bodily measurements and rules of treatment capture how people reinsert moral agency into the use of indicators in situations where these technologies fail to provide certainty.

The production of knowledge and social justice through indicators is also pertinent to the recent developments in economics and global finance. Indicators are playing an increasingly central role in microfinance as the system composed of myriad local lenders gives way to a global electronic marketplace. Barbara Grimpe examines recent developments in the field of microfinance – the practice of making small loans and other financial services to relatively poor people – as this global marketplace moves online. With the rise in the number of providers of small loans and services, there has been an expanding system of evaluating and measuring lenders according to their financial and their social performance, understood as contributions to well being. These indicators, along with online platforms, allow easy, quick comparison among programmes, the articulation of global standards, and thus the facilitation of choices for investors. Grimpe examines how these indicators are created and what they choose to measure or to ignore. The chapter asks to what extent the creation of a global marketplace for microfinance expands possibilities of understanding, oversight and interaction, and to what extent the inevitable selectivity in data collection and indicator creation exacerbates social conflict. In line with Bettina Heintz (2010), she points out that this is but one instance of the 'double-edged transformative power of quantitative comparisons'. Her ethnographic and structural analysis of microfinance highlights both the benefits of the transformation of microfinance into a global, commensurable market and the limited and misleading nature of many of the indicators upon which this market is based.

In his analysis of neoliberal economic indicators of competitiveness and wellbeing, William Davies traces the importance of moral values implied in economic quantifications. Rather than seeking to separate the economic and moral spheres of life, he argues, neoliberalism brings the principles of the market to all domains of social life by encouraging enterprise and competition as means of producing individual and collective wellbeing as a key moral value. These goals need to be quantified and measured in order to evaluate how well societies are doing in achieving both of these goals. After examining indicators of competitiveness and wellbeing, including happiness, he suggests that a new version of neoliberalism may be emerging which privileges wellbeing over competitiveness. In this lucid and provocative chapter, Davies suggests that there could be a move toward rival neoliberalisms based on competitiveness and wellbeing, each with its own form of quantification. These quantification systems are in some ways incommensurable, with the first emphasizing objective reality and comparison among countries, while the second is more populist and relative, since each person judges her happiness without reference to broader standards. He concludes that both kinds of indicators exist in the ambiguous space between expert knowledge that measures objective reality and the broader public's ideas, attitudes and values. Thus, his insightful analysis links the shifts in neoliberalism with changing ideas about how to measure and what to measure.

Andrew Farlow tackles the question of how financial indicators of risk and uncertainty, such as credit ratings and indicators of bank capital and liquidity, contributed to the financial crash of 2008. His analysis deftly demonstrates that financial indicators played an enabling role in the meltdown, even if they were not its principal cause. He argues cogently that global economic imbalances and underlying macroeconomic weaknesses interacted with the financial system and regulatory failures to foster the crash, and that, under these conditions, the failure of market efficiency allowed bad indicators to thrive. Farlow explores the contestation of the global financial regulatory space, in particular showing how large financial players shaped its key components like the Basel Accords and global accountancy standards.

He explains how credit ratings, capital adequacy rules and accounting standards hard-wired dangers into financial systems, and how this fragility enabled large financial players to reap the benefits of expected bail-outs. He shows how the apparent neutrality of financial indicators helped to render invisible the rise in systemic risk, the massive redistribution of wealth and the widespread effects of high-level corruption. As he turns conventional thinking about the role of credit rating agencies on its head, Farlow offers a very insightful and provocative analysis of the role that quantification played in the economic processes that led to the financial crash.

In addition to issues of accountability in governance, to quantifications of global health, and to measurements in finance and economics, climate change is another important field for understanding the workings of increasingly sophisticated quantification and calculation. Climate change vulnerability indicators are used, *inter alia*, by policy-makers and donors to develop programmes and allocate funding where it is most needed. At the same time, vulnerability is a particularly difficult concept to measure, as Till Sterzel, Boris Orlowsky, Hannah Förster, Anja Weber and Dennis Eucker point out in their chapter. The concept of vulnerability itself is very complex. It includes exposure, sensitivity to change and the ability to adapt. Moreover, the indicator must not only evaluate risk and the ability to adapt, but it must also quantify possible future harm, i.e. to identify, in some way, a quantity of potentially fundamental uncertainty and transform it into a calculable probability scenario. Sterzel *et al.* describe a variety of efforts to develop simple, aggregate indicators of climate change vulnerability. They point to the normative judgments embedded in apparently objective numbers and the lack of clarity in many indicators that have been developed over the past two decades. The chapter advocates creating locally specific, grounded assessments of relatively small places rather than broad measures produced at the national level. However, they also note that often donors, governments and policy-makers want broad, simple comparisons aggregated into a single number. Thus, creating useful climate change vulnerability indicators requires a painful navigation between providing accurate, detailed measures and broad, readily usable and comparative ones.

Alain Desrosières' chapter, the last one of this volume, links up with the ironic parenthesis opened in the first chapter by Theodore Porter. It takes the insights gained by metrology into the lion's den of quantification: the practice of statistics and the public role of statisticians and their institutions. He argues that in contemporary neoliberal orders, quantitative indicators increasingly have a direct influence, called 'retroaction', not only on those who are quantified, but eventually and unavoidably also on those who make the quantification. The concern that statistical accounts might partly result out of retroaction on quantified actors raises important questions about emerging contradictions in the disciplinary and professional ethos of statisticians. Against this background, his chapter argues that it is impossible to separate the concrete processes of measuring from the actual use of indicators and explores the black box of the production and the use of indicators.

In sum, this book is a contribution to metrology. It examines the making, the usage and the consequences of technologies of quantification in the production of governmental knowledge in globalized contexts through a series of theoretically guided case studies. In the words of Theodore Porter referred to above, the chapters are thick descriptions of thick practices which aim at thin, numeric descriptions of the world. They provide social scientific examinations of how quantifications – mainly indicators – affect the type of reality we inhabit and shape the way we understand, assess and act upon it. We argue that technologies of quantification, processes of neoliberal marketization and global governance combine into new figurations[8] which raise new and important questions. We hope to foreground how these figurations construct an epistemic space with particular evidentiary practices, institutionalized social forms and power relations facilitating confirmation and critique in globalized contexts of governance.

References

Berg, Marc 1997. *Rationalizing Medical Work: Decision Support Techniques and Medical Practices*. Cambridge, Mass.: MIT Press

Bijker, Wiebe, Thomas Hughes and Trevor Pinch 1987/1993. *The Social Construction of Technological Systems*. Cambridge, Mass.: MIT Press

Bloor, David 1976/1991. *Knowledge and Social Imagery*. 2nd edn, London: University of Chicago Press

Bowker, Geoffrey and Susan Leigh Star 1999. *Sorting Things Out: Classification and its Consequences*. Cambridge, Mass.: MIT Press

Bruno, Isabelle and Emmanuel Didier 2013. *Benchmarking: l'État sous pression statistique*. Paris: Éditions La Découverte

---

[8] Figuration is here used in the sense which Norbert Elias gave to this term, see primarily his chapter 'Figuration' in Kopp and Schäfers 1995: 75–8.

Bruno, Isabelle, Emmanuel Didier and Julien Prévieux 2014. *Statactivisme: comment lutter avec des nombres*. Paris: Editions La Découverte

Brunsson, Nils and Bengt Jacobsson (eds.) 2000. *A World of Standards*. Oxford: Oxford University Press

Callon, Michel, Yuval Millo and Fabian Muniesa 2007. *Market Devices*. Chichester: Wiley Blackwell

Carruthers, Bruce G. and Wendy Nelson Espeland 1991. 'Accounting for Rationality: Double-Entry Bookkeeping and the Rhetoric of Economic Rationality', *American Journal of Sociology* 97(1): 31–69

Daston, Lorraine 1988. *Classical Probability in the Enlightenment*. Princeton, N.J.: Princeton University Press

Desrosières, Alain 1998. *The Politics of Large Numbers: A History of Statistical Reasoning*, Cambridge, Mass.: Harvard University Press; original in French 1993

Espeland, Wendy Nelson and Michael Sauder 2007. 'Rankings and Reactivity: How Public Measures Recreate Social Worlds', *American Journal of Sociology* 113(1): 1–40

2014. *Fear of Falling: How Media Rankings Changed Legal Education in America*. Russell Sage Foundation, forthcoming

Espeland, Wendy Nelson and Mitchell L. Stevens 2008. 'A Sociology of Quantification', *European Journal of Sociology / Archives Européennes de Sociologie* 49(3): 401–36

Espeland, Wendy Nelson and Berit Irene Vannebo 2007. 'Accountability, Quantification and Law', *Annual Review of Law and Social Science* 3: 21–43

Foucault, Michel 1966/1973. *The Order of Things: An Archaeology of the Human Sciences*. New York: Vintage Books

Hacking, Ian 1975. *The Emergence of Probability: A Philosophical Study of Early Ideas about Probability Induction and Statistical Inference*. Cambridge: Cambridge University Press

1990. *The Taming of Chance*. Cambridge: Cambridge University Press

Heintz, Bettina 2010. 'Numerische Differenz. Überlegungen zu einer Soziologie des (quantitativen) Vergleichs', *Zeitschrift für Soziologie* 39(3): 162–81

Hetherington, Kregg 2011. *Guerrilla Auditors: The Politics of Transparency in Neoliberal Paraguay*. Durham N.C.: Duke University Press

Hopwood, Anthony and Peter Miller 1994. *Accounting as Social and Institutional Practice*. Cambridge: Cambridge University Press

Kopp, Johannes and Bernhard Schäfers 1995. *Grundbegriffe der Soziologie*. Wiesbaden: Verlag für Sozialwissenschaften; chapter on 'Figuration' written by Norbert Elias, pp. 75–8

Krüger, Lorenz, Lorraine J. Daston and Michael Heidelberger (eds.) 1987. *The Probabilistic Revolution*, vol. 2. Cambridge, Mass.: MIT Press

MacKenzie, Donald A., Fabian Muniesa and Lucia Siu 2007. *Do Economists Make Markets? On the Performativity of Economics*. Princeton, N.J.: Princeton University Press

Mennicken, Andrea and Hendrik Vollmer (eds.) 2007. 'Zahlenwerk. Kalkulation, Organisation und Gesellschaft', Fokus 'Herrschaft der Zahlen 1' and 'Herrschaft der Zahlen 2'. *WestEnd Neue Zeitschrift für Sozialforschung*

Merry, Sally Engle 2006. 'Transnational Human Rights and Local Activism: Mapping the Middle', *American Anthropologist* 108(1): 38–51

2011. 'Measuring the World: Indicators, Human Rights, and Global Governance', *Current Anthropology* 52(S3): 83–95

Merry, Sally Engle and Susan Coutin 2014. 'Technologies of Truth in the Anthropology of Conflict', *American Ethnologist* 41(1): 1–16

Meyer, John W. and Brian Rowan 1977/1991. 'Institutionalized Organizations: Formal Structure as Myth and Ceremony' in Walter W. Powell and Paul J. DiMaggio (eds.), *The New Institutionalism in Organizational Analysis*. Chicago, Ill.: University of Chicago Press, pp. 41–62

Miller, Peter 2001. 'Governing by Numbers: Why Calculative Practices Matter', *Social Research* 68(2): 379–96

Miller, Peter, Trevor Hopper and Richard Laughlin 1991. 'The New Accounting History: An Introduction', *Accounting, Organizations and Society* 16(5–6): 395–403

Osborne, Thomas and Nikolas Rose 2003. 'Do the Social Sciences Create Phenomena? The Example of Public Opinion Research', *British Journal of Sociology* 50(3): 367–96

Poovey, Mary 1998. *A History of the Modern Fact: Problems of Knowledge in the Sciences of Wealth and Society*. Chicago, Ill.: University of Chicago Press

Porter, Theodore 1986. *The Rise of Statistical Thinking 1820–1900*. Princeton, N.J.: Princeton University Press

1995. *Trust in Numbers: The Pursuit of Objectivity in Science and Public Life*. Princeton, N.J.: Princeton University Press

2012. 'Thin Description: Surface and Depth in Science and Science Studies', *Osiris* 27: 209–26

Power, Michael 1997. *The Audit Society: Rituals of Verification*. Oxford: Oxford University Press

Prince, Jane Ruth and Rebecca Marsland 2014. *Making and Unmaking Public Health in Africa: Ethnographic and Historical Perspectives*. Athens, Ohio: Ohio University Press

Rottenburg, Richard 2000. 'Accountability for Development Aid' in Herbert Kalthoff, Richard Rottenburg and Hans-Jürgen Wagener (eds), *Facts and Figures: Economic Representations and Practices*. Marburg: Metropolis-Verlag, pp. 143–73

2009a. *Far-Fetched Facts: A Parable of Development Aid*, Cambridge, Mass: MIT Press (first published in German in 2002)

2009b. 'Social and Public Experiments and New Figurations of Science and Politics in Postcolonial Africa', *Postcolonial Studies* 12(4): 423–40

2012. 'On Juridico-political Foundations of Meta-codes' in Jürgen Renn (ed.), *The Globalization of Knowledge in History*. Berlin: Max Planck Research Library for the History and Development of Knowledge, pp. 483–500

Shapin, Steven and Simon Schaffer 1985. *Leviathan and the Air-pump: Hobbes, Boyle and the Experimental Life*. Princeton, N.J.: Princeton University Press

Speich Chassé, Daniel 2013. *Die Erfindung des Bruttosozialprodukts*. Goettingen: Vandenhoek and Ruprecht

Strathern, Marilyn (ed.) 2000. *Audit Cultures: Anthropological Studies in Accountability, Ethics, and the Academy*. London and New York: Routledge

Turshen, Meredeth 1999. *Privatizing Health Services in Africa*. New Brunswick, N.J.: Rutgers University Press

CHAPTER TWO

THE FLIGHT OF THE INDICATOR

Theodore M. Porter

Etymologically, an indicator, like an index, has to do with pointing. Anatomically, the indicator muscle (*extensor indicis*) straightens the index finger. Logically, indicators detect, point or measure, but do not explain. An index in the social sciences typically combines or synthesises indicators, as with the 'index of leading economic indicators', which aims to maximize the predictive value of diverse measures whose movements anticipate the rise and decline of general economic activity. A quantitative index or indicator typically cannot measure the very thing of interest, but in its place something whose movements show a consistent relationship to that thing. Since its purpose is merely to indicate as a guide to action, ease of measurement is preferred to meaning or depth. The indicator ranks among the varieties of information whose ascent has been so steep within the intellectual economy of modern times, tending perhaps to crowd out those more exigent epistemic forms, knowledge and wisdom.[1]

We might even be tempted to categorize the indicator as an administrative or behavioral technology rather than as a mode of scientific understanding. Given the scientific hopes that have been invested in the design of effective indicators and the outpouring of scientific writing that has been brought to bear on them, this would be cavalier. Also, while managerial effectiveness is clearly not least among the stakes in

---

[1] Yaron Ezrahi, 'Science and the Political Imagination in Contemporary Democracies' in Sheila Jasanoff (ed.), *States of Knowledge: The Co-Production of Science and Social Order* (New York: Routledge, 2004) pp. 254–73.

a world of indicators, they are also pursued to promote informed action and decisions of a decentralized sort. For example, the Bureau of Agricultural Economics in interwar United States made strenuous efforts to anticipate harvests as a basis for estimating prices so that widely-dispersed farmers would not be wholly at the mercy of the companies whose agents showed up with an offer for their corn or wheat. On many matters, however, the knowledge of local people at the scene of the action, such as the manager of a factory, may be superior to that of executives in the head office, many miles away. Here, the availability of a numerical indicator, defining perhaps a standard of performance, can compensate somewhat for their informational disadvantage. Or finally, an official number might provide a neutral basis for adjusting contracts to changing circumstances. Cost-of-living measures began to be used this way in labor negotiations in the United States after the First World War, and later were even made automatic in some union contracts as well as social security payments.[2]

The enshrinement of measures by law or contract confers validity by fiat, making them more than mere indicators. Yet state ministries and boardrooms have limited power to dictate numbers so long as they continue to stand for something empirical. This is not because all the relevant actors automatically agree on such measures. Indicators, indexes and statistics are often sites of struggle and deception. These give the indicator its characteristic dynamism of disorderly opportunism leading sometimes to self-annihilation. Those subject to the verdict of the indicator are led almost ineluctably to exploit the gap between an imperfect measure and the sometimes shadowy entity it purports to capture. Judgment by numbers, and the deceit that comes with it, has been associated with the rise of neoliberal forms of governance. Indicators, indeed, have flourished under neoliberalism. Examining them from a historical perspective reveals that, to a degree, we have always been neoliberal. The indicator function is by no means limited to states and large organizations.

Indication as a reliable gesture, standing in for direct knowledge, has a multifaceted history, and no clear point of origin. In this chapter I follow some uses of the word 'indicator', supplemented at times with related ones such as barometer and index, to explore the ambitions and

[2] Emmanuel Didier, *En quoi consiste l'Amérique: les statistiques, le new deal et la démocratie* (Paris: Éditions La Découverte, 2009); Thomas Stapleford, *The Cost of Living in America: A Political History of Economic Statistics, 1880–2000* (Cambridge: Cambridge University Press, 2009).

hazards associated with this indirect basis for knowing and acting. Like *models*, whose prestige as a knowledge form rose rapidly from the early twentieth century,[3] *indicators* offer truth or validity in an abstracted or even fictionalized form, always presuming a sufficient degree of resemblance to a partly-accessible reality. The genealogy of the indicator, as I show here, passes through indicator birds in natural history, indicator diagrams in engineering, and diverse medical indexes in public health and therapeutic effectiveness, to the important economic indicators that have played so great a role in management and economic planning since the First World War. What may appear as rather whimsical instances of the indicator function may yet reveal how treacherous it can be to try to separate indicating from understanding and trust, or to look so intently to where it points that we neglect the reality and power of the indicator itself.

FEATHERY INDICATORS

On 13 October 1839, Leigh Hunt faced up to the problem of choosing a name for his new literary miscellany, one that would define the journal as modest, expressive, new and striking, that would 'comprise as many public interests as all the Christian names of a French or German prince'. On the second page of the journal he ran through a long list of odd and ridiculous titles that others had proposed to him. He gave no reason for the choice he made, not even a mention of what the reader would already have noticed at the head of page 1: *The Indicator*. The epigram, repeated each week for the first six issues, hinted at an explanation:[4]

> There is a bird in the interior of Africa, whose habits would rather seem to belong to the interior of Fairy-Land; but they have been well authenticated. It indicates to honey hunters where the nests of wild bees are to be found. It calls them with a cheerful cry, which they answer; and on finding itself recognized, flies and hovers over a hollow tree containing the honey. While they are occupied in collecting it, the bird goes to a little distance where he observes all that passes; and the hunters, when they have helped themselves, take care to leave him his portion of the food. – This is the Cuculus Indicator of Linnaeus, otherwise called the Moroc, Bee Cuckoo, or Honey Bird.

[3] Mary Morgan, *The World in the Model: How Economists Work and Think* (Cambridge: Cambridge University Press, 2012).
[4] Leigh Hunt in *The Indicator*, 13 October 1819, 1(1): 1.

Hunt's *Indicator* aimed, like the bird, to lead the reader into a garden of literary delights and temptations which Hunt evoked in a second epigram, three lines of verse from the English Renaissance poet, Edmund Spenser: 'There he arriving round about doth flie, / And takes survey with busie, curious eye, / Now this, now that he tasteth tenderlie.'[5]

Hunt's natural history was not merely fanciful. *Avibase: the world bird database* has a page for *Indicator Indicator*, as it is now named, the only species within the genus of honeyguides that reliably leads humans, as well as honey badgers, to beehives. Linnaeus's student Anders Sparrman is credited with the first description of the species in 1777, based on his observations in southern Africa. Dutch settlers already knew of these birds, calling them honey guides (*honig-wyzer* or *heuningwyzer*), and long before them, the Khoisan and other African peoples. Although these reports of the honeyguide's astonishing behavior are accepted by science, the bird seems to inhabit a world of natural theology or even of divine semiotics, far removed from seemingly sober social-science indicators. Yet African bee hunters, as Sparrman reported, behaved strategically in relation to their guides. They always left some honeycomb behind as a reward for the bird, but never enough to satisfy its hunger. 'The bird's appetite being only whetted by this parsimony, it is obliged to commit a second treason, by discovering another bees nest, in hopes of a better salary.' This passage from the *Philosophical Transactions* of the Royal Society of London was excerpted word for word two decades later, without attribution, in the May 1798 number of *The Sporting Magazine, or Monthly Calendar of the Transactions of the Turn, the Chace, and Every Other Diversion interesting to the Man of Pleasure, Enterprize, and Spirit*. The editors positioned it just after the explanation of 'The Game of Commerce, a card game for three to twelve players', and before the Law Proceedings in the Court of the King's Bench, 9 May 1798.[6] The bird, at least the female, was cunning in its own way, not only by enticing humans and badgers to assist in robbing the bees, but also by laying her eggs in the nests of other birds. This, we may presume, is why the first travelers, and Leigh Hunt afterwards, called it a cuckoo. In 1790, a French traveler defied his African hosts, who, he complained,

---

[5] Edmund Spenser, 'Muiopotmos, or the Fate of the Butterflie', quoting lines 169, 171, 173. In French, *indicateur* had already been in use for at least half a century as title for a miscellany.

[6] 'Description of a New Species of Cuckoo by Dr. Andrew Sparman [*sic*], of the Royal Academy of Stockholm', *Philosophical Transactions of the Royal Society of London* (1777) 57: 128–9. See also 'The Honeyguide' in *Sporting Magazine* (May 1798) 12: 89–90.

treated the birds as deities, and killed one in order to describe it rigorously, including the contents of its stomach. This, he determined, was no cuckoo at all, but a member of a genus that lives exclusively from honey and wax, and is endowed by the 'wonderful precaution of nature' with skin too thick and tough to be penetrated by a pin or by the sting of this 'most ingenious of insects', the bee.[7] Providence, too, took pleasure from agile maneuvers in the game of commerce.

Thomas Carlyle, in *Sartor Resartus*, brought together some of the economic aspects of the indicator with an ingenious perspective on the problem of misleading appearances. The authorial voice in *Sartor* invoked the indicator just once, in a disarming way that implied, implausibly, his disinterested posture in regard to the declarations he excerpted: 'We ourselves, restricted to the duty of indicator, shall forbear commentary.' What he pretended here to discuss neutrally was the determination of his fictional philosopher Teufelsdröckh to break apart the shell of a society that time and destiny had drained of its contents. The Latin phrase of Carlyle's title means 'the tailor retailored'. The book's many jokes about clothes make up a deadly serious meditation on appearance and reality. Fictions, for Carlyle, are necessary, like clothes, to maintain decency. The revolutionary antihero Teufelsdröckh, who respects nothing but naked reality, declares that the world has been reduced now to a 'rag-fair' of empty masks. We might as well yield to the inevitable, he declares, and unleash 'the monster Utilitaria' to 'tread down old ruinous Palaces and Temples' so that something new can be built over the ruins, something far better. Teufelsdröckh quotes the visionary Saint-Simon in French and then in English translation: 'The golden age which a blind tradition has hitherto placed in the Past is Before us.' But the indicator-author laces his report with acid irony, doubting whether merciless, unadorned truth is our best option. Can we be sure that a phoenix must rise from the ashes? A 'judicious reader', he adds, might expect a 'Professor in a University' whom *Society* has treated well to show more gratitude to his 'benefactress'. It is easy enough for Teufelsdröckh, secure in the Pinnacle of Weissnichtwo, to call for root-and-branch destruction, but others, quoth the prophet, will suffer terribly.[8] John Anthony Froude's canonical biography tells how

[7] François Le Vaillant, *Voyage . . . dans l'Intérieur de l'Afrique par Le Cap de Bonne Espérance, dans les Années 1780, 81, 82, 83, 84 & 85* (Paris: Chez Benoit Le Francq, 1790/1795), where the Indicator is described in vol. 1, pp. 371–2.

[8] Thomas Carlyle, *Sartor Resartus* (1833–34) Book III, ch. V; first published in *Fraser's Magazine for Town and Country* (June 1834) 9: 674. *Teufelsdröckh* may be translated as 'devil's dung'; *Weissnichtwo* as 'Knownotwhere'.

Carlyle came to reflect that clothes, like institutions and religious creeds, were not mere shams to be discarded at the first opportunity, but needful to cover the 'native nakedness of human creatures', who thereby were enabled 'to live harmoniously and decently together'. Varying as they do with the 'fashions and habits of life', clothes, for Carlyle, are 'the outward indicators of the inward and spiritual nature'.[9]

STEAM AND SPIRIT INDICATORS

The career of our pseudo-cuckoo as exemplary indicator gave way about 1840 to the regulation of steam engines. Watt's indicator diagram, as it has been designated, dates from about 1796. The recording indicator was not in fact Watt's invention, but that of his assistant John Southern. A decade earlier, in 1785, Watt was trying to make visible the motion and condensation of the steam inside the cylinder through experiments in a glass vessel. Subsequently he had recourse to instrumental means, placing a barometer in the cylinder, but this was hard to see and behaved erratically. He achieved better success through indirect means. Watt affixed to this cylinder a small piston and spring to indicate the changing level of pressure inside the cylinder as the engine went through its cycle. An attached pencil provided a record of the maximum and minimum of this pressure gauge. Southern's addition of a printer's plate that moved with the main piston enabled the automatic production of a closed curve that provided guidance to engineers looking to improve the efficiency of the engine. From the 1830s, the indicator diagram helped shape the emerging scientific field of thermodynamics. Watt and then his son kept the design of this instrument secret for as long as they could, and while its workings were known to other engineers, it was not much discussed in print. Dionysus Lardner's *Popular Lectures on the Steam Engine*, first published in 1828, gave only a cursory mention of the indicator until, in the seventh edition of 1840, he introduced a section on 'Watt's invention' of this instrument. There he explained how indicator diagrams permitted calculation of the 'whole mechanical effect' of the engine over a single stroke simply by averaging ten or a dozen measurements to approximate the area bounded by this closed curve.[10]

---

[9] James Anthony Froude, *Thomas Carlyle: A History of the First Forty Years of His Life, 1795–1835* (London: Longmans, Green and Co., 1882) vol. 2, p. 130.

[10] Dionysus Lardner, *Popular Lectures on the Steam Engine* (7th edn, London: Taylor and Walton, 1840). On Watt, Southern and the invention of the indicator see David Philip Miller, 'The

I have no evidence of any specific reasons for appropriating the word 'indicator' for this instrument. As with the flight and chirping of the honey guide, what we have here is indicating in the sense of betokening, pointing to the thing rather than seizing it. The indicator does not allow direct sensory access to the production of mechanical force or, as it would later be designated, work. It supplies merely an instrument reading. Yet, already in Watt's day, this diagram seemed to be indicating something of fundamental importance, more so than anything he could have learned from visual inspection of steam, boiler or cylinder, even if his vision were unobstructed. An early treatise on Watt's indicator emphasised that it shows more than 'the actual power of the engine...In fact, in the hands of a skilful engineer, the indicator is the stethoscope of the physician, revealing the secret workings of the inner system, and detecting minute derangements in parts obscurely situated.'[11]

From mechanical to spiritual indicators was a much smaller step than we might suppose, and by the later nineteenth century the indicator of Watt and Southern had become such a commonplace as to be readily available for metaphorical use. A book by the American Napoleon Bonaparte Wolfe, printed in 1874, exemplifies how thoroughly saturated with the wonders of technology these spiritualist discussions could be. In one dialogue recorded by Wolfe, 'Spirit' explains that he can be present only in a darkened room because light would agitate his electricity. Spirit, being fully up to date scientifically, recognizes the fundamental identity of electricity and magnetism. With the aid of the medium, he has the power to materialize in a magnetic sphere, 'as steam moves machinery'. When asked if the spirit world has any inventions not yet known to man, Spirit replies that all human inventions come from the spirit world, mentioning things that reach across great divides: the electric telegraph and the 'big bridge'. The greatest of the promised new instruments, destined to arrive in sixty years, will be the Thought Indicator, whose special contribution is to annihilate secrecy and in this way to disrupt criminal thoughts that are father to criminal deeds. The spirit world, like Carlyle's dystopia, allows nothing to be covered or concealed. The Thought Indicator there 'indicates

Mysterious Case of James Watt's "1785" Steam Indicator: Forgery or Folklore in the History of an Instrument', *International Journal for the History of Engineering and Technology* (2011) 81: 129–50.

[11] Thomas J. Main and Thomas Brown, *The Indicator and Dynamometer with their Practical Applications* (London: Hebert and Woodward, 1847) p. 5.

thought on paper as rapidly as if done by electricity – as rapidly as we think'.[12]

ADVANCING STATISTICS

The word 'indicator' does not seem to have been used as something quantitative until after 1900. Under labels such as 'barometer', 'yardstick' or 'index', however, statistical indicators set off about 1820 on a course of impressive expansion. Such indicators appeared on the scene more or less simultaneously with regular public statistics, requiring only that the numbers should stand for something larger than themselves, some object existing more durably than the fickle flow of data. We often nowadays give credit to statistics for the creation of such entities as crime or unemployment rates, but its role may sometimes have been more like that of a midwife. The prior existence of a broad concept is especially likely when a number, extending beyond its licensed perimeter as measurement, comes to be identified with social justice or level of civilization, or when it sounds the tocsin for an action of some kind. Rousseau spoke in his *Social Contract* of a growing population as the unfailing mark of a well-governed territory decades before the trajectories of European populations were known even qualitatively. The British state pushed aside proposals for a national census beginning in the mid-eighteenth century in part because its leaders feared they would be discredited by numbers revealing a decline of population.[13]

In the nineteenth century, some prominent advocates of public health argued that mortality rates or expected years of life provided the proof of sound policies. In Paris, the mathematician Joseph Fourier upheld the extension of life in preference to Rousseau's increase of population as a marker of public prosperity, while medical statistician René Villermé took differential rates of sickness and death in its various quarters of Paris as measures of social inequality. In England, Edwin Chadwick's 1842 *Report on the Sanitary Condition of the Labouring Class* singled out mean age at death as an appropriate index of health. William Farr at the General Register Office also favored a measure in terms of mortality rates. One so simple as Chadwick's, however, was

---

[12] Napoleon Bonaparte Wolfe, *Startling Facts in Modern Spiritualism* (Cincinnati, Ohio: no publisher given, 1874) pp. 393, 397–8.
[13] David V. Glass, *Numbering the People: The Eighteenth-Century Population Controversy and the Development of Census and Vital Statistics in Britain* (Farnborough: D. C. Heath, 1973).

flawed by its failure to take into account the age structure of the population. Farr preferred to use the general rate of mortality, even while recognizing that it too was subject (in lesser degree) to the same defect. This could only be remedied by measuring mortality on the basis of a life-table, which gave age specific mortality.[14] His reason for relying on a simplified measure, like Chadwick's, was to impress the public with a figure for all the avoidable deaths. The General Register Office from about 1842 to 1880 worked to put local health authorities in competition with each other, using a barometer to impress the public with their evidence of needless mortality. Farr put great emphasis on a standard of 'healthy districts', places where mortality was no higher than 17 per thousand. Why couldn't other regions reach the level of salubrity achieved by the top 10 percent? The Public Health Act of 1848 endorsed this form of indicator, requiring local authorities to establish health boards and implement reforms if their mortality exceeded 23 per thousand. Behind this parliamentary concern, Farr believed, was the force of public opinion. The GRO's 1872 *Annual Summary* called attention to the excess of deaths over the 'healthy standard', declaring that mayors and town councillors should work tirelessly to eliminate them. 'They are on trial. They will be questioned at the bar of public opinion.'[15]

Another barometer of the health and fitness of populations, one whose prominence expanded greatly over the nineteenth century, was the physical examination for military service. New practices of conscription tended to nationalize the measure itself, and unexpectedly high rates of rejection of young men for military service were a major source for the degeneration craze that began in the late nineteenth century. Cultural pessimists liked to blame urban civilization and factory conditions for a supposed decline of fitness, though their charges did not go unanswered. High rates of migration from country to city complicated the attempt to draw inferences from such numbers, and not all were favorable to rural life. In Switzerland, statistics showing the inferiority of recruits from the country by comparison to those from town and city created such a scandal that a veil of silence was drawn

[14] Gérard Jorland, *Une société à soigner: Hygiène et salubrité publique en France au XIXe siècle* (Paris: Éditions Gallimard, 2010) pp. 90, 96; John M. Eyler, *Victorian Social Medicine: The Ideas and Methods of William Farr* (Baltimore, Md.: Johns Hopkins University Press, 1979) pp. 69–72.

[15] Simon Szreter, 'The G.R.O. and the Public Health Movement in Britain, 1837–1914' (1991), reprinted in Simon Szreter, *Health and Wealth: Studies in History and Policy* (Rochester, N.Y.: University of Rochester Press, 2005) pp. 242–80, at pp. 245–50, quote from p. 248.

across all such figures. The medical examinations themselves were not at all straightforward, especially when the number of potential recruits per examining physician rose to such high levels. Doctors looked for straightforward indicators of health and fitness, with attention gradually focusing on simple bodily measurements. In contrast to our own era, they were more troubled by thinness than by corpulence. The scale invented by French military doctor Maurice Pignet in 1900, and adopted widely, was calculated by subtracting chest circumference and weight, suitably scaled, from height. Doctors rejected young men for insufficient weight and girth. This process depended on standardized measuring regimes. The medical examiners also had to guard against dissimulation, both by those who wished to elude conscription and those who were desperate to volunteer. In the face of such challenges the physical examination focused as much as possible on what was readily measured.[16]

INSANE INDICATORS

Physicians also required tight definitions of insanity and mental defect in order to gain some control over these dangerous domains of ambiguity. Insane asylums were among the most intensely statistical institutions to be found in the nineteenth century. Both the workings of the mental hospitals themselves and the lessons they offered regarding the larger polity were dense with numbers. At the same time, ambiguities abounded. All the normal statistical measures of mortality broke down within the hospital, where patients were admitted because of their need for medical care and would typically remain only for weeks or months. Sanitary indexes for hospitals were enveloped in controversy, in Farr's time and since, partly because the risk of dying is in no way proportional to the number of days spent in the institution, and partly because different institutions might well admit patients suffering from conditions of greater or lesser severity. To the extent that they treated patients for acute conditions, number of admissions was a more relevant variable than the average number of patients in residence. Although superintendents of mental hospitals disliked keeping long-term patients, the

---

[16] Heinrich Hartmann, *Der Volkskörper bei der Musterung: Militärstatistik und Demographie in Europa vor dem Ersten Weltkrieg* (Göttingen: Wallstein Verlag, 2011); Martin Lengwiler, *Zwischen Klinik und Kaserne: Die Geschichte der Militärpsychiatrie in Deutschland und der Schweiz 1870–1914* (Zürich: Chronos Verlag, 2000) p. 277; Daniel B. Bouk, *The Science of Difference: Developing Tools for Discrimination in the American Life Insurance Industry, 1830–1930* (Chicago, Ill.: University of Chicago Press, forthcoming).

institutions tended to fill up with the incurable insane, and the doctors had limited authority to discharge or transfer these needy souls. For them, it was possible to regard total population as the appropriate denominator for measures both of mortality and of effectiveness. The medical success of asylums was typically assessed by two numbers, a cure rate and a death rate, which functioned as indicators, though that term was not used.

During the first phase of the massive long-term expansion of European and North American asylum systems, from about 1815 to 1850, administrators and advocates of these institutions did not usually characterize these numbers merely as indicators, but as measures of reality. But the match between this quantitative language and the experience of asylum patients shows some definite shortcomings. On one side of the equation we have neat arrays of numbers, tables upon tables in annual reports subdividing patients as male and female and according to marital state, occupation, religious confession, date of admission, disease form, cause of illness, date of discharge, and outcome, whether cured, improved, unimproved or dead. On the other is a mass of noisy, suffering, disorderly bodies, some stripped naked to keep them from injuring themselves, howling and moaning or expressing discontent by spreading their own fecal matter on the walls of their cell, driving their more orderly and obedient fellow inmates to distraction, threatening always to turn the institutions into overflowing bedlams, and subject to a mix of constraints and incentives to control the chaos.

By the mid-nineteenth century, the asylum directors themselves began finding reason to doubt the adequacy of their numbers. Many institutions, especially the most aggressively upbeat ones in the United States, found that their cure rates were not advancing, but sinking. As they compared their results, not just with other institutions but also with the more favorable numbers from their own past, they began to realize how many factors stood in the way of accurate measurement of their medical effectiveness. First among these reasons was the medical and psychological condition of entering patients. The consequences of an undesirable patient mix could, to be sure, be partly neutralized by dividing the residents for statistical purposes between fresh, curable patients, and old ones, whose illness over time had penetrated more deeply into the brain tissues. Some institutions simply marked the entering patients as curable or incurable, and calculated separate cure rates for the former. State regulators, however, demanded general accounts as well, and whatever had been numbered lurked threateningly as a fact that might potentially be used against them. Asylum statisticians found themselves being judged against numbers reflecting looser accounting standards of the past, such as the practice of logging multiple cures for the same patient who was discharged, read-mitted and discharged again.[17] They hinted darkly that their colleagues in other institutions or other nations applied inordinately loose standards in determining when a patient was cured. They also complained when impatient relatives (who might be running out of money) forced them to discharge persons who were improving but not yet recovered, and who were likely to sink back into insanity if released before the cure was complete.

These were the opportunities for manipulation to which many institutions had recourse. With regard to death rates, too, the asylums shared with ordinary hospitals a limited but real capacity to improve their numbers through admission or discharge policies, even when sanitary conditions or medical treatments remained the same. But on some points, and especially in decisions as to which patients were to be admitted, they were more and more reined in. Especially at public institutions, the physicians were obliged to take in whatever patients were sent to them on the order of a judge or state official. Their plight had much in common with the modern situation of schools, which are judged by test scores that, in practice, depend more on family background than on anything the teachers know how to do. Deprived of the capacity to choose pupils or patients whom they regard as likely to benefit from what they have to offer, medical and educational professionals may very reasonably feel oppressed by the tyranny of indiscriminate indicators.

Beyond the institutions, insanity had another indexical dimension, as an indicator of the health of populations or the level of civilization. A high level of insanity meant an increase of human suffering and of private or state expenditure to maintain these needy, unproductive and sometimes dangerous persons. This bitter pill was somewhat easier to swallow for those who accepted the doctrine enunciated in 1816 by

---

[17] This point was raised many times, but most notably by Pliny Earle, *The Curability of Insanity: A Series of Studies* (Philadelphia: J. B. Lippincott Company, 1887), who confessed that he had counted his own patients this way from his former position at the Bloomingdale Asylum in New York City. Theodore M. Porter, 'Funny Numbers', *Culture Unbound* (online journal) (2012) 4: 585–98, available at www.cultureunbound.ep.liu.se/v4/a32/.

the celebrated Paris alienist (asylum doctor), Etienne Esquirol, that insanity was a disease of civilization.[18] By 1869, when the American George Beard introduced the diagnosis of neurasthenia for this incapacity to bear up to the pressures of modern life, civilization itself was coming to be viewed with deeper ambivalence, but Esquirol spoke rather slightingly of those backward, non-European cultures that, according to the most authoritative reports, had little or no experience of insanity. One might even feel a bit of national pride on account of a high rate of insanity. In any event, alienists were keenly interested in the causes of insanity, at a collective as well as an individual level, and many gave enthusiastic support to censuses of insanity. Merely counting the insane within institutions, they complained, was not science, but only medical administration, while a census could get at the genuine social or environmental causes. To be sure, there were administrative reasons also to measure the prevalence of insanity outside the institutions, and since censuses of the insane required considerable resources, it is unlikely that there would have been many of these without this practical imperative.

Ironically, it is far from easy to count censuses, especially censuses of the insane. There are many references in asylum reports and official census documents to volunteer or semi-official tallies of lunatics, counts that were begun but never brought to a satisfactory conclusion, and counts that were promptly buried in the files so that their results remained unknown. Clearly, though, many such efforts were made; the alienists spoke of insane enumerations going back to about 1800. In some jurisdictions, censuses of the insane were taken as often as every three or four years beginning, typically, in the 1830s. This is also when periodical national censuses by agencies dedicated to that purpose became common in the leading nations of Europe.

In the early nineteenth century, the prevalence of insanity was a wide-open question. The measured rate, however, grew alarmingly. By the 1830s, the highest ratios of insane to general population were found in Scotland, Norway and certain Swiss cantons. These were generally assumed to be the consequence of more complete counts rather than of intrinsically higher insanity levels. Esquirol, in particular, could not

---

[18] J. E. D. Esquirol, 'Folie' in *Dictionnaire des sciences médicales* (Paris: C. L. F. Panckoucke, 1816) vol. 16, pp. 151–240, at pp. 177–80. He already made this point in a slightly less epigrammatic way in his 1805 thesis, *Des passions considérées comme causes, symptômes, et moyens curatifs de l'aliénation mental*, thèse de médecine de Paris, no. 574, présenté et soutenue à l'École de Médecine de Paris le 7 nivose an 14 (Paris: L'Imprimerie de Didot Jeune, An XIV, 1805) pp. 14–15, 20.

bring himself to believe that a dispersed, mostly rural population so far north as Norway could exhibit a higher rate of this *disease of civilization* than did France or England. Thanks to a much-admired census by Fredrik Holst in 1828, Norway became a focus of medical attention, a model system for the statistics of insanity. Holst's results, as well as asylum reports and other social and medical investigations from Norway, were reprinted and translated into the great European languages and discussed in France and Britain, and especially in Germany. They eventually convinced most commentators that the basic rate of insanity, including 'idiocy', was not 1 in 1,000 or even 1 in 500, typical estimates for the larger nations of Europe from about 1820 to 1850, but more like 1 in 300. A particularly noteworthy investigation of insanity and its hereditary influences was conducted in 1859 by Ludvig Vilhelm Dahl, who exploited the detailed census information available on the geographical distribution of insanity in Norway. On this basis he pioneered the meticulous inventory of local communities, aspiring to identify every case (to get the ratio right) and every family member (to understand inheritance).[19]

The southwestern German state of Württemberg was another particularly bright star in the firmament of insanity science. Its mastery of census-taking reached a high point in an 1878 work by the director of the well-known institution of Zwiefalten, Julius Koch. Koch's book surveyed the history of censuses of the insane in Württemberg, in other German states, and in the rest of Europe and North America, arguing hopefully that each new census was able to draw on the accumulation of experience to reduce the error stemming from a subjective conception and, less hopefully, that better and more modern censuses increase again and again the number of the known insane. The Württemberg census involved an elaborate process of enlisting enumerators, to be arranged under a chief in each district, with the support and when possible the active participation of Protestant, Catholic and Jewish clergy. Its results, while not providing definitive answers to any of the questions that had troubled alienists, achieved a special authority comparable to that of the Norwegians. Koch was impressed by the forces in modern life, especially hereditary, that were tending to increase mental illness, and he concluded tentatively that while idiocy seemed to be

---

[19] Fredrik Holst, *Beretning, Betankning og Indstilling fra en til at undersøge de Sindsvages Kaar i Norge og gjøre Forslag til deres Forbedring i Aaret 1825 naadigst nedsat Kongelig Commission* (Christiania: Trykt hos Jacob Lehmanns Enke, 1828); Ludvig Vilhelm Dahl, *Bijdrag til Kundskab om de Sindssyge i Norge* (Christiania: Det Steenske Bogtrykkeri, 1859).

declining slightly, the picture for insanity was much darker. Still, he was not tempted to suppose that the high numbers for his own state implied a greater prevalence of mental disease. Their status as medical indicators was very much in doubt. They were a tribute, rather, to the excellent organization of its census.[20]

TAMING THE BUSINESS CYCLE

With economic measures of the early twentieth century, we return to indicators in name as well as in fact. Large corporations, especially in the United States, developed business indicators as part of their endeavor to reduce their vulnerability to fluctuations of economic activity. The aftermath of the Great War brought dismaying irregularities of prices as well as of demand and unemployment, and the favored term 'business cycle' seems an optimistic way of naming these disorderly movements. Indeed, one of the leading students of business cycles in the period immediately following the war, Warren M. Persons, found it impossible to distinguish irregular fluctuations reliably from cyclical ones.[21] In relation to the 1930s, this focus on regular cycles seems even more hopeful, though of course it wasn't clear at first that 1929 was the beginning of so deep and widespread a failure of the capitalist economies. The extraordinary prosperity of the period leading up to this collapse gave hope that rational planning could tame the business cycle. It was one of those moments of managerial exuberance that were destined to be criticized as hubris, and that have recurred as if in cycles. Faith in the predictive power of business indicators undergirded that confidence, and in this context the indicator became, for the first time, a focus of sustained research and discussion.

The use by Persons and his contemporaries of business 'barometer' interchangeably with 'indicator' clarifies the meanings. A barometer gives a measure of air pressure, but only an indication of the weather, and while the causality of the measuring was clear enough, prediction was highly imperfect and involved complicated notions of causality. The business cycle, a fashionable new preoccupation in 1920, was far from a new idea. Those who favored this conceptualization during the nineteenth century offered a variety of views as to what drove the

---

[20] Julius Ludwig August Koch, *Zur Statistik der Geisteskrankheiten in Württemberg und der Geisteskrankheiten überhaupt* (Stuttgart: Druck von W. Kohlhammer, 1878).

[21] Mary Morgan, *The History of Econometric Ideas* (Cambridge: Cambridge University Press, 1990) p. 60.

cycles. The sunspots of William Stanley Jevons and the influence of Venus theorized by Henry Ludwell Moore seemed outrageous, but perhaps not more so than supposing, as Marx and his followers were wont to do, that market processes or capitalism generated these unruly oscillations. Persons, an econometric pioneer, was willing to put aside for a time the question of cause for the sake of statistical techniques that would sort out the different movements to which business was subject. He fixed on four of these: long-term growth, seasonal cycles, business cycles and random fluctuations. Making intermittent use of the new biometric statistics of correlation, introduced by Francis Galton and Karl Pearson, while relying systematically on graphs of statistical series placed on an illuminated screen and viewed together in pairs, he sought a rule for how each element behaved over the course of a full cycle. Persons sought, in particular, the measure of correlation between different series, as well as their degree of anticipation or lag. A graph, titled 'The Index of General Business Conditions' effectively summed up the work and made it plausible. Here he merged a host of variables, functioning as indicators, into five groups, straightforwardly titled Group I, Group II, Group III, Group IV and Group V. The substances and even the units involved were almost bizarrely heterogeneous. Group III, for example, combined tonnage of pig iron, bank clearings, merchandise import values, unfilled orders of the US Steel Corporation, and Bradstreet's index of the number of business failures. Graphed along an axis of time, the lines were jagged and irregular, and went a bit haywire with the outbreak of the Great War. Yet they conveyed a general impression of lower-number groups anticipating higher-number ones, and a definite sense of Groups I and II reaching their peaks and troughs in advance of III, IV and V. He could not explain in any detail why it should be this way, yet he insisted that this kind of information had great practical value.[22]

A few examples give an idea of the ways the trade press took up business cycle indicators, and how business firms put them to use. In 1920, the *Practical Druggist and Spatula* instructed its readers to keep a record of business from year to year, since banks would want to see this indicator of the ups and downs of finance before deciding to extend credit. According to the *Iron Trade Review* in 1926: 'One of the most encouraging developments of recent years has been the increase in available

---

[22] *Ibid.* pp. 56–63; Warren M. Persons, 'An Index of General Business Conditions', *Review of Economic Statistics*, *Preliminary Volume* (April 1919) 2: 110–211, at p. 110.

statistics and measures of industry, together with the growing intelligent use of these valuable tools.' It attached that pronouncement to a specific discussion of indicators used in the trade. 'This index was chosen because it happens to be the business indicator which coincides most closely with the fluctuations of the business of the company with which I am connected.' Indicators, we learn, were included 'as part of the management week program arranged by Ohio State University. Mr. Smith has found that the Blast Furnace Index coincides more nearly with the fluctuations of his company than any other important business index.'[23]

At the annual meeting of the American Statistical Association in late December 1923, Persons and two colleagues organized a series of presentations on business forecasting. These appeared in an edited collection the following year. Most of the speakers had degrees in economics, statistics or related social sciences. Only a few held positions in private companies, but neither were there many university professors. Many were employed at government agencies like the US Geological Survey or the Department of Agriculture, and hence were closely engaged in promotion and regulation of the economy, without having as their highest priority the interests or the secrets of particular firms. Forecasting, as we have seen, had mainly to do with the business cycle. It relied heavily on indicators, whose justification was primarily grounded in correlation or correspondence of graphical form. Sometimes these made causal sense, as in agriculture where, as Henry Wallace remarked, corn prices are a better indicator of hog prices than the reverse. More generally, investors and financiers, collectively if not individually, somehow sniffed out the future direction of things before anyone else. If you want to anticipate agricultural yields, don't look to the sky or the weather bureau. 'The data seem to indicate that the stock market is the promptest indicator of probable demand for farm products', explained G. F. Warren and F. A. Pearson.[24]

---

[23] E. Fullerton Cook, 'Records: A Key to Business Success', *Practical Druggist and Spatula, Consolidated* (September 1920) 38: 27; *The Iron Trade Review* (1926) 79(2) 1243, at p. 1239. These lines, alas, are mere snippets on Google Ngram; I have not been able to access the original publications.

[24] H. A. Wallace, 'Forecasting Corn and Hog Prices' in Warren M. Persons, William Trufant Foster and Albert J. Hettinger (eds.), *The Problem of Business Forecasting, Papers Presented at the Eighty-Fifth Annual Meeting of the American Statistical Association, Washington D.C., December 27–29, 1923* (Boston, Mass.: Houghton-Mifflin Company, 1924) pp. 237–9, at p. 237; G. F. Warren and F. A. Pearson, 'Agricultural and Business Cycles' in *ibid*. pp. 250–64, at p. 258.

For a specific industry, the most valuable indicators were those that anticipated the cyclical movements of its own business. The main purpose of the collection, however, was to identify variables that reveal the direction of business activity generally. The value for this purpose of any particular statistical series, even if it was known to reflect intrinsic characteristics of the underlying commodity, depended on how carefully and for how long statisticians and economists had been observing it. Only extended experience could provide the background knowledge necessary to distinguish long-term increases from cyclical movements, and these from weather-related phenomena and other meaningless fluctuations. A group of authors led by George Otis Smith of the Geological Survey argued that electric power output was highly promising as a business indicator given its diversity of uses, but first its behavior had to be watched for a number of years. For the moment, they said, pig iron provided a more solid base of anticipation, since its behavior was known from long experience, and it was little subject to strikes or other 'accidental causes'. Some industries and products move in step with business cycles, others not, wrote L. D. H. Weld. As the best indicators, he listed railroad traffic, iron and steel, building construction, and AT&T, the telephone company.[25]

The statistical science of business indicators reached its zenith in 1929. The high level of confidence is epitomized by the title of a book by Monard V. Hayes, *Accounting for Executive Control*. Hayes insisted on the scientific character of business management and the need for accounting to come up to the same high level. For him, science meant prediction, plain and simple. Only on the basis of appropriate accounts could scientific managers predict accurately. 'If accounting is to serve management best it must accomplish the purpose of all science – that of prediction.' To highlight the problem of business prediction, he imagined a firm, the Mileage Tire Company, whose product will be free from fluctuations since it wears down uniformly. But every other business faces the problem of anticipation. 'This might at first appear to be an impossible problem, one to be "solved" by soothsayers and fortune-tellers, but it is not. This is just another business problem that has been and can be solved by scientific methods.' 'The general idea is to find some indices of business indicators which will serve as forecasting media

[25] George Otis Smith *et al.* (a footnote lists six further authors), 'Fluctuations in Mineral Output' in *ibid.* pp. 144–174, at pp. 150, 154, 174; L. D. H. Weld, 'Relating Manufacturing Policy to the Business Cycle' in *ibid.* pp. 93–9.

for a given industry or business.' Once management has identified 'a commodity or group of commodities, or some business indicator, which will show cyclical fluctuations which precede those of a given business by, say, three to five months, the administration of the business with regard to external business conditions then becomes a relatively simple matter'.[26]

A more visible event of 1929, still more auspicious for scientific management of the business cycle, was the inauguration of the brilliant engineer and manager, Herbert Hoover, as President of the United States. As Secretary of Commerce in the administrations of Harding and Coolidge, Hoover had worked out an 'associative' ideal of economic order, one to be formed and maintained by private industry, but not mainly through free, competitive markets. Rather, quasi-monopolistic corporations, little threatened by competition, were in a position to use their managerial expertise to set wages and prices in a way that served the common interest as well as their own. This idea of planning was not original to Hoover, having been taking shape for some time among the business corporations themselves. The sharp depression of 1920–1921 heightened the urgency of coordinating business activity, to which the new focus on business cycles was in part a response. Hoover's Commerce Department organized the collection of needed statistics, indicators of demand and production that would enable business to avoid shocks and surprises by planning ahead. This first flourishing of business indicators, while by no means synonymous with neoliberal governance, relied heavily on quantitative information to coordinate economic activity in a decentralized way. Even the data work, much of it performed by the National Bureau of Economic Research under Wesley Mitchell, was in some sense privatized. By 1929, they had it down to a system. An NBER report in the spring of 1929, coinciding with the first months of Hoover's presidency, celebrated 'the maintenance of our economic balance' for eight years of unmatched prosperity.[27]

Alas, it was not yet the end of 1929. The stock market crash and its aftermath undermined the strategies of decomposition of economic data and cast doubt on the transparency of indicators. On 6 July 1935,

---

[26] Monard V. Hayes, *Accounting for Executive Control* (New York: Harper & Brothers, 1929) pp. xi, 28, 338, 358.

[27] Stapleford, *Cost of Living*, n. 2 above, pp. 119, 138–9; Ellis W. Hawley, 'Herbert Hoover, the Commerce Secretariat, and the Vision of an "Associative State"', *Journal of American History* (1974) 61: 116–40; Guy Alchon, *The Invisible Hand of Planning: Capitalism, Social Science, and the State in the 1920s* (Princeton, N.J.: Princeton University Press, 1985).

the *Magazine of Wall Street* commented that the electric power index had almost returned to the high level of 1929. 'It need hardly be said that this is no longer a reliable business indicator, its high level contrasting so strikingly with continuing business depression.' Yet something, after all, was indicated by this number, namely, a great increase of home appliances, especially refrigerators.[28] In no way did the sting of Depression and Second World War undermine reliance on statistics, whose production, instead, reached unimagined heights. But the soft power of the indicator, treated as external to the firm, gave way to a more comprehensive, government-directed form of planning.

HISTORICAL POINTERS

The past does not repeat itself, and 2008 was not 1929. Neoliberal indicators of the era since 1980 presume a larger and more active social state than was to be found in the United States, or perhaps anywhere, in the 1920s. They also presume an economy, already highly corporatized by 1930, shaped by the power of finance. The indicator here assumed its role within a system of incentives that are supposed to mimic markets by functioning as artificial markets. Corporate capitalism means anything but the unadorned power of markets. It is rather a system of centrally-administered relations dressed up as markets, and, to be sure, sometimes disciplined by markets. Adam Smith characterized the logic of markets in terms of those butchers, brewers and bakers who supply us with our daily needs because we pay them for doing so. Some of our commercial relations are still like that, but big firms depend on a mix of direct monitoring and discipline with systems of artificial incentives. The artificiality of so much that passes as market behavior is the primary source of exploitable ambiguities that so often discredit the indicators.

The decentralizing moves of neoliberal governance left private firms and lower levels of government free to adopt the most advantageous means they knew to achieve desired ends, and to be compensated on the basis of the results they attained rather than the resources consumed.[29] It is an excellent system, provided the rewards are distributed only when contractors realise the actual purposes of the contract. But such goals are always subtle, with the indicator standing in place of a thing that is

---

28 *Magazine of Wall Street* (1935) 56: 281.
29 Alain Desrosières, 'Managing the Economy' in Theodore M. Porter and Dorothy Ross (eds.), *The Cambridge History of Science*, vol. VII, *Modern Social Sciences* (Cambridge: Cambridge University Press, 2003) pp. 553–64; see also Alain Desrosières, Chapter 13.

difficult or impossible to specify precisely enough to be legally enforceable. The world of indicators assumes that ends can be made crystal clear, and the means left to entrepreneurial ingenuity. But in real life, the ingenuity and enterprise of contractors may be exercised to evade these purposes and to fulfill their obligations to the letter (only) at minimal cost. If every contract for hand straps on subway cars requires eighty pages of detailed descriptions, then the much-reviled world of cumbersome bureaucracy gains very little from letting private firms with experience making this kind of product bid to carry out the contract. And in practice, eighty or even 800 pages is never enough, and often at the same time too much, to define workable, enforceable goals.

Indicator diagrams for steam engines were among the earliest of self-registering instruments, and left little opportunity for deliberate deception. Indicator birds knew what they were looking for, as did the honey hunters, though the relationship could break down if the honey hunters got too greedy, or if too many scientific explorers were impelled to collect too many specimens. In a system of government that lubricates contractual relationships with political contributions, there may not be much incentive to fulfill the real purposes of a contract. If schools, subject to the requirement to increase test scores to a certain level, achieve this by teaching very specific and useless testable skills rather than by raising educational levels (which are never easy to define), the results may not be happy. If banks pay their best bonuses for loans bearing the highest interest rates, or for profits that are only possible from highly leveraged transactions, they are asking for trouble. And if the good test results bring prestige to mayors, or if a portion of trading profits is passed along to top management, there is not much incentive to point out what the emperor is really wearing. Within such systems, those Spaces of Exploitable Ambiguity will be pushed ever wider, like water freezing and thawing in the fissures of a rock, until no one can say just where the indicator is pointing.[30]

On the other hand, it would be foolish and self-defeating to imagine that public ends must be achieved without some effective use of individual incentives. Emperors, we must understand, depend utterly on their adornments. On the one hand, there is always opportunity to spin webs of deception. On the other, the goals we aim for are never fully transparent, and never sufficient, until we take into account

---

[30] Porter, 'Funny Numbers', n. 17 above.

the by-products and implications of the actions they call for. Reduction to quantitative indicators may provide a rough solution, may be invaluable for achieving shared goals of public and private enterprise. And yet I see no prospect of achieving the utopia of self-regulated collective action without calling sometimes on moral and intellectual virtues that go beyond self-interested actors maximizing their profits. Such virtues would include understanding, communication and public responsibility.

CHAPTER THREE

NARRATING NUMBERS

Wendy Espeland

INTRODUCTION

This chapter examines one aspect of the logic that characterizes many indicators: the dynamic relationship between simplification and elaboration that is behind the production, circulation and interpretation of indicators. Indicators are appealing partly because they simplify complex organizations and processes in order to produce public, authoritative knowledge that makes them appear legible to outsiders. This simplification takes many forms but one way to characterize it is to understand it as the erasure of narratives: the systematic removal of the persons, places and trajectories of the people being evaluated by the indicator and the people doing the evaluation. This stripping away of narrative facilitates the circulation and insertion of numbers in new locations and their adaptability to new contexts. But as these new forms of knowledge move about and are re-appropriated or resisted by those being evaluated, they elicit new narratives, new stories about what they mean, how they unfold, if they are fair or unfair, or who made them

This chapter is a revised version of one presented at 'A World of Indicators: Knowledge Technologies of Regulation, Domination, Experimentation and Critique in an Interconnected World', 13–15 October 2011, Max Planck Institute for Social Anthropology, Halle, Germany. Thanks to prime movers Johanna Mugler, Sung-Joon Park, Richard Rottenburg, Bettina Mann and Sally Merry for their invitation and hospitality, and to all conference participants for their useful comments. Thanks especially to Cosima Rhughinis for her sage written comments. This chapter is based on research conducted jointly with Michael Sauder, a sociologist at the University of Iowa, and has been generously supported by fellowships and grants from the Russell Sage Foundation, Law School Admissions Council, the Radcliffe Institute for Advanced Study and the Wissenschaft-skolleg zu Berlin but does not reflect the views of those organizations.

and why. These narratives are important to analyse because they help us understand how actors make sense of their worlds, which is crucial for understanding the impact of quantification. Relying primarily on the examples of educational rankings, I consider this interplay between the erasure and invocation of narratives for different audiences in the production and reception of indicators.

An essay on narrative ought to start with a story. It is April, five or so years ago, and the Dean of a large, prestigious West Coast law school is dreading the 'town-hall meeting' he has felt compelled to schedule.[1] He was expecting scores of unhappy students well-schooled in the art of argument to attend. The reason the Dean called this meeting is that the *US News and World Report* (*USN*), an American news magazine, had just released its annual ranking of graduate schools, including US law schools. The school's rank had just dropped two notches.[2] His job at the meeting would be to explain why and try to reassure the students that theirs was still an elite school and that their careers were not jeopardized because of this decline in rank.

Law students are an articulate and anxious bunch, especially after the economic crisis shrivelled the market for attorneys; but even so students' reactions to the small drop in rankings at this school seem extreme, at first blush. According to students we interviewed, after news of the drop in ranking spread throughout the school in a matter of minutes, they went 'berserk'. News of the decline 'leaked into pretty much every conversation about school or the administration since then', according to Riley, a second year student. She reported that, 'It was all anyone talked about', so much so that student initiatives to change school policy, months in the planning, were put on hold because 'nobody cared about anything but rankings right now'. Many students, including Riley, were re-thinking their decision to attend this school, even though this was near the end of her second year of law school. According to Riley, 'I could have gotten almost a free ride at [an East Coast law school,] and instead I paid full tuition to come here because it was, "quote, unquote, a better school"'. Students were especially concerned because a local rival law school now fared slightly better in comparisons between the two schools' rankings than they had previously. Students worried that potential employers would look less favorably on

[1] References to particular schools or particular school rankings are deliberately left vague.
[2] Most people use language like 'dropping', or 'rising' or 'up' or 'down' to describe the trajectory of rankings even if, technically, rankings get smaller as they get better and larger as they get worse. With educational rankings, the normative trumps the accurate depictions of movements.

them because of this lower rank and that they would suffer in head-to-head comparisons with their regional rival. They *knew* that rankings mattered.

Now, the Dean of this particular law school knew that his school's decline, say from 15 to 17, or 14 to 16, was a statistically meaningless shift in the rankings. The algorithm that determined rankings, one devised by journalists at a for-profit magazine, was a formula so capricious it would flunk any statistical sensitivity test were one applied to its results. Since the scores of schools are so tightly bunched, even tiny adjustments to the weights of the various factors – reputation, selectivity, faculty resources and library quality – or small changes in raw numbers, would generate wild swings in rankings, the opposite of the desired characteristic that methodologists refer to as a 'robust finding'.[3] This Dean also knew that the law school had improved in so many ways over the past few years, reflecting an increase in its budget, more selective admissions and several prominent faculty hires. And he knew that, according to USN, his school remained firmly entrenched in the top twenty law schools in the country. Yet, he was also aware that the anxiety his students' expressed was real, that local media would report the school's 'decline', and that he would be called upon to account for this change as if it did reflect something real, something important. And his explanation for declining rank must include not just the concerns of students and faculty, but also his Board of Trustees, alumni, and even the firms who might employ his graduates. So, as much as he, like most deans, hated rankings, believing them to be misleading measures and dangerous for legal education, like all law school deans he was required to treat them with utter seriousness.[4]

The Dean's task at this meeting would be to explain why and how this 'drop' occurred, what the school was going to do about it, and to reassure students that their school's reputation and their professional futures would not be scarred by this new ranking. As another administrator put it, when rankings go down a notch or two 'You've got to give them the "I take your concerns very seriously but there, there, it will be alright" speech. And it's not just the students who need the speech.

---

[3] For methodological criticisms of law school rankings and USN educational rankings see Klein and Hamilton 1998; Lempert 2002.

[4] For example, we heard opinions like this one from many deans: 'The methodology is awful. I know when this first started that most of the deans at the accredited law schools stood up and said, "We will not comply with this." But then everybody started caving bit by bit and now it's a full-fledged business operation.'

Sometimes the faculty need it most of all.' But as this Dean knew, if his school dropped even one notch again next year, as one professor put it, 'Of course, all hell would break out.'

So, what is going on here? We can see rankings as part of a powerful global trend to render accountability and regulation in quantitative terms, one that makes it easier for outsiders to evaluate and compare schools, to note whether they are improving or not. One early example of this trend was the educational audits initiated by the Thatcher administration in the United Kingdom as part of its efforts to privatize government and reduce the influence of its most elite schools (Power 1994; Strathern 2000) and in US media outlets like the *USN*, *Business-Week* and *Financial Times* in their efforts to generate revenue and a distinctive identity. The attention that these new indicators garnered helped propel the proliferation of performance indicators, as did the European Union's efforts to integrate and standardize much policy and other globalizing processes. Today, the impact and reach of quantitative indicators is so powerful, it is hard to define accountability or performance in terms other than quantitative performance measures.

WHAT DO I MEAN BY INDICATORS?

Indicators are technologies of communication that are usually meant to address some practical problem. Indicators may be qualitative (e.g. letter grades, thumbs up or down, the canary in the mine-shaft) but for my purposes here, I restrict indicators to quantitative expressions that require or presume commensuration and integrate several measures (Davis, Fisher and Merry 2012). Indicators produce relationships among the things or people that they measure by sorting them according to a shared metric. The relations created by commensuration are at the same time precise and abstract; they simultaneously unite objects with this overarching metric and create precise distinctions among them that are subsumed as a matter of more and less (Carruthers and Espeland 1991; Espeland and Stevens 1998). So, for example, standardized test scores create a relationship among all those who have ever taken that test. That relationship is defined statistically, in terms of how well or poorly a particular test-taker does compared to everyone else. In this sense, every test-taker is joined to every other test-taker by virtue of having a test score and by the underlying assumption that the score measures some variable attribute such as intelligence, merit or whatever. This highly abstract relationship is inevitably reductive.

It does not take into account most characteristics of the people who take it or the context in which they take it. It reduces complex humans into test scores that are useful because they simplify and generate comparisons.

At the same time that standardized tests construct an abstract relationship that unifies test-takers, they also, like other quantitative indicators, create exact distinctions among the people they evaluate. By reducing a person to a test score we can compare her or him to everyone else who has ever taken that particular test. We know the specific relationship between all test-takers and we can construct statistics like averages or percentiles. Indicators are representations of something that requires interpretation and often serve as mechanisms of 'soft' power, as more or less legitimate means for distributing scarce resources. Quantitative indicators must be defended in terms of methodology and their usefulness. Often this usefulness is considered a public good.

To borrow Anne Swidler's metaphor (1986), indicators are cultural practices or signs that can be understood as handy tools that get moved around to new workers, new toolboxes and new worksites. Moreover, these tools leave their own marks on the places they go and the people that use them. Tools can be new things in the world, or they can seem new if they are put to new uses or used in new places, and they can be used to create new objects, or in our case, new kinds of people. If we think of indicators as 'tools' of communication, as a practice of representation, as cognitively significant, embedded in and constitutive of relationships among people and things, this helps us get at the array of changes indicators may elicit: in practical power, its communicative power, its constitutive power and so on. I would argue that we need to appreciate more seriously and systematically the *forms* that these relations take.

WHAT DO I MEAN BY NARRATIVE?

It is worth pointing out that the term 'narrative' comes from the Latin word, *narrare*, which means to recount. The kinds of narratives I am describing here are quite literally a re-counting of, or accounting for, important numbers. The narrative form is a structure of organization, basically that of a story in which there is usually a narrator, the people telling the story, protagonists, the people the story is about, a sequence of events or plot which often hinge on some problem. Narratives typically include stylized scenes or places in which the stories are located that help disclose important characteristics of the people or problem at hand. Narratives often begin with a catalyst that sets the events in motion and some sort of resolution.

Narratives have many purposes – to entertain, inform, persuade or to make sense of an experience – which is why, to paraphrase the literary scholar Kenneth Burke (1973), narratives are 'equipment for living'. They are a form of rhetorical discourse and can be organized as many different genres: the identity narrative; narrative poetry; narrative history; myth and so on. The narratives that indicators elicit are often causal and defensive, and often focus on unpacking some formalized aspect of identity that is a component of rankings. Some person or organization is telling a story and the story is a causal story that accounts for how events or entities are linked.

Why does it matter that people construct narratives around numbers that affect them? What can we learn from studying narratives as narratives? First, it is important to notice that they exist and are amenable to investigation. Second, analysing the narratives that indicators evoke helps us to better understand the effects of quantification because they are crucial means by which we make sense of ourselves and what is going on and this knowledge will complicate our understanding of indicators. Third, greater sensitivity to the narrative form can help us understand how quantification subverts narratives. And, finally, narratives are amenable to different strategies and tools for analysis than is quantitative information.

INDICATORS AS SIMPLIFICATIONS

One useful way to think about quantitative indicators is that they are technologies of simplification, strategies that make complex processes visible and easy to grasp, and make comparisons – across people, organizations, or time – easy. This simplification is both why we value indicators so much and why we often feel they misrepresent us. Many scholars have investigated the effects of such simplifications and there is an emerging consensus that indicators shape what people notice, how we think and make decisions, how we interact or fail to interact with each other, how power is expressed and politics is conducted, and whose expertise is included or excluded.[5] Quantification can be understood as

---

[5] Some of these scholars include Power 1994; Porter 1995; Espeland 1998; Espeland and Stevens 1998, Strathern 2000; Espeland and Sauder 2007; Mennicken and Miller 2012; Lampland and Star 2009; Davis, Kingsbury, and Merry 2012.

a systematic stripping away of the components of narrative: author, protagonist, scene and sequence in ways that are conventional, defensible and potentially reproducible to others.

Let me illustrate this point about simplification with an example of a merchant's 'account' of a business transaction from Forcalguier, in southeast France, in 1331 (Lopez, Raymond and Constable 1990):

> Owes Jacon, son of Astruc of Digne, 30 silver [deniers] Tournoise for 1 ½ cannas of canet of Carcassonne. To pay one half at the fair and the other at the beginning of Lent. And he took it – record by Chabaut – on May 8. Owes Jacon, in addition, s. 4 for some hose of blue [cloth] of Saint-Pons. To pay now. And he took it on the day and year written above. In the year of the Lord 1331, on May 9, I, Guillem Ortonlani, notary, acknowledge to you, Ugo Teralh, notary [and] merchant of Forcalquiet, that I personally have had and have received through purchase from you 1 ½ cannas of checkered [cloth] of Toulouse for the price of s. 24 at the rate of s. 16 the canna.

Notice that this account of two transactions takes the form of a simple narrative, with an author (Guillem Ortonlani, both notary and cloth buyer), protagonists (Jacon, the first cloth seller; Chabaut, notary or record keeper; Ugo Teralh the second cloth seller), and action that is organized sequentially, temporally, contextually: it occurs at the fair at which cloth was bought and recorded yesterday; notarized with an additional sale made today, with additional repayment due at the beginning of Lent; two actors are absent (Jacon and Chabaut), two are co-present (Ortonlani and Teralh); action includes making a down payment on cloth that is measured, described, identified by location: made in Carcassonne, or blue from Saint-Pons, or checkered and from Toulouse. Such accounts were common and served mainly as a private means for merchants to remember transactions and collect debts.

This form of accounting gradually changed with the advent of double-entry book-keeping, an accounting technique that was invented by unknown merchants in northern Italy in the late thirteenth or early fourteenth century and circulated in a treatise by Frater Lucas Pacioli in 1492. Scholars of capitalism such as Max Weber, Werner Sombart and Joseph Schumpeter describe double-entry book-keeping (DEB), a practice of recording each transaction twice, once as a debit and a credit, as a revolutionary practice that was essential for the development of capitalism. So Ortonlani's debt to Jacon would be rendered more concisely as two columns of numbers, with each number entered twice, once as a debit, once as a credit, with price expressed in a single currency. The narrative is stripped away such that all that remains are numbers, devoid of author, actors, timing, sequence or context. The simplification that DEB affords makes it much easier to glance at the account and know precisely how much was owed, paid, and what the balance is. It creates an indicator of financial wellbeing that we today convey, in common parlance and in arcane and complex formulations, as 'the bottom line'.

Among the technical virtues of DEB is that it permits merchants to calculate a running balance to make sure they are accurate. DEB also makes it possible to conceptualize business as a continuous rather than an episodic practice, so that books need not wait for the return of a ship or the end of a partnership for a balance to be struck. But advocates made even stronger claims for the value of DEB than their technical superiority (Carruthers and Espeland 1991). DEB could also make you a more disciplined person and thus enhance your reputation, which was crucial if you wanted credit or God's approval. In one of the earliest known explanations of DEB which appeared in the treatise entitled *Of Commerce and the Perfect Merchant* by Benedetto Cotrugli he exhorts:[6]

> The pen is an instrument so noble and excellent that it is absolutely necessary not only to merchants but also in any art . . . And when you see a merchant to whom the pen is a burden or who is inept with the pen, you may say he is not a merchant. And [a good merchant] not only must be skilled in writing, but also must keep his records methodologically . . . For no merchant ought to transact his business by heart, unless he were like King Cyrus, who could call by name every person in his entire army, which was innumerable.

The practice of accounting broadly, and DEB more specifically, gradually became associated with precision, accuracy and legitimacy of the business practices and the businessman under scrutiny. For a long time, precise quantification was understood as a means for forging and reflecting character, a means of self-improvement.

Theodore Porter (1995) describes the flip-side of the sort of simplification that DEB accomplishes, relying on Bourguet's investigation of

---

[6] Benedetto Cotrugli, first known as Benedikt Kotruljevic, was born in 1416 in what is now Debrovnik, lived as a merchant, diplomat, scholar in Naples for many years. He died in 1469. The better known conveyer of DEB is Luca Pacioli, whose famous treatise, Summa de arithmetica, geometria, proportioni et proportionalità, was published in Venice in 1494. The reason why Pacioli was thought to be the first written explanation of DEB was that Cotrugli's text was not officially published until 1573.

the failed census conducted by the French Bureau de Statistique in1800. Without a large, trained labor force, prefects were forced to enlist local elite volunteers to compile information about their regions. Instead of the quantitative information about economies, population and occupations using the designated categories that the prefects sought, volunteers submitted vast detailed monographs that were impossible for the Bureau to assimilate. Revolutionary France, it turned out, was still too divided by status and locale to fit into the neat categories prescribed by the statisticians. The simplification required for a census demanded a more centralized state, a more uniform populace and more compliant workers. Before it could be represented statistically, France had to be turned into a more standardized nation. What the examples of DEB and the failed census demonstrate is how powerful and difficult are the 'simplifications' wrought by quantification, by turning narratives into numbers.

In the case of law schools, rankings reduce a complex social institution into a formula that is based on a set of assumptions that reflect the mission and performance of an elite, national law school. Any deviations from this model, whether intentional or not, are not captured in the ranking, so that for many schools, rankings measure them for goals they do not share. For example, instead of a strong focus on maximizing selectivity based on high test scores, a school may wish to provide opportunities to under-represented groups or cater to students who want to perform public interest law. These missions do not matter with rankings. And the history, character and culture of a school is not conveyed in rankings, often among the qualities we most cherish in our organizations.

While each indicator will prompt some distinctive effects, there are broad patterns in how indicators simplify. I have already discussed some of the cognitive consequences of commensuration. In creating indicators, there is a strong preference for components that are already standardized and expressed in numbers. Features, which are hard or expensive to measure, are more likely to be excluded. So, for example, we determine merit based on standardized test scores rather than artistic expression or character. We assess a library not on the quality of the collection or the service provided by librarians but by the number of books in its holdings.

Another important attribute of quantification is that many audiences believe that it is more 'objective' than other forms of information and

therefore accord it a special 'scientific' authority. Part of this objectivity resides in the presumption that numbers are 'transparent' – that
they have clear, stable, universal meanings, such that they are forms of
public communication that transcend social, geographical and historical contexts; that they are, in Porter's words, 'impersonal'. Numbers that
seem impersonal have removed their connections to the people who
produce them, one important potential source of bias or contamination;
another source of this impersonality is that to produce them we rely
on the rules and examples of powerful others when we produce them,
which confers a technical and symbolic legitimacy that appeases critics
and justifies actions both within and outside of organizations and communities. The characteristics that we attribute to numbers and their
capacity to simplify information whose volume, pace and complexity
threatens to overwhelm us, are two reasons why numbers spread and
travel to so many places.

Another consequence of the commensuration of law schools that
rankings produce is that by attaching to each school a number, which
defines their precise relationship to every other school, rankings force
comparisons and magnify the competition among law schools. While
schools have always been competing for the best students, faculty
and jobs, rankings formalize the competition and create new forms of
competition. Instead of being concerned with how one fares against
local schools, schools now must compete with every other school and
changes in the ranking of one school can affect many. This leads to
intense scrutiny and a paranoia about what tactics other schools are
using to improve their numbers.

QUANTIFICATION AS STIMULATING NARRATIVE

I want to offer here what I think is a useful complement to this crucial
understanding of quantitative indicators as technologies of simplification. If the main job of indicators is to classify, reduce, simplify, to make
visible certain kinds of knowledge, indicators are also generative in
ways we sometimes ignore: they evoke narratives, stories about what the
indicators mean, what are their virtues or limitations, who should use
them to what effect, their promises and their failings. The stories told by
those subject to quantification often reclaim information that has been
stripped away, including reasons for numbers, their context and identity claims about their organizations. I believe that it is important for

those of us who investigate quantification, indicators or commensuration to account for the emergence, variation and effects of these narratives if we want to more fully grasp the meaning and power of numbers. Narratives are often a corrective to numbers; they are responses to what numbers cull and to the distortions or misrepresentations that people believe that numbers inflict.

Back to the 'town-hall meeting' I began with. The first thing to notice is that the Dean called this meeting. Because rankings are produced annually, and because they can go up and down, and are widely distributed by a media corporation, they are easily framed as 'news'. Often, local newspapers and television stations report the results of new rankings for regional schools, creating literal 'stories' about rankings. News about new rankings is reported in many other genres, too; they appear in blogs devoted to legal education and law, in memos sent to faculty and students, in emails, on webpages, in marketing brochures, in apps for mobile phones, and in tweets to friends. So it is not surprising that the Dean of this elite law school felt compelled to respond to this 'news' quickly. In this sense, rankings do seem to offer new tools and a regular occasion for holding law schools 'accountable', for explaining to various audiences why their school is improving or dropping in the rankings. Moreover, given the clear and very public 'trends' rankings create, anyone is qualified to comment on a school's performance because anyone can see if a number is higher or lower than last year. Where in the past, we might expect students to be deferential to their Dean, at least in public, rankings now offer a clear and legitimate means and time for confronting her or him, especially if the news isn't good. Complaints take on a new weight when they offer clear targets for mobilization and they are based on public indicators. Many deans we interviewed described how rankings have changed their interactions with students and applicants. As one Dean recounted:

> And we have even been in the position of having students call us to say, 'Why have you dropped in the rankings? I would never have applied if I had known that you were going to fall in the rankings.' In a lot of situations these people are not necessarily going to have had the opportunity to enjoy us wherever we may be ranked.

As this Dean suggested, even students who are unlikely to be admitted can challenge a school's ranking. Another Dean described the unpleasant experience of dropping to the bottom tier one year, a change that reflected a tiny and in his view unimportant change.

I remember when we went from third tier to fourth tier we heard that from students who wanted to know why and what was different this year from last year, and why it was and what could be done. So, yes, you hear from students. I think it really affects students. I think alumni are a little more detached from it currently. But for students that's the school they're going to right now and they're paying a lot of money to go to that school, and then they see in USN that somebody says that they're going to a mediocre law school.

For another school, the alumni were less detached about rankings. According to one administrator:

We briefly fell – for one year – into the third tier and the Dean got a lot of questions from alums, you know, 'What's happening?' And the truth is that we were kind of on that margin between the second and third tier and this was back before we cut the size of the class and so just a little fluctuation in class credentials and suddenly you're in a different tier.

But dropping a tier is a far more drastic event than slipping two notches for the highly ranked West Coast school. Even so, the pressure from students was resonant. I could not attend the town-hall meeting called by the Dean, but based on the interviews and emails with people at this school and others in similar situations I have a good sense of what likely happened. The Dean would have tried to reassure students that their school today was the same school as yesterday before the rankings came out and that it remained a stellar institution that enjoyed an excellent reputation. He would emphasize the wonderful jobs that recent graduates had obtained, the network of alumni that would continue to help them find employment, and the sense of community that endured among its alumni long after graduation. He would no doubt talk about the methodological flaws of rankings, and the wonderful characteristics of the school that they fail to take into account.[7] In asserting the uniqueness of their school, he would disentangle the unity that commensuration confers and perhaps help mitigate the competition students feel with their local rivals.

---

[7] A Dean at a different school described his approach to a drop this way: 'So I had to have a town meeting with the students in which I described how these things happen and how the rankings were "discovered" and tried to inculcate the appropriate skepticism in them and explain that a drop of whatever – forget it for a second – what does it mean? It means that somebody, namely USN, decided that they were going to rank seriatim the top 50 and then they're going to have second tier and third tier and not differentiate within those tiers. And now that's just an absolutely corporate decision…So you can go from 51st to 50th and you're suddenly a top tier school as if this has been a change.'

By now, the administrative staff in a flurry of activity would have dissected the new ranking and come up with some explanation for the drop. Perhaps fewer students returned their employment surveys, which would have lowered placement statistics. (If this was the reason, you can be sure the Dean would have used this 'teaching moment' to remind current students of the importance of reporting their employment status after they graduate.) Or maybe the school's yield went down slightly. Or perhaps all of the school's statistics either stayed the same or improved but other schools improved their numbers even more. Or perhaps the person in charge of calculating the statistics has been too conservative in how she or he interpreted employment. In any case, once the 'reason' for the drop was explained, the Dean would offer ways of improving the situation. The Director of Careers Services might be reprimanded for not being thorough enough or even fired, as has happened in several cases. Or schools would try to expand the number of applications they received through marketing or waiving application fees. Or they would offer additional help for students in preparing to take bar exams. In other words, the new ranking would elicit a public narrative from the Dean of the law school, one in which he reassured, explained, described new plans and offered an alternative account of the quality of their school, and reinforced their preferred organizational identity and how they understood their distinctiveness.

The narrative offered by the Dean would have been a collaborative effort, with contributions from Deans of Admissions, Directors of Career Services, and public relations experts. But for the narrative to be credible and compelling it must be seen as coming from the person in charge, the Dean, whose public performance, through time, words and an offering up of oneself, demonstrates his or her responsiveness to students' concerns and the seriousness of this accounting. The precipitating event in the narrative is the 'before' and 'after' of rankings. The event to be explained, the change in rankings, is being recast as a non-event: why what looks like change really isn't any significant change, along with the reassuring knowledge that the drop can be analysed and addressed.

Not all narratives are performed live, of course. Sometimes reactions to indicators such as rankings circulate as written texts. Consider the email that a Dean of a top ten law school that dropped one point several years ago sent the day rankings were made public. (It is wonderful to have informants who forward emails.) Sent to 'The [X] School Community', it begins by observing that the school's 'objective numbers' (its admissions, placement and resources statistics) have improved during the last year. It reinserts context by explaining the trajectory of the rankings for the past six years and reminding readers of how the school has overall improved its rank. And the email reasserts an identity that is not captured in the rankings and explains why:

> Our reputation among academics and practitioners as measured by US News is not commensurate with the increasing quality of our students, the scholarly impact of our faculty, and the expanding national and international employment of our graduates as measured by other rankings. As we have seen, reputations often lag objective results. This is especially true in a conservative field such as ours. We are clearly the most innovative of the top law schools; it takes time for innovation to be accepted and adopted by the profession. As more of our graduates have a chance to positively impact the industry throughout the world and as our faculty's discipline-based scholarship pushes academic research and influences public policy, I am confident that our innovative model, based on feedback from the marketplace, will be recognised as the standard in legal education.

The tenor of this reaction is that there is a logical reason for the current ranking but that the inaccuracy that lurks behind it – the lag in reputation – will correct itself over time. And while he reminds readers of the special qualities of his school, he does so with an implicit ranking, e.g. 'We are clearly the *most* innovative school'. Another implicit message contained in this email is that the Dean takes rankings very seriously and that he is confident that the school will continue to do well and improve. And while the invocation of community and all the 'we' talk acknowledges that the ranking affects everyone, that we are all in this together, the email also suggests that the Dean and the administration is working hard to improve the school despite what the rankings this year indicate. The email message ends with the new rankings and a list of specialties in which this law school does well, which is meant to be encouraging but also reinforces the legitimacy of rankings, as does the serious, reasoned tone of the message.

It is not just bad news that prompts the creation of narratives. Schools that rise in the rankings may also create narratives and collective occasions for celebrating them, with pizza or champagne, and expressions of gratitude in stories of hard work of the staff and faculty and its stellar students. Almost invariably, a Dean may urge caution against giving too much weight to rankings, but will nonetheless treat the ranking as affirmation of their school and something worthy of publicizing to alumni. In this way, celebratory narratives also elaborate the meanings of rankings by reinserting context, agency and moral values. So, when Dean Hiram Chodosh announced in 2009 that the University of Utah's Quinney College of Law has climbed six places in *US News* rankings, from 57th to 51st, he noted:

> We are well aware of the instrumental importance of rankings as a rough (albeit profoundly imperfect) proxy of value for applicants, peers, donors, employers, and others. As we celebrate this recognition and many other terrific achievements this year, let's continue to stay focused on what really matters in our pursuit to improve the world around us. If we take any pride and excitement from a boost in the rankings, let's be sure to channel it in service of our core objectives: the dedication to develop insightful research on the critical issues of our time, dynamic training of the next generation of leaders, and collaborative service contributions at the local, national, and global levels.[8]

If these public narratives are carefully crafted interpretations meant to reassure and offer reasons, in private members are less guarded in their reactions. The administrators and faculty that we interviewed often described how much they hate rankings, how rankings misrepresent their school, and informants complain about what poor measures they are, the bad behavior they encourage. They also often project motives and feelings onto *USN*. Some informants told us that rankings are best understood as a money-making vehicle for a 'lousy magazine', rather than some serious attempt to evaluate schools. They describe changes *USN* made in the methods used to classify information as strategies for producing volatility in the rankings because, if rankings stay the same, 'there is no reason to buy them'. And they tell stories of how things used to be better before rankings, or talk of the demoralizing effects of a poor ranking, of how they feel demeaned by them, or of how much time they waste on producing the information for *USN*, and how rankings have changed practices in ways that harm legal education. A small minority will explain why they believe rankings are useful in prompting schools to make more information public, create strategic plans or energize organizational members in ways that challenge inertia.

Narratives about rankings are not restricted to those being ranked. Those who produce the rankings also must create narratives about why

---

[8] See   https:////today.law.utah.edu/2009/04/college-of-law-climbs-six-places-in-u-s-news-ranking.

they are needed, why they are fair, and why law schools should accept them and provide accurate information to the magazine. USN has been the subject of scathing criticism of its rankings and so it, too, has been forced to defend them. Initially, this defence took the form of a creation story in which editors pointed out how many colleges and law schools there were, how bewildering it was for parents and students trying to decide among schools, and how uninformative school marketing was. As an external, objective observer, USN was providing a valuable service to those who needed it. Editors suggested that while people spend hours investigating which is the best US$100 CD player to buy, they spend far less time on the then US$100,000 decision of which law school to attend. In this way, potential law applicants are cast as consumers and the magazine as their champion.

Now, I'm not suggesting that all reactions to rankings take the form of narrative. Information can be conveyed in many ways and a slide show with bullet points may not have a narrative form. But if we look closely at the structure of reactions to quantification we can see that many take on something like a narrative, with many of the same components, and these narratives often put back the agency, context, identity, sequence, reasoning and emotions that quantification removes. Narratives offer a constrained agency to rebut rankings, the chance to reassert the distinctiveness of a school – its traditions, history, the emotional tenor of its community and the dangers of the reduction that rankings impose. It can be a means for assuaging anxiety about one's future and the competition that one might face. Narrative form, as we know, is supremely well-suited to the task of making sense of what has happened and for remembering.

NARRATIVES CHANGE OVER TIME

As criticism of its methods mounted, and as evidence emerged that some schools were misreporting or jiggering their numbers, USN gradually released more information about the methods it used to construct rankings, and made small changes in its formula and how to interpret the categories behind the statistics. The magazine also published the names of schools that reported more favorable numbers to the magazine than to the American Bar Association, law schools' accrediting organization. The responsiveness that the magazine prided itself on was later mobilized in defense of rankings, as USN argued that the methodological changes it made proved the magazine's willingness to listen to critics, its reasonableness, and demonstrated its commitment to continually improve rankings – an illustration of its adherence to scientific norms of always looking for ways to improve methods and measurement. And over new time, the claims made for rankings changed: not only did they provide useful consumer education, they also helped keep schools 'accountable' or even helped schools identify areas for improvement.

The changes in law school narratives over time reflect their very gradual and begrudging acceptance of rankings as an inevitable part of their educational landscape. Initially, professional organizations mobilized to try and discredit and stop rankings. A critical letter was signed by nearly every law school Dean and then sent each year to everyone who took the admissions exam. This letter pointed out the inappropriateness of the rankings, their methodological flaws, the self-interest of the magazine, and urged potential applicants to ignore them. But eventually, as schools were convinced of their popularity and their potency in steering students, efforts to stop rankings stopped, as a language of disapproving accommodation replaced that of resistance.

CONSTRAINTS OF NARRATIVE

I have argued that people often tell stories in reaction to rankings. The effects of these stories will, of course, vary. One way they vary is that not all narratives work. Narratives produced in response to rankings are constrained; for them to be successful in reassuring, persuading or reasserting a community that feels attacked, narratives must be viewed by their audiences as credible. The right person must be delivering them, they must seem reasonable, and they need to change in light of changing circumstances. For example, had law schools continued to exhort students to ignore rankings or to try to prevent USN from producing them, these efforts would have seemed unrealistic or even laughable. The concluding consensus of a panel on rankings featured at the annual meetings of the Association of American Law Schools was that 'rankings are here to stay'. When narratives explaining a poor ranking begin to sound too scripted and too self-interested, they are dismissed as 'spin' that administrators perform in order to mollify their constituents or cover their poor performances.

We can think of narratives as a means of 'talking back' to what might be termed the 'disciplinary power' of rankings (Sauder and Espeland 2009), the way rankings govern law schools indirectly through bureaucratic practices and internalized notions of self and subject. Stories about rankings are good for sense-making and for channelling emotions but as forms of resistance they are, in this case, weapons of the weak – not a characteristic that would typically have been applied to American law schools before rankings. The power of rankings stems from their widespread use by applicants, which in turn reflects their roots in a media corporation that is expert at the dissemination of information. Rankings have a much larger public than do the 'talking back' narratives law schools create and their audience includes a range of groups who discover they have 'an interest' in rankings, that they help groups solve practical problems, such as helping aspiring lawyers decide where to apply, offering reporters an easy story, providing employers a quick way to sort applicants, or offering Trustees a means of assessing the performance of their deans.

Another constraint that narratives about rankings face is that their terms are largely determined by the language of rankings: so such defenses need to invoke scientific authority in questioning *USN*'s methods by explaining what they exclude or criticizing their validity. More than one law student has noticed a whiff of hypocrisy in deans denouncing *USN* rankings as inadequate means for capturing the school's virtues, while simultaneously ranking students each semester. More broadly, narratives, as forms of information, lack the scientific authority we attribute to quantification, reflecting the suspect status of merely 'anecdotal' information. While many of us understand quantification as good at suppressing rather than extracting subjectivity – it is there but harder to find – that's not how most people understand quantification. When pressed, or when doing taxes, we understand that we can 'lie with statistics', but we more often take numbers at face value. We assume that narratives, as re-establishing agency, re-insert the person that quantification extracts, making them vulnerable to claims bias or sour grapes. So, like other forms, narratives are constrained by terms that shape the accounts they try to reinterpret.

CONCLUSION

We should not be surprised that quantification elicits narratives. Nor should we be surprised that there are patterns in the narratives they elicit. Such stories often put back what numbers remove, explain or explain away the numbers, describe how these indicators misrepresent the identities of schools, reassert the 'correct' identity, and help to evoke or channel emotions, whether these are celebratory or defiant.

While I think that understanding quantification as a radical and useful form of simplification is crucial, I am urging that as scholars of indicators we also look at the stories that numbers generate. These stories will help us understand how people who make and are governed by indicators make sense of them, understand the stakes of their simplification, and resist them. This is crucial for understanding the power of indicators. And in keeping with merchants' expectations for double-entry book-keeping, rankings change the people who use and confront them. Law school administrators report feeling more competitive, more anxious and more suspicious as a result of rankings. And Deans, faculty and students alike have begun to understand rankings as a status they cannot escape and sometimes eternalize. We often personalize the organizations we belong to, often by participating in the construction of organizational identities, identities that become part of how its members understand themselves. Talking back to rankings is a means of talking back to our 'selves'.

References

Burke, Kenneth 1973. 'Literature as Equipment for Living' in Kenneth Burke, *Philosophy of the Literary Form: Studies in Symbolic Action*. 3rd edn, Berkeley, Calif.: University of California Press, pp. 293–304

Carruthers, Bruce G. and Wendy Espeland 1991. 'Accounting for Rationality: Double-Entry Bookkeeping and the Rhetoric of Economic Rationality', *American Journal of Sociology* 97(1): 31–69

Cortruguli, Benedito 1990. *The Art of Mercatura Book (1484)*. Ugo Tucci (ed.), Venice: Arsenale

Davis, Kevin E., Angelina Fisher and Sally Engle Merry (eds.) 2012. *Governance by Indicators: Global Power through Classification and Rankings*. Oxford: Oxford University Press

Davis, Kevin E., Benedict Kingsbury and Sally Engle Merry 2012. 'Indicators as a Technology of Global Governance', *Law and Society Review* 46(1): 71–104

Espeland, Wendy and Michael Sauder 2007. 'Rankings and Reactivity: How Public Measures Recreate Social Worlds', *American Journal of Sociology* 113: 1–40

Espeland, Wendy and Mitchell Stevens 1998. 'Commensuration as a Social Process', *Annual Review of Sociology* 24: 312–43

Klein, Stephen and Laura Hamilton 1998. *The Validity of the U.S. News and World Report Rankings of the ABA Law Schools*, study commissioned by the

American Association of Law Schools, available at www.aals.org/validity.
html

Lampland, Martha and Susan Leigh Star (eds.) 2009. *Standards and their Stories: How Quantifying, Classifying and Formalizing Practices Shape Everyday Life.* Ithaca, N.Y.: Cornell University Press

Lempert, Richard 2002. 'Pseudo Science as News: Ranking the Nation's Law Schools', paper presented at American Association of Law Schools, New Orleans, 3–5 January

Lopez, Robert S., Irving W. Raymond and Olivia R. Constable 1990. *Medieval Trade in the Mediterranean World; Illustrated Documents.* Robert S. Lopez, trans., New York: Columbia University Press

Mennicken, Andrea and Peter Miller 2012. 'Accounting, Territorialization and Power', *Foucault Studies* 13:3–24

Pacioli, Frater Lucas 1969. *Treatise on Double-Entry Bookkeeping (1494).* Pietro Crivell, trans., London: Institute of Book-Keepers

Porter, Theodore 1995. *Trust in Numbers: The Pursuit of Objectivity in Science and Public Life.* Princeton, N.J.: Princeton University Press

Power, Michael 1994. *The Audit Explosion.* London: Demos

Sauder, Michael and Wendy Espeland 2009. 'The Discipline of Rankings: Tight Coupling and Organizational Change', *American Sociological Review* 74: 63–82

Schumpeter, Joseph 1950. *Capitalism, Socialism and Democracy.* New York: Harper Torchbooks

Sombart, Werner 1953. 'Medieval and Modern Commercial Enterprise' in Frederic C. Lane and Jelle Riemersma (eds.), *Enterprise and Secular Change.* Homewood, Ill.: Irwin, pp. 25–40

    1967. *The Quintessence of Capitalism.* M. Epstein, trans., New York: Howard Fertig

Strathern, Marilyn (ed.) 2000. *Audit Cultures: Anthropological Studies in Accountability, Ethics and the Academy.* New York: Routledge

Swidler, Ann 1986. 'Culture in Action: Symbols and Strategies', *American Sociological Review* 52(2): 273–86

Weber, Max 1927. *General Economic History.* New Brunswick, N.J.: Transaction

BY THEIR OWN ACCOUNT: (QUANTITATIVE) ACCOUNTABILITY, NUMERICAL REFLEXIVITY AND THE NATIONAL PROSECUTING AUTHORITY IN SOUTH AFRICA

Johanna Mugler

INTRODUCTION

Accountability is a watchword firmly established in contemporary politics, policies and organizational life in many countries world-wide (UN 2007; Espeland and Vannebo 2007; Power 2008: XV). Presently there are calls for greater and more expansive forms of accountability; rarely do we hear of calls for less. In the simplest sense, accountability describes situations in which people, who have been entrusted with power and money, are required to explain and justify their decisions – in other words, when their resource allocation and their professional and ethical reasoning are scrutinized. It is, however, only rarely that accountability scholars highlight the concept's obscurity, vagueness and its 'chameleon'-like character (except Sinclair 1995: 219; Boström and Garsten 2008: 5; Koppell 2005; Strathern 2000a). When, where, to whom and on what basis someone is made to be accountable can look very different, depending on the involved actors' understandings of the concept.

It is often pointed out that expectations of how accountability should be produced are never static (Dowdle 2006). Heated debates around the

I would like to thank Keebet von Benda-Beckmann, Kenneth Brown, John Comaroff, Julia Eckert, Amy Field, Barbara Grimpe, Sally Engle Merry, Sung-Joon Park, Theodore Porter, Richard Rottenburg and Olaf Zenker for their inspiring and insightful suggestions on earlier versions of this chapter. I gratefully would like to acknowledge the International Max Planck Research School REMEP, particularly Bertram Turner, and the Institute for Social Anthropology at the University of Bern for their support. Thanks also to my research participants in South Africa. This research would not have been possible without their incredible generosity and assistance.

'correct' way to ensure that public officials work in the best interests of the public and remain trustworthy are nothing new (von Dornum 1997). Over the last ten to fifteen years, however, various scholars have noted that the rapid increase of *quantitative* forms of accountability in many governmental settings world-wide are radically shifting these debates (Power 1997; Shore and Wright 1999; Strathern 2000a; 2000b). When being accountable becomes more and more synonymous with using quantitative measures and creating supposedly 'verifiable' accounts, then, scholars argue, our understanding of how accountability can be defined and rendered becomes narrower. People will be less accepting and convinced by other forms and it becomes difficult for institutions to otherwise practice accountability, that is, without performance indicators, rankings, benchmarking and/or audits and more deliberative forms of account-giving (Espeland and Vannebo 2007: 40; Rottenburg 2000).

Although quantitative forms of accountability are in high demand because they appear to have the capacity to simplify complex social phenomena and make these more accessible to outsiders and lay people, critics point out that the increased transparency achieved through this 'information reductionism' is illusory and counterproductive (Tsoukas 1997: 829). Illusory, because when complex phenomena such as 'justice', 'education' or 'health' are reduced to a few 'key' indicators chosen to represent the issue under scrutiny, equally important dimensions of these phenomena which are more difficult to quantify but which expert systems rely on to function, such as tacit and experiential knowledge, are lost in the quantification process (Power 2004: 774–8; Strathern 2000b: 313–14). This is especially so when the indicators become so pervasive and influential that they become synonymous with the measured phenomenon itself. In other words, critics warn that indicators do not only indicate to some aspect of reality, but are constitutive of this reality: they influence what people take to be real, what they pay attention to and how they act and react.

This can be counterproductive, it is argued, because people whose work is evaluated by and monitored with performance measurement systems soon change their behaviour, develop a 'compliance' or 'audit mentality', or game the numbers in order to promote their chances of receiving positive reviews – without necessarily improving the conduct the indicators and rankings are designed to measure (Power 1997: 16; Power 2003: 190; Strathern 2000a: 282–7). They thus then begin to manage the performance measurement systems instead of managing the underlying problems these systems were set up to deal with. Michael Power therefore refers to many of these audit practices as empty 'rituals of verification' (1997).

These points of concern and criticism are frequently repeated and restated when anthropologists and other social scientists talk and write about the consequences of numerical representations and quantitative forms of accountability.[1] Authors like Wendy Espeland and Michael Sauder (2006; 2007), and Sally Engle Merry (2011) illustrate in their exemplary work the harmful and detrimental effects of public law school rankings and globally circulating human rights indicators on many people's lives, respectively. However, a number of quantification scholars, including the aforementioned authors, point out that one needs to be cautious about simply assuming that 'numbers' have the same obvious effects in every organizational setting (Lampland 2010; Timmermans and Epstein 2010). They moreover call for studies, founded on careful empirical research, on how various forms of quantitative measures operate in distinct social domains. My study of how performance measurement systems shape South African prosecutors' understandings of accountability and their prosecutorial practices is an attempt to contribute more nuanced anthropological knowledge to this debate.

Prosecutors in many jurisdictions world-wide are equipped with extensive powers of discretion to initiate or discontinue criminal proceedings on behalf of the state, and are backed by the power of the state (Tonry 2012). By interpreting and establishing the accountability of people who committed crimes, they can be pivotal in assisting victims of crime to seek 'protection' and to get 'justice'. But their power can also be used to criminalize people and political opponents and hereby pursue own political interests, as was the case during most of the twentieth century in South Africa. Prosecutors played a central role in the daily administration of Apartheid's repressive, racist and exploitative social order. Close to 15 million people were prosecuted for pass laws and other influx control offences alone between 1948 and 1981 (Klug 1989: 201).[2] The white minority government furthermore made extensive use

---

[1] See also Alain Desrosières, Chapter 13, for a very insightful and concise summary of two different 'emerging critique[s] of statistics' and the associated 'crisis of confidence' in numerical representations since the 1990s.

[2] 'Pass laws' is a commonly used term in the legal and sociological literature about South Africa. The pass laws system entailed that all non-white South Africans had to carry a passport at all times. 'It was one of the key instruments of Apartheid and of the economic exploitation of African workers' as Klug points out (1989: 201).

of political trials to crush the country's resistance and dissent movements, as well as to publicly demonize their leaders as terrorists (Abel 1995; Lobban 1996). Extending prosecutors' accountability beyond the executive only became important after the transition to democracy in 1994.

This chapter begins with a historical overview of the practices of accountability-making established within the South African prosecution authority. I show that attempts to turn prosecutors into accountable 'lawyers of the people' in the new South Africa have relied on various forms of accountability. Quantitative accountability in the form of a performance measurement system was one form of accountability introduced at the turn of the new millennium. Thereafter I discuss examples of the role performance indicators, targets and rankings play for South African court prosecutors. How are they held accountable and how do they experience their accountability? This analysis is followed by a second set of examples which demonstrate what role the quantified performance information plays in the way more senior prosecutors and members of the National Prosecuting Authority (NPA) executive conduct their work, namely, managing the court prosecutors and running the NPA as a whole. Thus, my empirical analysis covers different organizational levels, namely, immediate prosecution and upper management.

While the evidence presented regarding these court and managerial prosecutors differs in specificity and depth, it demonstrates that quantitative accountability does not supersede or replace other existing forms of accountability in this particular organizational setting. The power of 'numbers' is, as I will argue, counteracted by alternative expressions of accountability like professionalism, ethics, responsibility and liability, and by the numerical competence of actors who are much more aware of the constructedness and constructiveness of quantifications than critics have often claimed. The independent professional self is, at least in this setting, not so easily turned into an 'auditable, competitive' self (Shore and Wright 1999: 569), who has to sacrifice 'quality' for 'quantity' and/or 'process' for 'substance' (Power 1997: 16).

BACKGROUND: FROM APARTHEID ADMINISTRATORS TO 'LAWYERS OF THE PEOPLE'

The accountability of prosecutors, and closely related to this, their independence, are topics of much debate in many countries world-wide

(Tonry 2012). How much freedom do prosecutors, who occupy a powerful position in any criminal justice system with their discretion to initiate and discontinue criminal proceedings on behalf of the state, need to do their job? To what extent this discretion should be limited in order to prevent misconduct or abuse was also a central question in the history of the prosecution services in South Africa (Schönteich 2001: 15–22). During the twentieth century, for example, the right and duty of prosecution was until 1926 vested in the Office of the Attorney General.[3] This independence and freedom from political control and interference was removed in 1926 when, after legislative amendments were initiated by the then government, the highest prosecutor of the country was placed under the control of the Minister of Justice, who was from then onwards authorized by law to reverse prosecutorial decisions and from 1935 onwards, after further legislative amendments, to act even as a prosecutor himself.

During the heyday of Apartheid in the 1970s, when strident protests took place against the country's racist and oppressive social order and the Apartheid government countered the resistance movement with escalated repression, including added pieces of repressive legislation, the 1935 position was reiterated in the then new Criminal Procedure Act of 1977. Formal separation of powers between the Attorney General and the executive were only reconstituted in 1992 via legislative amendment. The amendment, besides protecting the highest prosecutor in the country from interference from the executive, also provided security of tenure for this central state office until the age of sixty-five (Redpath 2012: 3).

For most of the twentieth century, the prosecuting authority was dependent on the executive, and demands for accountability to Parliament were silenced since the Apartheid government increasingly controlled all spheres of state and society. Thus, the executive-minded judiciary and the prosecution authority hardly provided a space for any legal protection or challenge against government repression. In turn, the courts obsessively enforced the racially discriminatory and exploitative Apartheid laws (Maylam 1990; Savage 1986; West 1982). As a result, courts and prosecutors were deeply distrusted by the majority of the population (Klug 1989: 177–80; Davis and Le Roux 2009).

---

[3] The Office of the 'Attorney General' can have different functions and responsibilities in different jurisdictions worldwide (Tonry 2012). In South Africa, the highest prosecutor of the country was called 'Attorney General' until 1998 and was then renamed in 1998, once the first national prosecuting authority was established, as 'National Director of Public Prosecution' (NDPP).

To be accountable only became an important and desirable good for the prosecution services after the transition to democracy in 1994. This was especially so from 1998 on when the country's first centralized, national prosecuting authority was established and came under pressure to legitimize itself in the eyes of those it had, until very recently, suppressed (Schönteich 2001: 30). Quantitative forms of accountability in the form of performance measurement systems did not feature much in the establishment of accountability procedures for the new prosecution authority until the beginning of the new millennium. Prior to this, other mechanisms were envisioned and used to make the prosecution services accountable in the new democracy, as we will see in the following section.

ACCOUNTABILITY AS SEPARATION OF POWERS, REPRESENTATION AND PROFESSIONALISM

Between 1994 and 1998, in the time period after the democratic transition and before the establishment of the NPA in 1998, accountability was initially hotly debated in terms of institutional independence. To whom is the head of the prosecuting authority answerable, and who has the final say in prosecutorial decision-making and policy? These questions were once again on the agenda because the separation of powers between the Attorney General and the executive, reintroduced in 1992, was perceived to be under threat (Redpath 2012: 1–10). South Africa's 1996 Constitution and the National Prosecuting Authority (NPA) Act No. 32 of 1998 provide the NPA with the 'power to institute criminal proceedings on behalf of the state' and further, to ensure 'that the prosecuting authority exercises its function without fear, favour or prejudice' (NPA Act No. 32 of 1998, section 2). But the Constitution also makes provisions for the country's President to appoint the head of the NPA, the National Director of Public Prosecution (NDPP). Opponents of this new constitutional clause questioned how far the country's highest prosecutor would be able to defend controversial prosecutorial decisions in which the NPA holds, for example, 'the powerful, rich and well connected to account', when there is institutional dependence on the executive (Schönteich 2001: 26–30). Proponents, in contrast, welcomed this institutional dependence because, at the time when the new constitution was drafted, most members of the prosecution services, especially those at the top, were old-order prosecutors and, as already mentioned, they were cemented into the system by the legislative amendment of 1992, an Act that secured their tenure until the age of sixty-five. At the time of the transition, there was concern amongst the new democratically-elected leaders that public servants who occupied central state functions during Apartheid might not be accountable and responsive to their commands, and might try to maintain the status quo (Redpath 2012: 10). The Constitutional Court decided in 1996 that the appointment of the NDPP by the President in itself does not contravene the doctrine of separation of powers, since the NPA is not part of the judiciary and the NPA Act No. 32 of 1998 and its provisions already had guaranteed prosecutorial independence (Schönteich 2002: 92).

A potential lack of responsiveness amongst the old prosecutorial guard was not only discussed as an accountability issue at the top of the new prosecution authority, but also in the context of the whole prosecutorial workforce of the country (Redpath 2012: 78–84). Being mostly white and male, there was also concern that they might not share the new leaders' vision for a democratic South Africa. Accountability was therefore also discussed in terms of creating a more representative workforce through affirmative action policies, for which the new Employment Equity Act of 1998 provided. It was also argued that an NPA more representative of the racial composition of South Africa would also help to overcome the mistrust and suspicion the wider public felt towards prosecutors. It would turn the prosecution services more convincingly into 'lawyers of the people', in the words of the first NDPP in 1998 (Schönteich 2001: 5).

While fresh and more representative faces were an important factor in creating a more accountable prosecution authority, in order to reach its organizational vision, the NDPP added 'a new breed of prosecutors', namely, those receiving extensive legal, professional and ethical training (Schönteich 2001: 5). The new constitutional set-up of South Africa in which the rights of the accused were drastically strengthened (for example, through the onus to prove the accused's guilt beyond reasonable doubt being moved onto the state) required a prosecutor with more sophisticated legal skills. A law degree therefore became the uniform entry-qualification to become a prosecutor.[4] Moreover, the

---

[4] During most of the twentieth century, many prosecutors had no tertiary legal education and were usually drawn from the ranks of the clerks, or in smaller towns, where local police officers were frequently used to conduct prosecutions on behalf of the state (Fernandez 1993: 120).

informal training practices of the past, in which clerks of the court would be authorized by magistrates to act as prosecutors and would be trained informally on the job, were replaced in 1997 with coherent professional training for aspiring prosecutors (Fernandez 1993: 120).[5] These courses were developed to prepare future prosecutors more adequately for the functions and responsibilities of prosecutors in court, and to acculturate them into professional legal values such as impartiality, objectivity and independence. Such courses were thus designed to act as an additional safeguard against prosecutorial misconduct and abuse (Schönteich 2001: 57). From 1998 on, there was also a focus on introducing more incentives for people to become career prosecutors, such as more attractive career guidance and remuneration systems (Schönteich 2001: 112). In the past, prosecutors were often withdrawn from the prosecutorial position to become magistrates after a relatively short period of time, or used the job as a springboard for private sector work.

That prosecutors' accountability was also talked about and secured in the form of performance measurement systems became an established practice only after the enactment of the Public Finance Management Act (PMFA) of 1999. This additional accountability demand came at a time when there was a general shift in attention in South Africa from policy development to 'efficient', 'effective' and 'friendly' service delivery, and to means of improving it (Chipkin 2011). A perceived growth in crime, and its wide discussion in the media especially, put the departments responsible for safety, security and justice under pressure to improve their performance (Leggett 2003; Ehlers 2008: 123). The PMFA requires that state departments cascade their five-year strategic plans into annual performance plans. In these plans they are required to report about anticipated service delivery targets and corresponding financial projections over the Medium Term Expenditure Framework (MTEF) period. The budget tabled in Parliament has to include measurable key performance indicators for both non-financial and financial performance information. By aligning plans and

Prosecutors were ranked as legal assistants in the Department's occupational classification system until 1979 (Fernandez 1993: 119). Then the professional group of public prosecutors was formally recognized by the Department of Justice, and in order to act in an official capacity as a prosecutor, a university-level legal qualification was required. However, police officers in the early 1990s were still used in rural areas to process postponements of cases or cases that involved petty offences (Fernandez 1993: 119). Only after the transition to democracy did this informal practice come to an end.

5 See www.npa.gov.za/UploadedFiles/Aspirant%20prosecutors%20graduate.pdf.

budget closer to each other, the PMFA is envisioned as assisting Parliament in making assessments of how well state officials implemented their department's annual performance plans based on the budget they received from treasury. That the NPA was able to conform relatively quickly to the requirement of the new Act was due to the 'court management unit'. It was established in 1998 at the national NPA head office in Pretoria and started to collect for the first time in the history of the country's prosecution authority 'court management statistics' in mid-1999.[6]

In 2002, the NPA submitted its first annual report for the 2001/2002 financial year, including performance indicators for Parliament and Minister of Justice and Constitutional Development. The following national statistics for individual courts were collected: (1) the number of court hours in session; (2) the number of outstanding cases on the courts' rolls; and (3) the number of finalized cases and how they had been finalized (for example, withdrawn; removed from the court roll; conviction or acquittal of the accused). So when the performance indicators had to be chosen and presented, the NPA were able to rely on this already existing administrative data. Over the last fifteen years, additional data was collected and more performance indicators have been created, but the ones relying on the above-mentioned statistics, remain, together with the number of received case dockets, the number of decision dockets, and the number of cases finalized with alternative dispute resolution mechanisms, the most important performance indicators for the National Prosecuting Services (NPS). The NPS is the largest business unit of the NPA, in which the bulk of the country's criminal cases are handled. Each court prosecutor in the country captures the data every day on the so-called 'prosecutor's daily court return' form. At the end of the month, the form is handed over to the court's control or senior prosecutor. All the data is then captured at the regional head office and is monitored and controlled by a chief prosecutor. The data from each court is calculated to arrive at an overall cluster efficiency rate, meaning the data from all the courts in one cluster are added to arrive at one aggregate rate, and then the different clusters in one province are ranked according to their achieved rates. It is important

---

[6] South Africa's Crime Information Analysis Centre (CIAC) started to collect information about South African courts' conviction rate from 1996 onwards. Other court-related performance statistics were not collected before that time. I traced the first parliamentary critique of the lack of commitment within the Department of Justice to collect statistical data on the work done by prosecutors to the late 1980s (Fernandez 1993).

to notice that the annual reports only contain national aggregated rates, so the court hours and the finalization or conviction rates of a specific prosecutor, court, cluster or province, for example, are not made public.

The following section gives an overview of what role the performance indicators, targets and rankings play in the way observed and interviewed prosecutors are held accountable. How have the quantitative measures shaped and influenced prosecutors' everyday work practices and their understandings of accountability?

By focusing on the NPA's performance measurement systems, I am not suggesting that the other forms of accountability presented here do not play a role in the NPA. It is important to keep in mind that different forms of and demands for account giving are not equally important at all times for all parts of the prosecuting authority, and that they can emerge from different constituencies and therefore have dissimilar effects on disparate parts of the organization. Accountability through representation was, for example, not a talking point when white prosecutors were working in the NPA's top investigative units to prosecute some of the country's 'top criminals' or 'serious gangsters'. When the same group of prosecutors initiated criminal proceedings against popular and highly ranked black politicians and government employees, all distinguished heroes of the struggle, the prosecutors' race became a topic of public conversation in relation to their accountability or more specifically as a sign of their lack of accountability (Matisonn 2001). Yet in other instances, accountability through institutional and political independence did not play an important role when the accountability of lower court prosecutors, who are mostly involved in the prosecution of 'petty criminals' (thieves, robbers, burglars), drunken rowdies or wife beaters, was discussed. It was more typical for accountability to receive attention when prosecutors were involved in more controversial prosecutions and when the NDPP was personally involved in the decision-making process. The prosecution of Jakob Zuma, the country's Deputy President from 1999 until 2005 and President of South Africa after 2008 was such a case in which the independence and accountability of the NPA was hotly debated. Critics questioned how independent the NDPP could be when he was appointed by a President who may again have to face serious corruption charges once his presidential terms ends (see Marais 2011). Quantitative forms of accountability were, in this high profile case, only a secondary concern. The amount of time and resources which went into the prosecution of Zuma is unprecedented. My research is concerned with a much less publicized side of the NPA:

the work of lower courts. Prosecutors in the lower courts deal with up to thirty cases a day, hundreds of cases per week, close to a thousand per month. Their cases are barely commented upon in the media, although this is the criminal justice system that the majority of South Africans encounter, if they encounter the national legal system at all.

NPA PERFORMANCE INDICATORS IN PRACTICE

Performance statistics, rates, indicators and targets were a common feature in the working world of most prosecutors I observed and interviewed over eighteen months of ethnographic fieldwork between 2008 and 2012.[7] They often discussed their work and their daily concerns in terms of NPA statistics or with regard to specific NPA performance rates and indicators, both with each other and with me. For example, lower court prosecutors would refer in these conversations to cases which could be finalized quickly, namely, cases where the offender pleaded guilty at first or second appearance or where the case would be mediated or diverted away from the criminal justice system, as 'good for the stats' or as 'assisting them in achieving their target'. Or when their court work was interrupted, for example, when attorneys, investigators or magistrates were not ready to proceed or were unavailable, or because there was a power failure so the court's recording machines could not function, prosecutors would comment 'there go the good stats out of the window'. What they meant by this is that court postponements and adjournments would often mean that they would be able to finalize fewer cases that day and would sit fewer hours in court, which in turn would then reflect poorly on their monthly 'finalization rate' and/or their 'court hours'. Likewise lower court and regional court prosecutors would, during interviews, or when I observed them screening their case dockets in which the police investigators, in their opinion, failed to link a suspect to the offence, complain that 'oh, no, they are chasing stats again' – 'they are pushing up our withdrawal rate' (prosecutors are instructed not to continue with a prosecution in cases which

---

[7] Eight prosecutors working at four different magistrate courts were shadowed on a regular basis over this period of time. Regular informal conversations and/or formal interviews were conducted with fifteen prosecutors working at regional and national head offices and additional magistrates and regional courts. Two former prosecutors, who act now as magistrates, were asked for comments on the research on a regular basis. For reasons of anonymity and protection of identity of research participants the geographical locations and names are not revealed in this study.

are not well-founded upon admissible and reliable evidence). Further-more, prosecutors' descriptions about 'working hard' would often make reference to a reduction or an increase of a specific performance indi-cator, for example, to the 'number of outstanding cases', also called the 'backlog rate'. In many of these conversations, interlocutors would also physically wave the statistical sheet(s) in my face.

Monthly and quarterly performance statistics also played a central role in meetings in which prosecutors would give accounts of their work to more senior prosecutors. For example, the monthly and bi-monthly management meetings I attended on a regular basis at local courts and at a NPA regional head office would almost without exception start with a prosecutor reading out loud the monthly performance statistics of the courts under discussion. These 'stats' (an abbreviation frequently used to refer to the information collected on the 'prosecutor's daily court return' forms) would always serve as a basis and starting point for the subsequent conversation in meetings on how the respective prosecutor, courts, cluster of courts or the whole province are 'doing'. Amongst prosecutors with managerial functions and with access to more aggregated performance rates and rankings, it was also common to use the NPA statistics in the description of their work and their daily concerns.

Comments like the following were made frequently during the infor-mal conversations and interviews I conducted with them: 'We are con-stantly working towards bringing down the numbers [of outstanding court cases]'; 'the [court roll] rates were out of control, they were sky-rocketing, a thousand outstanding cases, we took two prosecutors to screen the court rolls and identify pleas and it worked, we did seventy-five cases in that court that month'; 'If the conviction rate is 30 per cent, then there is something wrong, it may be an indicator that there is something wrong … the conviction rate is really to tell us how we are doing.' Lastly, prosecutors who held positions in the Strategy Office of the NPA, whose work includes the compilation of the NPA's annual performance plan and the creation of new or the adjustment of existing performance indicators, also referred to indicators frequently when talk-ing about their duties. The following statement of the head of the Strat-egy Office during an interview with me was exemplary: '[I]t's not busi-ness as usual. They [prosecutors] just actually want to have the leisure of just doing their job, but that's not good enough for government. There must be service delivery, and how do you get service delivery? It's by having good indicators. They drive performance.'

The above-mentioned observations and statements give an illustrative overview of the ways quantitative performance information forms a central part of the everyday language and account-giving practices of many prosecutors. They also show that prosecutors, depending on their rank and daily responsibilities in the organization (whether they hold a court-based or a managerial and/or executive position), talk and use them differently. The former use them to account for their monthly work, whereas the latter rely on them not only for attending to external accountability demands, but also for internal management accounting purposes. But what does it mean in practice when prosecutors' everyday work and thinking is shaped by performance statistics, rates and targets? When they ask themselves questions which focus on the quantity of their work, such as: 'am I finalizing enough cases?', 'how high is the outstanding number of court cases?', 'am I withdrawing too many cases?', what does it mean for their understandings and practices of accountability?

ALTERNATIVE ACCOUNTABILITIES: PROFESSIONALISM, RESPONSIBILITY AND LEGAL LIABILITY

The meaning of prosecutors' 'stats talk' and the effect of quantitative accountability on their prosecutorial practices can be best understood when it is placed in prosecutors' wider work environment and accountability relationships. In this section I show that when observing prosecutors at work it became clear that their understanding and practice of accountability was wider than simply having 'good stats'.

The NPA performance indicator 'conviction rate' is, for example, the indicator which receives the most media attention and is often central in debates in Parliament and portfolio committees in which the NPA's performance is evaluated (Broughton 2002; SANews 2013). Furthermore, the country's executives have celebrated the NPA's conviction rates in the past and used them to demonstrate their commitment to the country's 'fight against crime' (de Lange 2004). The opposition frequently adduces them to criticize the government and thereby also voicing their own commitment to a safer South Africa (Schafer 2012a; 2012b). The conviction rate, although such a publicly known indicator, was however something which played a more ambiguous role in prosecutors' everyday life at work in lower courts. Numerous prosecutors emphasized time and again in our conversations about their work or the outcome of a specific case that their primary aim is not to 'win cases' and obtain convictions or maximize sentence severity, but to assist the court in arriving at a just verdict and that it is unethical to suppress evidence or mislead the court in order to rescue one's case.

When I sat in on discussions between prosecutorial colleagues about their cases in their offices or over lunch and during tea breaks, it was apparent that they nevertheless liked or preferred 'winning' and that they took pride in achieving a conviction and a certain amount of punishment for the offender. The focus in these conversations was, however, predominantly on how they obtained the convictions, in what kinds of cases, and despite what kinds of obstacles. Their clever cross-examination tactics, the sophistication of their case strategies, or the styles of legal argumentation and case laws they used to 'take apart' the smart private defence lawyer, and the intricacies of the specific case, were in these conversations what counted most. Pride was attached to one's legal knowledge and prosecutorial technique, as well as the ease with which one navigates the country's criminal law and regulations. It was not the conviction in itself or the prospect of a higher conviction rate which made them visibly excited or turned them into well-performing prosecutors in their own and in their colleagues' eyes. Prancing around the court's corridors and bragging about their conviction rates and the severe punishments they achieved were actions I never witnessed. The working atmosphere that more senior prosecutors promoted in management meetings or when prosecutors came to them for advice in specific cases, time and again, was that an acquittal is as good as a conviction if the court found that this is the right result. Prosecutors were not punished or sanctioned for an acquittal. Thus there was also no institutional shame attached to losing a case. The following quote of a prosecutor in her early thirties and working for the NPA for the last five years, expresses well how many prosecutors felt about their performance indicators and what I observed during management meetings. She said:

> No one will lose his job if you have not made the target. I am not afraid of them. If you don't make it there will be questions and you have to give reasons, tell them what happened, you need to give reasons then it is ok, if you continuously don't make it, they will try to figure out why you didn't make it and if it is you, you might receive training sessions to assist you with your work, but you won't get fired for not reaching the target. And anyway the targets are realistic. I am not afraid of them.

It is also important to notice that none of the court prosecutors I worked with would describe 'trials', in which they have to prove the accused's guilt beyond a reasonable doubt and which is the most time-consuming and laborious way to finalize a case, as 'bad for the stats', meaning for their number of finalized cases. Being involved in trials is what almost all the observed and interviewed prosecutors enjoyed the most. They considered 'proper trials' – showing and using their legal litigation (and not their administration) skills as prosecutors as their core function – as their mandate.

That prosecutors viewed their job performance and accountability duties to a large extent in terms of adherence to the 'law', their legal profession and its code of conduct was common. While, for most prosecutors, professionalism meant conducting their actions in an unemotional, non-political and non-partisan way and complying with all applicable laws, rules and regulations, for a number of prosecutors, being professionally accountable included a personal commitment to improving the service delivery of the NPA.

For example, one senior prosecutor, who I shadowed at work between 2008 and 2009 frequently, saw her accountability as related to her strong commitment to fighting domestic violence in very poor and violence-ridden communities. While she worked as an ordinary senior prosecutor for most of her working hours, she also was involved in an 'NPA innovation project', which placed the prosecutor in direct contact with the community to play an active role in crime prevention. Increasing women's access to justice through regular awareness campaigns, workshops and meetings in and with these communities, but also during informal meetings with women when she visited schools or organized food kitchens and child-caring facilities, were particularly important to her. By using her interpersonal and legal skills, as well as her weight as a senior prosecutor, it was also observable how she actively coordinated the different state and non-state stakeholders in these communities to react more quickly and concertedly when protection orders were violated. She frequently quoted one of the NPA's service ideals which states that it is important to ensure that 'justice is not only done, but seen to be done' for these women.

When numbers of protection orders rose at the respective court in the area, for her, that was a sign that her work had made an impact and that more women were becoming aware of their rights and were more willing to speak out. At the same time, she also often explained that her work could not be easily measured. For example, when the number of domestic violence or rape cases rose, this could be interpreted not only as successful NPA outreach programmes, but also as simply a rise in occurrences of these crimes. When she talked about the project or wrote about it in the progress reports she included other forms of accounts, namely, direct feedback she received from members of the community and the police, her own experiences, observations and judgment, before and after photographs she took of specific hot spots of crimes to document her work, and survey data she received from an evaluator of the project. It is apparent that all these forms of account giving counted, in her eyes, as much to her as her 'stats' did.

For another prosecutor, to whom I paid daily visits throughout the entire time of this research, professional accountability meant that he needed to ensure high levels of courtesy for his 'customers', as he frequently called the complainants. No matter what time it was or how ill-informed and annoying the client's requests or complaints were, he tried to assist them. Although he was often not the person in charge of the cases people were inquiring about, he nevertheless tried to find out who was in charge, where they could find that person, and what was going on in their case. He would often say to me 'people like to complain, but it is their right to complain and to follow up their cases. What I am trying to say is called "Batho Pele",[8] "put people first". You need to follow up, fight for them in court, so they don't come and complain.' That he refrained at all times from any form of 'NPA gossip' and racist and/or moralistic and stereotypical conversations about colleagues and clients was another central dimension of how he defined and practised his professional accountability. He would rather try to change the topic of conversation or leave the room than participate in what was for him completely unethical and unprofessional behaviour.

When I asked him whether these time- and energy-consuming aspects of his work, which he perceived as so central for the delivery of justice, are captured in his monthly performance statistics, he said, 'no, it is taken for granted'. He pointed out that it does not bother him that these qualitative aspects are not measured and evaluated by NPA performance indicators, suggesting that it is 'common sense' for a prosecutor to treat his clients with respect, work with diligence and know his case law when appearing in court. He was of the opinion that these were

[8] 'Batho Pele' means in Sesotho 'People First'. It is also the name of a government initiative that was launched in 1997 to transform the inherited 'culture' of the South African Public Administration. Batho Pele is an approach to improve service delivery and turn public servants into people-friendly, efficient and problem-solving actors.

not prosecutorial work activities that had to be spelled out to everyone and measured every month. That would be too obvious. According to him, being a legal professional, a trained prosecutor and a public servant all are positions that require these qualities, which contribute to the delivery of justice.

While being committed to 'access to justice', 'women rights' or 'courtesy' and 'integrity' were individual expressions of prosecutors' professional accountability, another more commonly raised expression of professional accountability relied on legal accountability or liability. When observed prosecutors, for example, rejected requests from the police to *nolle prosecqui*[9] cases, or to sign a warrant of arrest in cases in which they had the feeling the investigators had not done their work properly, they explained why they could not accept 'short cuts' out of concern that they could be sued. Prosecutors widely commented on cases in which public servants were involved in internal disciplinary hearings or public cases in which the NPA and the Minister of Justice were sued for damages due to prosecutors' negligence or malpractice. Many prosecutors frequently quoted the so-called '*Carmichele* case'. It was one of the first cases in which a South African court found that the state could be held liable for damages arising out of the unlawful conduct of its civil servants (Davis and le Roux 2009: 167 ff.). Various prosecutors were also concerned that they would lose their jobs and their pensions in the event of a court holding that they acted negligently or abused their power.

These examples give evidence that the lower court prosecutors' understandings and practices of accountability are wider than simply having 'good stats' or working in a 'top ranked cluster'. Meeting their target of finalizing a certain number of cases per month or reaching a conviction rate of a certain percentage did not necessarily mean that these prosecutors felt that they were performing well and 'doing justice'. Concepts like professionalism, including adherence to an ethical code of conduct, public responsibility and responsiveness or legal liability were shaping prosecutors' work practices and the ways in which they explained and justified their decisions. More personal ideals of justice and public service were additional strong alternative expressions of their accountability. I argue, in other words, that lower court prosecutors had some control and flexibility over how their reputations were defined and what good prosecutorial performance should entail.

---

[9] *Nolle prosequi*: Latin term for the dismissal or termination of legal proceedings by the prosecutor.

That quantitative forms of accountability were prominent in lower court prosecutors' work lives, but that they were not exclusively indicative of prosecutorial performance, and were not the only legitimate measure of it, was, as I suggest, strongly connected to how their fellow professionals higher up in the organizational hierarchy defined performance and their accountability. As I mentioned before, when members of the senior and executive NPA management, who rarely do any direct court work, wanted to know how a specific prosecutor, court, cluster or whole province 'was doing', they would start their inquiries with a quick look at the respective performance statistics. These numerical representations were central in the way they received information about the people and courts they had to manage. They gave them access to perspectives and fields of vision in the organization that they would not have had otherwise. However, although the quantitative performance information was central for internal management accounting and for adhering to external accountability demands to Parliament, their understanding of performance and accountability was also not exclusively linked to 'bringing the numbers up' or 'down'. The following five quotations, all extracted from one to two hour interviews conducted with two Senior Prosecutors, a Deputy Director of Public Prosecution, a Director of Public Prosecution and a Deputy National Director of Public Prosecution, respectively, are exemplary for NPA senior and executive managers' more nuanced viewpoints about accountability:[10]

> You see you might achieve the 85 per cent target, for example in the District Court, but again you might just have been able to achieve 90 per cent, but you were not so good technically in what you did. What I am saying is some of the cases are guilty pleas and they do not go to trial so you might be achieving 85 per cent where 70 per cent of those were guilty pleas because they were so well investigated by the police and you as a prosecutor in the trial cases maybe achieved 15 per cent but that you should have achieved 20 per cent or 25 per cent to get 95 per cent. So it's not only convictions that we look at before we can promote you.

> You get the guys who are good at handling many cases fast and the ones which are driving when they bite themselves through more lengthy and complicated ones. The stats won't tell me their capacity to prosecute. That's my job to find that out and post them accordingly.

> We understand that sometimes a court can do one case for a month, because that's how justice works, we are not in a factory producing

---

[10] All quotes are taken from recorded transcriptions.

bottles... You know, we are busy with people's lives, we are busy with justice, when you become too focused on numbers in this game, you might lose sight of what we are busy with... It can never be, oh, you were supposed to have that amount therefore you didn't achieve it, therefore you failed, and then you are fired. It's not about that. It can't be about that you know, and that's the difference. In a factory you can do that, you can say this machine can deliver 100,000 stuff every month and these people should produce that... The conviction rate is a strange indicator; it's like a quality measurement although it's not really a quality measure, because we are not in the business of getting convictions.

There is a very sound argument that you put on the court roll what you can deal with, which is a maximum of three cases a day. But the problem is you then don't have any contingent planning so what it then requires, it requires a very effective criminal justice system. It requires a witness, that is subpoenaed, and comes to court, an accused who doesn't run away, a legal representative that is prepared and does come to court, a magistrate that is willing to sit, a prosecutor who is well prepared, and an investigating officer who did the case. You starting to see how many people it relies on? And it just needs one of those people not to play their role for the case not to proceed. It's been going on for more than a hundred years, so I don't know that it's going to change now and it's not unique to South Africa.

The only thing that we can really be held responsible for is quality prosecution, but the problem is, to measure a quality prosecution there are so many variables within it, that you would have to have a full-time staff compliment of 3,000 people to measure it, so therefore – and any rule to measuring is, if it is so cumbersome or so costly to measure, it's the wrong thing to measure and therefore – we measure things which are far easier to measure. They are not 100 per cent correct things.

The quotes of these five prosecutorial managers are presented here together because they are all examples which point to different aspects of the numerical knowledge and reflexivity which these actors exhibit when dealing with performance measurement information. First, they give an impression of managers' awareness that good prosecutorial work does not necessarily translate into high conviction rates or finalization rates and, accordingly, that high performance statistics in these categories do not always indicate excellent performance or desirable outcomes. In other words, it was clear to them that it is difficult to capture the actual complexity of a specific case, court prosecutors' skill levels, or the unpredictable and uncertain multi-actor environment in which they are managing with performance indicators. As a result these managers would not, for example, during meetings I attended, treat 'stats' as self-evident. They relied instead on certain experienced prosecutors' views on the data to decide how statistics should be read and interpreted. Prosecutors or courts with good statistics were in some cases determined to require further managerial attention and interventions and vice versa. Poor statistics were declared unproblematic after the numbers were accounted for and explained by a practised prosecutor. It was generally accepted by the managerial prosecutors that it is rarely clear whose problem or fault it was that a court case had to be postponed and could not be finalized, and that circumstances beyond the court prosecutors' control could and often did affect the results. Therefore, it was common that managers, as in three of the quotes above, expressed their hesitation to rely on the performance statistics to make far-reaching management and human resource decisions and emphasized that their own judgment and experience are needed when sanctioning, promoting or rewarding their staff.[11]

Secondly, the quotes make it clear that although managers work day in and day out with performance indicators which they use to improve or 'drive' the NPA's overall performance, they nevertheless held the opinion that their main task, namely, delivering 'justice' and 'quality prosecution', was not always straightforward and certainly not so easily measured. Although they used the performance indicators to understand 'what's going on', they often described them to me as good thinking tools to plan, strategize and prioritize the activities of the NPA. They furthermore still referred to the performance indicators as

---

[11] I explore the political economy of NPA performance indicators in detail elsewhere (Mugler 2014). The resource (re-)allocation on the basis of selective performance indicators is one of the main reasons why professionals in other organizational fields fear and loathe their performance measurement, especially when actors feel that the indicators are selected arbitrarily and fail to represent the core of their work (see e.g., Espeland and Sauder 2007; Strathern 2000a; Shore and Wright 1999). I show that in the organizational setting of the NPA this automated correlation between achieving 'high numbers' and receiving financial benefits, or achieving 'low numbers' and being sanctioned, did not apply. I argue there are two reasons for that. First, the institutional and legal set up of the prosecutorial work environment does not provide for straightforward competition for resources, funds and clients via numerical representations; second, I show that performance rewarding and sanctioning mechanisms, promotional aspects and salary increases and bonuses are today not tightly linked to the available performance indicators. While there were attempts around 1998 to implement this, long-lasting and intense negotiations over permanent salary increases for all prosecutors and more flexible salary bands pushed the talk about performance based salaries and bonuses into the background.

'strange' and 'not 100 per cent perfect' in capturing their main functions and responsibilities. That they viewed indicators just as indicators of the central issues in question, as something that hints at some but does not represent all aspects of their working reality, was not perceived as something problematic by most managers. They saw the making of indicators as something inevitable. In other words, it did not hinder their reliance on the performance information as sense-making and rationalizing tools to manage their staff and work towards something as complex as 'justice'.

Keeping these two points in mind I want to return to what I suggested earlier, namely, that lower court prosecutors' performance and reputation are not exclusively defined by performance indicators, but that other forms of accountability, in terms of professional, ethical, legal and public forms, are important as accepted and expected alternatives and additions of account giving in this organizational setting. I argue that this is the case because prosecutorial managers, who work daily with performance statistics, have a much more prudent, deliberative, yet ambiguous approach to dealing with them than is often described by scholars of social studies of numbers. While managers rely on them to see things they have not seen before, they are clearly aware of the constructedness and constructiveness of these numerical representations. I would suggest that their awareness of the numbers' shortcomings and limitations makes them more cautious when interpreting quantified information and gives lower court prosecutors greater control over their reputation, as well as flexibility in how they account for their work.

My deliberations are shaped and inspired by authors who explore how rationalization actually occurs in practice. They question how people communicate, collaborate and, in the end, accomplish social projects like improving public health (Geissler, Zenker and Rottenburg 2012); setting up urban water supply systems (Rottenburg 2009); modernizing agricultural production (Lampland 2010); or managing a powerful scientific laboratory (Law 1996; see also Alain Desrosières' analysis of European statisticians' 'fluid', 'implicit' and 'fuzzy' use of numbers, Chapter 13). These texts are all examples in which organizational actors acquired the reflexive competencies in order to juggle different and not always coherent institutional logics and accountabilities simultaneously. I would suggest that it is precisely the actors' use of both practical numerical knowledge and professional reflexivity which receives insufficient attention when one too hastily assumes that professional actors react to quantitative forms of accountability with unintended and harmful 'compliance' and 'audit' mentalities.

SUMMARY

Accountability, or the way people explain and justify specific social situations, 'is part of the general fabric of human interchange' (Strathern 2000a: 4). It is a concept of central importance in the understanding of social action. How quantitative forms of accountability shape the way people work and experience their accountability in different organizational fields is therefore an important social question worthy of more sustained investigation. In summary, I wish to make three points.

First, the meanings, uses and effects of quantitative accountability are context-dependent and time-specific. That knowledge is situational and relational is something which social anthropologists stress in most of their research settings. This professional invocation of context somehow seems to be less often applied when it comes to numerical representations. This is no doubt connected to the reason why numbers were or are propagated and used in many contexts in the first place, namely, that they appear to provide actors with a more objective, precise and impartial way of knowing, which is supposed to eliminate the importance of the contextual knowledge that is often associated with subjectivity, favouritism, or more generally with equivocality (Porter 1995). My research has shown, for example, that the prosecutors in this setting did not treat the quantified performance information as something with completely objective, precise and accurate meanings. In other words, they did not perceive them as simple and straightforward facts.

Therefore I would suggest, and this is my second point, that the dominance of quantitative forms of accountability depends upon how much power, faith and credibility powerful actors in an organizational setting give to numerical representations. As Vormbusch (2007: 61) writes, 'the power of numbers, to a large extent, relies on the social construction of calculations remaining hidden' (own translation). Being aware of this is 'the basis for a new, in a sense, clarified instead of enlightened handling' of numerical information; a sign for a more 'reflexive approach to numbers' in certain societal domains (Vormbusch 2007: 61). Prosecutors' awareness of the limits and shortcomings of the constructedness and constructiveness of the quantified performance information, their insistence on making their judgments, and their reliance on other forms of knowledge and accountability are signs, I argue, that professionals in this setting were not so easily disciplined into 'auditable selves'.

The numerical competence and reflexivity professionals are capable of and display in this organizational field are indeed phenomena which deserve further attention from social scientists in other settings. This would contribute to more specific answers to questions such as: Why are some professional practices and organizational fields more transformed by quantitative accountability than others? What are the factors which influence whether some professionals can free themselves and disengage from the power of numbers, where others struggle and cannot?

My last point, therefore, is simply that empirical research in this field is important. It provides the knowledge that can help move discussions of social studies of numbers beyond the point where numerical representations' 'reality-obscuring-capacity' is time and again emphasized. While a critical stance towards the quantification of complex social phenomena and quantitative accountability is no doubt essential, I argue that the 'taken-for-granted mistrust' in numbers, which is particularly prevalent among anthropologists, can be as damaging as the 'taken-for-granted validity of numbers' many scholars are rightly concerned about. If one focuses too narrowly on these poles when analysing people's interactions with numbers, then it becomes possible to miss the larger spectrum of locally relevant ways of working with numbers which exist in certain settings. I have just described, within an organizational setting, how prosecutors in the South African National Prosecuting Authority used indicators as valid sense-making and rationalizing tools. It did not, however, follow that they blindly trusted them when they made far-reaching decisions, nor did it follow that the indicators dominated what these actors paid attention to or took to be real. This nuance can assist us in seriously engaging with and trying to understand the context-specific meanings, uses and purposes of numerical representations. This is essential when living in a world surrounded by ever-increasing amounts of numbers and ever-expanding demands for quantitative accountability.

References

Abel, Richard 1995. *Politics by Other Means: Law in the Struggle against Apartheid 1980–1994*. London/New York: Routledge

Boström, Magnus and Christina Garsten 2008. *Organizing Transnational Accountability*. Cheltenham: Edward Elgar

Broughton, Tania 2002. 'Shocking: SA's conviction rate for rape', *IOL*, 10 December, available at www.iol.co.za/news/south-africa/shocking-sa-s-conviction-rate-for-rape-1.98486?ot=inmsa.ArticlePrintPageLayout.ot

Chipkin, Ivor 2011. 'Transcending Bureaucracy: State Transformation in the Age of the Manager', *Transformation* 77: 31–51

Davis, Dennis and Michelle le Roux 2009. *Precedent and Possibility: The (Ab)use of Law in South Africa*. Johannesburg: Double Story Publishers

De Lange, Jonny 2004. Address at the official launch of the Western Cape Community Courts, Gugulethu, 7 December, available at www.justice .gov.za/m_speeches/sp2004/2004%2012%2007_dmin_wccc.htm

Dowdle, Michael 2006. *Public Accountability: Designs, Dilemmas, and Experiences*. Cambridge: Cambridge University Press

Ehlers, Louise 2008. 'Frustrated Potential: The Short and Long Term Impact of Pretrial Services in South Africa', *Open Society Justice Initiative* (Spring) 121–40

Espeland, Wendy and Michael Sauder 2007. 'Rankings and Reactivity: How Public Measures Recreate Social Worlds', *American Journal of Sociology* 113(1): 1–40

Espeland, Wendy Nelson and Berit Irene Vannebo 2007. 'Accountability, Quantification, and Law', *Annual Review of Law and Social Science* 3(1): 21–43

Fernandez, Lovell 1993. 'Profile of a Vague Figure: The South African Public Prosecutor', *South African Law Journal* 110(1): 115–26

Geissler, Wenzel, Julia Zenker and Richard Rottenburg (eds.) 2012. *Rethinking Biomedicine and Governance in Africa: Contributions from Anthropology*. Bielefeld: Transcript

Klug, Heinz 1989. 'The South African Judicial Order and the Future: A Comparative Analysis of the South African Judicial System and Judicial Transitions in Zimbabwe, Mozambique, and Nicaragua', *Hastings International and Comparative Law Review* 12: 173–234

Koppell, Jonathan 2005. 'Pathologies of Accountability: ICANN and the Challenge of "Multiple Accountabilities Disorder"', *Public Administration Review* 65(1): 94–108

Lampland, Martha 2010. 'False Numbers as Formalizing Practices', *Social Studies of Science* 40(3): 377–404

Law, John 1996. 'The Manager and His Powers', paper presented at Mediaset Convention, Venice, 12 November

Leggett, Ted 2003. *What Do the Police Do? Performance Measurement and the SAPS*, Institute for Security Studies Paper 66

Lobban, Michael 1996. *White Man's Justice: South African Political Trials in the Black Consciousness Era*. Oxford: Oxford University Press

Marais, Hein 2011. *South Africa Pushed to the Limit: The Political Economy of Change*. Claremont: Cape Town University Press

Matisonn, John 2001. 'Yengeni hits out at "all-white" Scorpions', *IOL*, 5 October, available at www.iol.co.za/news/politics/yengeni-hits-out-at-all-white-scorpions-1.74762#.U-JK9RY8hd0

Maylam, Paul 1990. 'The Rise and Decline of Urban Apartheid in South Africa', *African Affairs* 89(354): 57–84

Merry, Sally Engle 2011. 'Measuring the World: Indicators, Human Rights, and Global Governance', *Current Anthropology* 52 (Supplementary Issue 3)

Mugler, Johanna 2014. *By their Own Account: An Ethnography of (Quantitative Accountability) and the National Prosecuting Authority in South Africa*. Ph.D diss., Max Planck Institute for Social Anthropology and Martin-Luther-University Halle-Wittenberg

Porter, Theodore 1995. *Trust in Numbers: The Pursuit of Objectivity in Science and Public Life*. Princeton, N.J.: Princeton University Press

Power, Michael 1997. *The Audit Society: Rituals of Verification*. Oxford: Oxford University Press

    2003. 'Evaluating the Audit Explosion', *Law and Policy* 25(3): 185–202

    2004. 'Counting, Control and Calculation: Reflections on Measuring and Management', *Human Relations* 57(6): 765–83

    2008. 'Foreword' in Magnus Boström and Christina Garsten (eds.), *Organizing Transnational Accountability*. Cheltenham: Edward Elgar

Redpath, Jean 2012. *Failing to Prosecute? Assessing the State of the National Prosecuting Authority in South Africa*, ISS Monograph 186. Pretoria: Institute for Security Studies

Rottenburg, Richard 2000. 'Accountability for Development Aid' in Herbert Kalthoff, Richard Rottenburg and Hans-Jürgen Wagener (eds.), *Facts and Figures: Economic Representations and Practices*. Marburg: Metropolis-Verlag

    2009. *Far-fetched Facts: A Parable of Development Aid*. Cambridge, Mass.: MIT Press

SANews 2013. 'NPA secures 88% conviction rate in High Courts', 1 March, available at www.sanews.gov.za/south-africa/npa-secures-88-conviction-rate-high-courts

Sauder, Michael and Wendy Nelson Espeland 2006. 'Strength in Numbers? The Advantage of Multiple Rankings', *Indiana Law Journal* 81(1): 205–27

Savage, Michael 1986. 'The Imposition of Pass Laws on the African Population in South Africa 1916–1984', *African Affairs* 85(339): 181–205

Schafer, Debbie 2012a. 'Conviction rate is not 90%', available at www.politicsweb.co.za/politicsweb/view/politicsweb/en/page71619?oid=303568&sn=Detail&pid=71619

2012b. 'NPA still missing the plot on conviction rate', available at www.politicsweb.co.za/politicsweb/view/politicsweb/en/page71619? oid=304570&sn=Detail&pid=71619

Schönteich, Martin 2001. *Lawyers for the People: The South African Prosecution Service*, ISS Monograph 53. Pretoria: Institute for Security Studies

2002. 'Court Room Warriors for Justice: History of the South African Prosecution Service', *Journal for Contemporary History* 27(3): 82–104

Shore, Chris and Susan Wright 1999. 'Audit Culture and Anthropology: Neo-Liberalism in British Higher Education'*Journal of the Royal Anthropological Institute* 5(4): 557–75

Sinclair, Amanda 1995. 'The Chameleon of Accountability: Forms and Discourses', *Accounting Organizations and Society* 20(2–3): 219–37

Strathern, Marilyn 2000a. *Audit Cultures: Anthropological Studies in Accountability, Ethics, and the Academy*. London/New York: Routledge

2000b. 'The Tyranny of Transparency', *British Educational Research Journal* 26(3): 309–21

Timmermans, Stefan and Steven Epstein 2010. 'A World of Standards but not a Standard World: Toward a Sociology of Standards and Standardization', *Annual Review of Sociology* 36(1): 69–89

Tonry, Michael 2012. *Prosecutors and Politics: A Comparative Perspective*. Chicago, Ill ./ London: University of Chicago Press

Tsoukas, Haridimos 1997. 'The Tyranny of Light: The Temptations and the Paradoxes of the Information Society', *Futures* 29(9): 827–43

United Nations 2007. *Accountability and the United Nations System*, Policy Brief No. 8 (Michael Fowler and SumihiroKuyama, United Nations University)

Von Dornum, Deirdre Dionysia 1997. 'The Straight and the Crooked: Legal Accountability in Ancient Greece', *Columbia Law Review* 97(5): 1483–1518

Vormbusch, Uwe 2007. 'Stichwort: Die Herrschaft der Zahlen (1)', *Westend Neue Zeitschrift für Sozialforschung* 4, Jg (Heft 2): 57–63

West, Martin 1982. 'From Pass Courts to Deportation: Changing Patterns of Influx Control in Cape Town', *African Affairs* 81(325): 463–77

FAILURE BY THE NUMBERS? SETTLEMENT STATISTICS AS INDICATORS OF STATE PERFORMANCE IN SOUTH AFRICAN LAND RESTITUTION

Olaf Zenker

> Government and public opinion have mainly measured the achievements
> of restitution quantitatively in terms of the number of claims settled and
> people who have benefitted, and the extent of land restored to claimants.
>
> Ruth Hall (2010: 28)

INTRODUCTION

On 30 March 2011, the South African Department of Rural Development and Land Reform presented its *Draft Annual Performance Plan: 2011–2012* to the Parliamentary Portfolio Committee on Rural Development and Land Reform. When referring to its land restitution programme, the presentation indicated that the 'purpose' of this programme was to settle land restitution claims under the Restitution of Land Rights Act (Act No. 22 of 1994) and to provide settlement support to restitution beneficiaries, further highlighting as 'key priorities' the reduction of the backlog of land claims and the settlement of all outstanding land claims (Department of Rural Development and Land Reform 2011a: 29). The presentation then displayed a table containing its annual targets for backlog claims to be implemented, totalling 360

My research was financially supported by the Berne University Research Foundation (2009–2011) as well as an Ambizione Research Fellowship of the Swiss National Science Foundation (2012–2014). Written for the 2011 Max Planck Workshop 'A World of Indicators: Knowledge Technologies of Regulation, Domination, Experimentation and Critique in an Interconnected World', this paper was also presented, in 2012, at the Department of Anthropology and Archaeology Seminar Series, University of Pretoria; at the Conference 'The New Public Good: Affects and Techniques of Flexible Bureaucracies', University of Cambridge; and at the Tuesday Research Seminar in African History of the Centre for African Studies and Basler Afrika Bibliographien, University of Basel. I am grateful for inspiring debates and for critical engagements, in particular, by Laura Bear, Chris Boonzaaier, Brenda Chalfin, Patrick Harries, Dag Henrichsen, Nayanika Mathur, Fraser McNeill, Sally Engle Merry, Johanna Mugler, Sung-Joon Park, Richard Rottenburg, Cherryl Walker and Julia Zenker.

claims, as well as 90 new outstanding claims to be settled (Department of Rural Development and Land Reform 2011a: 30). The title of the table column containing these numbers read: 'Performance indicator'.

Increasingly, we are living in a world informed by indicators. Indicators are statistical measures used to consolidate and standardize complex data into a simple number or rank that is meaningful to policy-makers, civil servants and the public (Merry 2011: S86). Thus constituting emerging technologies of knowledge quantification, indicators and their circulation support new forms of 'evidence-based' governance at the national, transnational and international levels (Davis, Kingsbury, and Merry 2010; Merry 2011). Embedded in epistemic environments that appeal to 'new governance' – a form of governance characterized by participation, flexibility, data-based monitoring and evaluation within an overarching 'audit culture' (Power 1997; Strathern 2000) – this recent upsurge of indicators is arguably based on a migration of basic technologies from corporate management and control into the realms of the state and civil society (Merry 2011: S90–S92). As a form of governance, indicators induce those subject to their measures to take responsibility for their own actions. They are meant to lead to forms of self-discipline and self-regulation that can be easily read and monitored from the outside, and as such, contribute to an increase in public accountability. Thus both reflecting and shaping the world they purport to measure, indicators constitute a world of their own – one about which, as Sally Engle Merry and others have recently argued (Davis, Kingsbury and Merry 2010: 1; Merry 2011: S85), relatively little is actually known. In contributing to an emergent ethnography of indicators, this chapter investigates the social life of settlement statistics in South African land restitution that have come to be interpreted as contested indicators of state performance.

In order to do so, this chapter first gives a brief overview of the legal and institutional set-up of the ongoing land restitution process in South Africa. Against this background, it focuses on the shifting relevance of restitution's settlement statistics, leading to their deliberate transformation into explicit indicators of state performance. This is a development that has paralleled recent global trends towards achieving more public accountability through indicatorization. While this has seemingly led to a remarkable 'success by the numbers' in dramatically reducing the amount of outstanding claims still to be settled, the next section highlights the contested nature of settlement statistics as performance indicators. The chapter refers to worrying inconsistencies in the numbers themselves, unpacks some of the local complexities that escape simple quantification, and discusses unintended consequences of indicatorization which, taken together, seem instead to point to an actual 'failure by the numbers'. While acknowledging some of the substantial criticism aimed against the indicatorization of settlement statistics in South Africa, the chapter moves on to discuss these figures as boundary objects. It is primarily this role of the figures that make possible in the first place the translation of various concerns and the switching of codes between claim-specific settings and the national arena of land reform. Emphasizing processes of autopoietic self-correction within the rational-legal logic of modern statehood, the text finally argues that indicatorization, at least in the case of South African land restitution, has indeed both increased state performance and made visible and processible, for the state and the public alike, worrying deficiencies that still persist. It is in this sense of probing the limitations and benefits that follow when the state operates 'by the numbers' – referring both literally to using technologies of quantification and, idiomatically, to doing things according to standard procedure or 'by the book' – that I make use of the phrases 'failure by the numbers' and 'success by the numbers' throughout this text.

INSTITUTIONAL SET-UP OF SOUTH AFRICAN LAND RESTITUTION

The current South African process of restituting rights in land that had been dispossessed on the basis of racially discriminatory laws originated during the negotiations of the transition to post-Apartheid democracy in the early 1990s. Ultimately, a balanced constitutional protection of both property rights and the right to land restitution emerged as a strategic compromise, enshrined in the new Constitution of the Republic of South Africa (Act No. 108 of 1996) (Walker 2008: 50–69).

Section 25(7) of the Constitution, for example, stipulates that a person or community dispossessed of property after 19 June 1913 as a result of past racially discriminatory laws or practices is entitled, to the extent provided by an Act of Parliament, either to the restitution of that property or to equitable redress.[1] The Act of Parliament in question, the

---

[1] This was the day of the promulgation of the Natives Land Act (Act No. 27 of 1913), which first legalized massive dispossessions country-wide by introducing racial zones of possible landownership and by restricting black reserves to only 7 per cent of South African land (later to be extended to 13 per cent).

Restitution of Land Rights Act (Act No. 22 of 1994), defines the legal framework for the actual restitution process and provides in section 2(1) a set of criteria according to which claimants are entitled to restitution. The claimant can either be an individual (or a direct descendant) or a community (or part of a community), whose rights in land were derived from shared rules determining access to land held in common by such group. The claimant had to have been dispossessed of a right in land after 19 June 1913 because of racially discriminatory laws and practices which were in effect during that time. Furthermore, claimants should not have received just and equitable compensation as stipulated in the current Constitution for the dispossession at hand. Finally, claimants also had to lodge their claims before 31 December 1998. As we will see below, this cut-off date was recently amended, thus re-opening restitution for lodging new claims until 30 June 2019.[2]

Importantly, restitution was not limited to former freehold ownership of land. Instead, the right in land to be restituted was defined quite broadly in section 1 of the Restitution Act, including unregistered interests of a labour tenant and sharecropper; a customary law interest; the interest of a beneficiary under a trust arrangement; and beneficial occupation for a continuous period of not less than ten years prior to the dispossession in question.[3] The Restitution Act further established as its key players the Commission on Restitution of Land Rights ('Land Claims Commission'), including the Chief Land Claims Commissioner and the Regional Land Claims Commissioners under the umbrella of the Department of Land Affairs (renamed Department of Rural Development and Land Reform in 2009), and the Land Claims Court, which took up their work in 1995 and 1996, respectively (Walker 2008: 5–9).

Since then, Commission officials have *prima facie* validated, gazetted and verified land claims, and then mediated between claimants and (usually) white landowners in order to settle on a largely market-oriented agreement whereby the state buys the land and, based on certain conditions, hands it over to the claimants. Originally, the Land Claims Court was established to grant restitution orders for all cases and to determine the conditions that had to be met before land rights could

---

[2] See below.
[3] These and other criteria or legal tests for specific entitlements to restitution have been further developed through jurisprudence. On the important role of the courts in defining the scope of restitution, which is often ignored in the literature on South African land restitution, see Mostert 2010 and Zenker 2011; 2014.

be restored. As discussed below, however, due to the slowness of the process of handling claims, amendments to the Restitution Act were made, shifting the approach from a judicial to an administrative one in 1999: since then, the minister, and by delegation the land claims commissioners, have had the power to facilitate and conclude settlements by agreement, and only claims that cannot be resolved this way take the judicial route through the Land Claims Court. This also entails the possibility of expropriation – an option that is also constitutionally enshrined (Hellum and Derman 2009: 128–31).

Since the inception of the restitution process, the total numbers of all lodged claims, as well as the figures slowly shifting from 'outstanding' to 'settled claims', have played an important role. Apart from informing the internal work of the Commission itself, these settlement statistics have also constituted an integral part of the annual reports, which the Commission is obliged to submit to Parliament according to section 21 of the Restitution Act, and subsequently must make accessible to the public. While these numbers have thus been compiled and worked upon for a long time, it is only in recent years that they have been explicitly referred to in terms of 'performance indicators'. The *White Paper on South African Land Policy* referred already in 1997, rather abstractly, to the need to develop 'service standards with clearly defined outputs, targets and performance indicators', when discussing the envisioned transformation of service delivery (Department of Land Affairs 1997: para. 6.5.2). However, it was only in the Department of Land Affairs' overall *Annual Report 2006/2007*, as well as in all its subsequent annual reports, that the settlement statistics for land restitution were explicitly referred to in terms of 'performance indicators' (Department of Land Affairs 2007a: 55). Correspondingly, the Land Claims Commission's own *Strategic Review Plan 2007–2008* began referring to the number of settled land claims as an 'indicator of success' for the purpose of monitoring and evaluation (Commission on Restitution of Land Rights 2007b: 14). Thus, in the recent annual reports for 2010/2011, 2011/2012 and 2012/2013, it has become standard procedure to refer to the number of claims settled in terms of 'output performance measures' and 'indicators', and to use these figures to retrospectively measure actual performance against target performance (Commission on Restitution of Land Rights 2011: 12; 2012: 13; and 2013: 12). It is to this process of the increasing indicatorization of South African land restitution with greater usage of settlement statistics as explicit measures of state performance that I turn now.

NATIONAL SETTLEMENT STATISTICS AS INDICATORS OF STATE PERFORMANCE: MOVING TARGETS ON SHIFTING TERRAINS

During the first term of the Commission on Restitution of Land Rights from 1995 until 2000, the state had to accomplish a number of challenging tasks and learn some difficult lessons. The Commission had to establish its national and regional offices, solicit claims, set up systems to register and investigate them, and finally, refer each one of them to the also newly founded Land Claims Court for finalization (Hall 2010: 26; Walker 2012). The task of identifying and settling all valid claims thereby turned out to be much more demanding than had initially been imagined. At the first working session of the Commission on 6 March 1995, the then Minister of Land Affairs Derek Hanekom projected that '[t]hree years from now the Commission will be rounding off its operation and we pray that its mission would have been successfully accomplished' (quoted in Walker 2008: 8). Yet in its 1997 *White Paper on South African Land Policy*, the Department of Land Affairs had to shift its deadlines for the restitution process, now providing for a three-year period for the lodging of claims (from 1 May 1995), a five-year period for the Commission and the Court to finalize all claims, and a ten-year period for the implementation of all resulting court orders (Department of Land Affairs 1997: para. 4.13). However, the deadlines for finalizing all of the claims proved elusive yet again. Thus, while in 2002 President Mbeki announced 2005 as the year when all claims would be settled, this deadline was again shifted back in March 2005 to March 2008 (Walker 2008: 21). In 2008, the deadline for finalizing all claims was reset for 2011 (Walker 2008: 21, 205), but in 2010, the Commission declared 2012 to be its target for winding up the restitution process (Commission on Restitution of Land Rights 2010: 13). However, in its *Strategic Plan 2011–2014*, the Department of Rural Development and Land Reform still foresaw financial involvement with restitution by the financial year 2013/14 (Department of Rural Development and Land Reform 2011b: 48, 65). Without all claims yet finalized, President Jacob Zuma then announced during his State of the Nation Address on 14 February 2013, that the government would re-open the lodgement of land claims and allow limited exceptions to the 19 June 1913 cut-off date to accommodate claims by the descendants of the Khoi and San. On 29 June 2014, President Jacob Zuma signed the Restitution of Land Rights Amendment Act (Act 15 of 2014), which re-opened the period for lodging land restitution claims and extended it until 30 June 2019. South African land restitution, it seems, is therefore going to stay for many years to come.

These moving targets have been directly linked to the sobering experiences of the frustratingly slow progress in settling land claims in South Africa. Especially during the first few years, the track record of land claims settlement was anything but promising: in 1997, the very first claim was settled by the court and it remained the only one for that whole year; in 1998, the total number of settled claims rose to seven, climbing to a total of forty-one settled claims in 1999 (see Table 5.1). Given that tens of thousands of people lodged claims (this number itself a shifting figure, as we will see below) and that many applications thus awaited their finalization in the file storage rooms of the Commission, settling claims at this rate would have taken a few thousand years, as Ruth Hall dryly observes (Hall 2010: 27). It was against this backdrop that the Minister ordered a review in 1998 of the restitution programme, leading to marked changes in the process. One such change was the above-mentioned 1999 amendment of the Restitution Act, which transformed the former judicial approach to the current administrative approach to restitution.[4] Furthermore, in 1999 the Commission became more closely integrated into the Department of Land Affairs (DLA) and the Chief Land Claims Commissioner was replaced, as was the Minister of Land Affairs under the new Mbeki administration. Under the leadership of the new Minister Thoko Didiza, the government's land reform priorities became reoriented in early 2000 (Walker 2008: 13). This policy reorientation has been described as a shift from an overtly pro-poor, rights-based approach to one prioritizing property rights and the production of a class of black commercial farmers, which led to a major exodus of senior staff in the Department of Land Affairs in 1999–2000 (James 2007: 36–40; Walker 2008: 12–14).

According to Deborah James (2007: 40), many of these departing staff members were English-speaking white activists on the left, who were frustrated by what they saw as a move away from the government's original land reform objective of securing livelihoods for the poor. However, as James elaborates, those remaining within the DLA's employ after 1999, who were mostly black, or white Afrikaans-speaking,

---

[4] For a detailed account of the unintended consequences of this de-judicialization, effectively outsourcing judicial review and creating 'all too flexible bureaucracies', see Zenker 2015.

TABLE 5.1 Official settlement statistics of South African land restitution

Numbers, as of date	Total of claims lodged	Urban %	Rural %	Claims settled[a] per year	Total of claims settled	Claims dismissed per year	Backlog claims finalized per year	Total of outstanding claims
March 1996	7,095	70	30	–	–	–	–	7,095
March 1997	14,298	81	19	1	1	43	n/a	14,254
March 1998	24,516	84	16	6	7	57	n/a	24,452
March 1999	63,455	≥80	≤20	32	41	42	n/a	63,372
April 2000	63,455	n/a	n/a	3,875	3,916	n/a	n/a	59,539
March 2001	68,878	72	28	8,178	12,094	293	n/a	56,491
March 2002	68,878	72	28	17,783	29,877	48	n/a	38,953
March 2003	79,694	n/a	n/a	6,609	36,489	n/a	n/a	43,205
March 2004	79,696	n/a	n/a	11,432	48,825	n/a	n/a	30,871
March 2005	79,696	n/a	n/a	10,634	59,345	n/a	n/a	20,351
March 2006	79,696	n/a	n/a	10,842	71,645	n/a	n/a	8,051
March 2007	79,696	82	18	2,772	74,417	n/a	n/a	5,279
March 2008	79,696	82	18	330	74,747	n/a	n/a	4,949
March 2009	79,696	82	18	545	75,400	108	n/a	4,296
March 2010	79,696	82	18	131	75,844	98	n/a	3,852
March 2011	79,696	82	18	714	76,023	257	1,318	3,673
May 2012	n/a	n/a	n/a	416	n/a	61	209	n/a
May 2013	n/a	n/a	n/a	602	77,334	37	376	n/a

[a] In the three annual reports published between 2009 and 2011, the total and/or per annum numbers of settled claims also included 'dismissed claims'. However, in the annual reports for 2011/2012 and 2012/2013, settled claims were again counted separately from dismissed claims.

Sources: Commission on Restitution of Land Rights 1996, 1997, 1998, 1999, 2000, 2001, 2002, 2003, 2004, 2005, 2006, 2007a, 2008, 2009, 2010, 2011, 2012, 2013 and Department of Rural Development and Land Reform 2011b.

officials, argued that 'the new approach is more pragmatic and realistic and has a greater chance of success' (James 2007: 40).

This shift within the overall land reform programme towards more 'pragmatism' and 'realism' also became reflected in a growing emphasis on service delivery and accountability regarding land restitution, as reflected in the settlement statistics. This reorientation showed its effects: between March 1999 and April 2000 the number of settled land claims rocketed from a mere 41 to a total of 3,916 settled claims, and substantially grew by impressive annual settlement rates over the next years (see Table 5.1).

However, it was not only the annual numbers for settled claims which rose over the years. The overall figure for lodged claims has also been demonstrated to constitute a shifting terrain upon which to manoeuvre. In the early years, the total number of claims naturally grew, when more and more people submitted their claim forms as the original cut-off date for lodgement (31 December 1998) approached. But even afterwards, the overall figure continued to increase until it stabilized into a total of 79,696 claims in 2004 (see Table 5.1). On the one hand, this was the case because the different provincial offices of the Commission had to work through the massive numbers of claim forms, and gain an overview of and count *prima facie* valid claims. On the other hand, the total number of lodged claims has also continued to change due to the very processing of land claims itself. In some cases, competing claims for the same land have been consolidated and fused into a single community or group claim. More often, however, the processing of group claims has led to fission, splitting such claims into separately counted claims of individual rights-holders or claimants desiring different outcomes of claims, such as those for the restoration of land or for financial compensation (Hall 2010: 28–9).

Against the backdrop of these shifting overall numbers for lodged claims, the Commission has made substantial progress in settling claims since the early 2000s: between March 1999 and March 2007, the annual rate for settling claims moved between a minimum of 2,772 claims (in 2006/2007) and an impressive maximum of 17,783 (in 2001/2002), adding up to a total of 74,417 claims reported as having been settled in March 2007, i.e. 93.38 per cent of the total of 79,696 lodged claims. In that year, the Commission also reported itself to be 'entering the most difficult part of the restitution process'. The Commission was only left with outstanding rural claims that often have been very complex and quite difficult to resolve (Commission on Restitution of Land Rights 2007a: 3), as they entail competing claims, extensive research, disputes among claimants, conflicts with traditional authorities, deadlocked negotiations with current land owners, and the time-consuming involvement of the Land Claims Court. Correspondingly, the rates have substantially decreased to only a reported few hundred claims settled *per annum* since 2007 (see Table 5.1). Nevertheless, the total number of only 3,673 outstanding claims, as reported in March 2011, seems to point to a considerable success in terms of state performance over the past decade.

This success by the numbers has been paralleled, if not made possible, by an increasing emphasis on figures and settlement statistics as actual indicators of state performance. As described above, in 2007 the Land Claims Commission and what was at that time still called the Department of Land Affairs started to make explicit and persistent reference to settlement statistics in terms of 'performance indicators'. This shift towards an increased importance attached to numbers rather than descriptive forms of representing and analysing the restitution process can be further traced to the transformed, and transformative, ways in which the Commission has presented its own work both to Parliament and the public in its annual reports. While some form of quantified information has been included in annual reports right from the beginning, its relative weight and importance has drastically grown only in recent years. Thus, even though a few spreadsheets on the numbers of claims lodged and settled were included from the start, the vast majority of pages in the first fifteen annual reports up until 2009/2010 were dominated by extensive reports from the national and regional offices, providing narratives of particular cases; descriptions of challenges and strategies devised to overcome them; verbal comments from restitution beneficiaries; numerous newspaper clippings; as well as tributes to claimants who passed away while waiting for their claims to be finalized. By telling contrast, the recent annual reports for 2010/2011 and 2011/2012 each contained only eleven sparsely covered text pages, including the obligatory 'Letter of Transmission', the 'Minister's Foreword' and the brief 'Chief Land Claims Commissioner's Overview', which were then followed by eighteen and thirty pages, respectively, of nothing but settlement statistics, in which the numbers of settled claims were explicitly referred to as 'indicators' measuring performance and service delivery. This trend was continued in the *Annual Report 2012/2013*, which is strongly centred on its twenty-three pages of settlement statistics, even though these figures are more extensively contextualized in narrative form by a total of twenty-six text pages.

This significantly increased importance of settlement statistics as explicit indicators of state performance also became evident in my conversations and interviews with officials working at the Land Claims Commission. For example, Isaac Peter, then Acting Director of the legal unit at the Commission's national office, confirmed that 'now, when the minister wants to give a report on restitution, he is more going to talk on statistics than talking about individual claims as we used to do in the past, when we talked about one project and raised issues of this one project. Now, the emphasis is on statistics'.[5] Themba Ntombela, another officer within the Land Claims Commission, further elaborated the point that the restitution budget recently became much more closely aligned to concrete target figures than had been the case before:

> There has been a major shift in how we report things and how we outline what we do. We learn from being in the commission and doing the work we do. These things are bringing a lot of heat on us, when we don't indicate how many claims we are settling. When we just issue a statement saying, 'there is a celebration, a handover', people will take note of the handover. But they want to know how many claims are being settled. When you come to parliament, the questions point to indicators, they want numbers. 'Why do you want so much of money? How many claims are you settling?' So that is how the shift [has been], we are starting to give them numbers now. 'With the money that you give us, this is what we are doing this year. This is what we will do next year.' That's why we have now indicators, to say: 'in a year, we are aiming at settling so many with the money that you are giving us'. Because we are trying to create a connection between the money granted and the work done . . . So our whole mindset and our whole work is now taking account of what is seen to be the questions raised, 'How many claims are you settling? What are you doing with the money? Why are you taking so long? Why are you continuously getting shifts in deadlines?' So, we are shaped by what cabinet and parliament and the general public are starting to ask.[6]

As this all shows, a profound indicatorization of South African land restitution has taken place over the past decade, in which a growing

---

[5] Interview with Isaac Peter, acting director of the legal unit at the national office of the Commission on Restitution of Land Rights, on 5 September 2011.

[6] Interview with Themba Ntombela, legal officer at the national office of the Commission on Restitution of Land Rights, on 5 September 2011.

emphasis on settlement statistics has been accompanied by an impressive acceleration in the actual settlement of land claims, dramatically reducing the number of claims that are still outstanding. Indicatorization, it would seem, has indeed led to a remarkable success by the numbers.

UNPACKING THE NATIONAL NUMBERS: DUBIOUS FIGURES, LOCAL COMPLEXITIES AND THE SOCIAL LIFE OF INDICATORS

This gospel of indicatorization and success by the numbers has, of course, not gone unchallenged. To begin with, worrying inconsistencies regarding the national numbers have been noted. Thus, if one compares the figures given in successive years (see Table 5.1), they do not necessarily add up to the proclaimed total of settled claims provided at a given point of time. For instance, in March 2004, 11,432 claims were reported as settled in the past year. If one adds these to the total of settled claims reported in March 2003 (36,489), however, one ends up with a new total of 47,921 settled claims rather than with the 48,825 reported in March 2004. One of the reasons provided by the Commission for such inconsistencies consists in the fact that 'the Database of Settled Restitution Claims is on an on-going basis subjected to internal auditing' (Commission on Restitution of Land Rights 2004: 44), which retrospectively leads to changes in the figures for lodged, settled and outstanding claims. However, other inconsistencies remain. Thus, for instance, the *Annual Report 2001/2002* actually reports two differing figures (17,918 and 17,783) for settled claims for that very year within the same report (Commission on Restitution of Land Rights 2002: 8, 12). Furthermore, it remains highly opaque whether dismissed claims have been excluded or included into the overall number of settled claims (see Table 5.1). Other irregularities concerning the numbers are also discussed by Cherryl Walker with regard to figures for land restoration in Mpumalanga Province, which are possibly related to fraud and corruption (Walker 2008: 206–7; see also Walker 2012: 17–20).

On 13 April 2011, the South African newspaper *Business Report* published an article entitled, 'Data on land reform faulty', in which the Director-General of the Department of Rural Development and Land Reform, Mduduzi Shabane, was reported as stating that, 'the department had realised at the end of May last year [2010] that the information it had could not be verified and the figures published in its annual report had no basis'; Shabane further explained that the existing figures 'remained the official figures until the department had concluded its "massive information management project", under which it would assess claim forms and the status of claims at land claim offices nation-wide'. Accordingly, the two most recent annual reports at the time of writing (March 2014), covering 2011/2012 and 2012/2013, only mentioned the annual figures for finalized backlog claims and newly settled claims, but without indicating the revised totals of claims lodged and still outstanding (Commission on Restitution of Land Rights 2012 and 2013).[7]

Besides such problems regarding the reliability of settlement statistics, the deeper issue of the ambiguous meanings of a 'settled claim' further complicates the restitution process (see Walker 2012: 19, 822–3). According to the *Annual Report 2001/02*, a 'settled restitution claim' is defined as a '[c]laim that has been resolved with a signed Section 42D submission [i.e. by ministerial approval of an agreement reached between the interested parties] or a Land Claims Court order'. This contrasts starkly with an actually 'finalized restitution claim', which refers to a 'claim that has been brought to completion with the transfer of land/funds to the relevant beneficiaries, i.e. all actions pertaining to a specific claim has been dealt with' (Commission on Restitution of Land Rights 2002: 81). In other words, when a claim is counted as being 'settled', it has not necessarily been finalized yet in terms of acquiring the land from the former (usually white) landowners and transferring it to the beneficiaries or providing alternative remedy to the claimants. As a matter of fact, the Commission only recently started making a distinction between outstanding claims to be settled, and the backlog of already settled claims still in need to be finalized as, for instance, in the presentation to the Parliamentary Portfolio Committee on Rural Development and Land Reform on 30 March 2011, mentioned at the very beginning of this text. Thus while an impressive 76,023 claims were counted as 'settled' in March 2011 (see Table 5.1), of these claims 18,297 were subsequently reported as still requiring finalization, hence constituting a considerable backlog for many years to come (Department of Rural Development and Land Reform 2011b: 40).

One might also ask, as Walker (2008: 209–11) does, whether speaking of 'settled claims' is of any real relevance for assessing actual state

---

[7] Although the *Annual Report 2011/2012* further announced the overall data verification process to be finalized in August 2012 (Commission on Restitution of Land Rights 2012: 9), the updated figures had not yet been released by March 2014.

performance in the restitution process, since the success or failure of settled claims as well as the disjuncture between numbers of claims and of actual beneficiaries (each individual claimant counts as one claim, whereas huge community claims often only count as one claim as well) obscure what is really happening on the ground. Take, for example, a case I have been studying of a number of competing claims on the so-called 'Kafferskraal' farm in Mpumalanga Province (see Zenker 2011; 2014; forthcoming). Due to ongoing conflicts between claimant groups, Commission officials told me in February 2012 that they were intent to start all over again with this case, even though the same claim had already been reported and counted twice as 'settled': first in 2003, when one portion of the farm had been handed over (Commission on Restitution of Land Rights 2003: 18), and again in 2010, after the remaining two portions had been acquired by the state (Commission on Restitution of Land Rights 2010: 61).[8] Given land claim cases like this, Walker is surely correct in emphasizing that many land claims are haunted by complexities that escape simple quantification in the form of settlement statistics.

Apart from dubious figures and local complexities on the ground, the indicatorization of settlement statistics has furthermore developed a social life of its own, producing unintended consequences with, in fact, adverse effects for the meaningful finalization of the land restitution process. Due to indicatorization, the pressure on the Commission has substantially increased to settle as many claims as possible in the shortest possible time. This has led to a prioritization of rather easy-to-solve cases, mainly urban claims, the bulk of which were settled quickly through financial compensation in form of Standard Settlement Offers (SSOs) which, unlike restitution in court, did not require the separate evaluation of each claim (Hall 2010: 27). Derided by some as 'checkbook' restitution, as Hall notes, this relatively rapid settlement of urban claims has involved 'overwhelming pressure on urban claimants to accept standard cash pay-outs that bear no relation to the value of what was lost or its current market value' (Hall 2010: 33). Such a prioritization has also kept the actual restoration of land at a rather low level and thus has contributed little towards the overall land reform goal of transferring white-owned land to black farmers.

---

8 The *Annual Report 2011/2012* for the first time acknowledged the problem of counting a single claim as 'settled' more than once, when emphasizing that backlog claims now finalized were 'not counted again' as they 'had been counted before when they were partly settled' (Commission on Restitution of Land Rights 2012: 7).

The Commission has also hastily 'settled' claims with sale agreements stating an accepted price at the time of settlement, without being able to immediately acquire the land. The backlog has led to the possibility of claims ending up in the Land Claims Court, not because the landowners necessarily oppose the validity of the claim, but because several years down the road with massively increased land prices, the owners feel they can no longer accept the original price of the agreement as this will prevent them from buying a comparable farm in order to continue farming.[9] Such backlogs thus create massive additional costs compared to the original settlement, not only in terms of the much delayed and hence much higher price the state ultimately has to pay in compensation for the land, but also for the additional administrative and legal costs.

Another unintended consequence of emphasizing the merely temporary nature of the Commission's work and of the pressure, generated through indicatorization, to close the Commission down soon has been a rather high staff turnover. This tendency has been further fuelled by the fact that until 2008, most Commission officials were only employed on contracts with considerable insecurity as to renewals of employment. The staff turnover that this created hit the Commission particularly hard, since the investigation of land claims often takes several years, and much of an official's intimate knowledge of a claim can only be superficially reflected in written form in the claim files. This means that, when this official leaves, much knowledge is lost. According to Peter Ntshoe, an official who has worked for the Commission since 1997, the increased pressure over the past years to settle more claims has also negatively impacted on the quality of research by the Commission.[10]

Given the numerous difficulties with existing settlement statistics, quantification's principal problem of leaving out so much of the marked specificity of each land claim and, finally, the adverse effects that indicatorization has had in actually obstructing South African land restitution, critics have pointed out that the promise of improving service delivery through indicatorization has, in fact, turned into a

---

[9] Hence, the *Annual Report 2011/2012* mentions the refusal of current landowners to implement backlogged agreements as one of the main reasons for the under-performance of finalizing only 209 backlog claims against the target of 360 such claims (Commission on Restitution of Land Rights 2012: 13).

[10] Interview with Peter Ntshoe, official at the Commission on Restitution of Land Rights, on 6 November 2010.

self-defeating prophecy. According to Walker, South African land restitution is haunted by a disjuncture between 'what the aggregate numbers purport to say about land reform at the national level and what the settlement of actual claims has achieved on the ground' (Walker 2008: 22). She also notes a discrepancy between the symbolic importance attached to the 'land question' at the national level of political rhetoric and 'the low level of actual commitment that the state has demonstrated for land reform in practice since 1994, particularly at project level' (Walker 2008: 19). Walker thus questions the adequacy of target deadlines and settlement statistics as the most significant measures of success, arguing that (2008: 23):

> the political emphasis on such national numbers detracts from the resource-heavy and time-consuming attention required of the state if it is to settle actual claims, rather than generic abstractions, in a way that benefits claimants in the longer term and addresses real concerns about their impact on local economies.

In other words, what has been propagated as a success by the numbers, namely, the indicatorization of settlement statistics in South African land restitution in order to enhance service delivery and public accountability, has actually produced a rather profound failure by the numbers.

SETTLEMENT STATISTICS AS BOUNDARY OBJECTS: TRANSLATING CONCERNS AND SWITCHING CODES BETWEEN LOCAL AND NATIONAL ARENAS

Such criticism is well taken, highlighting the necessity of providing more adequate and realistic resources for meaningfully finalizing all land claims, rectifying the unintended consequences of indicatorization, and improving the quality of national statistics in order to increase public accountability. Yet at the same time, such criticism is unlikely to fundamentally change the importance of settlement statistics, the role of quantification and the production of commensurability that have figured prominently, especially in recent years, in the ways in which the South African state has processed its land claims. In other words, the suggestion of settling 'actual claims', rather than 'generic abstractions', as Walker puts it in the above quotation, seems to propose a somewhat misleading alternative. Instead, it is precisely *through* generic abstractions that the state has been able to settle actual claims. As such, the official settlement statistics have played a crucial role as 'boundary objects'.

The notion of the 'boundary object' was first introduced by Susan Leigh Star and James Griesemer (1989: 393):

> Boundary objects are objects which are both plastic enough to adapt to local needs and the constraints of the several parties employing them, yet robust enough to maintain a common identity across sites...They have different meanings in different social worlds but their structure is common enough to more than one world to make them recognizable, a means of translation. The creation and management of boundary objects is a key process in developing and maintaining coherence across intersecting social worlds.

South African statistics on land claims can be interpreted as such boundary objects, which occupy the contact zone, or interstitial space, between local and national arenas, allowing for different concerns to be translated and divergent codes to be switched while still producing sufficient coherence for the overall land restitution process (Rottenburg 2005; 2008; 2009; Merry 2006a; 2006b).

Seen from within the local arena of one concrete land claim, or from between overlapping and potentially competing claims for the same land, the actual number of these particular claims in need of validation, settlement and finalization translates a specific concern with individual experiences of injustice into the national arena of rights restoration and reconciliation. As such, this specific figure embodies the constitutional duty of the state, for this particular case, to redress racial dispossessions of the past and therefore operates as a means of downward accountability of the state towards the affected parties. In the course of actually processing this individual case, however, the specific number of claims involved merely functions as the integument, the outer delineation of all the local complexities that, for the time being, are of crucial importance and make up the subject matter of 'the case'. Officials engage extensively with the marked specificities of each claim, in alignment with the procedures laid out in the Restitution Act and the Rules of the Commission (Department of Land Affairs 2007b: 102–15). Ultimately, they orient their actions towards the goal of letting the particular number of claims involved jump columns in national statistics from 'outstanding' to 'settled' and ultimately to 'finalized claims'.

At the same time, the number of land claims processed in the context of one case takes on a quite different life within the national arena of generalized and accumulated land restitution and state performance. Here, through quantification, greatly diverse land claims are stripped of their specificities and treated as commensurable, equitable and therefore calculable. In the form of numbers, concrete land claims are linked directly to other figures, such as the annual state budget for land restitution. In that way, new modes for communicating state action, monitoring and conducting evidence-based governance become possible, allowing for an upward accountability of state performance towards Parliament and the public. This may take the format of parliamentary hearings where, as Themba Ntombela has put it, the Commission tries to 'create a connection between the money granted and the work done'. Similar processes of retrospectively aligning actual performances with target performances can be observed in the annual reports of the Commission. In this way, quantification comes to operate as what Theodore Porter calls a 'technology of distance' (1995: ix):

> Since the rules for collecting and manipulating numbers are widely shared, they can easily be transported across oceans and continents and used to coordinate activities or settle disputes. Perhaps most crucially, reliance on numbers and quantitative manipulation minimizes the need for intimate knowledge and personal trust. Quantification is well suited for communication that goes beyond the boundaries of locality and community. A highly disciplined discourse helps to produce knowledge independent of the particular people who make it.

The way in which settlement statistics operate in South African land restitution can be further illuminated through shifting the analytical focus from boundary objects to the multiple social worlds, or 'meta-codes', in which such objects simultaneously live and maintain their divergent identities. A 'meta-code' refers to a *modus operandi* that emerges when participants cooperate under heterogeneous conditions. This cooperation creates incentives to bracket undesired complications, minimize contributing factors and relevant information to only those absolutely necessary, and resort to standardized forms of knowledge and procedures in order to get things done (Rottenburg 2005: 267–71). Furthermore, a meta-code typically purports to represent reality directly, objectively and universally, while dismissing other frames of reference as being only particular to local cultures, subjective in nature, and hence distorted (Rottenburg 2009: 198–200).

Such a meta-code is arguably at work within the national restitution arena where the main concern is with the legally correct and just, but also with the cost-effective and reasonable restitution of land rights by a modern state that is operating under a rational-legal bureaucratic logic (Weber 1978: 217–26, 956–1005) and, increasingly, within a generalized 'audit culture' (Power 1997; Strathern 2000). Under such conditions, it is indeed of principal importance to produce standardized, quantified and commensurable information on land restitution that is stripped of all potentially complicating specificities, thus enabling the processing of land claims within the national arena of accountable statehood. Within such a national meta-code, it becomes desirable to adhere to a 'mechanical objectivity' (Porter 1995: 4) whereby personal restraint, accountability and thus legitimacy are achieved by following collectively agreed-upon standards, rules and procedures. This emphasis on public accountability within the national arena has recently been even further enforced through the processes of indicatorization I have described here.

The workings of this national meta-code are aptly captured in James Scott's characterization of modern state 'legibility', in which the state, through both simplifying and transforming the world it purports to represent, hegemonically creates its own interested, standardized, aggregate and transportable 'facts' (Scott 1998: 1–83). Scott shows how many high-modernist schemes of authoritarian states failed because the gap between the simplified 'meta-code' of the state and the greatly varied and complex local realities proved simply too big to bridge (Scott 1998: 85–306). Arguing against the 'imperial or hegemonic planning mentality' of state legibility and its thin simplification, Scott instead makes the case for the indispensable role of *mētis*, or what he defines as 'practical knowledge, informal processes and improvisation in the face of unpredictability' (Scott 1998: 6, 307–57).

Applied to South African land restitution, Scott's critical depiction of the national meta-code and his favourable discussion of *mētis* as 'the missing link' (Scott 1998: 307) finds echoes in Walker's preference for 'actual claims' rather than 'generic abstractions'. Seen from the local arena, this criticism of an official misrepresentation (Scott 1998: 348) surely appears apposite, in that much of what is locally deemed important and relevant gets lost when the state nationally apprehends individual cases in its own terms. Yet as a differential ontology – opposing 'as real' a world lived, known and acted upon directly in particular localities with objectified knowledge detached from essentially transitory local processes (Walker 2012: 811, 815–16) – such a criticism, ironically, seems hoodwinked by the local code as simply *another meta-code*, in turn proclaiming its own objectivity and dismissing other codes (like the one of the national arena) as parochial, while merely operating according to different (usually less strict) standards, interests and demands.

In other words, state legibility is not a one-way street in that only the state 'misrepresents' local contexts, when framing them in terms that are meaningful to, and processible within, the state's own national meta-code. To the contrary, local meta-codes equally 'misconstrue' the principles and *mētis* of state officials in the national arena, when conceptualizing what the state 'actually' does in locally relevant terms. Put positively, such mutually transformative and expansive apprehensions between different meta-codes (arguably a crucial feature of any translation (Benjamin 2000/1923)) make use of boundary objects (like settlement statistics) in order to produce 'state legibility' that works in both directions: extending the reach of the state into localities, while making state activities more accessible and accountable to an equally expanded local vision.

Seen in this light, settlement statistics as boundary objects have allowed land restitution to be processed in both the local arena of individual injustices and private interests and in the national arena of public accountability and the common good. This has enabled the state to translate, and hence balance, rather divergent concerns by switching between different meta-codes, while simultaneously maintaining the appearance of overall coherence.

CONCLUSION

Since the beginning of the South African land restitution process in 1994, the national numbers of claims both lodged and settled have played an important role both for the internal processing by the state of individual claims within local arenas and for negotiating the public accountability of the state within the national arena. I have argued that in this process, settlement statistics have come to operate as boundary objects, linking both arenas and allowing for the translation of divergent interests, both private and public, into the respective code of the other arena. In recent years, a much more pronounced focus on the national numbers as explicit indicators of state performance has shifted this balance towards a much stronger emphasis on questions of public accountability, service delivery and cost efficiency within the national arena.

As I have shown, such an indicatorization of South African land restitution has been accompanied by considerable problems regarding the reliability of the numerical data and the danger of not counting what *really* counts in highly complex land claims. Furthermore, I have demonstrated how settlement statistics as explicit indicators have a social life of their own, often leading to undesirable, unintended consequences. Given these problems, for some critics, the recent indicatorization of land restitution clearly constitutes a failure by the numbers.

On the other hand, it seems undeniable that the growing emphasis on service delivery, cost efficiency and public accountability through indicatorization has also yielded impressive results: after the shift towards an increased trust in numbers in the late 1990s, the annual settlement rate drastically accelerated, leading to a situation in which 76,023 out of 79,696 lodged claims were reported as 'settled' in March 2011, i.e. 95.39 per cent (see Table 5.1). Critics might point out both that these figures for 'settled claims' hide the backlog of claims still not finalized and that, as reported above, even the Director-General of the Department of Rural Development and Land Reform, Mduduzi Shabane, in April 2011 acknowledged problems with the reliability of these figures. While these points are truly important, one could retort that these worrying facts have only been made visible as 'facts' *through* indicatorization. In other words, while it is evidently not the case that precisely 76,023 out of 79,696 lodged claims were settled in March 2011, it is without a doubt the case that the stronger emphasis in the national arena on public accountability through indicators has indeed massively sped up the whole process of settling land claims. Furthermore, the explicit need to justify its work in numbers has also forced the Commission to come to (numerical) terms with existing backlog claims. In this sense, indicatorization itself has contributed to making visible and processible those problems, which persist and are, with very good reason, criticized in public. The reliance on rule-bound, standardized and quantified procedures within the state bureaucracy has thus led to both a continuous internal data auditing and to forms of self-correction that informed, among others, the very shift towards indicatorization in the late 1990s, as Themba Ntombela put it: 'We learn from being in the commission and doing the work we do.'

However, this self-correction is, of course, to a considerable extent self-referential or 'autopoietic', to borrow Luhmann's (1995: 34–6) term. In other words, operating under a rational-legal bureaucratic logic, state officials are limited by that very logic in the ways in which they can actually change and improve their procedures. As I have argued, shifting towards settling 'actual claims', rather than 'generic abstractions' is thus simply not part of the available options. Instead, the national arena of processing land restitution by necessity relies on a meta-code that values standardized, quantified and commensurable information that can be connected to other numerical proxies (e.g. of state budget), and thereby satisfy public demands for evidence-based governance. This is not to say, of course, that the worrying deficiencies in state performance described earlier are negligible or not in need of addressing, but merely to point out that, one way or the other, quantification is likely to be part of any improvement and 'solution'. Obviously, this is also not to say that indicators will always and everywhere improve public accountability and state performance, and thereby lead to a success by the numbers. However, I do argue that, at least in the case of South African land restitution, the recent trend towards indicatorization has indeed both increased a more publicly accountable state performance – under conditions in which involved parties, including claimants *and* current landowners, are often quite concerned about poor state performance – and made visible, legible and hence processible in the first place, for the state, the public and observing social scientists alike, those disquieting deficiencies that still exist.

References
Benjamin, Walter 2000/1923. 'The Task of the Translator' in Lawrence Venuti (ed.), *The Translation Studies Reader*. London/New York: Routledge
Commission on Restitution of Land Rights 1996. *First Annual Report 1996*. Pretoria: Department of Land Affairs
    1997. *Annual Report 1996/97*. Pretoria: Department of Land Affairs
    1998. *Annual Report 1997/98*. Pretoria: Department of Land Affairs
    1999. *Annual Report 1998/99*. Pretoria: Department of Land Affairs
    2000. *Annual Report 1999/2000*. Pretoria: Department of Land Affairs
    2001. *Annual Report 2000/01*. Pretoria: Department of Land Affairs
    2002. *Annual Report 2001/02*. Pretoria: Department of Land Affairs
    2003. *Annual Report 2002/03*. Pretoria: Department of Land Affairs
    2004. *Annual Report 2003/04*. Pretoria: Department of Land Affairs
    2005. *Annual Report 2004/05*. Pretoria: Department of Land Affairs
    2006. *Annual Report 2005/06*. Pretoria: Department of Land Affairs
    2007a. *Annual Report 2006/07*. Pretoria: Department of Land Affairs
    2007b. *Strategic Plan Review 2007–2008*. Pretoria: Department of Land Affairs

2008. *Annual Report 2007/08*. Pretoria: Department of Land Affairs

2009. *Annual Report 2008/09*. Pretoria: Department of Land Affairs

2010. *Annual Report 2009/10*. Pretoria: Department of Rural Development and Land Reform

2011. *Annual Report 2010/11*. Pretoria: Department of Rural Development and Land Reform

2012. *Annual Report 2011/12*. Pretoria: Department of Rural Development and Land Reform

2013. *Annual Report 2012/13*. Pretoria: Department of Rural Development and Land Reform

Davis, Kevin E., Benedict Kingsbury and Sally Engle Merry 2010. *Indicators as a Technology of Global Governance*, Institute of International Law and Justice (IILJ) Working Paper 2010/2. New York: New York University School of Law

Department of Land Affairs 1997. *White Paper on South African Land Policy*. Pretoria: Government Printers

2007a. *Annual Report: 1 April 2006–31 March 2007*. Pretoria: Department of Land Affairs

2007b. *Restitution of Land Rights Act, No. 22 of 1994 as amended, and related documents*. Pretoria: Department of Land Affairs

Department of Rural Development and Land Reform 2011a. 'Draft Annual Performance Plan: 2011–2012', presentation to the Portfolio Committee on Rural Development and Land Reform, 30 March 2011. Pretoria: Department of Rural Development and Land Reform

2011b. *Strategic Plan 2011–2014*. Pretoria: Department of Rural Development and Land Reform

Hall, Ruth 2010. 'Reconciling the Past, Present, and Future: The Parameters and Practices of Land Restitution in South Africa' in Cherryl Walker, Anna Bohlin, Ruth Hall and Thembela Kepe (eds.), *Land, Memory, Reconstruction, and Justice: Perspectives on Land Claims in South Africa*. Athens, Ohio: Ohio University Press

Hellum, Anne and Bill Derman 2009. 'Government, Business and Chiefs: Ambiguities of Social Justice through Land Restitution in South Africa' in Franz von Benda-Beckmann, Keebet von Benda-Beckmann and Julia M. Eckert (eds.), *Rules of Law and Laws of Ruling: On the Governance of Law*. Aldershot: Ashgate

James, Deborah 2007. *Gaining Ground? 'Rights' and 'Property' in South African Land Reform*. Abingdon/New York: Routledge-Cavendish

Luhmann, Niklas 1995. *Social Systems*. Stanford, Calif.: Stanford University Press

Merry, Sally Engle 2006a. *Human Rights and Gender Violence: Translating International Law into Local Justice*, Chicago series in Law and Society. Chicago, Ill.: University of Chicago Press

2006b. 'Transnational Human Rights and Local Activism: Mapping the Middle', *American Anthropologist* 108(1): 38–51

2011. 'Measuring the World: Indicators, Human Rights, and Global Governance' (with CA comment by John M. Conley), *Current Anthropology* 52(S3): S83–S95

Mostert, Hanri 2010. 'Change through Jurisprudence: The Role of the Courts in Broadening the Scope of Restitution' in Cherryl Walker, Anna Bohlin, Ruth Hall and Thembela Kepe (eds.), *Land, Memory, Reconstruction, and Justice: Perspectives on Land Claims in South Africa*. Athens, Ohio: Ohio University Press

Porter, Theodore 1995. *Trust in Numbers: The Pursuit of Objectivity in Science and Public Life*. Princeton, N.J.: Princeton University Press

Power, Michael 1997. *The Audit Society*. Oxford: Oxford University Press

Rottenburg, Richard 2005. 'Code-switching, or Why a Metacode is Good to Have' in Barbara Czarniawska and Guje Sevon (eds.), *Global Ideas: How Ideas, Objects and Practices Travel in the Global Economy*. Malmö: Författarna och Liber AB

2008. 'Übersetzung und ihre Dementierung' in Georg Kneer, Markus Schroer and Erhard Schüttpelz (eds.), *Bruno Latours Kollektive: Kontroversen zur Entgrenzung des Sozialen*. Frankfurt am Main: Suhrkamp

2009. *Far-fetched Facts: A Parable of Development Aid*. Cambridge, Mass./London: MIT Press

Scott, James C. 1998. *Seeing Like a State: How Certain Schemes to Improve the Human Condition have Failed*, Yale Agrarian Studies. New Haven, Conn.: Yale University Press

Star, Susan Leigh and James R. Griesemer 1989. 'Institutional Ecology, "Translations" and Boundary Objects: Amateurs and Professionals in Berkeley's Museum of Vertebrate Zoology, 1907–39', *Social Studies of Science* 19(3): 387–420

Strathern, Marilyn (ed.) 2000. *Audit Cultures: Anthropological Studies in Accountability, Ethics and the Academy*. London: Routledge

Walker, Cherryl 2008. *Landmarked: Land Claims and Land Restitution in South Africa*. Athens, Ohio: Ohio University Press

2012. 'Finite Land: Challenges Institutionalising Land Restitution in South Africa, 1995–2000' *Journal of Southern African Studies* 38(4): 809–26.

Weber, Max 1978. *Economy and Society: An Outline of Interpretive Sociology*. Berkeley, Calif.: University of California Press

Zenker, Olaf 2011. *Land Restitution and Transitional Justice in post-Apartheid South Africa*, Working Paper No. 134. Halle: Max Planck Institute for Social Anthropology

2014. 'New Law Against an Old State: Land Restitution as a Transition to Justice in Post-Apartheid South Africa?', *Development and Change* 45(3): 502–23

2015. 'De-judicialisation, Outsourced Review and All Too Flexible Bureaucracies in South African Land Restitution', *Cambridge Journal of Anthropology* 33(1): 81–96

forthcoming. 'Bush-level Bureaucrats in South African Land Restitution: Implementing State Law under Chiefly Rule' in Olaf Zenker and Markus V. Hoehne (eds.), *The State and the Paradox of Customary Law in Africa*. Aldershot: Ashgate

CHAPTER SIX

DOING THE TRANSPARENT STATE: OPEN GOVERNMENT DATA AS PERFORMANCE INDICATORS

Evelyn Ruppert

> *Data is the new raw material of the 21st century; it allows citizens to hold governments to account, drives improvements in public services by informing choice, and provides a feedstock for innovation and growth.*
> Google Data Analytics Social Science Research (2012)[1]

INTRODUCTION

In 2010 the Cabinet Office of the UK government introduced its Transparency Agenda (TA) as a key part of its efficiency and reform programme and as a means of taking power away from Whitehall and putting it in the hands of the public. Through the oversight of the Public Sector Transparency Board, all Whitehall departments must publish key public data-sets, from expenses to business plans, on their websites in specified open data standards as a means of advancing a public right to data. A number of platforms then consolidate all of the data via online and interactive access points. In addition to spurring service delivery improvements and stimulating the digital economy, the TA is said to be liberating and making government data more accessible, interesting and dynamic via websites, mobile device apps and other platforms. Along with powerful visualization devices, quantitative data about the performance of the state is being rendered accessible and legible in innovative ways. Through the TA government data is on the move and travelling to myriad sites and even sceptics see the possibilities that are opened up by this 'big data'.

As the title of this chapter suggests, open government data constitute indicators of the state's performance just as indicators in general make

I would like to thank participants for their comments on an earlier version of this chapter presented at the workshop, 'A World of Indicators', Max Planck Institute for Social Anthropology, 13–15 October 2011. I would also like to thank Johanna Mugler for her editorial suggestions.

[1] The quote is from the introduction to the joint ESRC and Google research call on 'Google Data Analytics Social Science Research' announced on 20 August 2012.

phenomena visible so that they can be assessed, compared and ranked. The TA ostensibly renders the state visible to scrutiny such that the gaze is turned from the governed back onto the governors where subjects of 'dataveillance' now engage in 'sousveillance' – a 'watchful vigilance from underneath' (Dennis 2008). In a time of Wikileaks, MPs' expenses and open government data, it is tempting to conclude that 'seeing like a state' (Scott 1998) is being transformed into 'seeing a state'. However, rather than considering the TA as a practice of disclosure and oversight, I argue that the transparent state is being done by a changing configuration of mediators that is generative of data publics and multiple versions of the state and the very condition that it seeks to eradicate: distrust in the workings of the state.

To develop and unpack this argument I first step back to consider another kind of device that sought to make the workings of science transparent in the seventeenth century and constitute matters of scientific fact. Shapin (1984) writes an account of scientist Robert Boyle's experiments in pneumatics that involved constructing an elaborate air pump to demonstrate how a working vacuum could be created by emptying air from a cylinder. The experiments not only produced new knowledge of the behaviour of air but also established how legitimate knowledge and 'matters of fact' could be produced and evaluated by multiplying the witnessing of a sanctioned experimental practice. He writes:

> Boyle proposed that matters of fact be generated by a multiplication of the witnessing experience. An experience, even of an experimental performance, that was witnessed by one man alone was not a matter of fact. If that witness could be extended to many, and in principle to all men, then the result could be constituted as a matter of fact. In this way, the matter of fact was at once an epistemological and a social category.
>
> (Shapin 1984: 483–4)

Shapin identifies three ways that collectivizing and multiplying witnessing was achieved beyond the confines of the scientist's laboratory: demonstrations before authoritative male individuals; facilitating replicability and thus the repetition of demonstrations; and virtual witnessing. All were accomplished using three inter-related technologies: the material technology required for the operation of the air-pump; the social technology of scientific rules and conventions for considering knowledge-claims; and the literary technology of detailed experimental reports that could multiply witnessing beyond the laboratory. Shapin argues that the latter were most effective for multiplying witnessing. For one, material replications of experiments rarely succeeded even though Boyle intricately communicated how the pump worked and the necessary experimental procedures (Shapin 1984: 490). Thus, detailed experimental reports, and words and images, were more important as they enabled numerous readers to imagine experiments without direct witnessing or replication. A literary technology was thus central to the generation of both a scientific public and the constitution of matters of fact as a social category.

Shapin's account provides an interesting starting and reference point for thinking about how governments seek transparency about their workings and to establish matters of fact by disseminating data on the Internet and multiplying the 'virtual witnessing' of the state. Numerous governments are embracing Web 2.0 technologies to change the traditional ways of reporting on their doings, such as annual reports that communicate official statistics. Each seeks to 'liberate data' from the confines of administrative offices and make them publicly available along with applications and tools for imagined publics to do their own analyses of 'raw data'. Transparency, democracy, accountability, engagement, collaboration, participation – these are just a few norms politicians and administrators attach to providing open government data. For some, transparency represents a new 'freedom of information' and because it mobilizes interactive Web technologies constitutes Gov 2.0.

Like the technologies Shapin identified, the TA mobilizes all three kinds of technologies – material, social and literary – to establish facts about the performance of the state. But it is different in three ways that I summarize here and then elaborate below. First, instead of beckoning a virtual witnessing public, the TA generates 'data publics' who are not recipients of experimental reports, information or expert generated analyses and audits but are incited to do their own analyses through material, social and literary (especially visual) means. This is different from Boyle's literary technologies, which brought the public 'into the experimental scene' (Shapin 1984: 511) by calling upon them to reproduce experiments in their minds. Instead of learned and credentialled authoritative men of science, the TA calls forth data publics who can do their own experiments, establish matters of fact, see the state for themselves and disseminate their results to others. Witnessing is thus turned into doing, such that the literary technologies of auditor statements or government annual reports are displaced by myriad analyses conducted by imagined data publics. While disciplinary and organizational practices have legitimized the expertise of scientists such that there could be trust in their numbers (Porter 1995), trust in analyses of TA data is derived from the presumed openness and publicity of data whereby transparency is afforded moral superiority.

A second difference concerns the arrangements that constitute data publics. Like scientists, data publics are configured by the socio-technical arrangements of which they are a part. But the arrangements that make up data publics are quite distinct from the institutions, scientific rules and conventions, and disciplinary arrangements that configure the fact-making practices of scientists. Data publics are constituted by dynamic, complex and uncertain arrangements of actors mobilized and provoked by open data, such as technicians, bureaucrats, software technologies, data formats, and so on, or all of the material, social and literary technologies required to translate data into information. It is through a changing configuration of mediators that data publics are being produced and brought into being. For this reason I suggest these arrangements are best understood as 'agencements', a concept that captures how the agency and action of humans and technologies are mutually constituted.

Third, not only are data publics brought into being but it is through the relations and actions of never fixed people and things that the transparent state is being enacted or done; that is, the TA does not discover or reveal the state, but brings into being the 'real' and represented state simultaneously. But just as many data publics are generated, so too is the transparent state made multiple.[2] Indeed, the interactive and regularly updated data, the endless generation of new data and changing relations between myriad humans and technologies lead to multiple enactments. The performance of the state is thus never settled and the transparent state must be constantly replicated and done. Virtue is thus found in openness and in the constant generation of multiple accounts. Consequently, there can only ever be more to reveal and different accounts of the state to be generated. But this is complicated further: because the TA draws boundaries around what is to be included/excluded, displaces implicit knowledge and reconfigures bureaucratic recording practices, it is generative of distrust and leads to what Strathern (2000b) has called the 'tyranny of transparency'.

---

[2] In her book *The Body Multiple* (2002), Mol decentres the ontology of a disease (lower-limb atherosclerosis) by demonstrating how it is multiply enacted through myriad situated practices.

In the absence of trust and possibility of transparency, I conclude that what is needed is not more of the same but analytics that can attend to the normative and political assumptions embedded in the versions of the state that the TA elevates and makes possible. To begin I briefly outline the myriad data that make up the TA and suggest that they constitute two kinds of measurements of the workings of the state: transactional and evaluation metrics. I outline how these are different from the numerical accounts generated by audits and part of agencements that call forth imagined data publics, reconfigure expertise and social knowledge, and generate multiple enactments of the state.

TRANSPARENCY AGENDA

Notably, the TA was introduced in the wake of the 2009 MPs' expenses scandal, an online data exposé led by the media which involved public exposure of MPs' spending patterns on the Internet and led to more criminal convictions, resignations or decisions to stand down in a subsequent election than any other single event or controversy in recent history (Ruppert and Savage 2012). The TA needs to be understood in part as a reaction to this media exposure and as an effort to prevent such moral failures from happening again in the future (Harvey, Reeves and Ruppert 2013). Indeed, upon election one of the first actions of the Conservative-Liberal Democrat Coalition government was the establishment of the Public Sector Transparency Board in June 2010. The Board oversees the TA, including the setting of open data standards across the public sector and ensuring the opening up of data-sets in machine readable formats to allow for data linking and analysis.[3]

The TA is made up of eight key elements that extend concerns about MPs' expenses to the activities, expenditures and policies of every department.

(1) *Who does what in Whitehall.* All senior civil servants and their salaries are displayed in standard organizational charts that are

[3] Through their deliberations the data and information requirements of the TA have been specified and set out on the Cabinet Office website and the main open data government platform, data.gov.uk. To enable linked data, items in different data sources (e.g. a city) are given addresses on the web (URIs or uniform resource identifiers), and data is published about them in machine-readable formats. Members of the Board include Tim Berners-Lee (attributed with 'inventing' the World Wide Web), Professor Nigel Shadbolt (University of Southampton) and Tom Steinberg, founder of mySociety, which hosts TheyWorkForYou.com, an organization of volunteers that monitors elected MPs (speeches, attendance, ministerial statements, etc.), and the unelected Peers, and comment on what goes on in Parliament.

dynamic and interactive. For example, we can move about the Department of Business Innovation and Skills (DBIS) and learn that in 2010 the Permanent Secretary, Martin Donnelly, earned an annual salary of £160,000–164,999.

(2) *Who ministers are meeting.* Data is provided on all ministerial external meetings (who, purpose), hospitality (meals), gifts received (values) and overseas travel (where, how, purpose, cost). For example, in May and June 2010, we can learn that the Rt Hon Kenneth Clarke QC MP, Lord Chancellor and Secretary of State for Justice, received 'hospitality' from journalists at *The Times*, *Daily Mail*, Channel 4 and BBC. He also had 'introductory meetings' with external organizations such as the Metropolitan Police and a 'stakeholder meeting' with the Bishop of Liverpool. He travelled to Luxembourg from 3 to 4 June 2010 for a Justice and Home Affairs Committee Meeting via Eurostar that cost £782.

(3) *Government contracts in full.* A 'Contracts Finder' provides access for businesses, government buyers and the public to live contract opportunities, closed tender documentation, contract awards and contract documents for all procurements above £10,000. For example, in June 2012 English Heritage awarded Swift Fire & Security a £11,974 contract to replace two security bollards at Kenwood House, London.

(4) *How your money is spent.* Monthly expenditures of all central government spending over £25,000 broken down by department are provided. For example, on 12 May 2010, the Ministry of Justice paid £437,916.63 to Atos Origin IT Services UK Ltd for IT and Telecommunications. This is only one of sixty-four itemized expenditures made on that day.

(5) *Business plans.* Departments must monitor and provide monthly reports on their progress in meeting priorities set out in their business plans, which implement the government's 'structural reform plans'. For example, in February 2011 the DBIS completed the development of proposals to introduce loans for further education students and reported that work was ongoing to reform quality-related research funding.

(6) *All other government data.* Every department must have an information strategy explaining how it will share data and promote transparency. In addition to the above, input indicators are required on how the department will measure the efficiency of

its policies and expenditures, and impact indicators setting out measurements to evaluate policy outcomes. For example, the DBIS adopted the following input indicators: funding per student in higher education and total number of researchers in UK universities. The impact indicators include the qualification levels of the working age population in England.

In addition to these datasets, departments are also required to make available data that are used in their published reports and collected via various means such as surveys. For example, the DBIS provides spreadsheets on surveys of English businesses, and on building materials and trade union membership.

(7) *Transactions Explorer*. Introduced in late 2013, a database on transactional services compiles data on activities like vehicle licensing, passport applications, benefit claims and filing of company accounts.[4] Transactional services involve an exchange of information, money, licences, goods or services and result in a change in the records held by government organizations. Data is collected from departments every three months but only provided annually to balance out seasonal variations. As such, only one year is currently available (October 2012 to September 2013). For example, in this period the Department of Work and Pensions reported 113 million transactions, which are broken down by the specific service provided such as registration, information provision and benefit requests. Data is also provided on the percentage of transactions completed or partially completed through digital channels; average cost per transaction; total cost of transactions (including staff, IT and accommodation costs); and data coverage (proportion of requested data provided by each department).

(8) *MPs' expenses*. A final component follows from the MPs' expenses scandal mentioned above. Expenses are now compiled and released through the Independent Parliamentary Standards Authority (IPSA).[5] The IPSA transparency webpage provides data on annual expense totals for all MPs, itemizations of expenses for each MP (e.g. travel), and details for each transaction (e.g. origin-destination).

---

[4] See www.gov.uk/performance/transactions-explorer/all-services/by-transactions-per-year/descending.
[5] See http://parliamentarystandards.org.uk/.

All of the above data can be accessed through several portals and most of it via machine readable formats: the IPSA website just noted; the Office of the Prime Minister's Number 10 Transparency homepage; the transparency pages of departments; and through the open government data platform that is overseen by the Transparency Board, which as of September 2012 boasted some 8,667 data-sets, and by April 2014 over 18,000.[6]

What can we make of this myriad data? First, it can be understood as constituting two kinds of metrics or quantitative measurements to evaluate the performance of the state. One is a transactional metric and consists of data collected as a 'by-product' of service delivery (e.g. departmental purchases and contracts);[7] the activities of ministers (meetings, gifts); the remuneration of senior bureaucrats; counts of transactional services; and direct programme expenditures (e.g. total spend on museums). Most of this data is devoid of reference to the substance of government work and instead are simply the number and value of transactions. For example, little is revealed about the content of meetings, the reasons and uses of a purchase or a particular salary, and so on. Instead the data are detailed and granular quantitative registers of the heterogeneous doings of the state over time.

The second kind is an evaluation metric. This includes data on progress towards achieving business plans which can be tracked in 'real-time'; socio-demographic data on the performance of the population (e.g. health statistics); and input/impact indicators for policy decision-making and service delivery assessment. Instead of a language of targets (as established under the New Labour government) indicators are adopted to replace top-down systems and micromanagement. Rather than centrally defined targets, the assumption is that departments are best positioned to define and evaluate their performance according to indicators they establish. In general, evaluation metrics can be understood as measurements of the consequences of government transactions (meetings, expenses, programme costs) that implement policies (e.g. on the economy or health of the population).

Taken together, the TA consists of metrics of the everyday granular transactions of the state and their outcomes. It is because they are

---

[6] See http://transparency.number10.gov.uk; for an example of department data see www.bis.gov.uk/transparency/; many data-sets are also deposited on the open government data platform at http://data.gov.uk/.

[7] Minister Francis Maude has referred to this data as the 'by-products' of public services (Cabinet Office 2011: 3).

recordings of the state's doings and units for measuring, monitoring and evaluating its performance that I refer to the data as metrics. Furthermore, as I will describe later, rather than any one piece of data, it is through comparisons, rankings and the identification of patterns in the data that performance is revealed and assessed. In some ways, these metrics are similar to the measurements that constitute an audit, which Power (1999) argues exploded in the late 1980s and early 1990s and was in part about control and organizational transparency. Generally, auditing involves 'checking up' on public bodies through systems of verification. In an audit culture, indicators and benchmarks place responsibility on the performer, not the checker: 'Responsibility for compliance shifts to the monitored organisation, corporation, or country itself, which must not only seek to comply but also monitor and report the success of its efforts' (Merry 2011: S88). While Power's focus is on financial auditing, many practices engage in similar procedures of checking and reporting, such as those of university research assessment exercises (Burrows 2012; Strathern 2000a). Power argues that what exploded was less a standardized technique (there are numerous practices that are described as auditing), and instead an 'idea' about 'ritualized practices of verification' (Power 1999: 14). Rather than a weakness, he deems that this is what makes auditing so powerful as it refers to a 'style' of indirect regulation or control that can be configured in a variety of ways.

If Boyle required a witnessing public that could read texts and visualizations to verify and establish matters of fact, so too does the auditor when publishing his/her accounts. And both also involve responsibilizing and forms of indirect control. But there are important differences between the audit and the metric. For one, with the TA, ritualized practices of verification move from the offices of auditors and accountants to the online platforms of publics. And second, they move verification from paper ledgers, auditor statements and reports to detailed digital recordings that imagined publics can order, reorder and experiment with. These qualities constitute a ritualized practice that calls for different kinds of publics to verify matters of fact. While Boyle's experiments required a scientific public that could read and understand experimental reports, the TA requires data publics that can analyse and do things with data:

> But now statistics have become democratized, no longer the preserve of the few but of everyone who has a spreadsheet package on their laptop,

135

desktop or even their mobile and tablet. Anyone can take on a fearsome set of data now and wrangle it into shape. Of course, they may not be right, but now you can easily find someone to help you. We are not wandering alone any more.

(Rogers 2011)

PRODUCING DATA PUBLICS

Transparency devices are staged 'as if' everyone can easily participate and witness the inner workings of the state. Instead, as many studies have argued, these devices are implicated in the very production of digital inequality and a 'digital divide' along lines of class, gender, race and ethnicity.[8] Of course, the same could be said of other techniques through which states deliver data and information to publics, such as audits and annual reports, where differences in access and literacy also generate divisions and inequalities. The solutions put forward to reduce such 'digital divides' often include education, training and the delivery of publicly accessible technology. But such assessments and remedies treat technology as neutral and subjects as preformed, just as the quote above highlights a common interpretation that data, devices and publics are ontologically separate, independent and pre-formed rather than performed. As Halford and Savage (2010) suggest, these assessments separate 'technology, on the one hand, from social process, on the other' (Halford and Savage 2010: 937). Rather than assuming that 'pre-formed social groups "use" (or don't use) technologies', they identify a 'more complex process of mutual interaction and stabilization' where digital technologies are involved in constituting subjects in diverse and pervasive ways (Halford and Savage 2010: 952). For example, Wilson (2011) has shown how geocoding subjects with particular urban imaginations and cartographic visions are formed through technologies of citizen engagement such as handheld devices.

In this view we can think about the publics and technologies making up the TA as mutually constituting, as ontologically relational, rather than independent categories that come into play with each other (Halford and Savage 2010). As the quote above suggests, open government data requires particular kinds of publics who will not only look at data but analyse it alongside and with others. In many ways

---

[8] See discussion of these studies and critique of the 'digital divide' in Halford and Savage 2010.

it advances what eGovernment policies and projects have sought to produce: publics that can interact with governments through the use of information and communication technologies (ICTs) (Helbig, Gil-Garcia and Ferro 2009). With eGovernment interactive web-based platforms or Gov 2.0, publics are invited to manage their services, access information and communicate with various state agencies.

With the TA a new dimension is added that engages publics not as customers, service recipients, information gatherers or simple witnesses but as data analysts and interpreters enrolled in a citizen science of government. While most of the data released as part of the TA was previously available, much of it was buried in various online or paper files, and some would have required freedom of information requests in order to access. TA enables this data to travel. Furthermore, unlike paper-based methods or processes under freedom of information legislation, data is not simply to be seen but to be worked on by publics. Of course, prior to the launching of the TA, many organizations and individuals called for greater government accountability and transparency, made the release of open data a political issue and also worked with data that was already accessible.[9] Many also started digitizing government data and releasing it on the Internet, as in the *Daily Telegraph*'s exposé on MPs' expenses (Ruppert and Savage 2012). As such, we could say publics were in formation and 'coming into being' to take care of an issue that the government was not addressing (Marres 2005). However, by taking up the issue, the TA actively configures the subjectivities and agencies of these data publics through particular socio-technical arrangements. They are arrangements that can best be understood as agencements, a term that emphasizes that the agency and action of technological and human actors are mutually constituted.[10]

This understanding is implicit in Shapin's account of the witnessing public when he notes that literary technologies worked to produce a witnessing public that could read reports and expert accounts of experiments. Though establishing matters of fact involved a complex arrangement of three mutually dependent technologies only the literary was 'in

[9] There have been many active organizations in the United Kingdom, such as mySociety, a non-profit company that builds websites that provide tools and access to data so that people can make better use of the Internet for civic issues.
[10] The term is used instead of assemblage, which has a more passive connotation and for this reason has also been taken up by others, e.g. Hardie and MacKenzie 2007; McFall 2009; Ruppert 2011.

the hands', so to speak, of the witnessing public. Access to the material technologies needed to conduct experiments was limited and the ability to replicate experiments difficult and often leading to failure and the social technology of performing experiments before eyewitnesses was confined to select 'ingenious' and credentialled men. With the TA, multiple data publics are mobilized through relations to and engagement with all three technologies which make up the TA agencements: material technologies such as computer infrastructures, websites, apps and data; social technologies including rules, data formats, software protocols; and literary technologies such as visualizations, maps, photos, matrices and profiles. Yet, their relations to each of these is mediated: while wresting facts from experts and putting them in the hands of data publics, specific kinds of 'technical capital' – skills, resources and knowledge – are required to design and mobilize the necessary material, social and literary technologies. While the imagined public of the TA becomes multiple data publics who are active in the establishment of matters of fact, new mediators and gatekeepers are active in directing their capacities and competencies to 'work with data' either individually or collectively (Ruppert and Savage 2012).

RECONFIGURING EXPERTISE

For Prime Minister David Cameron, putting information that was previously held by a few into the hands of all will give rise to 'real people power' and a 'post-bureaucratic age' where government officials no longer are the keepers, arbiters and interpreters of data (Cameron 2009). Power over data will ostensibly reside with an imagined public. Yet most people lack the tools or expertise to make sense of the terabytes of data being released. Like other data sources such as those generated by social media, commercial, academic and scientific practices, open government generates 'big data' that can only be managed and interpreted with analytic and computational software. Tools for making sense of the data are needed because performance trends may be hidden in the details and only detectable in patterns. Thus, software developers are incited to develop apps and user-friendly interfaces for different publics to 'exploit' and interrogate the data. Organizations, volunteers and software developers have been incited to produce websites and applications that arrange and analyse the data or provide simple visualization tools. As of September 2012, about 230 tools and apps were promoted on the data.gov.uk platform and the following are some examples.[11] The website 'whoislobbying' was developed because the TA provides 'too much data'. It categorizes, ranks and then provides a simple visualization of the relative importance of types of meetings (e.g. introductory) and types of organizations attending meetings (e.g. industry). Others provide interactive tools on websites to visualize data such as 'Where does my money go', which 'aims to promote transparency and citizen engagement through the analysis and visualisation of information about UK public spending'.[12] The site has a tool that enables users to select their income and then use a slider to produce alternative visualizations of how their tax is being spent in different areas (e.g. health, education). Similar tools have also been developed for mobile devices such as the 'Numberhood' app. It compiles data on key indicators, with data charts and descriptions, enabling users to examine patterns and trends on how their local area is performing on issues such as unemployment and crime.[13] The 'Commons Performance Cockpit' app produces metrics on the performance of the House of Commons and individual MPs using data from the IPSA, Parliament.uk and data.gov.uk.[14] The 'OpenlyLocal' site provides access to local council data 'without having to poke around through dense, difficult-to-navigate websites'.[15] An open data 'scoreboard' identifies all local authorities that provide open data and a council dashboard compares expenditures and lists the biggest business and charity suppliers.

Yet another provider of analytic tools is the news media.[16] Government data sites are heralded as an opportunity to revitalize journalism through the analysis of open government data (Filloux 2009). Instead of relying on government or academic experts and reporting on their analyses, 'data journalists' do their own research and provide in-depth analyses of immigration, crime and finance data. In some cases they

[11] By April 2014 there were 325 apps.

[12] The website is produced by the Open Knowledge Foundation, a not-for-profit organization with the aim of opening up access to information and its re-use; see http://wheredoesmymoneygo .org/about/.

[13] Designed by Oxford Consultants for Social Inclusion (OCSI) who seek to 'develop and interpret the evidence base to help the public sector and other organizations deliver better services' (see www.numberhood.net/about/).

[14] See http://data.gov.uk/apps/commons-performance-cockpit. The site was designed by KeyBusinessInsight.

[15] See http://openlylocal.com/info/about_us. 'OpenlyLocal' is produced by Chris Taggart, founder of CountCulture with the aim of 'making local public data open and accessible'.

[16] See e.g., 'data journalist' Simon Rogers' Data blog page on the *Guardian* website: www.guardian.co.uk/news/datablog.

also provide interactive tools for publics to visualize, investigate and download data.[17] There are numerous other examples of apps and interfaces but one point I want to highlight is that data is organized into visualizations of the performance of the state in the form of rankings, dashboards, scoreboards, patterns and trends.

With the TA then, the production of data publics is mediated by software developers, journalists, think tanks, lobbyists, watchdog organizations, data visualizers and bloggers, who are the predominant experts rather than auditors, policy analysts, academics and statisticians.[18] But importantly and contrary to democratizing assumptions of open government data, these mediators are reconfiguring expertise and social knowledge. And, as indicated in the government's own assessments, they also tend to be the most active organizers and analysers of the data.[19] It is a reconfiguration that is also connected to the purported economic value of open data, which is intended to feed the digital economy through the stimulation of new analytics and applications. Big government data is not only a source of knowledge about the state but also worth billions of pounds. To that end, in late 2011 the UK government announced the formation of an Open Data Institute (ODI), now based in Shoreditch, London and forming part of what has been called the 'Silicon Roundabout'.[20] Its mandate is to demonstrate the commercial value of public data and to nurture innovative, data-driven businesses using open data.

Of course, the influence of IT professions in the work of governing is not confined to open data. Horrocks (2009) argues that the eGovernment agenda has increased the power and influence of IT experts and consultants who act as powerful agents. They both shape and control e-government policy and call for more 'experts', thus reinforcing a growing 'consultocracy'. Through a number of government policies the

---

[17] See e.g., an interactive visualization of crime in the United States, www.guardian.co.uk/news/datablog/interactive/2011/sep/30/crime-map-us-data.

[18] One 2010 survey (Davies 2010) identified developers as overwhelmingly male (6 to 1 in survey results), and generally split between micro-enterprise and SME business in the private sector, local and national public sector institutions, and academic institutions, with a very limited representation of voluntary sector workers.

[19] At the end of 2012 a government review reported that 80 per cent of visitors to the data.gov.uk website exit immediately without linking to data (see www.governmentcomputing.com/news/cabinet-office-to-improve-transparency).

[20] It is led by Transparency Board members Tim Berners-Lee and Nigel Shadbolt and opened in October 2012. As part of the Government's 'East London Tech City' initiative the area around the Old Street roundabout extending to Shoreditch and Hoxton is intended to serve as a hub for media agencies and digital technology companies such as Google's 'Campus London'.

role and influence of IT consultants and suppliers has increased while the capacity of the public sector to control and manage major policy areas has declined in a wide range of domains from health-care to security (Dunleavy et al. 2006). Open government data extends this policy influence and its democratic consequences to practices of knowledge production and how and what the public knows about government. But such influence needs to be understood in relation to the various other actors and technologies that are part of the TA agencements and the digital divisions of labour that make them up. For example, 'information infomediaries' are a faction of computer scientists and engineers who operate between data producers and users and undertake major computational tasks such as aggregating, standardizing, packaging, securing and processing data.[21] And code, algorithms and protocols are made up of complex sets of rules and relations written into hardware and software (Cheney-Lippold 2011). There is also incrementalism in the design of computational software such that new designs often depend on bits of pre-existing code accumulated over time (Goffey 2012). Thus, influence is much more complexly distributed and open government data is part of an emerging technoscience that is being made not simply by consultants but through practical efforts and relations between digital and other technologies, consultants, engineers, statisticians, computer scientists, technology firms, and so on; or, as I have been arguing, of multiple and complex agencements.

This includes the visualizations noted previously, which are a fundamental point of mediation. Like Boyle's literary technology, where images assisted the reader, visualization tools are more powerful than narratives and data tables. In the experimental report, visual representations could convey more detail, imitate reality and give 'the viewer a vivid impression of the experimental scene' (Shapin 1984: 492). Such visual technologies have been historically deployed to ostensibly minimize the mediation of the scientist and thus constitute objectivity (Daston and Galison 2007). However, while held up to have epistemic virtue, visual technologies always mediate objectivity. As Galloway (2011) argues in the case of the digital, visualizations are foremost depictions of principles and codes of production and only secondarily of raw data. But it is perhaps when visualization tools are in the

---

[21] This is a term coined by Cisco Systems to capture 'heavy lifting' data processing services provided by centralized companies for the information technology industry and forms part of what could be understood as a 'data ecosystem' (Harris 2012).

hands of publics that such codes become ever more blackboxed. Rather than visualizing an experimental scene, apps enable publics to see and analyse data right before their very eyes, as well as interact with, adjust, manipulate and experience the data. It is an experience of data mediated by technologies and screens that Knorr Cetina and Bruegger (2002) have called post-social in that subjects relate to screens not only as 'doers' but as 'experiencing, feeling, reflexive and remembering beings, as bearers of the sort of experiences we tend to reserve for the sphere of intersubjective relationships' (163). They show how screens bring dispersed phenomena such as the invisible market close to participants and render it interactionally present. In relation to the TA, the screen materializes the performance of the dispersed state and constitutes a post-social relation between the state and its publics. Thus, it is through screens that publics are not only produced but also that the state is made interactionally present and experienced.

But it is an experience that is generative of a particular kind of subjectivity much in the way that Hayles (2009) has written about the reconfiguration of human subjectivity by information-intensive environments such as context aware technologies. Human awareness and cognition are part of what she calls the 'cognisphere' made up of an assemblage of flows and agencies between people, animals and machines (48). The assemblage is part of how we live but of which we are often unaware (Hayles 2006). In a similar vein, Nigel Thrift (2004) has called this the technological unconscious of living in a world of performative infrastructures animated by intelligent technological environments that are 'producing a new sense of how the world shows up' (177). Because of the ubiquity of data, Kang and Cuff (2005) also suggest that subjects develop a 'datasense' about people, places and things that draws on myriad information and data not previously accessible. In this way TA agencements can be understood as producing data publics with a sense of the state's performance, a kind of subjectivity that is perhaps less analytic and more experiential. It calls forth data publics that can play with rankings, dashboards, cockpits, scoreboards and other visualizations, and from this acquire a sense about how the state is performing. On the basis of patterns and correlations, rather than numbers or narrative, publics can 'sense' things are getting worse/better or are suspicious/normal (Harvey, Reeves and Ruppert 2013). But it is a sense that is not fixed or stable; just as many data publics are generated so too is the transparent state made multiple.

ENACTING THE TRANSPARENT STATE

For Boyle, literary technologies relied to a large degree on visualizations of how things were 'really done' and what they 'really were'. This in part depended on experimental reports that stated things confidently as matters of fact, thus showing 'they were not of one's own making; they were, in the empiricist model, discovered rather than invented' (Shapin 1984: 496). In this regard, Boyle's air pump worked to achieve the appearance of matters of fact much like other scientific devices have worked to render knowledge objective (Porter 1995). TA similarly positions numbers, spreadsheets and visualization software as neutral technologies that enable the production of 'objective' accounts of 'facts' without the intervention of experts.[22]

However, as in the case of Boyle's air pump and other scientific devices, the TA does not simply represent or make the state transparent. As I have intimated in the previous section, it is made up of agencements of mutually constituting actors and technologies that *enact* the transparent state. That is, rather than producing a perspective or revealing something that is 'out there' that needs to be exposed, the reality and representation of the transparent state are simultaneously being done or enacted by the TA.[23] It is being done through the multiple and relational practices of myriad people and things, from the practices, technologies and relations between bureaucrats, policy analysts, politicians, computer technicians, administrators, and so on to data publics.[24] This understanding of the performativity of practices and the enactment of phenomena has been well developed in the social sciences. For example, Power (1999: 9) notes that audits are not simply descriptive 'but performative, projecting and enacting ideals', and once routinized in bureaucracies or written into law can be 'increasingly real and fateful' (Espeland and Stevens 1998; Porter 1995) and intervene in the 'happening of the real' (Verran 2012). There are many other examples and though the uses vary, overall they argue that representations and realities are enacted together in knowledge practices (Law 2011).

---

[22] This is the language of the Transparency Agenda; see e.g., http://data.gov.uk/blog/new-public-sector-transparency-board-and-public-data-transparency-principles.

[23] The argument follows approaches in science and technology, material semiotics or post-ANT (e.g. Law 2008; Mol 2002; Hacking 1999) that contend the real and represented are enacted simultaneously.

[24] Here I am drawing on Mol's (2002) study of ontology in medical practice where she argues that 'perspectivalism' assumes a unified object is viewed differently by different parties. Instead, an object is a 'precarious accomplishment', which needs to be studied rather than assumed, not a singular entity but a multiplicity and outcome of multiple practices.

Furthermore, such practices are changing as they are becoming increasingly digital, which has consequences for how phenomena are being enacted.[25]

However, enacting the transparent state is a process rather than an event. Like other digital technologies, the TA is generative of a 'newly coordinated reality, one that is open, processual, non-linear and constantly on the move' (Adkins and Lury 2009: 18). While gathering together particular elements and appearing relatively contained and coherent, the arrangements that make up the TA are not fixed. Relations are constantly changing as new data, applications, actors and relations are updated and added. Indeed, the first version of this chapter was written in 2011 and since then many changes have been made to the platforms, datasets, apps and other elements. Even though I have updated the account provided here it is inevitably out-of-date. The transparent state can thus be thought of as a moving target that requires ongoing monitoring because both the platforms and data are never finished as the following quote attests:

> [The Department of Education] will never be able to say that [all the data has been released and in every format possible], and nor will anyone else in the government. We accept that the role of government as a provider of information will never be finished, and it will never be perfect. No department will be able to guess every single need that people will have for the information it owns.
>
> (Cabinet Office Open Data Team 2012)

The state is thus never finally revealed and equally, like many digital knowledge practices, more actors are successfully enacting and often transmitting competing and innovative digital representations. The transparent state is thus being done by a style of repetition that Thrift (2004) has argued is 'more controlled and also more open-ended, a new kind of roving empiricism which continually ties up and undoes itself' (Thrift 2004: 186). While such multiplicity could be construed as positive, it is also generative of other effects. Strathern (2000b), for instance, argues that the accumulation of multiple accounts is based on the assumption that 'what is invisible is what is simply *not yet made* visible' and thus there is always more to be revealed and 'further realities to uncover' (Strathern 2000b: 312; italics in original). Furthermore,

---

[25] For example, recent work has extended performativity to the digital (Lash 2007; Mackenzie 2005; Marres 2010; Wajcman 2007). These arguments are more generally elaborated in Ruppert, Law and Savage 2013.

making some things explicit only displaces rather than erases what is implicit, all of the inner workings of government such as the values, interactions and experiential knowledge of experts. The TA displaces such implicit values, assumptions and working practices that have a potential to be data but inevitably cannot and do not make it into being data, just as much of social life escapes methods of knowing and is resistant to being gathered together (Law and Urry 2004). Yet experiential and implicit knowledge is crucial to the operating of expertise, which can only work if there is trust in practitioners (Strathern 2000b: 313). The matter then is not that everything could or should be made explicit but rather attending to the distrust that mobilized transparency in the first instance.

The explicit does not escape distrust as it involves drawing boundaries around what is to be included and thus always involves excluding. Making things explicit involves an economy of open government data where some data is excluded because of privacy and disclosure concerns, only released to approved researchers or only provided on a cost recovery and bespoke basis (United Kingdom Statistics Authority 2012). It also has a further effect: the doing of transparency also reconfigures practices of recording and counting. Civil servants have claimed that in relation to freedom of information legislation less information is being recorded and internal communications have become less detailed and informative (Wintour 2012). Thus, the very doing of transparency influences and configures data recording and counting practices. Together these effects tend to exacerbate the very condition that devices such as the TA seeks to eradicate – an absence of trust. For example, Freedom of Information requests in Scotland have had the paradoxical effect of fostering ever greater suspicion that government 'really' has something to hide (John 2010). Taken together, the accumulation of endless accounts, the drawing of boundaries, the displacement of the implicit, the reconfiguring of recording practices and the paradoxical relation to trust constitute what Strathern calls the 'tyranny of transparency'. But it is perhaps a tyranny that is sensed through experiencing flat visualizations generated by devices that smooth out and banish all of these constituting elements from the accounts of what the TA is and does. That is, because what is 'behind' the data is banished, viewers are left guessing what has been excluded and why.

Transparency is thus both done and an impossibility. It is done by elevating and naturalizing particular versions of the state; it is impossible because it inevitably blackboxes its own making and closes off alternatives. Yet it continues to be held up as a virtue despite voices of mistrust and criticism and claims that it has 'become an increasingly de-politicised technical process, where public participation has inconsequential political effects' (Karounos and Lampsa 2011). However, as I will argue in the concluding remarks, political effects need to be more broadly understood.

CONCLUDING REMARKS

While transparency has been politically and morally juxtaposed against secrecy, there is a symbiotic relation between the two. This is evident in decisions about what to disclose or when transparent data gets buried under volumes of data thus rendering it opaque (Birchall 2011). A politics of transparency must thus be understood in relation to a politics of secrecy, a relation also suggested in Strathern's formulation of transparency. An answer thus does not reside in extending the boundaries of the explicit as this will not lead to greater transparency or trust in the state. However, this tends to be the only criterion the state uses to assess its openness.[26] Indeed, such a strategy would only legitimize the technology of power through which the state has constituted transparency and through which it seeks redemption. Calls for more disclosure of the same reinforces the virtue and moral rightness of the TA and its authority and effectivity (Harvey, Reeves and Ruppert 2013). Rather, a politics of transparency needs to include contestation of the knowledge practices and their implicit normative assumptions that promote certain realities and eclipse others. If the transparent state is enacted rather than revealed then what versions does the TA make possible and what versions does it close off? And how might we evaluate the relative merits of alternatives? We could start by investigating the normative and political assumptions embedded in what the TA deems relevant and important indicators of the state's openness and performance. For one, as I have argued, the TA elevates metrics that track the granular transactions of the state. Thus, the transparent state is enacted in relation to what it does in much the same way that businesses and governments use transactions to identify, categorize and evaluate customers and citizens. Supermarkets track, accumulate and monitor detailed transactional data on purchases and border management agencies compile and

---

[26] The UK government produces 'openness scores' for all of its departments that measure their progress in meeting their open data commitments. In December 2012, the average openness was reported as 52 per cent.

analyse digital traces on movements to identify and categorize people on the basis of what they do. Does the TA then turn the granular movements and doings of government into indicators of its performance and the object of politics? If so, then what forms of politics are being displaced? These are the kinds of questions that the TA raises and which I suggest call for a different analytics of what open government data is and does.

References

Adkins, Lisa and Celia Lury 2009. 'Introduction to Special Issue "What is the empirical?"'. *European Journal of Social Theory* 12: 5–20

Birchall, Clare 2011. 'Introduction to "Secrecy and Transparency": The Politics of Opacity and Openness'. *Theory, Culture and Society* 28(7–8): 7–25

Burrows, Roger 2012. 'Living with the H-Index? Metric Assemblages in the Contemporary Academy'. *Sociological Review* 60(2): 335–57

Cabinet Office 2011. *Making Open Data Real: A Public Consultation*. HM Government.

Cabinet Office Open Data Team 2012. 'Open data initiative goes back to school', *Transparency Hub*, 2 February

Cameron, David 2009. 'A new politics: the post-bureaucratic age', *Guardian*, 25 May

Cheney-Lippold, John 2011. 'A New Algorithmic Identity: Soft Biopolitics and the Modulation of Control', *Theory, Culture and Society* 28(6): 164–81

Daston, Lorraine and Peter Galison 2007. *Objectivity*. Cambridge: Zone Books

Davies, Tim 2010. *Open Data, Democracy and Public Sector Reform: A Look at Open Government Data Use from data.gov.uk*, Masters thesis, Social Science of the Internet, Oxford

Dennis, Kingsley 2008. 'Keeping a Close Watch: The Rise of Self-surveillance and the Threat of Digital Exposure', *Sociological Review* 56(3): 347–57

Dunleavy, Patrick, Helen Margetts, Simon Bastow and Jane Tinkler 2006. *Digital Era Governance: IT Corporations, the State, and e-Government*. Oxford: Oxford University Press

Espeland, Wendy and Mitchell Stevens 1998. 'Commensuration as a Social Process', *Annual Review of Sociology* 24: 313–43

Filloux, Frédéric 2009. 'Can Data Revitalise Journalism?', *Monday Note: Media, Tech and Business Models*

Galloway, Alexander 2011. 'Are Some Things Unrepresentable?', *Theory, Culture and Society* 28(7–8): 85–102

Goffey, Andrew 2012. 'Breaking the Laws of Code: Programming as Sociotechnical Praxis', paper presented at the CRESC Annual Conference, Manchester, 6 September

Hacking, Ian 1999. *The Social Construction of What?* Cambridge, Mass.: Harvard University Press

Halford, S. and Mike Savage 2010. 'Reconceptualizing Digital Social Inequality', *Information, Communication and Society* 13(7): 937–55

Hardie, Ian and Donald MacKenzie 2007. 'Assembling an Economic Actor: The Agencement of a Hedge Fund', *Sociological Review* 55(1): 57–80

Harris, Derrick 2012. 'How Cisco Wants to Make Big Data a Community Affair', *GIGAOM*

Harvey, Penny, Madeleine Reeves and Evelyn Ruppert 2013. 'Anticipating Failure: Transparency Devices and their Effects', *Journal of Cultural Economy* 3: 294–312

Hayles, N. Katherine 2006. 'Unfinished Work: From Cyborg to the Cognisphere', *Theory, Culture and Society* 23(7–8): 159–66.

2009. 'RFID: Human Agency and Meaning in Information-Intensive Environments', *Theory, Culture and Society* 26(2–3): 47–72

Helbig, Natalie, J. Rarmón Gil-Garcia and Enrico Ferro 2009. 'Understanding the Complexity of Electronic Government: Implications from the Digital Divide Literature', *Government Information Quarterly* 26(1): 89–97

Horrocks, Ivan 2009. '"Experts" and E-Government: Power, Influence and the Capture of a Policy Domain in the UK', *Information, Communication and Society* 12(1): 110–27

John, Gemma 2010. 'Transparency in Motion: Freedom of Information in Scotland as Ends and Means', paper presented at the Law and Society Annual Conference, Chicago, Ill.

Kang, Jerry and Dana Cuff 2005. 'Pervasive Computing: Embedding the Public Sphere', *Washington and Lee Law Review* 62(1): 93–146

Karounos, Thodoros and Paulina Lampsa 2011. 'Introduction: Contested Transparencies', Special Issue, *Re-public: Re-imagining Democracy*

Knorr Cetina, Karin and Urs Bruegger 2002. 'Traders' Engagement with Markets: A Postsocial Relationship', *Theory, Culture and Society* 19(5/6): 161–85

Lash, Scott 2007. 'Power after Hegemony: Cultural Studies in Mutation', *Theory, Culture and Society* 24(3): 55–78

Law, John 2008. 'On Sociology and STS', *Sociological Review* 56(4): 623–49

2011. 'Collateral Realities' in Fernando Domínguez Rubio and Patrick Baert (eds.), *The Politics of Knowledge*. London: Routledge, pp. 156–78

Law, John and John Urry 2004. 'Enacting the Social', *Economy and Society* 33(3): 390–410

Mackenzie, Adrian 2005. 'The Performativity of Code: Software and Cultures of Circulation', *Theory, Culture and Society* 22(1): 71–92

Marres, Noortje 2005. 'Issues Spark a Public into Being: A Key but Often Forgotten Point of the Lippmann-Dewey Debate' in Bruno Latour (ed.),

Making Things Public: Atmospheres of Democracy. Cambridge, Mass.: MIT Press, pp. 208–17

2010 'Frontstaging Non-humans: The Politics of "Green" Things and the Constraint of Publicity' in B. Braun and S. Whatmore (eds.), *Political Matter: Technoscience, Democracy and Public Life*. Minneapolis, Minn.: University of Minnesota Press, pp. 177–210

McFall, Liz 2009. 'The Agencement of Industrial Branch Life Assurance', *Journal of Cultural Economy* 2(1–2): 49–65

Merry, Sally Engle 2011. 'Measuring the World: Indicators, Human Rights, and Global Governance', *Current Anthropology* 52(S3): S83-S95

Mol, Annemarie 2002. *The Body Multiple: Ontology in Medical Practice.* Durham, N.C.: Duke University Press

Porter, Theodore 1995. *Trust in Numbers: The Pursuit of Objectivity in Science and Public Life.* Princeton, N.J.: Princeton University Press

Power, Michael 1999. *The Audit Society: Rituals of Verification.* Oxford: Oxford University Press

Rogers, Simon 2011. 'Data journalism at the Guardian: what is it and how do we do it?', *Guardian*, 28 July 2011

Ruppert, Evelyn 2011. 'Population Objects: Interpassive Subjects', *Sociology* 45(2): 218–33

Ruppert, Evelyn, John Law and Mike Savage 2013. 'Reassembling Social Science Methods: The Challenge of Digital Devices', *Theory, Culture and Society, Special Issue on The Social Life of Methods* 30(4): 22–46

Ruppert, Evelyn and Mike Savage 2012. 'Transactional Politics', *Sociological Review* 59(S2): 73–92

Scott, James 1998. *Seeing Like a State: How Certain Schemes to Improve the Human Condition have Failed.* New Haven, Conn./ London: Yale University Press

Shapin, Steven 1984. 'Pump and Circumstance: Robert Boyle's Literary Technology', *Social Studies of Science* 14(4): 481–520

Strathern, Marilyn 2000a. *Audit Cultures: Anthropological Studies in Accountability, Ethics and the Academy.* London/New York: Routledge

2000b. 'The Tyranny of Transparency', *British Educational Research Journal* 26(3): 309–21

Thrift, Nigel 2004. 'Remembering the Technological Unconscious by Foregrounding Knowledges of Position', *Environment and Planning D: Society and Space* 22(1): 175–90

United Kingdom Statistics Authority 2012. *Monitoring Review: Public Availability of Official Statistics – Three ONS Datasets.* London: UKSA

Verran, Helen 2012. 'Number' in Celia Lury and Nina Wakeford (eds.), *Inventive Methods: The Happening of the Social.* London: Routledge, pp. 110–24

Wajcman, Judy 2007. 'From Women and Technology to Gendered Techno-science', *Information, Communication and Society* 10(3): 287–98

Wilson, Matthew W. 2011. '"Training the Eye": Formation of the Geocoding Subject', *Social and Cultural Geography* 12(4): 357–76

Wintour, Patrick 2012. 'Freedom of Information Act has not improved government, says MoJ', *Guardian*, 13 February

CHARTING THE ROAD TO ERADICATION: HEALTH FACILITY DATA AND MALARIA INDICATOR GENERATION IN RURAL TANZANIA

Rene Gerrets

INTRODUCTION

Speaking at a gleaming office building in midtown Manhattan two days before the start of the sixty-sixth General Assembly at United Nations headquarters, Jakaya Kikwete, President of Tanzania and Chair of the African Leaders Malaria Alliance (ALMA), announced the launch of the ALMA Scorecard for Accountability and Action (depicted in part in Figure 7.1, green/yellow/red/grey colors in original replaced with grey scale).[1] Underscoring the significance of this event, President Kikwete explained that the ALMA Scorecard would be an excellent tool for advancing malaria research and control efforts in sub-Saharan Africa, where the continent bears the brunt of the mosquito-borne affliction:

> We, the leaders of Africa, are ultimately responsible for keeping our citizens safe from malaria. With the help of this new tool, ALMA is committed to delivering on our promise to end malaria deaths for our

I would like to thank Dr Mkikima, District Medical Officer of Rufiji District at the time of this research, for giving permission to conduct observational research in the Rufiji government health system. My gratitude goes to health facility staff in Rufiji District for welcoming myself and my research assistant Bunzigwa Salum Bofu to observe routine diagnostic and registration practices at their facilities. Finally, I am deeply grateful to Dr Caroline Jones (Kenya Medical Research Institute, Kilifi) and Dr Melanie Renshaw, ALMA Chief Technical Advisor, for offering much-appreciated feedback on earlier drafts of this chapter. This research conducted under COSTECH Research Permit 2005–74-NA-2004–06.

[1] The original traffic-light colored ALMA Scorecard can be viewed at www.alma2015.org/ alma-scorecard-accountability-and-action?page=1.

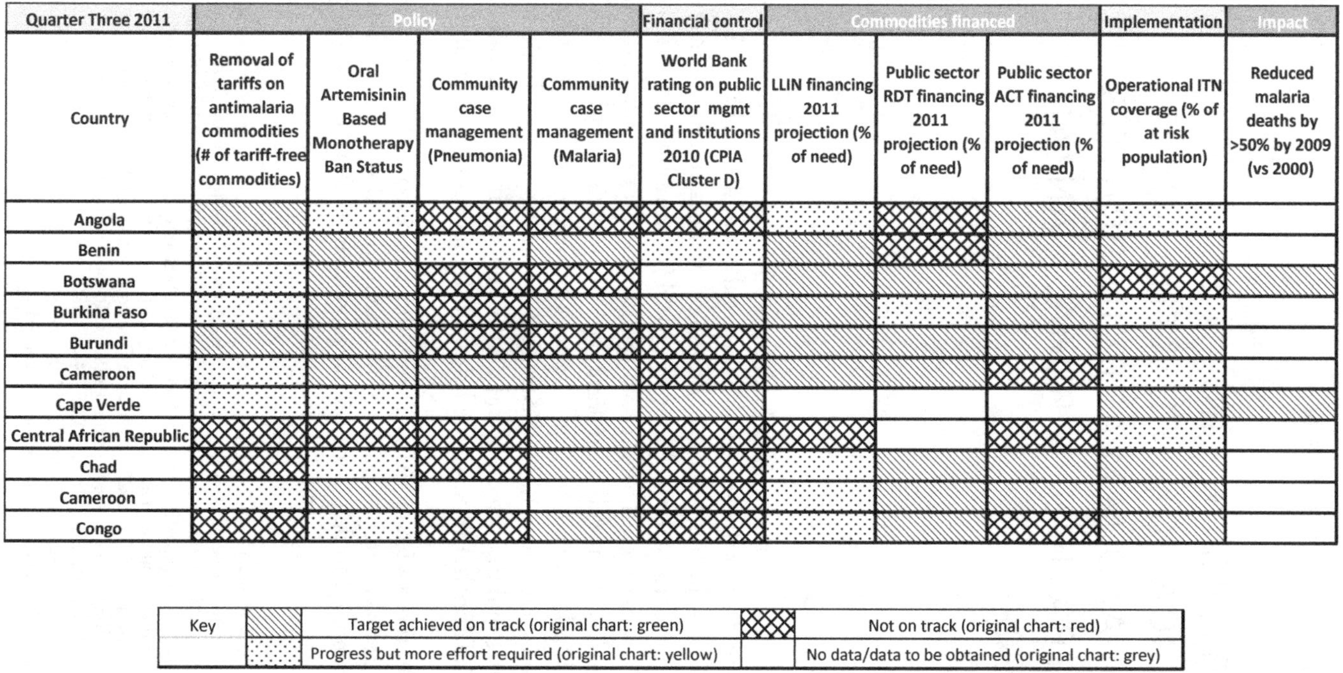

Quarter Three 2011										
	Policy				Financial control	Commodities financed			Implementation	Impact
Country	Removal of tariffs on antimalaria commodities (# of tariff-free commodities)	Oral Artemisinin Based Monotherapy Ban Status	Community case management (Pneumonia)	Community case management (Malaria)	World Bank rating on public sector mgmt and institutions 2010 (CPIA Cluster D)	LLIN financing 2011 projection (% of need)	Public sector RDT financing 2011 projection (% of need)	Public sector ACT financing 2011 projection (% of need)	Operational ITN coverage (% of at risk population)	Reduced malaria deaths by >50% by 2009 (vs 2000)
Angola										
Benin										
Botswana										
Burkina Faso										
Burundi										
Cameroon										
Cape Verde										
Central African Republic										
Chad										
Cameroon										
Congo										

Key:
- Target achieved on track (original chart: green)
- Not on track (original chart: red)
- Progress but more effort required (original chart: yellow)
- No data/data to be obtained (original chart: grey)

Figure 7.1 Portion of ALMA Scorecard for Accountability and Action (converted to grey scale), published 19 September 2011.

citizens and for all of Africa. The ALMA Scorecard for Accountability and Action measures progress, but it also inspires action by African Heads of State and Government.

(ALMA 2011)

The endorsement by over forty African Heads of State and the African Union of the ALMA Malaria Scorecard, which depicts country achievements on various core indicators and targets, illustrates the striking transformation of malaria during the past decade from a neglected disease to one that is commanding considerable resources and political action. Updated every four months, the ALMA Scorecard, divided into fourteen columns, each depicting a particular malaria-related indicator, is intended as a handy visual tool for African leaders and policy-makers. It deploys a 'traffic light color scheme' to identify areas where more effort is needed: green (signified by ▨▨▨ in the modified ALMA chart in Figure 7.1) indicates that a country is on track for that indicator; yellow (signified by ▦▦▦ in Figure 7.1) alerts that more effort is required; while red (signified by ▬▬▬ in Figure 7.1) warns of (impending) failure. The fourteen indicators depicted in the Scorecard are selected from a much larger 'dream list' of potentially relevant indicators which ALMA aims to include when consistent and reliable data from internationally recognized sources become available. Through its color-coded simplicity, the ALMA Scorecard aims to usher African leaders and policy-makers down a mutually agreed-upon path toward the ultimate goal: eliminating malaria as a public health problem in sub-Saharan Africa.

Tools such as the ALMA Malaria Scorecard used to be uncommon in international health and their recent proliferation in this domain results from three interrelated shifts: the rapid rise of results-based financing since 2000; skyrocketing donor funding for infectious disease research and control efforts in low-income countries (LICs); and mounting concern with fostering accountability and transparency (Chan *et al.* 2010; COIA 2014; Ravishankar *et al.* 2009; Shore 2008; Strathern 2000). This development spurred the spread of monitoring and evaluation (M&E) procedures, enumerative technologies for auditing and performance-measurement that were widely used in the business world and that recently began spreading into different domains of global governance (Merry 2011). Proliferating along with these M&E procedures, indicators are rapidly acquiring a core place in priority setting and decision-making since these quantified representations are deemed central to comparing and ranking (complex) phenomena (Davis, Kingsbury and Merry 2010).

In malaria research and control efforts across the world, M&E procedures and indicator production rapidly became a dominant feature during the past decade. As a well-known malaria expert told me at the 2011 Global Health Metrics Conference in Seattle: 'Nowadays indicators and targets are everywhere ... they are dictating increasingly what we can and can't do.' This growing centrality is even more striking when considering that global funding for malaria interventions has increased twenty-fold since the late 1990s (Ravishankar *et al.* 2009), propelling an enormous expansion of activities that has been credited with substantially lowering mortality and morbidity rates in many affected areas (Pigott *et al.* 2012). However, principal donors behind this funding boom (notably, the Global Fund to Fight AIDS, Tuberculosis and Malaria (Global Fund) and the Presidential Malaria Initiative (PMI)) place steadily growing demands on recipient organizations and countries to monitor and evaluate interventions at regular intervals (Chan *et al.* 2010). A consequence of this mounting pressure is that good performance is increasingly regarded as doing well in terms of M&E measurements and indicator-centered comparisons (Davis, Kingsbury and Merry 2010). Consequently, in this context wherein organizations and countries are compelled to demonstrate measurable performance and improvements, indicators, as the core tools for comparing and ranking in M&E procedures, quickly gained importance, both in malaria research and control efforts, and across global health more generally (Merry 2011).

While the rapid embrace of indicators in the 'malaria world' was spearheaded by donors, other actors certainly contributed to this process. To development organizations, (international) non-governmental organizations (NGOs), multilateral organizations and (as the ALMA Scorecard illustrates) government, indicators constitute a valuable form of 'comparable translocal knowledge' that they can use to assess or to influence the goals and implementation of interventions and projects, facilitating their governance at a distance (Rottenburg 2009). However, the meaning of such translocal indicator-based knowledge is not necessarily fixed or self-evident, and discussion about its possible interpretations can open up opportunities for stakeholders to steer interventions closer toward their particular goals and agendas (Rottenburg 2009). Such discussion about possible interpretations is in part related to the simplified nature of indicator-based data as 'statistical measures that are used to consolidate complex data into a simple number or rank' that simplify and ignore context and specificity, and collapse these into standardized categories (Merry 2011). By combining apparent transparency with numerical certainty and simplicity into standardized categories, indicators are 'easy to think with' (Holland and Quinn 1987; Needham 1973), to experts and policy-makers as well as the public (Merry 2011).

The presumed numerical certainty, simplicity and transparency of indicators obfuscates their heterogeneity as well as the uncertainties and complexities that surround their definition and production. For example, indicators differ substantially with regard to their ability to numerically represent the phenomenon they are said to represent. Some indicators involve phenomena that, at least on first sight, appear to be readily countable, such as column 9 in the ALMA Scorecard ('Operational ITN coverage as % of population'), which refers to the proportion of a population that possesses insecticide-treated nets (ITNs). Under real-world conditions, enumerating 'readily countable' phenomena such as ITNs oftentimes is less straightforward and more complicated than apparent at first sight. For instance, if an ITN is lost, neatly folded in a cupboard or drawer to protect it from damage, or suspended above a bed but not used after dusk because it hinders ventilation during the hot season, how does it get counted (or not) for the ALMA indicator 'Operational coverage'? Adding another layer of complexity, while quantifying 'readily countable' phenomena can be challenging, these issues are magnified for indicators of phenomena that do not seem straightforward to count. Gender equality, labor discrimination, sexual abuse or corruption are examples of multifaceted, fluid and context-bound phenomena that must be transformed into stable quantifiable units in order to make enumeration possible.

Similarly, as will be explored further in the second half of this chapter, the category 'malaria' – a foundational building block of many malaria-centered indicators – is not always easily countable or stable, especially in field conditions under which a lot of data are collected. Take for instance the (impact) indicator in column 10 of the ALMA 2011 Q4 Scorecard, 'Reduced malaria deaths by ≥50 per cent by 2009 vs 2000' (a target recently increased to ≥75 per cent reduced malaria deaths by 2015). This indicator centers on the category 'malaria deaths', a seemingly self-evident notion that masks various complexities involving the determination and enumeration of malaria-specific mortality. However, health experts have long agreed that identifying and measuring malaria-specific mortality is extremely difficult and fraught with errors due to three interrelated challenges. First, accurately diagnosing malaria can be daunting for prevalent symptoms (such as fever, head-aches, respiratory difficulties) often resemble those associated with common afflictions such as pneumonia or gastrointestinal infections (Källander et al. 2004; Perkins et al. 1997). Without appropriate tests it is almost impossible to identify the etiological agent, parasitic protozoans of the genus Plasmodium that invade and destroy red blood cells. Second, determining malaria-specific mortality is hard since the disease is both a direct and an indirect cause of death. It can kill on its own, but especially in areas where the disease is endemic and people generally develop a degree of immunity, recurrent or chronic malaria infections weaken and undermine patients, rendering them more susceptible to other infections (Guyatt and Snow 2001; Molineaux 1997). Disentangling which of these infections contributed most to a person's death (a hierarchy of causality implied by the notion malaria deaths) involves highly skilled persons with appropriate expertise and equipment, which oftentimes are not readily available in many LICs, particularly in rural areas. Third, and intimately related to the preceding point, mortality statistics are notoriously inaccurate in many LICs since health information infrastructures for systematic collection of mortality statistics are inadequate, dysfunctional or non-existent. As a consequence a considerable proportion of deaths in these countries is not recorded while determination of cause of death is rarer still (AbouZahr and Boerma 2005; AbouZahr et al. 2009; Setel et al. 2007; Snow et al. 1999). These interconnected challenges involving determination of malaria-specific mortality are compounded in settings where health workers are inadequately trained or poorly supported, and where appropriate diagnostic tools are in short supply, conditions encountered across much of rural sub-Saharan Africa (Bhattacharjee et al. 2012; Deressa et al. 2007; Mpimbaza et al. 2011; Snow et al. 1999). Cognizant of these multifaceted hurdles, experts regularly develop novel approaches to obtain more reliable malaria-related morbidity and mortality burden estimates, innovations that at times stir up heated debates when such calculations differ substantially from estimates obtained through conventional procedures (Brieger 2010; Hay et al. 2010; Murray et al. 2012). Taken together and framed in more general terms, the issues outlined above raise questions to what extent indicators actually reflect the phenomena they (are said to) represent and, by extension, about their validity and reliability as numerical shorthands for these phenomena.

Debates about the (un)countability and (ir)representability of (social) phenomena through indicators are not merely an academic exercise; the recent massive expansion of infectious disease research and control activities in LICs, the associated M&E boom, and effects in the health systems are just beginning to be explored. A key consequence of this boom is the exponentially increased demand for data to produce indicators for monitoring and evaluation. However, as mentioned above, many LICs are facing huge obstacles in terms of generating health and disease-related data. On scores of issues, data are absent. If data are available, these are often deficient in terms of quantity and quality (Setel *et al.* 2007). Moreover, the limited number of health information systems (HISs) that produce high quality data seldom generate the diverse kinds of data needed to produce a larger panel of indicators (AbouZahr and Boerma 2005). This 'data gap' – the difference between data needs and actual availability and production capability – characterizes many contexts wherein contemporary M&E efforts are taking place. A veritable health survey industry has sprung up in recent years to fill this data gap, and although support for strengthening HIS has increased, significant weaknesses remain especially in the public sector (AbouZahr and Boerma 2005; Boerma and Stansfield 2007). Unsurprisingly, given the persistence of weak data production capabilities, many low-income countries are struggling to meet the growing demand for data resulting from the proliferation of indicator-based M&E procedures attending the expansion of disease research and control efforts.

The issues and tensions outlined above serve as the entry point for this chapter. Drawing on ethnographic fieldwork conducted in a rural area of southern Tanzania, it examines how on-the-ground realities in health facilities are influencing routine data production on malaria – a key data source for indicator generation and M&E assessments. The Tanzanian context reflects these recent shifts in many regards: since the late 1990s, funding for combating the mosquito-borne disease soared 100-fold to around US$100 million annually in 2011 (personal communication, Presidential Malaria Initiative (PMI) Tanzania). Most of this funding comes from two external donors, the Global Fund and the Presidential Malaria Initiative, whose reporting procedures include submission of data that are used for M&E and indicator generation. The steadily expanding malaria data need to satisfy indicator-based M&E activities in Tanzania inspires the following question, which this chapter seeks to answer. How do daily practices at health facilities in rural Tanzania shape malaria-related diagnostic and recording practices, and how do these practices influence the production of data that is needed to generate indicators involving the mosquito-borne infection?

To situate this chapter, it begins with a brief historical overview of institutional malaria control efforts in Tanzania followed by a section that describes malaria control activities during the past decade. The focus then shifts to a rural health system in southern Tanzania, sketching the range of issues that health workers grapple with in their daily practices, and how these influence malaria diagnostic practices. The final section traces knowledge practices at health facilities and shows that the category 'malaria' entered into the government health information system often differs from the biomedical definition of the disease, but that these differences are exceedingly difficult to identify or correct retroactively. This raises the question as to what HIS data about malaria actually refer to and, by extension, what indicators generated from these data purport to represent. What is foregrounded and what is sidelined in indicator-driven knowledge production? Pushing these issues further, how do indicator-centered metrics shape the planning and the implementation of health interventions across the world? Conversely, how does the growing centrality of indicator-based information shape knowledge about health-care interventions?

SHIFTING HISTORICAL LANDSCAPE OF MALARIA CONTROL IN TANZANIA

Malaria's reputation as the leading health problem affecting Tanzania dates back to the colonial conquest of the area by the Germans in the 1880s. The disease was the principal killer of European newcomers and sickened so many Africans that it was widely viewed as the principal obstacle to economic development of German East Africa. Advised by the eminent bacteriologist Robert Koch, German colonial authorities commenced malaria control activities in 1901 by mandatorily treating with quinine Africans residing in and migrating to the cities of Dar-es-Salaam and Tanga (Ollwig 1903). This approach was unpopular among Africans due to its intrusiveness, and failed to lower the prevalence of disease appreciably, ultimately defeating Koch's goal of eliminating malaria (Clyde 1967).

Following their conquest of German East Africa during the First World War, the British gradually resumed malaria control activities in urban areas and set out to increase access to curative services for Africans, especially those living in rural areas, by laying the groundwork for a rudimentary health system. Colonial records indicate that in large parts of Tanganyika (the British name for the territory) malaria was the leading health problem in terms of the number of patients diagnosed and treated (Clyde 1967). Similarly, these records regularly comment that malaria was a major cause of death, however, actual mortality figures were only available from a handful of hospitals where post-mortems were conducted. Quite like today, most malaria mortality occurred out of sight from government authorities and the health sector, and the cause of death was seldom determined (de Savigny *et al.* 2004).

This bleak picture began to change during the 1950s, when the British authorities replaced quinine with chloroquine, a cheaper and more potent antimalarial with fewer side-effects and easier to use. Chloroquine quickly became the corner-stone of malaria treatment, its use rising further after independence when Tanzania's first president, Julius Nyerere, embarked on a huge expansion of the rural health system. Suppressed by these interventions and by rising living standards, malaria receded steadily during the 1970s and gradually came to be viewed as a relatively minor public health issue (Beck 1970; Iliffe 1979). This trend was reversed when economic crisis engulfed Tanzania during the 1980s, progressively crippling the health system at a time of spreading parasite resistance to chloroquine, rendering malaria more difficult to treat and deadlier (Coulson 1982; Turshen 1999). Meanwhile, the Tanzanian government, facing bankruptcy, was compelled to implement an International Monetary Fund structural adjustment programme, steps that further eroded the public health system and all but ended government involvement in malaria control activities. The gap left behind by retreating Tanzanian government institutions attracted a wave of NGOs which paid little attention to malaria and focused mainly on problems such as the devastating AIDS epidemic (Turshen 1999). Inexorably, the disease reclaimed its position as the leading cause of death and sickness and health facility attendance in Tanzania (Abdulla *et al.* 2001). Alarmed by this trend, the Tanzanian Ministry of Health (MoH) established the National Malaria Control Program (NMCP) to counter the resurging disease. However this organization, hamstrung by extreme shortages of funding and skilled staff, could do very little until the late 1990s when malaria once again became a priority issue on the international stage and more external funding for combating the disease became available (Kiszewski *et al.* 2007).

The dawn of the twenty-first century witnessed a surge of activity involving diseases of poverty, a shift that culminated with the establishment of new organizations such as the Gates Foundation and the Global Fund, and the launch of novel initiatives such as the PMI. Malaria, along with AIDS and tuberculosis considered among the three deadliest infectious diseases, became a key focus of attention and funding for researching and fighting the affliction began to rise sharply. By mid-decade, these new entities had become the dominant financiers of malaria research and control activities world-wide, contributing around 85 percent of global funding for the disease (Roll Back Malaria 2010). As will be explored in the following section, the key organizations behind this global funding boom greatly shaped the expansion of malaria control activities and M&E procedures in Tanzania.

SPREAD OF M&E AND INDICATORS IN CONTEMPORARY TANZANIAN MALARIA CONTROL EFFORTS

The rapid expansion of malaria research and control efforts in Tanzania during the past decade generated a soaring demand for data, propelled largely by increasingly elaborate M&E procedures that require data on a steadily growing number of indicators in order to track the 'inputs', 'outputs' and 'outcomes' of interventions. Although this demand for M&E data derives primarily from the reporting requirements of the two principal external donors Global Fund and PMI, which provided 98 per cent of the total funding for malaria control in 2010, with the remaining 2 per cent paid by the Government of Tanzania (NMCP 2010), it would be misleading to claim that the spread of indicator-centered M&E procedures was imposed by these donors. Leading Tanzanian stakeholders, notably the National Malaria Control Programme, embraced these approaches well before the malaria funding boom commenced. This shift can be traced to development interventions during the mid-1990s that tested the World Bank propagated notion 'evidence-based' disease management and health planning at the district level (World Bank 1993), a novelty at the time in Tanzania where such decisions usually were politically motivated (Neilson and Smutylo 2004). Considered successful by influential donor organizations such as Canada's International Development Research Centre, these interventions fostered a greater role for sound data in decision-making and public policy in the Tanzanian health sector (Neilson and Smutylo 2004), and, in the longer run, contributed to creating an institutional environment which, at least officially, claims to be receptive to promoting efficiency, accountability and transparency. Tracing how the Tanzanian government gradually adopted indicator-based M&E procedures goes well beyond the scope of this chapter, so instead the following section briefly sketches this process in policy documents issued by the National Malaria Control Programme (NMCP). Analysis of these documents suggests that the push for promoting indicator-based monitoring and evaluation was not homegrown, but can be traced to several new players in the global malaria world whose converging ideas about a perceived need to foster cost-effective and evidence-based health interventions based on quantifiable benchmarks and targets dovetailed with the development agenda outlined in the Millennium Development Goals (MDGs), an overarching framework that emerged out of the 2000 United Nations Millennium Summit which the Government of Tanzania endorsed and is keen on showing progress towards (Dodd and Cassels 2006).

Examination of successive Tanzanian Malaria Control Strategies issued by the NMCP during the first decade of the twenty-first century shows not only the growing role assigned to indicators and M&E procedures, but also the influence in this process on organizations such as the Global Fund to Fight AIDS, Tuberculosis and Malaria (GFATM) and the Roll Back Malaria (RBM) Monitoring and Evaluation Reference Group (MERG), an advisory body comprised of experts from key organizations in the global malaria world that provides guidance on malaria-centered M&E issues including indicators and targets. The support from foreign institutions was much appreciated by the NMCP, which in the late 1990s was very tiny and faced acute constraints with regard to (human) resources, office facilities, transport, etc., a state of affairs that reflected the limited amount of funding available for malaria at the time (in Tanzania as on the global plane), as opposed to, for instance, HIV/AIDS (Gerrets 2010; Roll Back Malaria 2010; Shiffman 2006). One of the earliest NMCP policy documents that sets specific targets for reducing the impact of malaria and discusses possible indicators for monitoring and evaluating progress towards these goals is the National Malaria Medium Term Strategic Plan 2002–2007 (NMMTSP-1), a document co-produced by 'many [unspecified] stakeholders [including] bilateral and multilateral partners, sectoral ministries, NGOs, the private sector, institutions and individuals' (NMCP 2003). NMMTSP-1 outlines specific targets for reducing malaria that largely reflect the milestones set by Roll Back Malaria and in the Abuja Declaration of 2000, wherein forty-five African governments committed themselves to reduce by 60 per cent various aspects of the malaria problem (Roll Back Malaria 2000). Specifically, NMMTSP-1 set the goal to reduce 'malaria mortality and morbidity in all 21 regions by 25 per cent by 2007 and by 50 per cent by 2010', citing five specific targets through which this objective would be pursued (not listed here, see NMCP 2003). To determine progress toward reaching these targets, NMMTSP-1 contains a section dedicated to M&E that lists thirty-three relevant indicators, though their actual use remains unclear while the authors caution that 'many sources of malaria data are available but a number of constraints remain that threaten the acquisition of robust and reliable data' (NMCP 2003). Both the targets and the indicators are framed overwhelmingly in quantitative terms, reflecting the overarching approach and the standards spearheaded in the MDGs (Molyneux 2008; Sachs 2005). NMMTSP-1 was deemed successful in terms of results achieved, and it sprouted a successor policy plan for the period 2008–2013, NMMTSP-2. Since NMMTSP-2 formulated even more ambitious goals which constitute the backdrop for the findings that will be presented in this chapter, they are quoted in full (NMCP 2010: 9):

(1) reduce the prevalence of malaria by 50 per cent by the end of 2013 from current levels (as determined by indicator values at the point of last measurement);
(2) 80 per cent of malaria patients are diagnosed and treated with effective antimalarial medicines, artemisinin-based combination therapy (ACT), within 24 hours of the onset of fever;
(3) 80 per cent of all pregnant women receive 2 or more doses of intermittent preventive treatment (IPTp);
(4) 80 per cent of people in malarious areas are protected through the use of insecticide-treated nets (ITNs);
(5) 80 per cent of people in target areas are protected through the indoor residual spraying (IRS);
(6) early detection and containment of 80 per cent of malaria epidemics within two weeks from onset.

In order to measure (lack of) progress toward reaching these targets, the Tanzanian NMCP developed a comprehensive Monitoring and

Evaluation Plan (MEP) which elaborates on the indicators described in NMMTSP-1, drawing heavily on the M&E procedures and recommendations developed by the MERG and on the Global Fund Monitoring and Evaluation Toolkit (Global Fund 2009; NMCP 2010). Significantly, the MEP is a stand-alone document that can be used for a variety of malaria-specific monitoring and evaluation activities. Hence it is not only designed for use in NMMTSP-2, but also for general development activities such as the Tanzania Health Sector Strategic Plan III (2008–2015) or the National Strategy for Economic Growth and Poverty Reduction, and to measure progress regarding the MDGs (NMCP 2010). This transformation from an aspirational section in NMMTSP-1 to a stand-alone MEP that accompanies NMMTSP-2 illustrates the growing reach of indicators and M&E procedures among Tanzanian institutions.

A critical look at the MEP reveals several core themes and taken-for-granted assumptions. Predictably, indicators (and targets) occupy a central place in the MEP, for it is through these calculative devices that phenomena are turned into countable units that can be ranked and compared, a principal aim of monitoring and evaluation (Davis, Kingsbury and Merry 2010). The MEP is furthermore laced with language that frames M&E in terms of cost-effectiveness and efficiency as the following quote illustrates: 'It will be essential to monitor and evaluate all of the national malaria control strategies implemented in Tanzania under NMCP to ensure that resources are being used in the most cost-effective manner' (NMCP 2010). Likewise, the central role of indicators as the preferred tools for monitoring and evaluating interventions is taken for granted and undisputed in the MEP. Abundant use of technical idiom and the passive voice obscure the (at times contentious) decision-making that accompanies the selection of an indicator for a particular task, and such decisions typically are presented as deriving from expert reasoning. The following verbatim excerpt illustrates the matter-of-fact technical language in which the centrality of indicators in the MEP is framed:

> Indicators selected for monitoring will be different depending on the reporting level within the health system and the epidemiological situation of the country. At the global level, the main focus of the monitoring process is outcome indicators to monitor trends in coverage of recommended interventions, as elaborated above. At the national and sub-national levels, the emphasis will be on utilizing programmatic records,

health system data, and sentinel site data to monitor inputs, processes, and outputs.

NMCP (2010: 13)

Descriptions such as this are typical in (Tanzanian) policy documents, which tend to be co-produced by 'stakeholders' from various local and foreign institutions whose perspectives and interests are not readily discernible in this consensus text.[2] While indicators feature centrally in NMMTSP-1, the document reveals little about their specific role in M&E procedures. To understand the role of indicators in M&E activities, it is necessary to unpack the MEP further.

The MEP presents a conceptual M&E framework that distinguishes five classes of indicators: input indicators, process indicators, output indicators, outcome indicators and impact indicators. As its name suggests ('RBM coverage indicator', see Figure 7.2), the framework derives from Roll Back Malaria, the WHO-based partnership that was launched in 1998 as a global malaria coordination and advocacy platform (Brundtland 1998). This RBM framework mirrors the one used by the Global Fund, an organization that played a seminal role in propagating M&E performance-based approaches since its launch in 2002. Each of these five classes of indicators (their names suggest as much) corresponds with a particular facet of interventions and its relation to the overarching M&E framework. The purpose of and relation between each class of indicators in this M&E framework is depicted in Figure 7.2 (NMCP 2010: 13).

The five classes of indicators comprising the M&E framework are sub-divided into three clusters of performance indicators and two clusters of evaluation indicators. Each of the five classes furthermore contains sub-sets of indicators that are devised to enumerate and track a specific phenomenon. In total, the basic M&E framework in the MEP lists twenty-six different indicators that are shown in Figure 7.3 to illustrate their diversity (NMCP 2010: 14).

As the names of these twenty-six indicators suggest, they cover disparate phenomena. While some of these phenomena appear to be quite

---

[2] For the MEP, the MoH was the lead stakeholder on the Tanzanian side, with contributions from experts representing other levels of government (eight district medical officers (DMOs), seven regional medical officers) and several malaria NGOs, while on the international side it involved experts from large international NGOs (such as World Vision, Population Services International and the Clinton Foundation), globally-oriented public health institutions (e.g., US Centers for Diseases Control, the Johns Hopkins University), multilateral institutions (World Health Organization and UNICEF), donor agencies (USAID) and US government-driven initiatives (e.g. PMI, the International Health Initiative) (NMCP 2010).

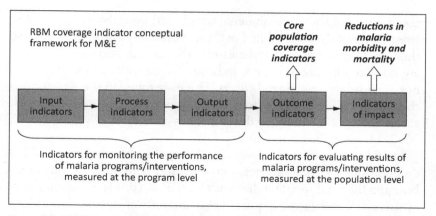

Figure 7.2 M&E framework of the National Malaria Control Programme, Tanzania.

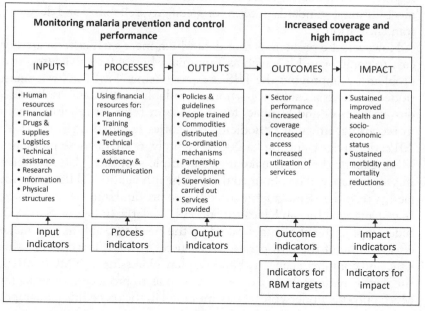

Figure 7.3 Basic indicators of the M&E framework of the National Malaria Control Programme, Tanzania.

countable, e.g. the input indicator 'Drugs and supplies' (column 1) or the output indicator '[number of] People trained' (column 3), other ones do not seem to be readily reducible to numbers, e.g., the process indicator 'Planning' (column 2) or the outcome indicator 'Sector performance' (column 4), pointing toward the challenges surrounding the

165

countability of these phenomena, which will be elaborated on below. Irrespective of the countability of these indicators, the breadth of topics they aim to cover gives an indication of the amount and sort of data that are needed. Of note, the basic indicator framework shown above does not describe any specific indicators. These are found in the Appendix to the MEP in a set of tables listing the fifty-six process and output indicators that the NMCP has developed or intends to develop (NMCP 2010: 44, table shown in part as Table 7.1).

In addition to these 56 process and output indicators, the MEP lists an additional 47 'key impact, outcome and confounding indicators', bringing the total to 103 indicators (NMCP 2010: 44). Producing each of these 103 indicators requires large amounts of diverse data. Moreover, it requires data that meet particular criteria. Since indicators require comparable units for measuring and ranking, these data must meet minimal standards in terms of specificity, reliability and degree of standardization.

However, the problem is that data which meet such criteria are not easy to come by in LICs such as Tanzania, where efforts to address this problem by improving the HIS are progressing slowly. As was mentioned earlier, a sizeable proportion of available health data display serious weaknesses and lacunae, for instance in terms of reliability, gaps in recording, irregular periodicity, categories reported on (Braa *et al.* 2012; de Savigny and Binka 2004). Acutely aware of these problems, M&E experts therefore make use of multiple sources of data, combining, for instance, data obtained through health facilities (HIS or health facility records), demographic surveillance sites and stand-alone surveys (e.g. Demographic and Health Surveys, Malaria Indicator Surveys). Sidestepping the challenges raised by the need to combine and make effective use of these disparate data sources (the MEP recognizes this issue and contains a capacity building plan addressing it: NMCP 2010), the deployment of diverse data sources so as to produce indicators for M&E purposes underscores the point raised in the preceding paragraph: the rising importance of M&E, and the concomitant production of indicators, is generating a colossal demand for data. A sizeable proportion of these data are supposed to be generated by institutions such as public-sector health facilities which, especially in rural areas, often are poorly resourced, overburdened and understaffed (Chandler *et al.* 2009; Dieleman *et al.* 2009; Leshabari *et al.* 2008). Improving health data and HIS requires substantial investments, for instance, to buy and maintain equipment such as computers which in turn need reasonably

TABLE 7.1 Output and process indicators of the M&E framework of the National Malaria Control Programme, Tanzania

Information Education and Communication (IES) & Behavior Change Communication (BCC)

		Data source
PROCESS	1. Number of IEC/BCC materials produced	Monthly monitoring report/participating partners
	2. Number of people trained in IEC/BCC	Monthly monitoring report/participating partners
OUTPUT	3. Number of districts receiving IEC/BCC materials	Commodities Tracking

Diagnosis and case management

PROCESS	4. Number of health facilities that reported no RDT stockout for more than one week	Health Facility Survey/Sentinel Surveillance/ IMPACT 2
	5. Number of health facilities that reported no ACT stockout for more than one week	Health Facility Survey/Sentinel Surveillance/ IMPACT 2
	6. Number RDTs distributed to health facility	Commodities Tracking/IMPACT 2
	7. Number of malaria cases treated	Health Facility Sentinel Surveillance/HMIS/IMPACT 2
	8. Number of pregnant women who received their second dose of IPTp	Health Facility Sentinel Surveillance/HMIS
OUTPUT	9. Number of health facilities equipped with diagnostic facilities	Health Facility Sentinel Surveillance/HMIS
	10. Number of children with fever	Health Facility Sentinel Surveillance/HMIS
	11. Number of malaria microscopy slides taken	Health Facility Sentinel Surveillance/HMIS
	12. Number of malaria RDTs taken	Health Facility Sentinel Surveillance/HMIS/IMPACT 2
	13. Number of anti-malarial drugs distributed in health facilities for malaria treatment	Commodities Tracking/IMPACT 2

stable electricity supplies in order to operate reliably, not an easy task in many remote rural areas. Moreover, given the multitude of challenges that health facilities face, improving HIS is not necessarily accorded high priority (AbouZahr and Boerma 2005; Maokola *et al.* 2011).

This brief overview of structural issues surrounding (malaria) data collection in the Tanzanian health system raises a range of questions, two of which will be explored in the remaining sections of this chapter: How does the growing data demand for indicators and M&E mesh with daily practices in rural Tanzanian health facilities? How might weaknesses involving data generation in the health sector influence data generation for indicator-based M&E procedures? To answer these questions, the following two sections draw on ethnographic fieldwork conducted in Rufiji District since 2004 to trace how on-the-ground challenges that health facility staff confront during their daily work activities influence the diagnosis and treatment of malaria, and by extension, the data that are produced for generating malaria indicators and M&E-based assessments.

CONTEXTUAL HURDLES AND DATA PRODUCTION AT RUFIJI HEALTH FACILITIES

Although indicator-based M&E activities across Tanzania have multiplied since 2002, the implementation of plans outlined in NMMTSP-1 was slow, difficult and uneven as structural issues in health facilities and health information systems, among other things, often hindered, corrupted or derailed these efforts (NMCP 2010). Many of these structural issues have affected the health system for a long period and can, for instance, be traced to IMF-mandated structural adjustment programs in the 1980s, neoliberal reforms that took off during the 1990s, and a continuous stream of health sector interventions emanating from the international 'development apparatus' (Cooper and Packard 1997; Turshen 1999). Issues such as staff shortages, difficult working conditions, low and delayed salaries, heavy patient loads, recurrent medicine shortfalls and absent or faulty equipment have not gone away, especially in the public sector, and influence both the motivation of health workers and the quality of care that patients receive at health facilities (Chandler *et al.* 2009; Leshabari *et al.* 2008; Manongi *et al.* 2006; Songstad *et al.* 2011). To many health workers I spoke with during fieldwork, these problems appeared to be perennial and intractable, notwithstanding a continuous flow of interventions, usually spearheaded by foreign 'partners' such as NGOs or universities, that promise improvements which rarely can be sustained in the long run (Cooke and Kothari 2001; Mercer 2003; Mubyazi *et al.* 2007; Pfeiffer 2003). Such structural problems present all kinds of hurdles and can complicate, disrupt or upend even the simplest kinds of activities. Working under the shadow of these problems can at times be trying and present unique challenges for M&E activities including data generation for indicators. The following section explores one of these trenchant structural problems that has profoundly affected the functioning of government health facilities – the provision of drugs and medical supplies.

In Tanzania, the Medical Stores Department (MSD), a privatized, semi-autonomous branch of the Ministry of Health (MoH), is in charge of and responsible for provisioning the approximately 5,400 facilities in the government health system on the mainland with drugs and medical supplies. However, shortages and stock-outs have persisted in Tanzania since MSD was founded in 1993, notwithstanding repeated restructurings that aimed to improve procurement and distribution procedures. Over time, these recurrent shortages elicited far-reaching effects in health facilities, shaping not only patient treatment seeking behavior but also the motivation and behavior of health facility staff. A substantial literature reports that patients bypass health facilities and go straight to stores to buy their drugs (if they can afford to do so) when they (their relatives, friends, neighbors, etc.) notice, hear or suspect that medicines are in short supply or about to run out (Hetzel *et al.* 2008; Ishengoma *et al.* 2009; Kangwana *et al.* 2009). Health workers often found these drug shortages and outages very frustrating and demotivating in the long run, so I learned in the course of fieldwork. Bi Kulsum, for instance, a nurse in Jaribu, explained to me in 2006 during a study exploring the ramifications of drug stock-outs in the area:

> How can I treat people when medicines have run out? What kind of nurse am I, if all I can do is tell people to go to the store and buy this and that kind of drug? Making matters worse, few people let me know if they succeeded in buying the medicines I prescribed. This makes me feel very bad.

The sentiment described by Bi Kulsum was not atypical among health workers at government health facilities in Rufiji District, an impoverished rural area some 180 kilometers south of Dar-es-Salaam, the bustling commercial capital of Tanzania. Especially in more remote dispensaries serving relatively large populations, where certain drugs (e.g. gentamycin, an antibiotic) almost always ran out well before the new MSD shipment would be delivered, some staff regularly complained to me about the inadequacy of the government drug supply system. Others shrugged their shoulders in dismay, and some mumbled wryly '*watu wakubwa wanakula sana*' (literally, 'big people eat a lot'), an often heard trope in Tanzania (and other sub-Saharan countries) which in this case derides persons for being more interested in 'eating' (i.e. stealing) than in making sure their organization runs well (Bayart 1993; Smith 2007).

Commonly occurring situations such as the recurrent stock-outs of medicines commented on by Bi Kulsum matter for M&E efforts and indicator production if these events are not necessarily, or consistently, entered into health facility records, as happened in Rufiji District. Since health facility records constitute a vital data source, they could influence indicator production and monitoring and evaluation activities. Take, for instance, target 2 in NMMTSP-2 (80 per cent of malaria patients are diagnosed and treated with effective antimalarial medicines, artemisinin-based combination therapy (ACT), within 24 hours of the onset of fever) and the accompanying indicator for measuring progress toward this goal, called MAL-T8: the proportion of 'people with uncomplicated or severe malaria receiving antimalarial treatment according to the national guideline' (Global Fund 2009). According to NMMTSP-2, which follows the Global Fund Monitoring and Evaluation Toolkit, data for indicator MAL-T8 ought to be collected on a quarterly basis using 'health information systems or facility records' (Global Fund 2009: 226). Since the vast majority of government health facilities in Rufiji did not have electricity at the time of the research, there was no computer-based HIS and hand-written facility records provided the main source of health data in the district. Keeping the points raised here in mind, we now return to Bi Kulsum's reaction and focus on two issues raised during drug shortfalls: first, stock-outs and the 'vanishing' of malaria medicines and patients, which sheds light on the usefulness of health facility records for M&E activities and indicator production; and second, difficulties surrounding the diagnosis of malaria in rural health facilities, which filter into and shape the content of health facility records.

A peculiar feature of drug and medical supply shortfalls at government health facilities is that although they are predictable to a certain extent, the impact of these events on record-keeping can vary significantly from one location to another. When operating as planned, MSD trucks fan out across Tanzania from national and zonal warehouses on a three-month cycle to distribute medicine kits to each health facility across the country. Likewise in Rufiji, which at the time of my encounter with Bi Kulsum had largely transitioned from a centralized 'push' system, wherein each health facility received a kit containing a standard allotment of medicines, irrespective of the actual usage at that facility, to a decentralized 'indent' (or 'pull') system that gives 'in-charges' of health facilities a standardized budget from which they can decide on the quantity of medicines (and supplies) to order (Shretta 2005). Within budgetary limits, determined by the type of health facility (e.g. a hospital gets a larger budget than a dispensary) the indent system gives the in-charge more freedom when ordering supplies, for instance enabling her to balance remaining supplies and anticipated demand of a drug. Thus the indent system aims to promote planning, greater autonomy and more efficient utilization of limited resources. In practice, however, it does not always work as planned. Doctors and nurses regularly showed me kits that lacked an item or that contained less than had been ordered. At times, ordered items also failed to arrive in the subsequent delivery, three months later. As mentioned earlier, certain drugs such as gentamycin were never shipped in sufficient quantities even when specifically requested. Since MSD rarely communicated to health facilities that shipments differed from orders submitted, let alone how the shipment differed from the placed order, clarity came when the kit was opened. While discovering that MSD had not shipped an item could be disappointing or irritating, this did not automatically mean that it would not be available during the coming three-month period: Rufiji, unlike many other districts in Tanzania, had a so-called 'cascade system', established in the late 1990s as part of externally-funded project, the Tanzanian Essential Health Intervention Project (TEHIP), that enabled in-charges to bridge or shorten drug shortfalls by requesting or borrowing supplies from other facilities. However, the cascade system no longer works effectively, because after the TEHIP project closed down financial support for 'cascade officers' to travel between health facilities dwindled, making it more difficult to quickly transport medicines from one site to another. Hence, in Rufiji as in many other parts of rural Tanzania, drug shortages were, and remain (Mikkelsen-Lopez et al. 2014a; 2014b), a fact of life. Health facility staff dealt with this fact of life in various ways. For example, when faced with dwindling supplies some clinicians and nurses kept on prescribing a medicine as usual until it ran out. Others decided to ration the remaining drugs. Dr Shabani, for example, the in-charge of Hanga dispensary, told me that he initiated a form of triage and reserved medicines for pregnant women and children. Staff at other health facilities reportedly reserved medicines for relatives and friends. Yet whichever distribution strategy was chosen, over time supplies could only be stretched for so long, and eventually a medicine ran out, at which point patients had to look for it elsewhere. During such shortfalls, clinicians continued to diagnose and write prescriptions for patients that came to their facility. However, upon approaching such a health facility it was immediately apparent that it had run out of essential drugs, for the familiar long lines of patients had vanished.

An important ramification of drug shortfalls is a pronounced 'decoupling' between diagnosing, prescribing and treating ailments, raising the question if and how such events appear in health facility records. Returning to the drug stock-out example, Bi Kulsum may diagnose a sick child with malaria and prescribe antimalarials, but when she instructs the care giver to buy the drug elsewhere she does not know with certainty if the child has actually acquired medicines, let alone taken them as prescribed – so how does she enter this encounter in the health record? This example may seem exceptional, but in the course of fieldwork it became clear that such decoupling was neither rare nor limited to particular events or locations. Take, for instance, nurse Mwajuma, who ran the dispensary in Ubunju by herself for months on end, for lack of a clinical officer who was supposed to head the unit. Mwajuma was devoted to her community and worked very hard but on many weekdays the number of patients seeking attention was simply too large to handle. On such busy days, when several hundred patients visited the clinic, nurse Mwajuma expedited matters by diagnosing, treating and prescribing patients one after another, postponing record-keeping until all patients were gone, usually towards sunset. Frank, the clinical officer who paid (bi-)monthly supervisory visits to Mwajuma and other dispensaries in his cascade, acknowledged in an unusually frank conversation that the records generated at Ubunju dispensary at times 'did not have much detail', and hinted that these may not give an accurate reflection of the actual diagnostic and treatment events at that health facility. Then, as if to locate blame elsewhere, Frank said that 'Mwajuma was not supposed to treat or diagnose anyway, since she was not a clinical officer'. Obviously, Frank was correct in this regard, but if Mwajuma had stuck to official guidelines, then patients in the area could no longer be diagnosed or treated at the dispensary in Ubunju (at least until a clinical officer settled there), forcing them to travel to a village 12 kilometers away to access government health-care. Although both involve different situations and causes, the examples of Um Kulsum and Mwajuma point toward similar questions. Drawing from the cases of Um Kulsum and Mwajuma, which involved two context-specific forms of 'decoupling' of the relationship between diagnosing, prescribing and treating (attributed respectively to drug shortages and high patient loads): What other forms of context particular 'decoupling' between diagnosing, prescribing and treating ailments might occur at health facilities, and how might these occurrences influence health facility knowledge practices? How are such 'decoupled events' entered in health facility records? Are these events entered differently into records than 'regular' treatment encounters wherein diagnosis, prescription and treatment are recorded as procedure requires? Can decoupled events actually be identified in health facility data-sets, and isolated and disaggregated for subsequent analyses? If the answer to these questions is 'no', then the presumed relationship between diagnosis and treatment is not only unclear and variable in health facility records but also untraceable. Such untraceable variability might render health facility records a problematic source of data for M&E and production of indicators. Take, for example, indicator MAL-T8 which aims to measure the relationship between diagnosis and prompt treatment with appropriate medicines. In light of the above described decoupling between diagnosis, prescription and treatment during drug outages, how do traces of such events embedded within health facility records influence the production of data for indicator MAL-T8?

DIAGNOSING AND RECORDING *MALARIA* AT RURAL HEALTH FACILITIES

Since health facility records constitute a source of data for M&E efforts and the generation of indicators, it is worthwhile to deepen our examination of record-keeping practices. Again drawing on ethnographic fieldwork conducted in Rufiji, we take a closer look at the influence of diagnostic practices on data generation about the category 'malaria' – a basic building block in the production of various malaria-centered indicators such as MAL-T8 and for M&E assessments more generally.

As in any other Tanzanian District, in Rufiji the Council Health Management Team (CHMT) (the government entity in charge of health-related matters at the district level) is responsible for ensuring that health facility record-keeping is up to par with standards set by the MoH. To achieve this goal, the CHMT regularly organizes training for clinicians and nurses on record-keeping, and routinely monitors these activities on-site. Such training and supervision occurs both through routine supervisory visits to each of the sixty health facilities in the district and through unscheduled inspections, usually to follow up on problems discovered after reviewing of records at CHMT headquarters in Utete.

Yet notwithstanding ongoing efforts by CHMT to standardize recording practices at health facilities, in practice these seldom were uniform. In fact, recording practices differed not only from facility to facility, but also from person to person, and over time. These variations had multiple underlying reasons, but the consequences of persistent staff shortages featured prominently in Rufiji. The example of Mwajuma, the nurse who ran Ubunju dispensary by herself, was not unique. In other facilities with large numbers of patients, clinicians and nurses were often so overworked that record-keeping was sometimes done in a rush, or pushed toward the end of the day after the queues had dwindled. Dispensaries located at some distance from the main road faced particular issues. Typically, clinical officers who graduated from government sponsored colleges must serve at least two years in a rural health facility but many resented 'living in the woods' (*kuishi porini* in KiSwahili), making recruitment and retention of staff very challenging. In Rufiji, around 40 percent of positions for clinical officers were vacant during the study period, and most of these vacancies were at unappealing dispensaries located 'in the woods'. Hence a sizable number of these facilities were run by a nurse or a nurse assistant for prolonged periods rather than by a clinical officer as government regulations stipulated. Moreover, in some dispensaries, village health workers dispensed medicines and helped with simple diagnoses. However, nurses received limited formal training in diagnosing infectious diseases and record-keeping, and village health workers none to speak of. Given these contextual constraints, it should come as little surprise that inexperienced nurses sometimes faced difficulties in establishing clinically correct diagnoses.

To explore how such contextual constraints influence the diagnosis and recording of malaria in rural health facilities in Rufiji, the focus now turns to the different technologies through which the parasitic disease was identified. Caused by Plasmodium parasites that invade and destroy red blood cells, malaria is invisible to the naked eye while, as

174

mentioned earlier, its symptoms often resemble those of common ailments (e.g. heat stroke, measles, headache, joint ache, some bacterial and viral infections). Due to these characteristics, the 'gold standard' diagnosis involves assessment of symptoms plus a confirmation that malaria parasites are present in a patient's blood. For the purposes of the argument that follows, the gold standard diagnosis is considered to yield *malaria* which ontologically approximates the biomedical definition of malaria. The gold standard involves laboratory testing, which is available in few rural health facilities in Tanzania. Hence, in much of the country malaria diagnoses were made based on clinical symptoms, an inaccurate method because symptoms are unspecific and could very well result from other ailments. Clinical diagnosis can be seen as picking up a mixture of malaria plus an unspecified number of 'malaria-like illnesses', a category that will be called +malaria+ in this analysis. This mixture of malaria and malaria-like illnesses is not stable, but can vary from place to place, and over time. Thus, the category +malaria+ is variable in a context-particular manner. Clinicians, public health experts and malariologists have long been aware of the difficulties surrounding accurately diagnosing malaria, and their aim to develop diagnostic technologies that can better distinguish between malaria and malaria-like illnesses in resource-poor settings has inspired various innovative solutions. One of these innovations was a 'diagnostic algorithm' which facilitates health workers in differentiating between symptoms typical of malaria and those associated with other diseases. Essentially, the algorithm is a flowchart comprised of a specific sequence of questions about a patient's illness history and steps to differentiate symptoms, based on which a health worker can more easily distinguish between uncomplicated and severe malaria and, for instance, upper respiratory infections. If properly used, the algorithm can be more accurate than clinical diagnosis and reduce the number of 'false positive' diagnoses (caused by illnesses other than malaria) by up to 50 per cent (CREHS 2009). Thus, when deployed consistently and precisely, the algorithm can be considered as yielding ^malaria^. The category ^malaria^ is bigger than *malaria* (obtained with the more precise gold standard) but smaller than +malaria+ (which results from clinical diagnosis, the least accurate procedure). Rufiji was the first Tanzanian district where the algorithm was tested, as part of a broad-based strategy called Integrated Management of Childhood Illness (IMCI), which identified and addressed causes of child mortality at the community, health facility and health system level. Considered an improvement over clinical diagnosis when coupled to IMCI (Armstrong Schellenberg et al. 2004), the algorithm was rolled out across the district during the late-1990s as the preferred method for diagnosing malaria (except in several larger health facilities where laboratory testing was available). However, for various reasons its utilization across the district was uneven. Health facility staff cited inadequate training, staff shortages and absences, and heavy patient loads as key reasons why they were unable to use the algorithm consistently or effectively. Studies exploring the algorithm elsewhere reported similar findings, and noted that such contextual influences greatly diminish the effectiveness of the diagnostic tool (Chandramohan et al. 2002). Such suboptimal application of the algorithm can be seen as yielding the diagnosis °malaria° – a variable cluster of malaria-like illnesses that is larger than the category ^malaria^ (derived from optimal application of the diagnostic algorithm) yet smaller than +malaria+ (obtained through clinical diagnosis). Crucially, these 'four malarias' refer to different though partially overlapping illness clusters. When imagined as a Venn diagram, the category +malaria+ refers to the largest cluster of illnesses, one that includes those called °malaria°, which in turn envelops those named ^malaria^, which encompasses those called *malaria* – the category that ontologically approximates the biomedical definition of the disease most closely. It is important to underscore that this distinction between these four malarias is an analytical one, in order to highlight that in daily practices these diagnostic technologies produce ontologically different malarias (Mol 2002).

In the daily realities of Tanzanian health workers, however, these four categories do not exist as such for they enter the outcome of each diagnostic procedure into a single column in the health facility record: (uncomplicated) malaria. This conflation of ontologically different malarias into a single category in the health facility record in conjunction with the variable implementation of diagnostic methods across Rufiji District shapes health facility records in three fundamental ways. First, it results in over-reporting of the number of patients that supposedly have *malaria*. Second, it misconstrues as *malaria* what actually is a contextually variable mixture of +malaria+, °malaria°, ^malaria^ and *malaria*. Third, since variations in the implementation of diagnostic practices are not recorded, health facility record-derived data on *malaria* cannot be disaggregated into the constitutive elements of the admixture (comprised of +malaria+, °malaria°, ^malaria^, and *malaria*).

This ethnographic sketch of diagnostic practices resulting in onto-logically different malarias that are conflated into a single category through recording practices suggests that a key building block for indi-cator generation and M&E assessment – the category malaria itself – is highly fluid and context-bound in terms of its actual content, rather than the universally stable category that biomedical doctrine supposes it to be. This analytic finding probably would not differ substantially if this study had been conducted elsewhere in Tanzania, for the following reasons. Not only were many districts less well managed than Rufiji but the national roll-out of the diagnostic algorithm that commenced in 2004 ran into multiple obstacles (e.g. lack of funding for training, weak and irregular supervision), resulting in erratic and poor implementa-tion across the country, thus thwarting the objective to replace clin-ical diagnosis with the supposedly more effective algorithm (CREHS 2009). In these areas, where many health workers became insufficiently accustomed to using the algorithm, many likely reverted (at times) to clinical diagnosis, the least accurate method. Further complicating this picture, Tanzania has been transitioning to a different diagnostic test for malaria, so-called rapid diagnostic tests (RDTs). An antibody test that detects malarial antigens, markers of a current or past infection, these RDTs are somewhat less accurate than the gold standard (Ishengoma *et al.* 2011). Echoing what happened during the implementation of the diagnostic algorithm across Tanzania, the roll-out of RDTs has been fraught with challenges, resulting in highly variable availability and implementation of this technology across the country (Masanja *et al.* 2010; McMorrow *et al.* 2008). The variable implementation of RDTs added yet another layer to the already fluid landscape of malaria diagnostic technologies, rendering the range of ontologically different malarias that these technologies yield still more complex and fluid.

More examples could be furnished but for the sake of wrapping up this chapter I will briefly recapitulate the main findings presented in this section. Through an ethnographic examination in the Rufiji health system, it has shown how health system-related context-specific variations shape diagnostic and recording practices, and by exten-sion, data production about malaria. Investigation of knowledge prac-tices involving health facility records shows that data generated about malaria are ontologically variable, yielding multiple malarias that corre-spond to varying degrees with the biomedical definition of the disease. Furthermore, health facility record data about malaria actually refer to a contextually variable admixture of malaria-like illnesses whose composition cannot be disaggregated because the uneven implementation of diagnostic procedures at the root of this variability is not documented and therefore unavailable for scrutiny. This finding that malaria data produced in the health system are unreliable is not novel; 'untrustworthiness' of health data is a long-standing concern that has prompted numerous calls to strengthen health (information) systems (e.g. AbouZahr and Boerma 2005; Chilundo et al. 2004; Gimbel et al. 2011; Maokola et al. 2011). Since achieving this goal requires substantial resources and time, experts – who need data now – regularly sidestep health system data and resort to data obtained through stand-alone surveys (such as Demographic and Health Surveys, DHS). While many experts I spoke to affirmed that stand-alone survey data were generally considered more reliable, an important downside is that they are collected infrequently (every three to five years), whereas health system data, although more problematic, are more or less continuously generated. Hence, in practice experts resort to different kinds of data for different purposes. This 'juggling' by experts of different data sources raises obvious questions that this study does not answer: When do (malaria) experts use which data-sets to pursue what ends? For which purposes do experts choose to use stand-alone and/or health system data? How do experts mobilize different data sources in the generation of various indicators and in monitoring and evaluation efforts more generally? Finally, recalling the preceding discussion of ontologically diverse malarias, since health facility records constitute a source of raw data for M&E and indicator generation: How does using health system data consisting of a disaggregable admixture of malaria and malaria-like illnesses shape the production of malaria-centered indicators such as MAL-T8, and M&E assessments more generally?

CONCLUDING COMMENTS

This chapter took the simplicity of the ALMA Scorecard as an entry point for examining several issues evoked by the ongoing rapid expansion of indicator-based M&E assessments in malaria research and control efforts world-wide. The growing centrality of M&E in contemporary global governance is eliciting, and hinging on, a phenomenal expansion of data production in low-income countries such as Tanzania so as to produce steadily expanding panels of indicators, used for measuring and comparing inputs, outputs and impacts of interventions. However, as this study showed, obtaining sufficient and sufficiently reliable data can present daunting challenges in these settings, and data collection and recording activities are profoundly shaped by highly variable, context-specific structural hurdles that shape daily routines in the health system. Examination of contextually variable malaria-centered diagnostic practices at rural health facilities revealed that entering diagnoses into health facility records is the key step in transforming diagnostic uncertainty and ontological fluidity into a seemingly stable category. This category is referred to as 'malaria' but actually consists of an admixture of biomedically defined malaria (i.e. parasites of the genus Plasmodium) plus 'a lot of other stuff', a contextually variable part that cannot be identified retroactively from aggregated health facility records. Importantly, in this study such variations in diagnostic and record-keeping processes were rarely if ever the result of deliberate fabrication or falsification of data; rather they typically occurred *despite* health workers' attempts to uphold procedures and protocols, efforts that regularly foundered and eventually failed when converging challenges related to the context in which they worked prompted them to modify routine activities. Pushing these findings further, one could therefore argue that these health workers are inadvertently engaged in producing new forms of knowledge. This knowledge is different from biomedical conceptions, even if on the surface it appears to be dealing with 'malaria' and thus carries a biomedical gloss.

Since health facility records contained little meaningful information as to how context-specific variations might have influenced the implementation of a diagnostic procedure, it is very difficult if not impossible to ascertain from these records how diagnostic uncertainty and ontological fluidity shaped the content of the category 'malaria'. The Rufiji case examined in this chapter suggests that this category encompasses 'malaria plus a lot of other stuff'. Leaving aside the question what this 'other stuff' might be (except for being context particular and as such variable and fluid), the ambiguous content of 'malaria' data in health facility records raises questions about indicators produced from these data, particularly with regard to the phenomena that they are said to represent. To what extent are indicators produced from such data about 'malaria' or about 'other stuff'? How does this 'other stuff' influence the production and the content of 'malaria' indicators? How do actors understand, use and mobilize these indicators, both at national

179

and international levels? At these levels, does it matter if some malaria indicators are to a large extent about 'other stuff', and if so, how does this matter?

At this point I am unable to answer these questions, however they do point us back to the 2011 ALMA indicator chart that inspired this chapter, specifically the right-most column titled 'Reduced malaria deaths by 50 per cent by 2010 (versus 2000)'. A quick glance at this column shows that most blocks are 'empty'/⬚, as opposed to the other indicators which mainly consist of 'filled' blocks (those marked with ▨, ▦ or ▧, corresponding respectively with green, yellow and red in the original traffic-light). According to an expert involved with ALMA, the preponderance of 'empty' blocks for the indicator 'Reduced malaria deaths by 50 per cent by 2010 (versus 2000)' reflects the paucity of internationally validated data on malaria mortality for these countries, the production of which, as discussed in this chapter, is fraught with complex challenges. Strikingly, in the most recent ALMA chart (first quarter 2014: to view this chart, follow link in footnote 1), the number of countries that reported malaria mortality data barely increased (from seventeen to eighteen) while the color ratio of blocks stayed more or less the same (around half was green/▨, half yellow/▦, none were red/▧). This marginal progress in terms of both reporting on and reducing malaria deaths contrasts markedly with the other columns in the 2014 ALMA chart which, barring some exceptions, have become increasingly green/▨ between 2011 and 2014, thus signaling progress for those indicators. What does this relative lack of progress with regard to malaria deaths mean?

A skeptic might suggest this means that showing progress in terms of diminishing malaria deaths is not as important as demonstrating improvements for other indicators in the ALMA chart. However, such a reading would be facile, for a recent flurry of publications suggests that demonstrating measurable reduction in infectious disease mortality is anything but a trivial matter. For example, the Global Fund (itself a key driver of the performance-based turn) has been faced with growing pressure since the 2008 financial crisis to show results from its multi-billion dollar investments in fighting AIDS, tuberculosis and malaria (Akachi and Atun 2011; Komatsu et al. 2010). In one of several publications about lives saved by Global Fund-sponsored interventions, the authors estimate that around 130,000 deaths from malaria were averted between 2003 and 2007 (Komatsu et al. 2010). Continuing in this vein, another publication co-authored by representatives from different organizations estimates that the scale-up of malaria interventions between 2000 and 2010 had prevented around 842,000 deaths in forty-three African countries (e.g. Eisele *et al.* 2012). These are impressive achievements, but the point I want to focus on here concerns the data used to generate these publications: the figures presented are estimations which are largely based on sophisticated modelling of mortality trends and primarily derive from survey data (such as the DHS). In contrast, health system-derived mortality statistics were of minor relevance in the calculations. This reliance on stand-alone data sources such as DHS in the saving lives publications, combined with the persistence of 'empty' blocks for the ALMA indicator 'Reduced malaria deaths by 50 per cent by 2010' raises the question if what takes place at health facilities and at the local level actually get reflected in these estimations and indicators.

Several experts I talked with spoke of a discernible trend at the global level, wherein issues that can be measured reliably tend to get more traction than those for which reliable data are harder to come by. Obviously, such 'trust in numbers' has a deep history (Porter 1995), but the growing number of publications that concentrate on performance measurement appears to be informing if not fueling the trend that malaria experts referred to (Chan *et al.* 2010; Zhao *et al.* 2011). Should this trend continue or intensify (there is no way of knowing at this point so I am speculating here) then it is conceivable that 'readily countable' phenomena which can be quantified quite easily and reliably could gain more attention than phenomena that are difficult to quantify accurately. Pushing this point a bit further, one could further imagine that in an indicator-driven world increasingly preoccupied with quantifying 'readily countable' phenomena, goals such as the number of insecticide-treated nets distributed or ACT doses financed (columns number 2 and 8 in the ALMA chart) could be viewed as more amenable to action than goals centering on issues for which obtaining accurate figures is more problematic. Such a shift, whether it unfolds intentionally or unintentionally, can over time elicit problematic effects and, for example, usher attention away from the problem underlying poor quality malaria mortality data – the need to improve weak health (information) systems – or making it less likely that issues which happen and matter at the health facility level will filter through to the global level.

Finally, extending this musing to the column titled 'Reduced malaria deaths by 50 per cent by 2010 (versus 2000)' in the ALMA chart, how might a growing preference for 'readily countable' phenomena at the global level influence perceptions of this overarching goal in indicator-driven interventions? Various malaria experts assured me that notwithstanding this shift, diminishing deaths will always be the top priority in contemporary interventions. If and how their expectations materialize deserves further investigation, also because examining the growing attention in contemporary malaria interventions to 'readily countable' categories such as 'number of antimalarials financed' will enhance our understanding of the ways in which indicator-driven knowledge practices are shaping the current system of global health governance.

References

Abdulla, S. *et al.* 2001. 'Impact on Malaria Morbidity of a Programme Supplying Insecticide Treated Nets in Children Aged under 2 Years in Tanzania: Community Cross Sectional Study', *British Medical Journal* 322(7281): 270–3

AbouZahr, C. and T. Boerma 2005. 'Health Information Systems: The Foundations of Public Health', *Bulletin of the World Health Organization* 83(8): 578–83

AbouZahr, C., L. Gollogly and G. Stevens 2009. 'Better Data Needed: Everyone Agrees, But No one Wants to Pay', *Lancet* 375(9715): 619–21

Akachi, Y. and R. Atun 2011. 'Effect of Investment in Malaria Control on Child Mortality in Sub-Saharan Africa in 2002–2008', *PLoS One* 6(6): e21309

ALMA 2011. *African Leaders Make New Commitment to Accountability and Action Against Malaria.* New York: African Leaders Malaria Alliance, 19 September, available at www.alma2015.org/sites/default/files/events/almascorecard_pressreleasefinal.pdf

Armstrong Schellenberg, J. *et al.* 2004. 'The Effect of Integrated Management of Childhood Illness on Observed Quality of Care of Under-Fives in Rural Tanzania', *Health Policy and Planning* 19(1): 1–10

Bayart, Jean-François 1993. *The State in Africa: The Politics of the Belly.* London: Longman

Beck, Ann 1970. *A History of the British Medical Administration of East Africa, 1900–1950.* Cambridge, Mass.: Harvard University Press

Bhattacharjee, J. *et al.* 2012. 'Estimation of Malaria Mortality of a District in India During 2010 by Using Three Models', *Journal of Communicable Diseases* 44(1): 1–7

Boerma, J. Ties and Sally K. Stansfield 2007. 'Health Statistics Now: Are We Making the Right Investments?', *Lancet* 369(9563): 779–86

Braa, Jørn, Arthur Heywood and Sundeep Sahay 2012. 'Improving Quality and Use of Data Through Data-Use Workshops: Zanzibar, United Republic of Tanzania', *Bulletin of the World Health Organization* 90(5): 379–84

Brieger, William R. 2010. 'Before We Count Malaria Out We Must First Learn to Count', *Africa Health* 32(4): 15–19

Brundtland, Gro Harlem 1998. 'Reaching Out for World Health', *Science* 280(5372): 2027

Chan, Margaret *et al.* 2010. 'Meeting the Demand for Results and Accountability: A Call for Action on Health Data from Eight Global Health Agencies', *PLoS Med* 7(1): e1000223

Chandler, Clare I.R. *et al.* 2009. 'Motivation, Money and Respect: A Mixed-Method Study of Tanzanian Non-Physician Clinicians', *Social Science and Medicine* 68(11): 2078–88

Chandramohan, Daniel, Shabbar Jaffar and Brian Greenwood 2002. 'Use of Clinical Algorithms for Diagnosing Malaria', *Tropical Medicine and International Health* 7(1): 45–52

Chilundo, Baltazar, Johanne Sundby and Margunn Aanestad 2004. 'Analysing the Quality of Routine Malaria Data in Mozambique', *Malaria Journal* 3(1): 3

Clyde, David F. 1967. *Malaria in Tanzania*. London: Oxford University Press

COIA 2014. *Accountability for Women's and Children's Health: Report on Progress to May 2014*. Geneva:World Health Organization

Cooke, Bill and Uma Kothari (eds.) 2001. *Participation, the New Tyranny?* New York: Zed Books

Cooper, Frederick and Randall M. Packard (eds.) 1997. *International Development and the Social Sciences: Essays on the History and Politics of Knowledge*. Berkeley, Calif.: University of California Press

Coulson, Andrew 1982. *Tanzania: A Political Economy*. New York: Oxford University Press

CREHS 2009. *IMCI Implementation in Tanzania: Experiences, Challenges and Lessons*. London: London School of Hygiene and Tropical Medicine, Consortium for Research on Equitable Health Systems

Davis, Kevin E., Benedict Kingsbury and Sally Engle Merry. 2010. *Indicators as a Technology of Global Governance*, Institute of International Law and Justice (IILJ) Working Paper 2010/2. New York: New York University School of Law

De Savigny, Don and Fred Binka 2004. 'Monitoring Future Impact on Malaria Burden in Sub-Saharan Africa', *Am. J Trop. Med. Hyg.* August (71): 224–31

De Savigny, Don, Kasale H., Mbuya C. and Reid, G. 2004. *Fixing Health Systems*. Ottawa: International Development Research Centre

Deressa, Wakgari, Mesganaw Fantahun and Ahmed Ali 2007. 'Malaria-related Mortality Based on Verbal Autopsy in an Area of Low Endemicity in a Predominantly Rural Population in Ethiopia', *Malaria Journal* 6: 128

Dieleman, Marjolein, Barend Gerretsen and Gert Jan van derWilt 2009. 'Human Resource Management Interventions to Improve Health

Workers' Performance in Low and Middle Income Countries: A Realist Review', *BioMed Central* 7: 7

Dodd, Rebecca and A. Cassels 2006. 'Health, Development and the Millennium Development Goals', *Annals of Tropical Medicine and Parasitology* 100(5–6): 379–87

Eisele, Thomas P. *et al.* 2012. 'Malaria Prevention in Pregnancy, Birthweight, and Neonatal Mortality: A Meta-analysis of 32 National Cross-sectional Datasets in Africa', *Lancet Infectious Diseases* 12(12): 942–9

Gerrets, Rene 2010. *Globalizing International Health: The Cultural Politics of 'Partnership' in Tanzanian Malaria Control.* New York: Anthropology, New York University

Gimbel, Sarah *et al.* 2011. 'An Assessment of Routine Primary Care Health Information System Data Quality in Sofala Province, Mozambique', *Population Health Metrics* 9: 12

Global Fund 2009. *Monitoring and Evaluation Toolkit.* Global Fund to Fight AIDS, Tuberculosis and Malaria

Guyatt, Helen L. and Robert W. Snow 2001. 'Malaria in Pregnancy as an Indirect Cause of Infant Mortality in Sub-Saharan Africa', *Transactions of the Royal Society of Tropical Medicine and Hygiene* 95(6): 569–76

Hay, Simon I., Peter W. Gething and Robert W. Snow 2010. 'India's Invisible Malaria Burden', *Lancet* 376(9754): 1716–17

Hetzel, Manuel W. *et al.* 2008. 'Obstacles to Prompt and Effective Malaria Treatment Lead to Low Community-Coverage in Two Rural Districts of Tanzania', *BMC Public Health* 8: 317

Holland, Dorothy C. and Naomi Quinn 1987. *Cultural Models in Language and Thought.* New York: Cambridge University Press

Iliffe, John 1979. *A Modern History of Tanganyika.* New York: Cambridge University Press

Ishengoma, Deus S. *et al.* 2009. 'Health Laboratories in the Tanga Region of Tanzania: The Quality of Diagnostic Services for Malaria and Other Communicable Diseases', *Annals of Tropical Medicine and Parasitology* 103(5): 441–53

2011. 'Accuracy of Malaria Rapid Diagnostic Tests in Community Studies and Their Impact on Treatment of Malaria in an Area with Declining Malaria Burden in North-eastern Tanzania', *Malaria Journal* 10(1): 176

Källander, Karin, Jesca Nsungwa-Sabiiti and Stefan Peterson 2004. 'Symptom Overlap for Malaria and Pneumonia: Policy Implications for Home Management Strategies', *Acta Tropica* 90(2): 211–14

Kangwana, Beth B. *et al.* 2009. 'Malaria Drug Shortages in Kenya: A Major Failure to Provide Access to Effective Treatment', *American Journal of Tropical Medicine and Hygiene* 80(5): 737–8

Kiszewski, Anthony *et al.* 2007. 'Estimated Global Resources Needed to Attain International Malaria Control Goals', *Bulletin of the World Health Organization* 85(8): 623–30

Komatsu, Ryuichi *et al.* 2010. 'Lives Saved by Global Fund-Supported HIV/AIDS, Tuberculosis and Malaria Programs: Estimation Approach and Results Between 2003 and End-2007', *BMC Infectious Diseases* 10: 109

Leshabari, Melkidezek T. *et al.* 2008. 'Motivation of Health Care Workers in Tanzania: A Case Study of Muhimbili National Hospital', *East African Journal of Public Health* 5(1): 32–7

Manongi, Rachel N., T. C. Marchant and I. C. Bygbjerg 2006. 'Improving Motivation Among Primary Health Care Workers in Tanzania: A Health Worker Perspective', *Human Resources in Health* 4: 6

Masanja, M. Irene *et al.* 2010. 'Health Workers' Use of Malaria Rapid Diagnostic Tests (RDTs) to Guide Clinical Decision Making in Rural Dispensaries, Tanzania', *American Journal of Tropical Medicine and Hygiene* 83(6): 1238–41

McMorrow, Meredith L. *et al.* 2008. 'Challenges in Routine Implementation and Quality Control of Rapid Diagnostic Tests for Malaria: Rufiji District, Tanzania', *American Journal of Tropical Medicine and Hygiene* 79(3): 385–90

Mercer, Claire 2003. 'Performing Partnership: Civil Society and the Illusions of Good Governance in Tanzania', *Political Geography* 22(7): 741–63

Merry, Sally Engle 2011. 'Measuring the World: Indicators, Human Rights, and Global Governance', *Current Anthropology* 52(S3): S83–S95

Mikkelsen-Lopez, Inez *et al.* 2014a. 'Essential Medicines in Tanzania: Does the New Delivery System Improve Supply and Accountability?', *Health Systems* 3: 74–81

2014b. 'Beyond Antimalarial Stock-Outs: Implications of Health Provider Compliance on Out-of-Pocket Expenditure During Care-seeking for Fever in South East Tanzania', *BMC Health Services Research* 13: 444

Moakola, W., Willey, B.A. *et al.* 2011. 'Enhancing the Routine Health Information System in Rural Southern Tanzania: Successes, Challenges and Lessons Learned', *Tropical Medicine and International Health* 16(6): 721–30

Mol, Annemarie 2002. *The Body Multiple: Ontology in Medical Practice.* Durham, N.C.: Duke University Press

Molineaux, L. 1997. 'Malaria and Mortality: Some Epidemiological Considerations', *Annals of Tropical Medicine and Parasitology* 91(7): 811–25

Molyneux, David H. 2008. 'Combating the "Other Diseases" of MDG 6: Changing the Paradigm to Achieve Equity and Poverty Reduction?',

Transactions of the Royal Society of Tropical Medicine and Hygiene 102(6): 509–19

Mpimbaza, Arthur *et al.* 2011. 'Validity of Verbal Autopsy Procedures for Determining Malaria Deaths in Different Epidemiological Settings in Uganda', *PLoS One* 6(10): e26892

Mubyazi, Godfrey M. *et al.* 2007. 'Community Views on Health Sector Reform and Their Participation in Health Priority Setting: Case of Lushoto and Muheza Districts, Tanzania', *Journal of Public Health* 29(2): 147–56

Murray, Christopher J.L. *et al.* 2012. 'Global Malaria Mortality Between 1980 and 2010: A Systematic Analysis', *Lancet* 379(9814): 413–31

Needham, Rodney (ed.) 1973. *Right and Left: Essays on Dual Symbolic Classification.* Chicago, Ill.: University of Chicago Press

Neilson, Stephanie and Terry Smutylo 2004. *The TEHIP "Spark": Planning and Managing Health Resources at the District Level.* Toronto: IDRC

NMCP 2003. *National Malaria Medium Term Strategic Plan 2002–2007.* Ministry of Health and Social Welfare, Tanzania

2010. *National Malaria Control Program Monitoring and Evaluation Plan 2008–2013.* Ministry of Health and Social Welfare, Tanzania

Ollwig, H. 1903. 'Die Bekämpfung der Malaria', *Zeitschrift für Hygiene und Infektionskrankheiten* 43: 133–55

Perkins, B.A. *et al.* 1997. 'Evaluation of an Algorithm for Integrated Management of Childhood Illness in an Area of Kenya with High Malaria Transmission', *Bulletin of the World Health Organization* 75(Suppl 1): 33–42

Pfeiffer, James 2003. 'International NGOs and Primary Health Care in Mozambique: The Need for a New Model of Collaboration', *Social Science and Medicine* 56(4): 725–38

Pigott, David M. *et al.* 2012. 'Funding for Malaria Control 2006–2010: A Comprehensive Global Assessment', *Malaria Journal* 11: 246

Porter, Theodore 1995. *Trust in Numbers: The Pursuit of Objectivity in Science and Public Life.* Princeton, N.J.: Princeton University Press

Ravishankar, Nirmala *et al.* 2009. 'Financing of Global Health: Tracking Development Assistance for Health from 1990 to 2007', *Lancet* 373(9681): 2113–24

Roll Back Malaria 2000. *The African Summit on Roll Back Malaria. Abuja, Nigeria, 25th April 2000,* available at www.rollbackmalaria.org/docs/abuja_brf2702.htm

2010. *Malaria Funding and Resource Utilization: The First Decade of Roll Back Malaria,* Progress and Impact Series. Geneva: WHO

Rottenburg, Richard 2009. *Far-fetched Facts: A Parable of Development Aid.* Cambridge, Mass.: MIT Press

Sachs, James D. 2005. 'Achieving the Millennium Development Goals: the Case of Malaria', *New England Journal of Medicine* 352(2): 115–17

Setel, Philip W. *et al.* 2007. 'A Scandal of Invisibility: Making Everyone Count by Counting Everyone', *Lancet* 370(9598): 1569–77

Shiffman, Jeremy 2006. 'Donor Funding Priorities for Communicable Disease Control in the Developing World', *Health Policy and Planning* 21(6): 411–20

Shore, Cris 2008. 'Audit Culture and Illiberal Governance', *Anthropological Theory* 8(3): 278–98

Shretta, Rima 2005. *Participation in a Rapid Assessment in Tanzania for the President's Malaria Initiative, August 8–12, 2005: Trip Report*, submitted to the US Agency for International Development by the Rational Pharmaceutical Management Plus Program. Arlington, Va.: Management Sciences for Health

Smith, Daniel J. 2007. *A Culture of Corruption: Everyday Deception and Popular Discontent in Nigeria*. Princeton, N.J.: Princeton University Press

Snow, R. W. *et al.* 1999. 'Estimating Mortality, Morbidity and Disability Due to Malaria Among Africa's Non-Pregnant Population', *Bulletin of the World Health Organization* 77(8): 624–40

Songstad, Nils G. *et al.* 2011. 'Perceived Unfairness in Working Conditions: The Case of Public Health Services in Tanzania', *BMC Health Services Research* 11: 34

Strathern, Marilyn 2000. *Audit Cultures: Anthropological Studies in Accountability, Ethics, and the Academy*. London: Routledge

Turshen, Meredeth 1999. *Privatizing Health Services in Africa*. New Brunswick, N.J.: Rutgers University Press

World Bank 1993. *World Development Report 1993: Investing in Health*. Washington, D.C.: World Bank

Zhao, Jinkou *et al.* 2011. 'Indicators Measuring the Performance of Malaria Programs Supported by the Global Fund in Asia, Progress and the Way Forward', *PLoS One* 6(12): e28932

CHAPTER EIGHT

'NOBODY IS GOING TO DIE': AN ETHNOGRAPHY OF HOPE, INDICATORS AND IMPROVIZATIONS IN HIV TREATMENT PROGRAMMES IN UGANDA

Sung-Joon Park

'One world, one hope' Theme of the 11th International AIDS Conference in Vancouver in 1996

INTRODUCTION

Uncertainty in HIV treatment

'AIDS is not over', warn Michel Sidibé, Peter Piot and Mark Dybul, representatives of the principal organizations of global health,[1] in a commentary published in the *Lancet* (Sidibé, Piot and Dybul 2012). A lot is contained in their short claim. The authors explain that 8 million people world-wide were receiving antiretroviral medicines by 2011. AIDS-related deaths have been decreasing as a result of the large-scale provision of antiretroviral therapy. Most of these global health achievements were made in sub-Saharan African countries, which bear the brunt of the global burden of disease. Despite this 'good news', one of the reasons why these authors refrain from an optimistic view of the future of the AIDS epidemic is that today, still too many HIV positive people lack access to these medicines.

The research for this chapter has been funded by the Max-Planck-Institute for Social Anthropology in Halle/Germany and the German Research Foundations' Priority Program 1448 'Creativity and Adaptation in Africa'. I am very grateful for the critical and inspiring comments on this chapter made by Sally Engle Merry, Amy Field Craven, Richard Rottenburg and Rene Umlauf.

[1] These authors are the executive directors of the most important organizations in the fight against HIV. Michel Sidibé is the executive director of UNAIDS (the Joint United Nations Programme on HIV and AIDS). Peter Piot is a former executive director of UNAIDS and currently the director of the London School of Hygiene and Tropical Medicine. Mark Dybul is since 2012 the executive director of the the Global Fund to Fight AIDS, Tuberculosis and Malaria.

Currently, the most important global framework to articulate such claims to access to antiretroviral therapy is the Millennium Development Goals (MDGs) project, which defines a set of targets and indicators to measure progress toward the most important development goals of the twenty-first century. Under this project, 'universal access to treatment' is defined as one of the targets to 'combat HIV/AIDS, Malaria and other diseases'.[2] The official list of indicators promoted by UN organizations posits that universal access to treatment is reached when at least 80 percent of the 'population with advanced HIV infection [have] access to antiretroviral drugs'.[3] The attribute 'universal' refers not to all people with HIV, but only to those who, according to official treatment guidelines, are in an advanced stage of HIV infection and thus need treatment. Even with this definition, 8 million is only half of the target to reach 15 million people with access to antiretroviral therapies by 2015 (see also United Nations 2014: 36). Yet, the global prevalence of HIV is actually much higher, currently estimated to be 34 million, as the authors remind us in their review of these indicators (Sidibé, Piot and Dybul 2012: 2058). However, current funding levels of donor aid are not sufficient to cover the 15 million. Health economic models projecting the long-term costs of antiretroviral therapy demand an annual US$22 billion to run treatment programs world-wide, of which US$12 billion alone would be earmarked for the purchasing of antiretrovirals (e.g. Schwartländer et al. 2011; UNAIDS 2012). But for the last couple of years funding has been stagnating at an annual US$8.2 billion, raising serious concerns about the future of access to antiretroviral therapy (Sidibé, Piot and Dybul 2012: 2058).

I begin with this review of these influential global health policy-makers as it raises several questions which I examine in this chapter. In what follows, I will discuss how the calculation of patient numbers, antiretroviral drugs, and the production of numeric representations to measure access to treatment are enacted by treatment programmes in Uganda. In addition, I explore how indicators are used to make an inherently uncertain future more predictable, which is of fundamental importance for the provision of access to antiretroviral

---

[2] This goal comprises three targets. The first is to 'have halted by 2015 and begun to reverse the spread of HIV/AIDS (Target 6a)'. The second goal is the above-mentioned target, to 'achieve, by 2010, universal access to treatment for HIV/AIDS for all those who need it (target 6b)'; and the third goal is 'Have halted by 2015 and begun to reverse the incidence of malaria and other major diseases (target 6c)'.

[3] See 'Official list of MDG Indicators', available at http://millenniumindicators.un.org.

therapy as a global health routine in countries like Uganda. Antiretroviral therapy is not a cure. It turns HIV from a deadly disease into a chronic condition, requiring a life-long supply of relatively expensive antiretroviral medicines. Antiretroviral therapy therefore constitutes a life-long financial commitment for international donor agencies, which currently provide the largest portion of funding for antiretrovirals in sub-Saharan African countries. This new type of long-term commitment to maintain HIV as a chronic condition is a distinctive problem of global health, as it raises the question how access to treatment can be sustained in the future, and by whom.

One of the allures of indicators is to reduce uncertainty not only by producing better facts, but by making gaps visible and thereby stimulate individuals, organizations and countries to perform better, as Sally Engle Merry argues (Merry 2011: S89). Asserting that 'AIDS is not over' in the above-mentioned review is indeed a reminder and an alert 'to do more – and do better – to achieve the AIDS-free generation the world is waiting for', and to counter resignation and pessimism arising out of the uncertainty about the future of antiretroviral therapy (Sidibé, Piot and Dybul 2012: 2059). In contrast to these teleological accounts of the future of the AIDS epidemic inscribed into technologies to measure progress, I wish to broaden the view on indicators and global health infrastructures by considering the concept of hope. My main concern in this chapter is to illustrate how the use of numbers constitutes an embodied and situated practice in dealing with the uncertainties in the supply of antiretrovirals – a practice which, as I will show, produces hope as part of an agentive rather than as a passive strategy for the improvisation of therapy.

AN ETHNOGRAPHY OF HOPE AND INDICATORS

My approach to the future of global health from the perspective of hope draws on my field research in Uganda between 2009 and 2012, during which I observed a dramatic shortage of antiretrovirals (Park 2013). In the months between 2009 and 2010, the most common antiretroviral regimen, AZT/3TC/NVP, and many other regimens were out of stock at various treatment programmes in the country. These so-called 'stock-outs' made fragmentations and instabilities in current global health infrastructures visible, which raised questions such as: How far does the planning of scaling up of access to antiretroviral go? Who, in future, will have access to treatment? How does the stock-out of antiretrovirals affect patients' hopes for a normal life with HIV? And more importantly, what kinds of local futures are produced by today's global health regimes?

The notion of hope I am interested in differs from the above-mentioned use of indicators to mobilize actors to do more and better in order to realize a vision of a generation free of AIDS. The hope inscribed in this vision underwrites the 'excessive optimism' typical for the broader field of development aid (van Ufford *et al.* 2003: 8). The optimism nourished by indicators is neither objective nor neutral. Quite the opposite, it rests on a modernist notion of progress necessitating the use of quantitative technologies to render the future as a series of temporally discrete steps, which can be measured and tracked (Richard Rottenburg and Sally Engle Merry, Chapter 1). Instead of challenging this optimism by questioning the hidden politics of indicators, which in my view carries the danger of prompting a pessimistic and even tragic account of a hopeless future, I wish to ask what kind of hope arises in the context of radical uncertainty. This understanding of hope is influenced by my ethnographic approach. Hope, as I maintain, is often captured inadequately as a kind of universal concept or emotion. Instead, my point of departure is to understand hope as a form of agency to live with the contingencies and the uncertainties surrounding the provision of free access to antiretroviral therapy.

I argue in this chapter that the use of indicators and other measures constitutes a distinct experience when actors improvise treatment in order to maintain the current conditions of care under constantly changing circumstances. I support this argument by describing the efforts of patients, health workers and doctors to maintain hope during the stock-out of antiretrovirals at a treatment programme, located at the centre of Kampala, which I will call Clinic U. Such efforts in the improvisation of therapy have been frequently noted as responses to the moral dilemmas emerging out of impoverished African public health systems (Feierman 2011). There is no need to romanticize these efforts, which are a 'defining feature of biomedicine in Africa', as Julie Livingston writes (Livingston 2012: 6). Improvisations to maintain the best possible level of care reflect what the pragmatist philosopher John Dewey describes as 'moral courage' in distinguishing hope from optimism (Dewey 1920). Moral courage contrasts with rationalist notions of knowledge, which underlie the optimistic belief in technological progress. As Dewey argues, it captures a more fundamental 'experimental and re-adjusting form of intelligence' (Dewey 1920: 97).

Intelligence, as Dewey uses this term in conjunction with the notion of moral courage, provides us a clue in terms of how to define improvisation as a distinct knowledge practice, 'in constant process of forming, and its retention requires constant alertness in observing consequences, an open-minded will to learn and courage in re-adjustment' (Dewey 1920: 97). Such practices go beyond a purely instrumental understanding of indicators, and capture how these specific technologies of quantification constitute embodied knowledges employed to make sense of bodily conditions.

Moral courage as a disposition of hope is close to Jarrett Zigon's description of hope as an ethics which asks affected individuals to 'keep going' in difficult situations and live through the world as it is found (Zigon 2009: 258). Antiretroviral therapy, in this regard, demonstrates more vividly that hope has its own ethics of care. In mass HIV treatment programmes, it is ethically impossible for doctors and patients to imagine giving up, regardless of how impossible therapy may appear in a particular moment. Without hope, there would be no reason to take the pain of improvising and no reason at all to care when organizations fail to supply these life-prolonging medicines. During stock-outs, when no one knows when the next drug supplies will be delivered, the seemingly endless waiting for supplies does not necessarily lead to resignation or paralysis (Crapanzano 2003; Zigon 2009). Waiting does not mean that nothing happens, but actually quite the opposite: doctors have to decide about switching patients to other regimens or adjust measures to improvise therapy, as I will describe below.

Often the term improvisation connotes arbitrariness rather than intentionality. In contrast, as I will show below, actors are *carefully* trying not to undermine the level of care necessary to keep hope alive in the improvisation of therapy. Being careful expresses the reflexivity necessary for adjusting measures, redefining rules, and other practices of improvisation in living with uncertainty as a condition.[4] The concept of hope is useful in understanding how this reflexivity is directed toward a 'future goodness', particularly in situations of uncertainty in which technologies like indicators fail to orient decisions over life and death (see also Lear 2006: 103).

---

[4] See also Wendy Espeland and Michael Sauder's discussion of reflexivity to capture how quantitative measures are made effective and how reflections on the experiences of the reality destabilize such measures (2007: 35).

In what follows, I will first situate my discussion of stock-outs and improvisation of therapy within ongoing debates in the anthropology of global health and the latent biopolitics in antiretroviral therapy. The critical impulse and the analytical limitations of Michel Foucault's notion of biopolitics in approaching contemporary biomedicine in Africa have been frequently discussed in the scholarly literature (Comaroff 2007; Geissler, Zenker and Rottenburg 2012). In this chapter, I do not aim to offer another reading of this debate with respect to the use of indicators in the provision of access to antiretroviral therapy in Uganda. Instead, I argue that the analysis of numbers and indicators, which are described in Foucault's work on biopower as political technologies in the 'administration of bodies and the calculated management of life' (Foucault 1978: 140), signals the pressing need to elaborate on the problem of agency for which the notion of hope may provide a crucial point of departure (Miyazaki 2004).

BIOPOLITICAL FUTURES OF ANTIRETROVIRAL THERAPY

In the first years of antiretroviral therapy in Uganda, antiretrovirals were too costly to be a realistic option for most patients and their wider social networks in Uganda. For the activists and physicians like Alex Coutinho, then working for The AIDS Support Organization (TASO) in Uganda, it was unacceptable that treatment was purely a matter of 'some families [who] were lucky enough to access ARVs versus those not so lucky' (Coutinho 2004: 1929). Non-governmental organizations (NGOs) like TASO in Uganda or the Treatment Action Campaign (TAC) in South Africa were mobilizing people and money to provide access to treatment on a broader scale. Organizations like TASO promoted a notion of hope in the form of a model of care termed 'positive living', which for example encouraged patients to disclose their HIV-status to others. More importantly, this model of care included the provision of material support, and the distribution of medication for opportunistic infections to strengthen people's hope when lifesaving antiretrovirals were unaffordable. The anthropologist Hanne Mogensen emphasizes that being hopeful in the early years of the AIDS epidemic also meant 'talk[ing] carefully', which could include being silent about a disease 'one could do nothing about'. This hope was not entirely passive. It enabled people to care for sick relatives by 'holding on to other things' (Mogensen 2010: 69).

Ideas like positive living were not only meant to strengthen people's hope, but were a very successful model of care, which furnished the public with scientific evidence that HIV care in Africa can be effective (e.g. Kaleeba *et al.* 1997). Such evidence, in turn, allowed for the assertion of better moral arguments against the high costs of antiretrovirals and for the challenging of donor organizations' reluctance to provide aid for antiretroviral therapy in African countries. Here, indicators were crucial technologies to produce scientific evidence of the effectiveness and accountability of antiretroviral provisioning in African countries, which led to the paradigmatic shift toward the scale-up of access to treatment as a human right (Robins 2006; Hardon 2012). As a result, patient numbers increased rapidly. In Uganda, patient numbers increased dramatically from 10,000 patients in 2002 (WHO 2003: 6) to 96,000 in 2006 (Katabira and Oelrichs 2007: S6). In terms of the MDG to reach universal access to treatment, Uganda had reached 46 per cent coverage of treatment by 2006. But for the following years, the scale-up rate was flat for a variety of reasons, which I will discuss in a moment.

One of the more subtle reasons for the rapid increase in patient numbers in the first years of free access to antiretroviral therapy and their subsequent stagnation originates in a shift from newly emerging logistic infrastructures to provide relief for humanitarian emergencies, toward more ambitious global public health infrastructures (Redfield 2013). For disasters and other short-term emergencies, humanitarian relief organizations like Médicins-Sans-Frontières had to be able to react quickly and move large quantities of life-saving devices to any place in the world. This operational principle fostered the development of 'mobile infrastructures' by simplifying relief-giving in the form of a standardized repository of essential items needed during emergencies, as Peter Redfield describes in his work on Médicins-Sans-Frontières (Redfield 2013: 81). In contrast to short-term emergencies, the chronicity of HIV, the high costs of treatment and, moreover, the sheer scale of the AIDS epidemic fostered the use of indicators to simplify treatment and, more importantly, to simplify the calculation of the distribution of treatment. These simplifications are essential for procuring expensive antiretrovirals more efficiently. In logistical terms, mass HIV treatment programmes in Uganda 'pull' antiretroviral medicines from national and international drug suppliers, unlike other medicines, for example antibiotics, which are 'pushed' from the drug warehouses down to the health facilities. That is, mass HIV treatment programmes order the amount of drugs they need to provide patients with antiretroviral therapy.

The use of indicators allows for an exact quantification of demand to regulate the distribution of antiretrovirals. This regulation is premised on the simplification of therapy. Usually patients are not immediately started on treatment. First, patients are registered as clients. Over the course of an HIV infection, the number of CD4 cells continuously decreases, which means that a patient's immune system is weakening. Once the CD4 count falls below a numerical threshold, patients are regarded as eligible for treatment. Over the past few years this threshold has been constantly elevated. The WHO's *Rapid Advice for Adults* (2009) recommends 'starting antiretroviral treatment in all patients with HIV who have CD4 count <350 cells/mm^3 irrespective of clinical symptoms' (WHO 2009: 10). The current tendency is to start treatment 'earlier' at a CD4 count of 500 (WHO 2013). The elevation automatically increases the number of eligible patients. This means that treatment programmes require more antiretrovirals and, of course, more funding, if programmes in fact strictly follow the updated treatment guidelines.

In principle, these simplifications make it possible to calculate the 'need' for antiretroviral therapy easily, as patients have to take pills daily once they are started on treatment. All patients are started on the standard first-line regime 'AZT/3TC/NVP',[5] which requires the consumption of two pills a day, with sixty pills per month making up one pill bottle. Such numbers can be simply multiplied for whole programmes in order to calculate the needed stock of antiretrovirals and estimate the quantity of bottles for bi-monthly drug orders.

In practice, however, mass HIV treatment programmes in Uganda 'pull' antiretrovirals from a variety of sources, like the US President's Emergency Program for AIDS Relief (PEPFAR), the Global Fund to Fight HIV/AIDS, Malaria and Tuberculosis, the Clinton Foundation, and most importantly from the National Medical Stores, which is mandated to supply the national public health system in Uganda. The pull system, enacted by novel funding mechanisms in global health, is however too fragmented, giving rise to new uncertainties and inequalities in the provision of HIV treatment in Uganda (Whyte *et al.* 2013).

---

[5] AZT/3TC/NVP is a so-called fixed-dose combination comprising Zidovudine, Lamivudine and Nevirapine. A monthly pack today costs only US$10. This is comparatively low. In contrast to these first-line regimens, second-line regimes refer to patent antiretroviral regimens, which are significantly more expensive.

The AIDS researchers Tony Barnett and Alan Whiteside noted early on that organizations define and use indicators in different ways, reflecting donor countries' 'politics of how to count patients, and [...] most importantly how to count a program's effect' (2006: 2). Antiretrovirals were pulled from different sources with different mechanisms to count patient numbers, and more importantly, to account for the distribution of the drugs. Indicators used to track the progress towards universal access to treatment were also travelling through separate information infrastructures – to PEPFAR, the Global Fund, to UNAIDS, but not to the Ministry of Health in Uganda. These numbers were irregularly aggregated on a national level and thereby lacked the accuracy necessary for organising a reliable and continuous supply of antiretrovirals.

When I asked Joy Kabayaga,[6] a public health official working at the Ministry of Health in Uganda, about the lack of accurate data on patients and drugs, she pointed out that the introduction of antiretroviral therapy was not the only public health intervention in the more recent past. All these interventions significantly undermined the establishment of a comprehensive national health system (see also Pfeiffer 2013):

> Over the years, many countries and organisations had developed interventions and methods of handling the health problems caused by diseases of public health concerns. All these had different methods of measuring the successes or failures of the interventions depending on the vision and mission of the particular organisations. The measurements were covering specific interests of individual countries or organisations, and it had become difficult to *see the global picture* of these attempts to combat the diseases.[7]

(emphasis added)

The fragmented logistics and the lack of accuracy were occasioned during a countrywide shortage of antiretrovirals between 2009 and 2010. The provision of antiretroviral therapy is, as in many other fields of development aid, carried out by a great number of projects, which are often limited in terms of time. As Joy explained, specific interests of these projects were incompatible with each other. Even if data on key indicators like patient numbers were, in principle, defined in the same way, each project may have calculated them differently and asked for

---

[6] All names in this text are pseudonyms.
[7] Interview, 3 October 2009, Ministry of Health, Kampala.

separate reports, which led to an exhausting amount of paperwork to produce data, as Joy pointed out to me.

Accurate data on patient numbers is not only important for tracking progress toward universal access to treatment, but also for calculating the need for antiretroviral therapy and projecting the costs of treatment in the country. Thus, the multiplicity of projects and the complexity of existing indicators in the field also undermined the national public health system in terms of its ability to offer coordinated antiretroviral therapy and to manage the supply of medicines as a routine function. During the months between 2009 and 2010, when most hospitals were experiencing severe stock-outs, information on how many patients were receiving the medicines, how many patients were in need, or how many treatment sites were providing these medicines through which sources was not available.

The uncertainties arising out of the shortage of medicine in current efforts to scale-up access to treatment resonate with the biopolitics of population, which Vinh-Kim Nguyen describes in his ethnography of the early years of antiretroviral therapy in West Africa (Nguyen 2010). In the first years of antiretroviral therapy, the pressing need to develop rules for distributing these expensive and scarce antiretroviral drugs inaugurated novel relations between health and subjectivity. Nguyen captures the specificity of the rationing of antiretroviral drugs with the term 'triage', referring to those practices of determining certain lives to be more worth to be saved than others in the context of scarce resources (Nguyen 2010: 133). This form of rationing antiretrovirals is cobbled together with technologies of the self, for example, the practice of disclosing one's status, constituting new forms of therapeutic citizenship (Nguyen 2010: 6–7). The emergence of therapeutic citizenship in contemporary mass HIV treatment raises the question of what specific *biopolitical futures* are taking shape in this unprecedented humanitarian experiment. According to Nguyen, the analysis of these novel forms of biopolitics raises the following questions about the future of antiretroviral therapy:

> Can the emergence of therapeutic citizenship and triage be attributed to the peculiarities of the local character or were they imposed from the outside? Are they historical aberrations that will wither away as mass treatment programs are deployed to address the crisis? Moreover, what are the implications of the introduction of these novel mechanisms that sort people out based on their need for treatment?
>
> (Nguyen 2010: 110)

These biopolitical futures rest on the use of a broad array of technologies of quantification to administer the antiretrovirals, which remain scarce in spite of frequent portrayals of an abundance of resources for HIV treatment. Unlike the early years of antiretroviral therapy, when the drugs were scarce because people in African countries could not afford the high costs, the scarcity produced by stock-outs reflects a persistent infrastructural problem, a conjoined lack of data and donor aid money, which together inhibit these life-saving medicines from being distributed free-of-charge. During stock-outs, practices of rationing emerge when the next delivery is uncertain: hospitals wait and must dwindle down the remaining stock of antiretrovirals. During these stock-outs, antiretroviral therapy is improvised, most notably by adjusting indicators for treatment decisions to ration medicines.

Foucault's notion of biopower, which he provocatively framed as an act of 'making live and letting die' (Foucault 2003: 247), provides an answer to the question of what future is emanating from the rationing of scarce antiretrovirals. According to Didier Fassin, the latter part of the definition of biopower – the 'letting die' – has often been ignored (Fassin 2009), as scholarly attention has been paid mostly to the productive dimensions of novel forms of biopower.[8] Fassin thus emphasizes that biopolitics is not only about the improvement of bodies and the health of a population, but that 'to "make live" actually presupposes implicit or sometimes explicit choices over who shall live what sort of life and for how long', which ultimately mean that some patients are 'rejected into death', for which the rationing of antiretrovirals may be considered as a case in point (Fassin 2009: 53; see also Foucault 1978).

Seen from the perspective of biopolitics, the rationing of antiretrovirals resulting from stock-outs is inherently linked to the deployment of statistics and indicators as political technologies in the regulation of free access to antiretroviral therapy. The purpose of using these technologies is to produce a minimal degree of fairness in the distribution of scarce antiretrovirals. In this regard, stock-outs arising out of the infrastructures of contemporary global health point toward a future

---

[8] Anthropologists' attempts to bring the new forms of biopower into view include an elaboration of biopolitics as a 'politics of life itself'. Relevant for the discussion in this chapter is Nikolas Rose and Carlos Novas' suggestion that a political economy of hope is emerging around projects addressing 'life itself' typically organized around hope for a cure of conditions, which have yet to be developed, have yet to be clinically tested, or which are simply too expensive to be realized (Rose and Novas 2005; see also Hardon 2012).

characterized by the emergence of new inequalities, which are biopolitical. Practices of rationing by determining those who must receive treatment now and those who can wait may imply more generally who in the future may be left without treatment, to paraphrase Nguyen's description of triage (Nguyen 2010: 9).

The biopolitics inscribed into the use of technologies to administer the distribution of antiretrovirals calls the hope invested into the future of HIV treatment into question. Hope is unevenly distributed in global health, as the anthropologist Ghassan Hage notes more generally for contemporary neoliberal regimes of governance (quoted in Zournazi 2003: 152). Yet, conditions of radical uncertainty are not necessarily characterized by hopeless-ness. For one thing, hope, as Zigon argues, 'does not arise in good times' (Zigon 2009: 262). Rather, it is precisely exceptional circumstances, such as when indicators and other technologies in the fragmented infrastructures of global health fail to generate practical certainty, which give rise to hope. An emphasis on the biopolitical nature of the shortage of antiretrovirals loses sight of the ethics of care in which hope constitutes a form of agency to live with the contingencies and uncertainties both surrounding and emerging out of free access to antiretroviral therapy.

As the following account of the stock-outs of antiretrovirals will show, waiting for the next supply to arrive is not a passive stance but rather entails a number of improvisations. Even the rationing of antiretrovirals requires improvisations of treatment guidelines and measures. Moreover, these improvisations are quite common for the Ugandan health infrastructure in order to maintain a minimum level of care in situations of radical uncertainty. What is crucial about these improvisations is that they articulate a capacity to endure crises which do not have a clear end. To borrow from Theodor W. Adorno, this hope expresses its own minimal morality to live through emergencies and crises, knowing that the only certainty is that everyone will at some point die, as my ethnographic account of antiretroviral stock-outs in the following sections wants to describe (Adorno 1951: 224).[9]

---

[9] Adorno's notion of hope aptly captures the minimal morality distinctive of contemporary humanitarianism. 'So, when we are hoping for rescue, a voice tells us that hope is in vain, yet it is powerless hope alone that allows us to draw a single breath. All contemplation can do no more than patiently is trace the ambiguity of melancholy in ever new configurations.' ['So sagt uns eine Stimme, wenn wir auf Rettung hoffen, daß Hoffnung vergeblich sei, und doch ist es sie, die ohnmächtige, allein, die überhaupt uns erlaubt, einen Atemzug zu tun.'] Adorno 1951: 224; see also Jackson 2011: xiii; Redfield 2013: 235.

IMPROVISING THERAPY AT CLINIC U

In order to elaborate on the concept of hope as expressed in the improvisation of therapy, the following sections will focus on treatment decisions in the context of antiretroviral stock-outs. In these situations of uncertainty, when no one knows when the next supplies will arrive, the use of indicators and numeric thresholds in treatment decisions is better understood as an embodied and situated practice in the rationing of antiretrovirals. My description of these improvisations of therapy focuses on one treatment programme in Uganda, which I shall here call Clinic U.

Waiting for antiretrovirals

During my field research I regularly visited Jamila, the pharmacist of Clinic U, to discuss the logistics of antiretrovirals because this clinic was exemplary in terms of the exceptionality as well as the partiality of global public health in Uganda. Clinic U was built explicitly to provide 'high-quality' care and treatment services free-of-charge. The statutes of this clinic envision 'a healthy Africa, free from the burden of infectious diseases', while the clinic's official mission is, 'To build [the] capacity of health systems in Africa for the delivery of sustainable, high quality care and prevention of HIV/AIDS and related infectious diseases through training, research, and advanced clinical services'. In 2009, treatment numbers at Clinic U had reached 6,500 'active patients' on free antiretroviral therapy. In total, some 12,000 clients were reported as having officially registered there. It is one of the largest clinics in Kampala: it operates outreach programmes, offers training programmes for the larger East African region and, moreover, has considerable scholarly output in terms of formal research articles.

With the national roll-out of antiretrovirals in 2004, Clinic U became one of the 'pockets of excellence' in the provision of antiretroviral therapy, attracting funding from several international sources, as Dr Niwagaba, the head of Clinic U, explained to me. This funding, however, was not used solely for treatment. Only 1,000 patients were receiving antiretrovirals procured with PEPFAR money. The other 5,000 patients were receiving medicines procured from the National Medical Stores and paid for by the national health budget. At Clinic U, these antiretrovirals had different names, and were dispensed from different windows. Yet, as patients complained, these drugs treat the same condition.

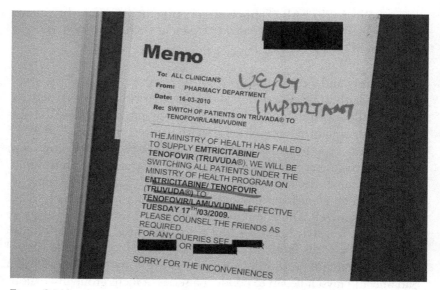

Figure 8.1 Announcement to switch patients on Truvada to Tenofovir/Lamivudine. This announcement of the pharmacists is an example of the improvisation of therapy by switching patients from one antiretroviral regimen, which the National Medical Stores had failed to supply, to an equivalent regimen. Photo taken by the author.

From early 2009 on, the supplies from the National Medical Stores were becoming irregular and led with growing frequency to stock-outs, to the extent that Clinic U was running its treatment programme in crisis mode. Clinic U, like many other clinics in the country, had to improvise therapy in order to provide treatment. Jamila, the pharmacist of Clinic U, for example, switched patients to other regimens (see Figure 8.1). Further, she dispensed only half of the monthly dosage, two weeks only. Most importantly, Jamila borrowed antiretrovirals from the PEPFAR source, which was more stable than the National Medical Stores. However, after several months of stock-outs, Clinic U had exhausted its PEPFAR source, and Jamila was not able to borrow any more medicines.

When Clinic U had exhausted its limit for borrowing medicines, it had to ration medicines more strictly by stopping the enrolment of new patients, as Dr Niwagaba explained to me in our discussion of the situation. But he also questioned the borrowing of medicine from PEPFAR. Dr Niwagaba insisted that 5,500 patients at his clinic should be provided with antiretrovirals from the national health system instead of depending on PEPFAR. 'This is a government hospital', he argued, and 'after all, who should pay for Ugandans' treatment, if not this government'.[10]

CD4 counts and a normal life

The longer the clinic had to wait for new stock, the fewer patients were enrolled into free antiretroviral therapy programmes. After discussing this situation with various health workers of Clinic U, I asked how patients experienced the situation and how they were going about managing the uncertainties surrounding the shortage of antiretrovirals. Nelson Bahame, the chairperson of the Client's Council at Clinic U, urged that I conduct focus group discussions as forums in which to ask the patients myself. I first hesitated, but Nelson insisted, 'this is the way we conduct research here'. Dr Niwagaba, the head of Clinic U, also supported the focus group discussions. He thought the public should know that patients were still waiting for antiretrovirals. Thus, Nelson Bahame and myself began to conduct a series of focus group discussions at Clinic U. I prepared a question guide and was told to bring money to pay for participants' transportation and to buy some 'little eats'. Nelson went through the clinic's records to identify clients who had not been started on treatment and who had a CD4 count below 200.

In our first focus group discussion, after Nelson welcomed all clients as the chairperson of the clients' council and after I introduced myself, clients immediately began to ask questions about the average life expectancies with antiretroviral therapy – before we even approached the topic of stock-outs.[11] The emerging dialogue was revealing in the ways that indicators like the CD4 count come to embody definitions of normal life and death. One participant wanted to know 'the longest life span on ARVs'. Other participants responded by pointing to 'a man called Major Rubaramira,[12] who claims to live for over twenty years now and that he has an almost zero viral load'. Many other popular figures taken from newspapers were quoted as examples of living a 'normal life'. In these discussions, a normal life with HIV was expressed in terms of an average CD4 count, comparable to the CD4 count of a person without HIV. But, a normal life with HIV has to follow what Meinert

---

[10] Interview AK, 19 March 2010, Kampala.

[11] I conducted five focus group discussions between 11 February 2010 and 19 April 2010 at various ART clinics in Kampala. In this chapter I will only summarize one focus group discussion.

[12] Major Rubamira is a prominent critic of Museveni's AIDS politics, who publicly declared his HIV status early.

and others term 'the rules of ART' to maintain this average CD4 count (Meinert, Mogensen and Twebaze 2009). These rules of ART refer to a set of practices, which are thought to help improve patients' adherence to treatment. As one participant said, 'if you take the drugs regularly and take the right types at the right times you can live up to 62 to 70 years, which is normal like others'.

This participant also mentioned a list of practices that would boost the functioning of his immune system: 'enough rest', 'eating well', 'eating fruits and greens', 'avoid getting exhausted', 'avoid stress', 'always use condoms to avoid re-infections', 'chew raw garlic and if somebody complains that you are smelling, don't worry for you it is your life'. Most importantly, participants all argued to 'take Septrin[13] consistently'. These practices are also understood as boosting the immune system. Participants were confident that they had the ability to increase their CD4 levels without treatment. 'I know the reason why it [a CD4 count 175] has gone below and I told the doctor that I will raise it up with my diet', as one participant explained. However, as other participants cautioned, these instructions were not always easy to follow. 'You need money to eat properly or everyday life problems like paying school fees or fights with wives are creating too much stress.'

Participants' accounts of their CD4 counts reflect how these technologies embody a range of knowledge practices, which help them understand and manage their own bodily conditions by following the rules of ART, specifically in terms of practices of disclosure, living positively and having a treatment supporter. The CD4 count is, moreover, a central indicator for determining when patients are supposed to start treatment because it specifies a particular numerical threshold. In Uganda, the threshold for starting treatment has been constantly elevated over the past years: from 150 in the first years of antiretroviral therapy (WHO 2003), to a threshold of 350 in the latest official treatment guidelines (WHO 2009). Alongside the changes of treatment guidelines, recommended thresholds may vary between different clinics depending on the availability of treatment at drug suppliers. By contrast, in the context of drug shortages, the CD4 count, which is normally used to calculate the need for scaling-up access to treatment, is used to ration antiretrovirals by adjusting the threshold to start treatment to the shortage of drugs.

[13] Septrin is an antibiotic and prescribed as a prophylaxis before patients are started on antiretroviral therapy. Similar to antiretrovirals, patients are counselled to adhere strictly to Septrin, that is, twice a day and always at the same time.

All participants of the focus group discussion should have already been started on treatment. When Nelson and myself asked the group about their CD4 counts and if they knew when they were supposed to start treatment, participants responded that they were all eligible for treatment based on their CD4 counts, but that they had been told by the clinic to wait. As one man said, 'my CD4 now is at 175. They told me that they give ARVs when you are sick and your CD4 is 50. The doctor said that I'm now ready for ARVs but they are not there and he told me that now they have reduced to 50, that is when I would start.' Another confirmed that Clinic U had reduced the threshold to start treatment because of the stock-outs of antiretrovirals. 'They have again checked me and told me that the CD4 count has reduced. They told me it is 117. They told me that I had to start on ARVs, but the drugs were not available.' Somebody else mentioned, 'I got ready long ago because I had to start in December but each time I come they tell me that I should have started on the drugs, but it is not yet available.'

The threshold to define a client's eligibility for treatment is usually based on recommendations issued by treatment guidelines. The implementation of this recommendation differed from hospital to hospital. As one client, for example, told us, 'there is something I cut out of the newspapers, you see this government of ours, this was 4th of September 2009, and they were saying 250 and the minister was saying differently, 350. I even asked the doctor and he said, "Ah! The ministry does its things and for us we do our things".' In addition to the variable implementation of the official treatment guidelines, antiretrovirals were rationed at Clinic U by lowering the threshold to start treatment step-by-step in order to slow down the enrolment of new patients until the next supplies would arrive. The adjustment of this numeric threshold demonstrated how measurement systems were used to recalculate treatment during drug shortages, instead of instantly stopping the enrolment of patients into treatment.

'Nobody is going to die'

All participants were concerned about the stock-outs, but not everyone was eager to start treatment at all and, instead, many claimed to have already improved their health conditions without antiretrovirals. Suddenly, one participant, whom everybody called the 'young man', started to cry and asked, 'Am I going to die?' He explained that his CD4 count was at 98. He had followed all the instructions given by the social workers in mandatory counselling sessions. He had been living cautiously, eating properly, taking Septrin and using condoms. Now, he said, he was ready for treatment, but the doctors told him there were no drugs. The group was silent. Although the situation was serious, everybody had been so far smiling or even making ironic jokes. 'Nobody is going to die', Nelson Bahame responded harshly, breaking the few milliseconds of silence. 'Nobody has been dying at this clinic', he reminded everyone, 'because it takes care of its clients'. Nelson told the young man that this clinic was about to launch its start-up programme for young entrepreneurs. The young man could be in the first group of clients getting a start-up loan. 'Nobody should lose hope', Nelson added.

Nelson's comment meant that normally no one at Clinic U dies of AIDS. Starting patients on treatment, providing support and following up on patients' adherence to live a normal life are routines at Clinic U, which are predicated upon a steady supply of antiretrovirals. In the context of drug shortages, however, his comment demonstrated more drastically that HIV can be managed as an ordinary chronic condition if a set of logistical, technical, economic and political conditions for the supply of antiretrovirals are put into motion. But Nelson's hopes, as expressed in his response to the upset patient, went beyond a discussion of public health infrastructures, which nobody really trusts in Uganda. Stock-outs of medicines are common experiences of the national public health system in Uganda (see e.g. Jitta, Whyte and Nshakira 2003). Yet unlike for other diseases and medicines, access to antiretroviral therapy is rigidly standardized to control the risks of sudden stock-outs, which might undermine patients' adherence to treatment and thus increase the risk of drug resistance.

Nelson's hope that 'nobody is going to die' highlights the relationship between CD4 counts as quantitative measures, and patients' personal health conditions. This relationship cannot be fully grasped by inquiring into official treatment guidelines, health infrastructures, and how they determine access to treatment. Instead, one must consider how the relationship between numbers and health is embodied in the provision of care. To care meant to respond to clients' fears by strengthening hope that Clinic U will do something during the stock-outs, as each and every life counts at this clinic.

More importantly, the embodiment of the relationship between numbers and hope in reflecting upon the stock-outs highlights that HIV treatment is not only about patients' survival, but treatment is about the possibilities for living a normal life with a normal death. 'Of course everyone is going to die at some point', Nelson told me later after we closed the focus group discussion. But, as Nelson continued to say, 'once you start on antiretrovirals, you take them until God calls you'. Nelson's attempt to keep clients' hope alive was referring to a future goodness, which transcended the humanitarian understanding that antiretroviral therapy is saving lives. Nelson's reassuring words that nobody will die includes a hope that everyone will die a normal death. This hope is not a passive trust in Clinic U, but reflects a capacity to persevere until the next supplies will arrive. As the following account of stock-outs shows, waiting for antiretrovirals is not a passive stance. Rationing entails a range of improvisations, like the adjustment of measurement system, which elicits moral reflections about care under conditions of limited resources.

'Ethical thresholds'

A few days after the focus group discussion on the stock-outs, Nelson told me that he had managed to squeeze the young man into a treatment programme of Clinic U. He had talked to the doctors about the young man. He assured me that the 'young man is safe'. Had the doctors listened to Nelson? What about the other patients with much lower CD4 counts? How rigid was the rationing of antiretrovirals at Clinic U?

After conducting the focus group discussions, I had to report back to Dr Niwagaba, the head of clinical services at Clinic U. I did not have to raise the point that patients were worried about the delays in starting treatment. Instead, I emphasized the uncertainties surrounding the use of CD4 counts in determining eligibility for treatment. Furthermore, I reported that not only were patients who returned for each appointment frustrated with not being started on treatment, but that the treatment supporters accompanying the patients were also disappointed. Each postponement made it more difficult to convince supporters to join them for the next visit.

Dr Niwagaba countered that he would not officially announce that patients should only start treatment if they are severely ill with CD4 counts less than 50, 100, or anything else:

> I don't want to frustrate our patients, such that they lose hope. We are not going to formalise the CD4 count of 50. It is scientifically and ethically wrong. What is the difference between 50 and 100? This is an arbitrary definition. This is our *ethical threshold*.
>
> (emphasis added)[14]

---

[14] Interview AK, 2 April 2010, Kampala.

During stock-outs, doctors adjust the rules of ART, which are configured by a complex arrangement of logistical, technical and bureaucratic elements according to the availability of medicines at the pharmacy. But how far can the rules of ART be bent? How low can CD4 counts go without putting life at risk? What is the most ethical conduct when medicines are not there and nobody knows when the supplies will arrive?

As Dr Niwagaba continued to explain, regardless of whether CD4 counts are at 50 or 100, clinically, patients are already at great risk. But Dr Niwagaba insisted that as long as the supplies remain unstable and unpredictable, 50 was considered to be the clinic's ethical threshold. His decision to start treatment at a CD4 count of 50 in turn was a form of triage (Nguyen 2010), used for determining which individuals must receive treatment and when by introducing an ethical threshold. With this threshold, the moral dilemmas revolving around the rationing of antiretrovirals could be routinized. However, routinization did not mean that Clinic U was indifferent towards patients' worries. Quite the opposite, Dr Niwagaba bitterly explained. Once patients are started on treatment at a CD count of 50, all kinds of opportunistic infections may have to be treated at the same time, which increases the cost of treatment. Delaying the recruitment of patients, thus, might turn out even more expensive. As he stated, with regard to patient costs, it did not make sense to wait until patients developed severe opportunistic infections because this would require a range of other medicines that would make antiretroviral therapy even more expensive. With regard to patients' rights for treatment, it did not make sense to have a national free treatment programme at all if only a few patients could be provided with treatment. Dr Niwagaba and the pharmacists' challenge was to compare any new patients with the 6,500 active patients at this clinic who relied on the stable supply of antiretrovirals in order to continue therapy. Furthermore, he stated, 'it makes my life easier. I don't want to discuss each and every case with the pharmacist, who tells me that we do not have the drugs. We start at 50, whether the drugs are there or not, without any discussion.'[15]

During the prolonged stock-out of antiretrovirals at Clinic U, the adjustment of the threshold to enrol patients into treatment routinized the rationing of antiretrovirals. The routinized rationing was premised upon the assumption that Clinic U would, at some point, receive new

[15] Interview AK, 2 April 2010, Kampala.

antiretroviral supplies through the national public health system – although nobody knew exactly when this would happen. This improvisation of measures was not a blind attempt to deal with drug shortages. The ethical threshold to keep hope alive illustrates how hope works as a form of moral courage to reinsert agency into situations of radical uncertainty. The rationing of antiretrovirals put patients' lives at risk, but viewed from the perspective of hope, even this form of rationing constitutes an improvised form of care used to gain valuable time until the next supplies could arrive.

Repairing measures and the next years of antiretroviral therapy
The stock-outs were also reflected in the data on the indicators deployed to track Uganda's progress toward universal access to treatment, which I described in the first part of this chapter. From 2006 to 2009, data for measuring progress to universal access to treatment showed an increase from 41 per cent to 54 per cent. However, in the following year, this scale-up rate dropped to 50 per cent (MoFPED 2013: 27). The previous section on the rationing of antiretrovirals described some of the reasons for the decrease in patient numbers. At the same time, treatment guidelines officially recommended starting patients earlier on treatment, which immediately elevated the number of people eligible for treatment. In addition, actual patient numbers were not only stagnating, but also quite inaccurate as a result of the various improvisations of therapy, most notably because of the borrowing of antiretrovirals. As a result, numbers had failed to provide a full account of the progress toward universal access to treatment as well as the extent of the stock-outs in the country.

But in the following year, in 2011, Jamila, the pharmacist at Clinic U, told me with great relief that the 'drugs are there'. At some point early 2010, antiretrovirals from an emergency procurement,[16] worth US$4.25 million, arrived in the country and were distributed to Clinic U. Treatment programmes immediately absorbed these medicines. Thus, in May 2010, another disbursement of about US$5.9 million was made in order for clinics to procure additional antiretrovirals. In the meantime, PEPFAR had started its second funding phase, though much

---

[16] One of the reasons for the stock-out of antiretrovirals was the suspension of Global Fund grants in Uganda, worth US$200 million, after a corruption scandal. Until the suspension was revoked in 2011, the Global Fund made only two emergency remittances to stop the stock-out of antiretrovirals in the country (GFATM 2009; Ministry of Health 2011).

of the funding was allocated for other goals.[17] Finally, the National Medical Stores resumed supplying antiretrovirals using the national health budget with approximately US$9 million for antiretroviral therapy per year, with the effect that treatment programmes like Clinic U could resume the scaling-up of access to treatment.

Funding alone, though a key factor for the availability of medicines, is not enough to make access to antiretroviral therapy more predictable. Over the past years, the complex infrastructural fragmentations of global public health, in which treatment programmes like those run at Clinic U were supplied by two or even more sources, had undermined the calculations of the need for antiretrovirals in the country, as health professionals frequently pointed out. Patient numbers were scattered across the many organizations managing the logistics in the country.

From 2010 onwards, I had attended a series of workshops which attempted to address the infrastructural fragmentations in the supply of antiretrovirals. Toward the end of 2011 these workshops eventually led to a final meeting, 'Harmonization of the supply side of antiretrovirals in Uganda'. Dr Isaac from the Ministry of Health gave a PowerPoint presentation on this topic. He showed two slides that depicted the idea of the harmonization of the different infrastructures in the supply of antiretrovirals in Uganda. The slides demonstrated how the harmonization would resolve the infrastructural fragmentation (see Figure 8.2).

The first slide in this presentation gives an abstract picture of infrastructural fragmentations in the supply of antiretrovirals (see Figure 8.2, first slide), in which HIV treatment programmes were receiving medicines from at least three different sources. As the second slide (see Figure 8.2, second slide) concludes, the duplications in the supply lines had contributed to an 'inefficient use of resources' over the past years. The second slide suggests that the harmonization ('one site – one source' as it proclaimed) would reduce the 'overlappings', 'fragmentations' and ultimately the 'confusions' produced in practices of ordering medicines.

During the stock-outs between 2009 and 2010, treatment programmes had been borrowing and sharing HIV medicines with other programmes, and were moreover 'double-dipping' in various sources. These practices of borrowing and sharing antiretrovirals during these stock-outs eventually reinforced fragmentation by undermining the rigid reporting system instituted to yield precise monthly calculations

---

[17] See *Status Report on the Global Fund Grants in Uganda* (Ministry of Health 2011).

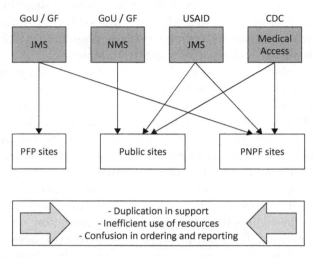

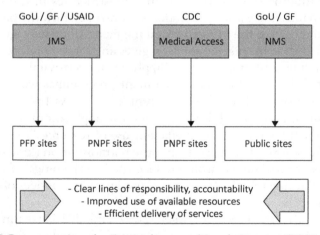

Figure 8.2 Presentation on the 'Rationalization of Supply Lines', AIDS Control Programme, Uganda.

of the need for antiretroviral therapy in the country. As Dr Isaac explained:

> From a technical point of view this is a necessary precondition to increase accountability for all involved parties. Moreover mechanisms that enhance accountability lead to clear assignments of responsibilities, which is particularly important to manage such a complex and uncertain domain like free ART. There is no alternative in this complex setting other than all parties knowing about what the other parties do and can rely on their commitments and their responsibilities ... If all fail to agree on the ways to make the supply side of ARVs more accountable, then ultimately all parties, not only individual parties, will fail to be responsible, if problems like stock-outs occur again. But this holds also in the opposite direction: if all parties are efficiently supplying ARVs, then individual organisations' performance are disappearing in the current complexities in the supply of ARVs. So, one important result of the harmonisation would be that each organisation's efficiency in supplying drugs would be made more visible.[18]

All major stakeholders – the major suppliers in the country (the National Medical Stores, Joint Medical Stores, Medical Access), major donor organizations (PEFPAR, the Clinton Foundation, USAID), and government agencies (the AIDS Control Programme, Ministry of Health) – participated in this workshop. The shortage of these medicines had turned the many organizations in the supply of antiretrovirals into a collective unit of fate. As Dr Isaac recapitulated after the meeting, 'everybody was happy and even surprised that we reached an agreement. They were asking three times "do we all agree?" – Now it is agreed.'

During the workshop, the organisers provided a new list of all treatment sites, the respective patient numbers and through which sources they were supplied. Such a list was remarkable, as nobody had seen such a comprehensive list before. The list showed that exactly 274,789 people had access to antiretroviral therapy in 2011. The harmonization would not have been possible without numbers believed to be accurate. All supply organizations had to know how many patients they would have to supply after the harmonization. Clinic U, for instance, would either have to put all patients supplied by PEPFAR on medicines supplied by the national health system, or (the other way around) put all patients on medicines supplied by PEPFAR. Either way, the shift would

---

[18] Interview Dr A, 20 January 2012, Kampala.

depend on an agreement between PEPFAR and the Ministry of Health on the overall number of sites and patients they would like to supply.

One of the key questions of this meeting, however, was the future of HIV funding. 274,789 patients, though a presumably accurate count, was too low with regard to the MDG of reaching universal access to treatment by 2015. In 2011, when Dr Isaac presented his projections, the public sector lacked the US$2.27 million needed to scale up access to treatment for 44,000 people, and would thus have to reduce its annual targets to 33,000 patients for the financial year 2012/2013. In 2014, accordingly, there would be no funds for the scale-up at all. The private sector, that is, all donor organizations, lacked about US$19 million to reach this scaling-up target of 44,000 people, as the most important donor agency PEPFAR would exceed its funding level already in 2013 due to higher current consumption figures of the previous years. With the remaining funds, the larger private sector would be able to scale up access to treatment to only 11,000 people by 2014.

These calculations did not even cover the period after 2015, when the target for universal access to treatment should be reached in Uganda and elsewhere. As other countries like South Africa or Central African Republic also report a lack of funding or even antiretroviral stock-outs, the rationing of antiretrovirals, which I described in the Ugandan context, may be indicative of the kinds of biopolitical futures arising out of mass HIV treatment programmes.[19] These calculations and the projections of the cost of treatment highlight how much the future of antiretroviral therapy depends on donor aid. The stock-outs of antiretrovirals, at the same time, demonstrate how uncertain such dependencies can be.

HOPE AND IMPROVEMENT

In their seminal work on risk, Mary Douglas and Aaron Wildavsky's answer to the question of whether we can know all the risks we face now or in the future is: 'no, we cannot; but yes, we must act as if we do' (Douglas and Wildavsky 1982: 1). This answer aptly captures the logics driving the improvisations of therapy, ranging from the practice

[19] For a recent discussion of antiretroviral stock-outs in the Central African Republic, see David 2014. For more media reports on South Africa and Kenya see 'Stock-outs rock world's biggest HIV treatment program', available at www.irinnews.org/report/99233/stock-outs-rock-world-apos-s-biggest-hiv-treatment-program; or 'HIV funding worries in Kenya', available at www.irinnews.org/report/100419/hiv-funding-worries-in-kenya.

of rationing of antiretrovirals to the calculations to project the costs of treatment described in the previous section. Moreover, Douglas and Wildavsky's approach to an inherently uncertain future provides an intriguing point of departure to account for the concept of hope in juxtaposition with scientific notions of anticipatory knowledge. The calculative practices, described in the last section, aim at making an inherently uncertain future of HIV treatment more predictable by making gaps visible and thereby create funding commitments. In these practices numbers and indicators appear to be a more rational basis for decision-making, because they are neutral (Merry 2011: S85). Indicators and other technologies of quantification thus provide a framework of rationality in which actors can predict other actors' decisions, coordinate the distribution of expensive pharmaceuticals and ultimately anticipate outcomes, which are more likely than others, if all actors agree on the representations of access to treatment (see also Rottenburg 2009a).

However, the neutrality of numbers and indicators is not a given but instead underwrites a teleological notion of progress to improve the human condition through modern science.[20] In this modernist understanding of scientific knowledge, quantitative indicators, targets and goals underwrite a distinction between 'before' and 'after' in establishing what counts as progress in the scale-up of antiretroviral therapy by providing a framework to describe the future of antiretroviral therapy in terms of an increase in patient numbers. Targets to reach universal access to treatment and the use of indicators to measure access to treatment define with apparent exactness the road toward a future in which no one dies of HIV. These indicators count patients, monitor drug prices and CD4 cells, all of which are regarded to be indispensable to project the costs to fulfil the commitment to a future without AIDS.

Within this framework, there are many reasons to doubt that Uganda and other countries will reach universal access to treatment. One can also call the usefulness of indicators into question if tracking progress and the encouragement to perform better ignores the fact that basic questions like the future funding of HIV treatment remain uncertain. Indicators, however, are not only deceptive and capable of failure because of a lack of accuracy; they also shape access to treatment,

[20] This understanding of predictability is premised upon Max Weber's work on the rationalization of life, which he regarded as a key characteristic of modernity. Instead of predictability, Weber uses the term formal 'calculability' (in German *Berechenbarkeit*), which more aptly captures the way quantitative modern regimes of governance deploy technologies like indicators to 'administer' the provisioning of any service to large populations formally without the need to know how indicators work exactly as long as they enable public life (Weber 1922: 128).

which in turn raises the question of what kind of biopolitical future will arise out of the current state of global health. In this respect, the distinction between 'before' and 'after' which obscures that access to treatment constitutes a financial life-long commitment which global health organizations and governments are not taking up. Moreover, people's accounts of their experiences of stock-outs suggest that the meaning of the future of the AIDS epidemic has profoundly changed since the introduction of HIV treatment. Goals, targets and indicators are only one of the many ways to think about and reflect on the future of antiretroviral therapy.

In my discussion of the variety of indicators used to organize access to treatment, I contrasted the neutrality of indicators with the worries, fear and anger about the fragmentation and the lack of predictability, which characterize contemporary global health infrastructures. More importantly, I emphasized the embodiment of hope in the improvisation of therapy under conditions of radical uncertainty. The notion of hope captured in my discussion of indicators and technologies of quantification used in antiretroviral therapy differs from an understanding of the future as a series of temporally discrete steps defined by the targets and goals of frameworks, such as the MDGs. Such definitions are crucial, but the underlying notion of the future activated in technologies of quantification fails to take account of the contingencies in human practices. These contingencies, by contrast, ask how unfulfilled hopes of the past can 'pull' practices in the present, as Miyazaki aptly writes (Miyazaki 2004: 139).

Rationing antiretrovirals puts patients' lives at risk, but viewed from the perspective of hope, we gain important insights into the improvisation of treatment, comprising the adjustments of regimens, measures and numbers, as well as the character of a distinctive ethics of care. It is precisely this form of hope – in caring for people in spite of the uncertainty when the next supplies will arrive – which should inform reflections upon the future of antiretroviral therapy and the larger field of global health. The improvisations in rationing antiretrovirals at Clinic U were premised upon the need to keep going until the national public health system would supply drugs – although no one knew exactly when this would happen.

In this context, hope as a method of knowing reveals the enormous reflexivity expressed in improvising treatment to maintain care. Neither Nelson, Dr Niwagaba, nor the many clients waiting for antiretrovirals could know who was predestined to survive, for how long, and who would die. Hope motivates improvisations through which patients and doctors can keep on providing care. In this kind of hope, the only certainty is that everyone is going to die at some point, as Nelson the chairperson of the Client's Council said.

Hope propels improvisations of therapy by adjusting measures and introducing new numeric thresholds, which foster reflection of uncertainty as a basic human condition. This hope transcends the quantitative projections of a future and instead points to the moral courage expressed in making decisions over life and death when calculations fail to make the supply of antiretrovirals predictable. Following John Dewey's notion of 'meliorism', improvisations like the ones I have described here can be understood to express hope as a capacity, which not only resists both a fatalistic attitude and a blind trust in scientific progress, but which also subscribes to the belief that all situations, 'be they comparatively bad or comparatively good, in any event may be bettered' systematically (Dewey 1920: 178; see also Whyte 1997: 232). In my account of adjusting measures to the stock-outs described above, the endeavour for systematic improvement of conditions meant rationing medicines carefully. Being careful involved reducing monthly dosages to distribute the shrinking amount of medicines diligently and setting priorities or reducing the threshold step-by-step in order to gain time, instead of suspending the provision of treatment immediately and leave patients without it.

Dewey's pragmatist notion of knowledge draws our attention, on the one hand, to people's faith in a better future, and on the other, to how actors reinsert agency into the moral reflections and confrontations of radical uncertainty, as Susan Whyte argues (Whyte 1997: 232). A pragmatist notion of knowledge highlights the intimate and irreducible relationship between hope and care by capturing 'what is at stake' in specific situations of antiretroviral shortage (Kleinman and Kleinman 1991: 277). The stock-out of antiretrovirals demonstrates how this relationship is embodied and situated reflexively in the improvisation of measures – as the case of Dr Niwagaba's introduction of an ethical threshold showed. I described this reflexivity in medical improvisations as a form of moral courage which runs against the assumption that hope dies with occurrence of stock-outs. Many things have to be done during stock-outs. Hope has its own ethics and logics of care. One just cannot be passive and wait when patients need treatment. Nelson, as the chairperson, urged me to run focus group discussions on clients' experiences of stock-outs. Dr Niwagaba's decision to ration drugs and suspend the enrolment of patients, as the awaited drugs failed to arrive, required the continuous improvisation of therapy in order to provide care under conditions of severely limited resources. Even the repair work to fix the measurement systems in order to then manage the supply of medicines is only provisionally finished and necessitates further maintenance work in the near future, because global health funding will probably always be uncertain. It is precisely these improvisations of treatment which counter false optimistic views on the future of antiretroviral therapy, and simultaneously prevent us from concluding that the future of antiretroviral therapy is utterly hopeless.

References

Adorno, Theodor W. 1951. *Minima Moralia*. Frankfurt a.M.: Suhrkamp (English translation: Adorno, Theodor W. 2005. *Minima Moralia: Reflections on a Damaged Life*. London/New York: Verso)

Barnett, Tony and Alan Whiteside 2006. 'HIV/AIDS, Mobilizing and Spending: Current Purposes and Problems', paper prepared for the High-level Meeting on Trans-Atlantic Collaboration organized by the Center for Strategic and International Studies (CSIS) and Ministère Des Affaires Etrangères, Paris, 12–13 March

Comaroff, Jean 2007. 'Beyond Bare Life: AIDS, (Bio)Politics, and the Neoliberal Order', *Public Culture* 19(1): 197–219

Coutinho, Alex 2004. 'Capturing the HIV/AIDS Epidemic', *Lancet* 364(9449): 1929–30

Crapanzano, Vincent 2003. 'Reflections on Hope as a Category of Social and Psychological Analysis', *Cultural Anthropology* 18(1): 3–32

David, Pierre-Marie 2014. 'Towards the Embodiment of Biosocial Resistance? How to Account for the Unexpected Effects of Antiretroviral Scale-up in the Central African Republic', *Global Public Health* 9(1–2): 144–59

Dewey, John 1920. *Reconstruction in Philosophy*. New York: H. Holt and Company

Douglas, Mary and Aaron B. Wildavsky 1982. *Risk and Culture: An Essay on the Selection of Technical and Environmental Dangers*. Berkeley, Calif.: University of California Press

Espeland, Wendy and Michael Sauder 2007. 'Rankings and Reactivity: How Public Measures Recreate Social Worlds', *American Journal of Sociology* 113(1): 1–40

Fassin, Didier 2009. 'Another Politics of Life is Possible', *Theory, Culture and Society* 26(5): 44–60

Feierman, Steven 2011. 'When Physicians Meet: Local Medical Knowledge and Global Public Goods' in P.W. Geissler and C. Molyneux (eds.),

Evidence, Ethos and Experiment: The Anthropology and History of Medical Research in Africa. New York: Berghahn Books, pp. 171–96

Foucault, Michel 1978. *The History of Sexuality*. New York: Pantheon Books
2003. *Society Must be Defended: Lectures at the Collége de France, 1975–76*. New York: Picador

Geissler, Paul Wenzel, Julia Zenker and Richard Rottenburg 2012. '21st Century African Biopolitics: Fuzzy Fringes, Cracks and Undersides, Neglected Backwaters, and Returning Politics' in P.W. Geissler, J. Zenker and R. Rottenburg (eds.), *Rethinking Biomedicine and Governance in Africa*. Bielefeld: Transcript, pp. 7–22

GFATM 2009. *Follow up Review of the Global Fund Grants to Uganda*. Office of the Inspector General Uganda

Hardon, Anita 2012. 'Biomedical Hype and Hopes: AIDS Medicines for Africa' in P.W. Geissler, J. Zenker and R. Rottenburg (eds.), *Rethinking Biomedicine and Governance in Africa*. Bielefeld: Transcript, pp. 77–96

Jackson, Michael 2011. *Life Within Limits: Well-being in a World of Want*. Durham, N.C.: Duke University Press

Jitta, Jessica, Susan Reynolds Whyte and Nathan Nshakira 2003. 'The Availability of Drugs: What Does It Mean in Ugandan Primary Care', *Health Policy* 65: 167–79

Kaleeba, N., S. Kalibala, M. Kaseje, P. Ssebbanja, S. Anderson, E. Van Praag, G. Tembo and E. Katabira 1997. 'Participatory Evaluation of Counselling, Medical and Social Services of The AIDS Support Organization (TASO) in Uganda', *AIDS Care* 9(1): 13–26

Katabira, Elly T. and Robert B. Oelrichs 2007. 'Scaling Up Antiretroviral Treatment in Resource-Limited Settings: Successes and Challenges', *AIDS* 21: S5–S10

Kleinman, Arthur and Joan Kleinman 1991. 'Suffering and Its Professional Transformation: Toward an Ethnography of Interpersonal Experience', *Culture, Medicine and Psychiatry* 15(3): 275

Lear, Jonathan 2006. *Radical Hope: Ethics in the Face of Cultural Devastation*. Cambridge, Mass.: Harvard University Press

Livingston, Julie 2012. *Improvising Medicine: An African Oncology Ward in an Emerging Cancer Epidemic*. Durham, N.C.: Duke University Press

Meinert, Lotte, Hanne O. Mogensen and Jenipher Twebaze 2009. 'Tests for Life Chances: CD4 Miracles and Obstacles in Uganda', *Anthropology and Medicine* 16(2): 195–209

Merry, Sally Engle 2011. 'Measuring the World: Indicators, Human Rights, and Global Governance', *Current Anthropology* 52(S3): 83–95

Ministry of Health 2011. *Status Report on the Global Fund Grants in Uganda*. Ministry of Health, Republic of Uganda

Miyazaki, Hirokazu 2004. *The Method of Hope: Anthropology, Philosophy, and Fijian Knowledge*. Stanford, Calif.: Stanford University Press

MoFPED 2013. *Millennium Development Goals Report for Uganda 2013*

Mogensen, Hanne 2010. 'New Hope and New Dilemmas: Disclosure and Recognition in the Time of Antiretroviral Treatment' in Ute Luig and Hansjörg Dilger (eds.), *Morality, Hope and Grief: Anthropologies of AIDS in Africa*. New York: Berghahn Books, pp. 61–80

Nguyen, Vinh-Kim 2010. *The Republic of Therapy: Triage and Sovereignty in West Africa's Time of AIDS*. Durham, N.C.: Duke University Press

Park, Sung-Joon 2013. *Pharmaceutical Government: An Ethnography of Stock-Outs and the Institutionalization of Free Access to ART in Uganda*, Ph.D thesis. Department of Anthropology, Martin-Luther University Halle/Germany

Pfeiffer, James 2013. 'The Struggle for a Public Sector' in Joao Biehl and Adriana Petryna (eds.), *When People Come First: Critical Studies in Global Health*. Princeton, N.J.: Princeton University Press

Redfield, Peter 2013. *Life in Crisis: The Ethical Journey of Doctors Without Borders*. Berkeley, Calif.: University of California Press

Robins, Steven 2006. 'From "Rights" to "Rituals": AIDS Activism in South Africa', *American Anthropologist* 108(2): 312–23

Rose, Nikolas and Carlos Novas 2005. 'Biological Citizenship' in S. Collier and A. Ong (eds.), *Global Assemblages, Anthropological Problems*. Malden, Mass.: Blackwell Publishing, pp. 440–63

Rottenburg, Richard 2009a. *Far-fetched Facts: A Parable of Development Aid*. Cambridge, Mass.: MIT Press

2009b. 'Social and Public Experiments and New Figurations of Science and Politics in Postcolonial Africa', *Postcolonial Studies* 12(4): 423–40

Schwartländer, Bernhard, John Stover, Timothy Hallett, Rifat Atun, Carlos Avila, Eleanor Gouws, Michael Bartos *et al.* 2011. 'Towards an Improved Investment Approach for an Effective Response to HIV/AIDS', *Lancet* 377(9782): 2031–41

Sidibé, Michel, Peter Piot and Mark Dybul 2012. 'AIDS is Not Over', *Lancet* 380(9859): 2058–60

UNAIDS 2012. *AIDS Dependency Crisis: Sourcing African Solutions*, Issues Brief

United Nations 2014. *Millennium Development Goals Report 2014*

Van Ufford, Quarles, Ananta Kumar Giri and David Mosse 2003. 'Interventions in Development: Towards a New Moral Understanding of Our Experiences and an Agenda for the Future' in Q. van Ufford and A. K. Giri (eds.), *A Moral Critique of Development*. London: Routledge, pp. 3–40

Weber, Max 1922/1976. *Wirtschaft und Gesellschaft*. 5th edn, Tübingen: Mohr

Whyte, Susan Reynolds 1997. *Questioning Misfortune: The Pragmatics of Uncertainty in Eastern Uganda*. Cambridge/New York: Cambridge University Press

Whyte, Susan Reynolds, Michael A. Whyte, Lotte Meinert and Jenipher Twebaze 2013. 'Therapeutic Clientship: Belonging in Uganda's Mosaic of

AIDS Projects' in João Biehl and Adriana Petryna (eds.), *When People Come First: Anthropology and Social Innovation in Global Health*. Princeton, N.J.: Princeton University Press

World Health Organization 2003. *Scaling Up Antiretroviral Therapy: Experience in Uganda*, WHO Perspectives and Practice in Antiretroviral Treatment. Geneva: WHO

2009. *Rapid Advice: Antiretroviral Therapy for HIV Infection in Adults and Adolescents*, available at www.who.int/hiv/pub/mtct/advice/en/

2013. *Consolidated Guidelines on HIV Prevention, Diagnosis, Treatment and Care for Key Populations*. Geneva: WHO

Zigon, Jarrett 2009. 'Hope Dies Last: Two Aspects of Hope in Contemporary Moscow', *Anthropological Theory* 9(3): 253–71

Zournazi, Mary 2003. *Hope: New Philosophies for Change*. New York: Routledge

CHAPTER NINE

FINANCIAL INDICATORS AND THE GLOBAL FINANCIAL CRASH

Andrew Farlow

In 2007 and 2008, large swathes of the global economy were plunged into the biggest financial crash and economic recession since 1929. Problems surfaced first in countries with large banking sectors and those that had heavily gorged themselves on private-sector debt, especially in the United States and Europe, with some Middle-Eastern and emerging economy flavouring. The trigger for previous major 'global' recessions had usually been some sort of shock: an oil price spike, war, inflation, a technological disturbance. This time, collapse was linked to the malfunctioning of the financial system itself. It was aggravated by financial firms engaged in an intense battle to redistribute the fruits of economic activity towards themselves.

There is value in viewing the financial crash through a fresh lens, that of the indicators at the heart of the financial system. We start with the metrics used to measure and manage risk. We proceed to credit ratings, manufactured by specialist agencies to a set of recipes, seasoned with their own opinions, and applied to just about anything of financial interest. Then, we turn to the information generated by markets in financial instruments, such as Asset-Backed Securities (ABSs), and derivatives, such as Credit Default Swaps (CDSs, a form of insurance). With the 'market' being increasingly used to manage and regulate financial behaviour, such 'market-based' prices were taking an ever more central role. Finally, regulators relied upon a range of indicators of bank capital and (not especially) bank liquidity (i.e. the ability to convert assets into cash at little notice).

We immediately face a puzzle. If financial indicators pointed to dangers and yet were ignored, that would be one thing. However, just before the crash, all the standard financial indicators declared the financial system safe. Credit ratings for financial firms flashed up strings of As. The prices of CDSs (i.e. the cost of insurance) on bundles of loans, especially subprime mortgages, were at record lows. Banks were deemed well capitalized, and regulators were proving adept at looking tough. A Eurozone crisis was even more unlikely, according to the ratings of, and interest rates charged on, the sovereign debt of Ireland, Greece, Spain, Italy, Cyprus and others, and the costs of insuring such sovereign debt against default as expressed in the prices of CDSs on it.[1] Even just a year or two before it happened, this was the crash that was not to be. How could *this* be? Even more puzzling for economists, why did poor financial indicators survive given that standard economic narratives of 'efficient markets' said they should not?

The mid-2000s were, by conventional measures, some of the most stable on economic record. It was the era of the 'Great Moderation'. According to recent legend, not only had gyrations in inflation, GDP and unemployment been confined to economic history, but so too had financial crises.

Ironically (we now see, the fog having finally lifted), it was those balancing atop the giddying pinnacles of high finance who were being congratulated for this happy turn of events. That prodigious storyteller himself, Alan Greenspan, declared (at an appropriately safe distance before the crash): 'The use of a growing array of derivatives and the related application of more-sophisticated approaches to measuring and managing risk are key factors underpinning the greater resilience of our largest financial institutions' (Greenspan 2005). Central bankers were keen to share in the praise too. Ben Bernanke, the soon to be new chair of the US Federal Reserve, added that: 'Improvements in the execution of monetary policy can plausibly account for a significant part of the Great Moderation' (Bernanke 2004). The economic syrup had tasted good and, to keep it flowing, the general public had time and again voted in those who tempted economic disaster (until disaster happened, and the public were suitably

---

[1] The difference (i.e. the 'spread') between the costs of CDSs to insure Eurozone periphery sovereign debt and CDSs to insure the 'risk-free' sovereign debt of, for example, the United States, was extremely low.

outraged). Words of a crash – rarely, if ever, whispered in the hallowed corridors of Treasuries and Central Banks, or the inner sanctums of media outlets – were those of a tiny group of ungrateful and uncouth intelligentsia.

Yet, the dangers were clear to anyone with a care to scratch the surface. The financial sector had swelled enormously, and was increasingly concentrated into a few very large banks, with low rates of entry and exit. Globally, in 2008 just 145 banks controlled at least US$100 billion each in assets, 85 per cent of the assets of the biggest 1,000 banks in the world, and between 1998 and 2008, the fraction of global banking assets held by the five largest global banks doubled, from about 8 per cent to 16 per cent (Haldane 2010). In the United States between 1990 and 2005, the largest ten banks increased their market share from 25 to 55 per cent (Jones and Oshinsky 2009). There was even animated talk of the 'financialization' of a number of economies, as the share of their GDPs shifted towards their financial sectors. For example, in 1947 manufacturing accounted for 25.6 per cent of the GDP of the United States, and finance (including insurance and real estate) for only 10.4 per cent; by 2009, the figures were 11.2 per cent and 21.5 per cent, respectively. There was an astonishing build-up of debt, especially *inside* the financial sector itself. Maturity transformation (referring to the way short-term 'liquid' funds are used to support long-term 'illiquid' assets, many based on overvalued real estate) was becoming increasingly stretched, making the balance sheets of financial firms ever more fragile (Hellwig 2009). Lending was becoming more supply- and less demand-driven (Shin 2009), a symptom of so-called secular stagnation, as investment opportunities struggled to keep up with savings (and real interest rates were not allowed to be negative) (Teulings and Baldwin 2014). Global economic imbalances fed global financial imbalances, and encouraged an increasingly lax attitude towards financial quality (Farlow 2013: Part I).

Why were signs of danger so often ignored, especially by those with the power to act? One key reason was the collective declaration of safety being issued by the financial market indicators. Rattling through all this is the uncomfortable question: for all their self-conferred markers of smartness – high salaries and enormous bonuses – were those working in the financial sector really ignorant of the dangers, or much more knowing? Did they fall, or were they pushed? Or, worse, did they even jump?

RISK AND ITS INDICATORS

The principal purpose of a financial system is to efficiently distribute savings and investment across economic sectors and over time, against a blanket of uncertainty. Keynes drew the distinction between 'irreducible uncertainty' which cannot be calculated accurately, and 'risk' which can, between the majority of economic cases when at best only an 'interval estimate' is possible and the few cases when probability can be calculated to a single number (a point estimate) (Keynes 1921). Knight got a whole book out of the distinction between uncertainty and risk, observing: 'You cannot be certain about uncertainty' (Knight 1921; Turner 2008).

Sadly, true 'Knightian' uncertainty never proved an easy concept to model, let alone measure. Increasingly, the burgeoning academic disciplines of economics and finance required uncertainty that was – well – much more certain. And so, unmeasurable 'uncertainty' was made measureable, in the shape of 'risk', and true uncertainty skulked off into the peripheries of the discipline, where the strong socializing forces of academic economics and finance kept it appropriately restrained.

Investors worry about a range of risks. A few stand out. First, there is the chance that borrowers will default, and investors will not get their money (i.e. their 'principal') back at maturity. Second, they worry about interest rates, which determine the present value (i.e. expressed as a lump sum now) of streams of future payments. Third, increasingly, they worry about liquidity risk: at moments of crisis, there are many sellers of assets who have no choice but to sell, but there are not many buyers, and asset prices fall without warning. To complicate matters, appetites for holding risk vary; if investors *en masse* become more willing to accept lower payments (i.e. 'risk premiums') for holding financial products, this could either be because their risk appetites have not changed but the risks embodied in financial products have genuinely fallen, or because investors' appetites for bearing given levels of risk have risen. If the latter, the issue then becomes whether this is rational, perhaps the sign of a more efficient financial system, or instead based on 'irrational' market psychology.

Risk is a constructed concept, based on a model or models, of how economic worlds work. This necessitates that economic uncertainty – a notion that resides, invisible, inside the heads of investors, managers, consumers and others – be converted into a set of externally-verifiable parameters and mathematized. The shift in the academic discipline of finance towards this analytical, mathematical, economics-focused approach started in the 1950s, especially from within US business schools, and grew strongly in the 1960s and 1970s, paralleling similar developments in economics. It was aided and abetted by advances in computing that allowed financial theories for the first time to be tested (Mackenzie 2006).

Before the crash, the view was widespread (after all, bankers and regulators had eagerly championed it) that those working in finance had developed sophisticated risk management models. However, at the heart of these sat a range of questionable assumptions.

First, the risk of holding stocks, bonds, housing and other assets was modelled on the basis of the volatility of their prices, and the degree of diversification of the portfolios in which they sat. This had strong ideological roots: if markets are always 'right', the use of market prices is the 'efficient' way to go. As a consequence, the less volatile are asset prices and interest rates, the more certain are the prices of stocks and bonds, and the higher are their present values. In the years before the crash, when interest rates hit (till then) record lows, this helped to boost to historically high levels the recorded capital positions and profitability of financial institutions.

Such thinking backfires at times of 'irrational exuberance' (Shiller 2000), when always-expanding asset price bubbles artificially suppress asset price volatility and generate measures of low apparent risk. This justifies higher credit ratings, which encourage capital to enter and banks to expand, which pumps asset price bubbles some more, which makes the apparent low risk, for a while, self-sustaining. In a collapse, the process goes into reverse. In hindsight, it seems pretty dumb to allow periods of apparent economic stability to sow the seeds of future instability (Minsky 2008), but it was encouraged by many financial firms, and tolerated by regulators. And the public was happy enough.

Second, there was the habit of using past patterns of price movements to infer probability distributions over future patterns of price movements. This involved taking a technique from physics, in which a random sample is drawn from a definitely existing universe of events to determine the probability characteristics governing future random samples. This was methodologically unsound in the world of social and economic relationships where apparent correlations are based on configurations of economic forces and players, the possible persistence of which requires some economic, and indeed historical, judgment.

Third, probability distributions over price movements were presumed to be normal. Yet, we have known for a long time that financial-market price movements have 'fat tail' properties which are somehow linked to the sudden synchronization of investors. That is, there are many more price movements than is normal in the tails of the probability distribution of financial-market price movements (Mandelbrot and Hudson 2004; Taleb 2007); and that these 'fat tails' are somehow linked to the sudden synchronization of investors. Risk models stuck to idiosyncratic behaviour, and the notion that the actions of each individual can be safely treated as having negligible impact on any other individual and on overall market behaviour.

Fourth, treating risk in terms of asset price movements and portfolios took attention away from who was holding different risks. For example, the capacity to absorb liquidity risk is greater when there is more time to sell an asset, which suggests that a financial system is safer if liquidity risks are held by, for example, pension funds. Instead, rules about mark-to-market valuations (whereby the 'fair value' of an asset or liability is based on its current market price or that of similar assets and liabilities) that shaped capital requirements, short-term solvency and risk, positively discouraged pension funds from holding the liquidity risks they were best suited to hold. Meanwhile, the capacity to absorb credit risk is higher if there is a wide array of uncorrelated credit risks that can be pooled together. When, instead, large consumer banks laid off their credit risks onto non-banks, such as hedge funds, pension funds and insurance companies, who wanted the extra yield but had limited ability to hedge the credit risk and no requirement to hold capital against concentrated credit risk, the whole financial system became less safe. The emphasis on quantitative models and measurement took attention away from more qualitative dimensions of risk management, involving information flows and the motives and incentives of those holding risks (Blommestein, Hoogduin and Peeters 2009).

Greenspan was at the scene of the final fantasy:

> In recent decades, a vast risk management and pricing system has evolved, combining the best insights of mathematicians and finance experts supported by major advances in computer and communications technology … The whole intellectual edifice, however, collapsed in the summer of last year because the data inputted into the risk management models generally covered only the past two decades, a period of euphoria.
>
> (Greenspan 2008)

In the case of real estate, the data series used were of even shorter durations; in the United States, the risk models presumed that US house prices could not fall, on the slenderest of foundations that they never previously had. With even less history to go on, new financial products were underpriced because of a lack of historical data, insufficient grasp of systemic risk and plain poor judgment.

Risk was not just a mathematical concept. In the years before the crash, 'risk' was increasingly turned into its own asset class, traded on markets, and the prices generated used as 'market-based' indicators. Two products stand out.[2] The first, Asset-Backed Securities (ABSs), of which Mortgage-Backed Securities (MBSs) are a subcategory, involves slicing, dicing and re-bundling debt to suit different investors' tastes. Instead of holding loans on their books to maturity, financial institutions got to bundle and offload them, in a process called 'securitization', at a single point in time, and pocketing a payment to reflect all of time. The second, Credit Default Swaps (CDSs), involves the purchaser of a CDS paying a regular premium to the writer of the CDS, in exchange for which the writer of the CDS promises to pay a specified sum should the underlying security specified in the contract default.

The justification for securitization is that it opens up risk assessment to 'the market.' The prices of the new bundles, as determined by the market, supposedly reflect the risks contained therein. Meanwhile, the collective price-discovery process in the market for CDSs generates new indicators of credit risk.[3] If a bank is making loans with high risks of default, this is reflected in higher costs to insure itself via CDSs. At some point, it might decide to tame its risky activities. Both securitization and CDSs supposedly reduce the concentration of credit risk in the financial system by allowing non-banks to bear some of it, making financial firms and the economy more resilient to shocks.

In truth, as a consequence of securitization, a lot of the tasks that hitherto got performed by the credit risk departments within financial firms got shifted onto credit rating agencies external to them. Few questioned whether the external expertise was any better than the internal expertise it replaced. Meanwhile, the CDS market allowed mortgage banks to offload their credit risks to non-banks, including companies such as AIG, who could get exposure to an underlying credit instrument without committing significant funds to actually buying it. In

---

[2] There are others, but there is insufficient space to cover all possibilities here.
[3] For example CDSs spreads, for example, over 'risk free' US Treasury bonds, were used in internal credit models.

their turn, those who took on the credit risk via CDSs were not regulated like banks, and so did not need to fund themselves with the levels of capital a bank would have to. The owners of AIG did agreeably well out of charging too little for their insurance services because, although they made huge profits while nobody made a claim against them, it was taxpayers who paid up when all the claims eventually came tumbling in.

Such market-based financial indicators relied on markets always being liquid, with no constraints ever on buyers or sellers. This proved to be one assumption too far. When, starting in 2006, the US housing market turned, the prices of securitized bundles of loans based upon it collapsed, and the obligations in the defaulting CDS contracts became so unclear that any informativeness that CDSs might have had as indicators was destroyed.

Working together, securitization and CDSs, with the help of credit ratings, fashioned a particularly egregious example of (what we might call) 'responsibility shifting'. Banks first transformed mortgage debt, much of it of poor quality, into layers, or tranches that included an unjustifiably large number that were triple-A rated. With the quality of the underlying debt exaggerated upwards, the level of regulatory capital needed to support it got dragged downwards. Then they got the capital requirement near to zero with insurance, via CDSs, that shifted the credit risk on to others, such as AIG. Such insurance practices, combined with the faulty credit rating practices we will shortly discuss, gave banks the confidence to lend to those who would not repay. Again, we hit the question: were those operating in such markets stupid, or knowing?

Excessive risk-taking was linked to limited liability. Limited liability serves a useful purpose. Many high-payoff, high-risk investments fail, but the successful few more than outweigh the failures; imposing limitless liability on bankers will hold back the successes. But limited liability has a big downside.

An important source of limited liability comes courtesy of government insurance of banks, often implicitly and for free or at a very low cost, and often forced onto governments by banks being Too Big To Fail (TBTF). There is deposit insurance to protect banks' retail deposits, liquidity insurance to protect their wholesale deposits, and capital insurance to protect their equity. While such measures stop depositors and investors panicking when they see others withdrawing deposits or terminating their investments, this creates moral hazard; knowing they get to take the upside and leave the downside to the insurance 'fund', banks take bigger risks, which increase the chances of financial crashes.

The danger is especially high when bankers' rewards are aligned with those of bank shareholders, for example, through bonuses and options linked to shareholders' rewards (with no ability to claw bankers' rewards back later). This incentivizes bankers to tank up on debt (in the sense of ownership stakes of bondholders in their banks) per unit of bank shareholder equity (that is, to increase their leverage) so as to pump their own returns. So long as nothing out and out illegal is done (or bankers are not careless enough to get caught), the punishment if things go wrong is at most the loss of a bonus. With compensation biased on the upside, being overly optimistic in risk assessments was also more profitable than being pessimistic.

When making a mess of a financial system, it is generally best to go the whole hog. Governments are far less inclined to bail out half-hearted failures than they are complete and utter fiascos. To maximize the expected value of this takes skill and no small amount of imagination, but the key is to push up the chances of getting an outcome in the extreme 'tail' of the distribution over outcomes, that is, to increase the 'tail risks', by making the banking system deliberately, not accidentally, more fragile. As well as increasing bank leverage, other common strategies included holding larger trading books, taking on more tail-heavy financial instruments, engaging in greater business diversification, and writing deep 'out-of-the-money' options (such as CDSs) (Haldane 2010). The mission was aided by risk metrics that were incapable of alerting to the dangers of tail risks. In their enthusiasm to eke more profit out of every unit of initial bank capital by leveraging it with ever more debt, banks multiplied the repercussions of poor credit rating practices, to which we now turn.

CREDIT RATINGS

Perhaps the best-known, and most ubiquitous, financial market indicators are credit ratings – each, supposedly, an impartial, objective assessment of the creditworthiness of a debt obligator, or, more crudely put, of whether or not a borrower is likely to default. Sadly, credit ratings were victims of all the risk modelling faults described above and, for good measure, added a few of their own (Standard & Poor's 2001).

The role of credit ratings is to offset the asymmetry of information between borrowers and lenders, and to economize on evaluation and monitoring costs: a bank is more informed about its own quality than those investing in it, each of whom cannot expend resources on evaluating the bank's quality; those buying fancy new financial products can't be expected to evaluate the risks of all the parts that go into the securitization process; and millions of investors don't have the know-how and resources to model the financial health of nations. Instead of investors (that is the 'market') being left to form their own judgments based on masses of information, credit rating agencies became key centres of calculation to which many, and the market, deferred for judgment.

It seems that nothing is not fair game to be rated: banks, financial instruments, governments and firms. Ratings, supposedly, standardize knowledge across investors, and allow all investment options to be measured, compared and ranked not only within an instrument class, but across different instrument classes.

In theory, ratings also discipline. The more likely a firm is to default, the lower its credit rating, the higher its costs of finance, and the lower its share price; a low rating incentivizes a firm to reduce the riskiness of its activities. The lower the credit ratings on securitized bundles of mortgages, the higher the risk premium that needs to be paid on them, and the fewer such bundles will be created. The lower a country's credit rating, the harder for that country to access financial markets to roll-over its debt, and the higher its costs of borrowing, and the more likely it will try to avoid being in such a situation in the first place.

With the rise of debt of many sorts, the need for credit ratings rose. In the case of Mortgage-Backed Securities (MBSs), securitization divided the income streams from the underlying mortgage debts into different layers, or tranches, the credit ratings of which reflected their qualities, with a rule for allocating progressive default losses on mortgages. Investors with different risk profiles could choose the tranches that most suited their needs. The first income streams got allocated to the tranches rated AAA, with the (supposedly) lowest risks of default. Investors who were more risk-averse or required by regulators to hold only AAA-rated assets, would take these. With the 'good bits' rated AAA, investors no longer felt the urge to check the underlying quality for themselves. Those prepared to take the risk that they would not get paid or get paid less than expected, took lower-rated tranches, in return for a higher payment in those states where payment was made. To those who took the AAA-rated bundles, the remaining 'bad bits', a necessary by-product to get their hands on all the 'good bits', conveniently were someone else's problem. Ratings aided and abetted responsibility shifting. Banking supervisors, managers and accountants deferred to credit rating agencies to avoid having to do their own checks. Investors did not feel the need to peek inside the wrappings of subprime-based MBSs because the rating agencies had already declared the contents good. This was all a bit too convenient.

Yet, the AAA-rated bundles turned out to be unusually unsafe in a crash. AAA securities carry more systemic risk than lower-rated securities because they only lose value in a systemic crash; at such times their decline in value forces onto their holders a much greater need for new capital than is the case for those holding BBB-rated securities (which already pay more to compensate for higher expected losses, and their risks are idiosyncratic and more diversifiable). Much of what passed for AAA was a mirage (Farlow 2013: 106).

It is the instruments, not their issuers, which are given credit ratings. For corporate bonds the distinction hardly matters. For Asset-Backed Securities it does. A corporation is a dynamic entity. Facing a potential downgrade, it can if necessary inject fresh capital to avoid default. For a corporation, the loss of a reputation for creditworthiness will raise its future borrowing costs; a corporation has no incentive to default on its debt, if under neutral conditions it would stay creditworthy. In contrast, ABSs are based on the performance of a static pool of assets. If the quality of the pool deteriorates – for example, because house prices are collapsing and mortgage defaults are rising – nobody expects the original issuers to improve the quality of the pool by a costly act like injecting their own capital.

Corporate debt ratings involve firm-specific judgments, based on long historical records. A firm's long-run condition needs to be teased out from the fluctuations of the business cycle, to determine if an industry downturn is temporary or permanent, and to what degree a firm can withstand a temporary downturn. In contrast, ABS ratings involve macroeconomic forecasts and estimates of how sensitive losses are to those forecasts, both of which are vulnerable to errors. With no 'real world' records to judge performance against, the ratings of ABSs involved imagined 'possible' worlds. The ratings agencies, without history or context, and in need of a few assumptions, were subject to the same 'conventionality' bias prevalent in economics and finance. In particular, their core models presumed stable financial markets.

As the numbers of securitized products exploded, regulatory inertia (rules took years to negotiate and involved large sunk costs, making it hard to change direction) rubbed up against the huge private benefits to be had by continuing to apply the logic of corporate credit ratings to the credit ratings of ABSs.

It is easy to be harsh on credit rating agencies. Yet, they were warning for a long time about the possibility of a housing market downturn in the United States. However, in their ratings of MBSs, they massively underestimated the scale of the potential downturn and compounded this by failing to spot the falling quality of the underlying mortgages.

Actually, it was worse. To protect investors, each MBS tranche came with a 'credit enhancement', a buffer posted against potential losses. A credit rating on an MBS tranche is a rating agency's assessment that conditions will deteriorate to the point that losses on the tranche will exceed its credit enhancement. If the enhancement is bigger, it takes much more deterioration for losses to exceed the enhancement, and this justifies a higher credit rating. To stabilize credit ratings 'through the business cycle' (avoiding upgrades in booms and downgrades in busts), rating agencies adjust the amount of the credit enhancement required in new financial products at any given rating. In the case of MBSs, the required enhancement fell when the housing market rose, making mortgage financing cheaper and encouraging speculation and higher house prices. When the required enhancement rose when the market fell, this, naturally enough, amplified the crash. Thus, the attempt to make credit ratings less volatile made the required credit enhancements more volatile. The dangers of this were largely ignored.

Odd though it may look now, rating agencies also conditioned their ratings on their expectations that banks would be bailed out by their governments. Thus, when Icelandic banks were engaging in some very risky behaviour, the rating agencies made it clear that their ratings were as much about the solvency of the Icelandic government as of the country's banks. Then, after the crash, when many financial institutions suffered downgrades, those financial institutions that were treated more leniently by their governments saw their credit ratings more quickly upgraded.

The procyclical consequences extended also to how credit ratings got used. Counterparties on derivative (and many other) contracts, i.e. those who were obligated to pay out in particular circumstances dictated in the contracts, had to post collateral, in the shape of assets or cash, as 'security' to protect those on the other side of such contracts. The level of required collateral was linked to the credit ratings of the counterparties. So, for example, when the credit rating of AIG was downgraded in September 2008, this triggered the need for AIG to post extra collateral to support the CDSs it had entered into. AIG's efforts to do so exacerbated a downward spiral of falling asset prices, falling access to funding, an even lower credit rating for AIG, more need for AIG to sell assets to generate collateral, and so on. Such built-in ratings-based triggers depressed the value of the collateral of other financial firms, forcing similar problems onto them.

Credit ratings, like the risk models used in their derivation, reflected the systemic stability of the moment, and not the potential systemic instability. Their comfort zone was standard idiosyncratic risk, and the rating agencies made minimal effort to incorporate system-wide, cyclical risk. As one of the rating agencies put it: 'Moody's believes that giving only modest weight to cyclical conditions serves the interests of the bulk of investors' (Moody's Investors Services 1999: 6–7). The onus was on regulatory agencies, not the rating agencies, to act against system-wide risk, a responsibility they had little enthusiasm to fulfil.

In the build up to the crash, credit ratings failed spectacularly to flag the growing dangers, and encouraged the misallocation of capital on a grand scale. In the crash, credit rating downgrades and the system-wide forced selling of assets this triggered, created a self-fulfilling spiral that reinforced collapse. Credit ratings were a placebo when the patients were already sick, a poison when they were on their deathbeds.

Credit ratings performed poorly in part because of the conflicts of interest that credit rating agencies faced. Ratings are expensive to produce, but also public goods (once produced, everyone gets to see them for free). To avoid their under-provision, they are created by specialist bodies, the rating agencies, and paid for by the issuers whose products are being rated.

Issuers shopped around, across both rating agencies and the liabilities structures of the ABS they were seeking to get rated (Fender and Kiff 2004), and the rating agencies obliged by giving to pools of loans ratings that were far too generous (Shin 2009). Furthermore, the rating agencies, clients of those they sort to discipline, earned generous fees from consultation on how to construct securities to achieve particular ratings at the lowest possible cost. Fee rates on complex financial securities were more than double those on simpler corporate ones; no wonder then that, on the eve of the crash, Moody's operating margins were more than 50 per cent. With the explosive growth in debt-based instruments in need of 'expert' assessments, demand for the services of credit rating agencies boomed, and they faced little need to worry about the falling quality of much of what they rated. The rating agencies were also an oligopoly. Though their role was to help enforce capitalist pressure on others, they felt less of the same pressure on themselves. To some, this was 'the final nail in the coffin' (Ashcraft and Schuermann 2008). For competition authorities vested with the job of enforcing competition, on this particular oligopoly there seemed little enthusiasm to lift the lid.

Credit ratings became part of the broader movement towards risk management and regulation by 'the market'. Though ratings are derived by rating agencies (or internally within financial firms according to their own risk models), in all cases it is 'the market' that determines the fates of those being rated. Yet, for all the rhetoric, credit ratings replaced 'market-based' processes with processes based on fallible institutions and their opinions. As loans based on long-term relationships (such as between home buyers and mortgage banks) were bundled and turned into securities and traded on markets, those markets relied on institutions, not markets, to be the arbiters of the quality of the underlying loans. And so credit ratings found themselves at the heart of a grand tautology. Credit ratings were mythologized as somehow from outside, over and above, the 'market', helping to discipline 'the market' to be efficient. Yet, credit ratings were controlled by the market. For example, the test of the validity of the AAA ratings of subprime MBSs came from the market (which actually signifies the collective mass of investors) that traded in MBSs. This 'market' was inefficient, and therefore poorly disciplined the credit rating agencies and encouraged laxity in their MBS ratings. This allowed institutions, in the shape of banks themselves, to drive much of the action under the cover that it was the ratings that exercised ultimate authority.

It is easier to pass on to the rest of society the costs of a collapsing asset price bubble if it is based on debt than if it is based on equity. Though prices on a stock market move around in response to new pieces of information, this does not trigger a systemic collapse and the need for a bail-out. In contrast, the 'prices' of debt contracts, in response to new information reflecting their risk of default, do not move around, but the prices of equity-like securities built out of such contracts do. This builds bail-out commitments into such securities *ex ante*. Many of the securities that failed in the crash were based on credit-rated debt. Did the creation of misleading indicators, especially credit ratings, cause the proliferation of these products, exploiting weaknesses? Or did a financial system, dominated by big financial firms and lending-supply pressures that emphasized quantity over quality, and bursting with equity-like securities that were in fact based on debt, end up needing a lot of credit ratings?

ACCOUNTANCY RULES AGGRAVATE

Risk models and credit ratings depend on accounting and disclosure practices. In the run up to the crash, regulatory reforms pushed in the direction of mark-to-market (also known as fair value) accounting. In the past, accountants would recognize cash only when it had been received or legally committed to be paid. With assets and liabilities mark-to-market, future expected profits, spread over long periods of time, could be treated as if they had already been earned, and taken right away. It was argued that this allowed 'the market' to form an ongoing 'opinion' on, and discipline, the investments of firms.

However, the introduction of IFRS (International Financial Reporting Standards) 'mark-to-market' accounting practices exacerbated the focus on short-term profits and created new opportunities for wealth extraction. In particular, bankers were motivated to encourage asset price bubble; the more difficult to detect the bubble, the easier it was to take false profits before their true identity was realized. The effect could be enhanced hugely by leverage, by holding more assets that are marked to market than are not marked to market, and by treating profits by mark-to-market accounting standards while leaving losses on balance sheets as long as possible. This had the flavour of a Ponzi scheme,[4] with early investors extracting wealth from later investors, or rather, from those who would have to bail the system out.[5]

Then, such accounting practices aggravated the fall in the value of bank balance sheets when the crash came. Instead of an economic

---

[4] A Ponzi investment scheme pulls new investors in by offering returns that beat alternative investments, but then makes good on this promise by using the investments of the later rounds of investors to pay off earlier investors. In the case here, it is taxpayers who eventually pay the returns of earlier investors. Charles Ponzi was so notorious for running such a scheme that they named it after him. In recent years Bernard Madoff perfected the approach, but is yet to be given such an accolade.

[5] Incidentally, such behaviour also drained aggregate demand from the future. But that, as they say, is a story for another day.

shock gradually impairing a loan and marking down its losses steadily over time, mark-to-market practices force financial firms to mark losses down right away. Thus, when the subprime bubble burst, many mortgage defaults that were off in the future got priced into Mortgage-Backed Securities right away. An 'efficient markets' perspective would suggest that the ability for losses to show early and in such damaging fashion would encourage bankers to take less risk. As we now know, such logic mattered not one jot; those who took the profits did not have to pay back bonuses when losses materialized. This was not just a function of accounting practices. Ethnographic analysis reveals just how insecure are the typical workplaces of investment bankers; those who may be let go by their firms at any moment are apt to more heavily discount potential future losses caused by their actions (Ho 2009).

INDICATORS OF BANKING CAPITAL AND LIQUIDITY

When a bank makes losses, they first eat into the ownership stakes of its equity holders (i.e. the capital of the bank's shareholders), and then, when that has gone, into the ownership stakes of its bondholders (i.e. creditors who hold debt in the ownership structure of the bank) in order of their seniority. Bank depositors have no ownership stakes, and so are usually protected against losses. So long as bank owners do not expect to be saved by taxpayers, banks are kept safe by the efforts of their shareholders to discipline them not to take excessive risks that might wipe out their ownership stakes. Shareholders also vote on who runs banks, and lose when share prices fall if risk-taking is judged by the market to be excessive.

A bank's capital ratio is the amount of private capital in the bank as a proportion of its assets (i.e. its loans and investments). A higher ratio means there is more private capital to absorb losses. To the extent this makes a financial institution safer, this improves its credit rating, which helps it to raise funds more cheaply.[6]

But what is the 'optimal' capital ratio from society's perspective? The literature on 'capital adequacy' finds that this is all about mitigating the moral hazard consequences of government insurance of banking (Kim and Santomero 1988; Furlong and Keeley 1989; Rochet 1992; Besanko and Kanatas 1996). Banks pool funds from the rest of society and lend

---

[6] Both supply and demand are at work here. If the wholesale market expands dramatically, this may drive the cost of capital lower for any given credit rating. There is much mythologizing about the costs of equity capital, which is nicely dispelled by Admati et al. (2013).

to long-term projects, allowing individual members of society to access their funds at shorter notice than the length of the projects. The average returns are greater, both for society and for financial institutions, than if only short-term projects are possible. Society and those in banking split the gain. However, this arrangement is vulnerable to bank runs, when many demand their funds back at once, and central banks are forced to intervene. To illustrate, imagine that at one extreme the capital ratio is so high and banks' strategies so safe, that the chance of a bank run is negligible. However, this generates very poor returns and low welfare for society. At the other extreme, the capital ratio is so low and risk-taking so high, that when things do not go wrong, society's welfare is high, but when things go badly, such as in a financial crash, society's welfare is so reduced that, on average (including the high-welfare states), society's welfare is very low.[7] Somewhere between these two extremes, bank strategies are neither too safe nor too risky, the chances of a crash neither too low nor too high, and society's welfare maximized.

To further complicate matters, one bank's capital benefits other banks by reducing the chances of a systemic crash caused by collective behaviour. Like other (positive)[8] public goods, it may go underprovided. If those in banking reason that the state will bail them out in a crash, the incentive to hold capital for public good reasons is even lower.[9]

Over the years, a set of rules, the Basel Accords, were issued by the Basel Committee on Banking Supervision (BCBS), Switzerland, regarding the minimum levels of regulatory capital (a mixture of bank shareholder equity and other reserves and financial instruments) to be held relative to a financial institution's total risk-weighted assets.

Basel I, negotiated between 1974 and 1988, laid down two uniform minimum capital ratios to risk-weighted assets of 2 per cent for Core Tier 1 capital and 8 per cent for Core Tier 1 plus Tier 2 capital (and thus a ratio of average total assets to total Core Tier 1 and Tier 2 capital of 12.5). Bank assets were classified according to their credit risk (i.e. the risk of the borrower defaulting) into five groups, given risk weightings that ranged from 0, for home-country Treasury bonds, cash and

---

[7] Strictly speaking, this is a function too of how investors feel about the riskiness of the 'go-wrong' and the 'not-go-wrong' outcomes.

[8] For there are negative ones too, such as pollution and financial instability.

[9] Even this simplifies. In a full-blown crash, there will never be enough capital or liquidity in banks, and governments will intervene. The point is to make reaching that intervention point much more demanding.

bullion, to 100 per cent for most corporate debt. Securitized assets, such as MBSs, because of their top-notch AAA credit rating, carried just a 20 per cent risk weighting.

Prompted by the Asian financial crisis of 1997–1998, Basel II, negotiated between 1999 and 2004, on the face of it was more sophisticated and, supposedly, tougher. Its goals were to incorporate also operational and market (and not just credit) risk, to make (or so the large international banks argued) capital allocation even more risk-sensitive by allowing large international banks to use their own internal risk models to generate risk weightings, to enhance disclosure requirements so that investors could assess the capital adequacy of particular institutions, and to do more to prevent regulatory arbitrage (i.e. banks getting around the rules).

The alert reader will spot already a number of contradictions between these rules and what we now know in light of the crash. First, MBSs were not at all safe, and did not justify their low 20 per cent weighting. Second, Eurozone banks, required by regulators to hold large amounts of their own governments' Treasury bonds in their capital bases because such bonds were deemed so safe as to be zero weighted, instead exposed themselves to the Eurozone crisis when those countries struggled to repay their bonds. Third, rather than being more risk sensitive, large international banks used the flexibilities of internal models to greatly understate their risk exposures. Fourth, leverage ratios were well above 12.5. Finally, the rules expressed no concern for illiquidity, which turned out to be key to several crash propagation mechanisms (Farlow 2013: ch. 4).

Just for good measure, this was the era of 'light-touch' regulation, facilitated by the myth that the market would discipline bankers far better than any 'man-made' rules. As Greenspan put it in 2005:

> But those unregulated and less heavily regulated entities generally are subject to more-effective market discipline than banks...In essence, prudential regulation is supplied by the market through counterparty evaluation and monitoring rather than by authorities.
>
> (Greenspan 2005)

If regulation had previously been deemed a substitute for monitoring (Dewatripont and Tirole 1994), it quickly followed in Greenspan's logic that the market was a substitute for regulation. And so Basel II emphasized self-regulation. Large international banks convinced leading regulators that only they were expert enough to understand their complex business practices, and (their strongest card of all) that if they got their internal risk weightings wrong, the market would punish them. As a side-effect, regulatory practice came to reflect the dominant paradigm, focusing on the individual ('microprudential') and not the systemic ('macroprudential'), with capital ratios attached only to risks a financial institution inflicts upon itself, and not rising with its contribution to systemic risk.

In response, the incentive for large financial firms was to get as many assets as possible classified as low-risk weighted, so that their balance sheets could be as big as possible, and the return to bank equity as high as possible. In particular, many investment banks overdid their holdings of residential mortgages because these needed less regulatory capital than other types of loans. Both sellers and buyers of MBSs were happy to oblige, because neither of them was particularly interested in the quality of what went into each bundle. Credit ratings certified risky bundles as being of low risk, and the capital adequacy rules authorized investors to hold them. What was there not to like about that?

With zero weighting on off-balance sheet (i.e. they did not appear on a bank's balance sheet) exposures with maturity of less than one year, the rules could be circumnavigated via stand-by loan commitments with rolling maturities of less than one year. These were used to support the activities of (so-called) shadow banks, a motley collection of hedge funds, private equity funds, money market funds, monolines, conduits, structured-investment vehicles (SIVs), and so forth. The rate of growth in the assets of shadow banking was much higher than that of traditional banking (Tobias and Shin 2009), such that shadow banking came to play a significantly larger role than depository institutions. However, though they were functionally very similar to banks, shadow banks did not take deposits, held very little capital, and were not subject to any meaningful prudential requirements as regards their leverage, liquidity or the features of their assets and liabilities. They had few reporting obligations and, being mostly privately held, were accountable to few governance standards.

Just in case shadow banks got into difficulties, their (regulated) sponsoring banks put in place arrangements to provide liquidity or – to avoid costly reputational damage – to take the offending problems back. This meant that shadow banks had indirect recourse to government insurance, even though neither they nor their sponsoring banks had paid for it (in the costs of the sponsoring banks' own capital and liquidity holdings).

In contrast to decades of work on harmonized capital ratios, hardly any effort had gone into harmonized liquidity ratios, and there were no operational liquidity indicators. Many financial firms, especially investment banks, felt they could hold ever more MBSs funded from short-term borrowing, because some MBSs could always be sold quickly in liquid markets if needs be. However, 'liquidity through marketability' only works for individual financial firms facing idiosyncratic shocks. In the crash, when delinquencies and defaults on subprime mortgage started to turn up, many financial firms tried simultaneously to sell assets, and this inflicted lower asset prices on all. This, with the helping hand of fair value accounting, pushed up the leverage of financial firms (the ratio of the value of their loans and investments to the value of their assets), lowered their credit ratings, forced further asset sales, and intensified the initial liquidity problem. Governments felt their arms being twisted to make huge liquidity injections into banking because of the systemic dangers of not doing so.

Was lack of attention to liquidity due to a failure to perceive dangers, or something much more willing? After all, the shadow banking system was built to exploit the lack of regulation of liquidity while still keeping within the capital rules. This was easy to spot at the time, but dealing with it was not part of the mindset of those in positions to act.

INDICATORS AND REGULATION

Being regulated is a precondition – part of the social contract between those working in finance and the rest of society – for financial firms and financial markets to exist in the first place. The financial firms at the heart of the crash were therefore, ostensibly, highly regulated. The Federal Reserve, in the United States, was the most powerful, best-resourced, and best-informed financial regulator in the world. Yet, the crash happened right under its nose. The problem was that regulation was process-oriented, not results-oriented, an exercise in legal compliance that paid too little attention to how banks made their profits. In spite of appearances of there being many international bodies, there was no global regulatory or governance body: the International Monetary Fund and the World Trade Organization had no mandate to force international cooperation to constrain banks; the Financial Stability Board was a talking shop between domestic regulators; and the Bank for International Settlements could recommend but not force.

Financial indicators did not come into being by 'natural market pro-cesses'. They were negotiated: between regulators and the bankers, financiers and associated elites who built the system that collapsed. Those who got to shape the indicators, got to shape the future powers and profits of financial firms and markets. Contestation of the regula-tory space, in the shape of the Basel Accords and global accountancy standards, was at the transnational, not the local level. This made it easier for bad regulation and poor financial indicators to crowd out the better (from society's perspective). Unlike local regulators, those who devised the Basel Accords were not formally accountable within those countries where the Accords were to be applied. This made it very diffi-cult for officials to use public interest grounds to block the negotiation process, especially in its late stages. This gave those representing dom-inant well-resourced financial players an incentive to get their propos-als on the table early, preferably at the agenda-setting stage (the use of firms' own risk measurement systems to derive their internal ratings was put on the agenda of Basel II even before any negotiations, and then lobbied hard). This created a first-mover advantage, and pushed up the sunk cost of regulators at later stages of negotiation (Lall 2014).[10]

In the long negotiations that shaped the Basel Accords, the officials who framed them were frequently less expert than those who were to be subject to them. Officials came to rely upon the superior technical skills of those representing large international banks and, in some cases, they had themselves come from the higher echelons of such banks. There was no role in this for the public or civil society as, for example, had been the case in agenda-setting and policy-making at the WHO. Negotiations were reserved for unaccountable 'experts', whose delib-erations were technocratic and often informal, creating an environ-ment conducive to 'conventional' and 'group' thinking, and intellectual capture.

Basel II was biased towards large well-resourced international banks, who understood a thing or two about economic rent seeking. Rent seek-ing refers to the expenditure of scarce resources to acquire (for example, by securing monopoly power) payments that are above and beyond the minimum payments that otherwise would have been accepted to provide a particular service. In rent-seeking games, regulators are at a

---

[10] Lall (2014) argues that other stakeholders, especially small banks, US community banks and banks from emerging economies, only became aware of the push towards internal credit risk models at the second draft stage of the Accords in 2001, by which time, Lall argues, it was too late.

disadvantage. For large banks, it is worth spending up to the expected value of the economic rent that will be gained. In contrast, regulators, notably in the United States, have to go through a political process to secure their resources. Even if the spending of regulators prevents a lot of rent seeking, it does not get valued on a market. In particular, the avoided costs of a crash never register with the public, but the costs of avoiding a crash do. There was, anyway, low incentive to invest political capital in reforming regulatory frameworks when everything seemed to be working just fine. Indeed, many central banks lost their banking supervisory roles to other bodies, and were increasingly made to concentrate on monetary policy objectives alone.[11] It took a crash to expose the costs of rent seeking and the value of avoiding a crash – by which time, it was too late.

The ability of large international banks to manipulate their capital requirements lower (passing on any negative side-effects to the rest of society) gave them a big competitive advantage over those, such as smaller regional banks, community banks and banks in emerging economies, that had insufficient resources to develop their own internal risk models and who therefore were required to stick to the standardized approach based on the external ratings of credit rating agencies.

Large international banks put themselves and the financial system at risk when they lobbied for Basel II. For all its apparent sophistication, and twenty or more years in the making, it, along with 'mark-to-market' accounting, hard-wired dangers into the financial architecture. This was understood in advance, but ignored (Danielson et al. 2001; Goodhart and Segovino 2004; Goodhart and Taylor 2007; Gerlach and Gruenwald 2007). Big international banks, realizing they were going to be regulated anyhow, did not threaten but instead went along with, and did their best to shape, an approach that looked tougher than it really was, to avoid something genuinely tough.

In September 2009, at the G20 Summit in Pittsburgh, global political leaders agreed that a new set of capital adequacy rules, including extra capital requirements on banks deemed systematically important, was needed. In December 2009, the BCBS, quickly on top of its task,

---

[11] There was some logic to this. First, concentrating on the 'one tool one goal' approach was designed to make the role of central banks more technical and less political. Second, it took away some conflicts of interest, including, e.g. the temptation to use inflation to help rescue a failing bank system (by inflating the burden of its debts away), or to save insolvent banks because of the need to help the economy.

released its preliminary 'Basel III' proposals. However, large international banks were equally quick off their blocks. Their main lobbying front, the Institute of International Finance (IFF) heavily promoted the claim that if large banks were forced to hold more bank equity this would be costly for society, merrily ignoring the distinction between the private and public benefits of more capital (in particular, society's benefit from avoiding crashes), and taking an equally cavalier attitude to financial theory (Admati *et al.* 2013). By late 2010 significant increases in capital levels had been toned down by the BCBS. The minimum Core Tier 1 capital ratio, on an amended definition of capital, would rise to 4.5 per cent, but this was still less than half of what large banks had managed to achieve just before the crash. In the face of opposition from smaller banks, community banks, credit unions and emerging-economy banks, the IFF was equally good at lobbying for large international banks to be allowed to continue using their own internal ratings models, and for the new capital surcharge on systematically important banks to be non-binding and well below the level proposed by the (hardly radical) Federal Reserve.

Like its predecessor, Basel III was prompted by an international crisis that was widely blamed on the pursuit of neoliberal policies such as financial market deregulation (Basel Committee on Banking Supervision 2009). Each time, as the initial political impetus faded, cries of reform were gently, but firmly, smothered by the powerful and better resourced.

INDICATORS AND COMPLEXITY

One might think that if something got so complicated that few, if any, could understand it, the fear of being fooled to part with one's money would act as some sort of corrective. Instead, complexity became synonymous with safety.

Yet, complexity wrought vulnerabilities in its wake. First, complexity made it easier to hide risk and poor quality, not just from regulators, but also from management. In accounts of the crash, especially those of the more blow-by-blow variety (Sorkin 2009), it is noteworthy how many of those in the most senior positions in banks did not know about the risks they had taken on and the parlous states of their own banks' balance sheets.

Second, complexity made it difficult to model, and to verify, default risks. When the financial system crashed, the values of many securities based on bundled debt collapsed, because it was near impossible to work out the risks contained therein and to value them. Any buyer dipping into the pool of failing securities risked drawing an adverse selection from it. This, naturally enough, made the crash worse. Credit ratings, which depended on modelling default possibilities, became even harder to derive.

Third, complexity aided and abetted misselling. It was far easier to avoid legal risk via complexity than it was via humdrum dishonesty (try explaining to a jury, if ever a case got that far, how complex risk models were used to conceal the truth behind a curtain of sophistry). In a boom there is even less incentive to question complexity, and misselling goes even more undetected. Assuredly, for those crippling the poor under a burden of subprime mortgages, the trips and traps would not break *their* bones, and the short-term gains were worth it.

Fourth, complex financial structures facilitated tax avoidance and, in turn, tax avoidance encouraged complexity. According to the US Government Accounting Office and the Tax Justice Network, in every country the largest users of tax havens have been financial firms. For example, hedge funds, an important source of funds into 'shadow banking', were usually allowed to treat themselves as sourced and resident offshore, even if managed in New York or London, allowing profits and distributions to be lightly (if at all) taxed. Politicians representing leading financial centres were too afraid to act for fear it would frighten lucrative business away and weaken their claims to being the most finance-friendly cities in the world.

Finally, complexity benefited large international banks because, by creating complex regulatory challenges, it biased the negotiation process towards those who represented such banks when regulators came along in search of 'help' from experts.

EFFICIENT MARKETS?

In principle, regulators could have ignored credit ratings they deemed unfit for purpose, poked around inside the internal risk models being used by large international banks, and set higher capital requirements than any ratings models said were necessary. Or they could have sought to change the rules of ratings to capture more systemic risk, and created incentives for banks to hold more capital for systemic reasons. Instead, the myth was spread that ratings provide discipline, though they clearly could not in a systemic manner. At the same time, those arguing that markets were getting unstable faced a barrage of financial indicators that said the opposite.

Why would smart, long-term investors not profit from setting up 'better' financial indicators? After all, the loss of global economic output that could potentially have been avoided, in the region of US$10–20 trillion, was astronomic.[12] Sadly, capture was as much by ideas as it was by interest groups. The intense negotiations that led to the adopted financial indicators had, as their background, an intellectual consensus. According to the 'efficient markets hypothesis' (Shiller 2000 ch. 9; Malkiel 2003) financial markets will always correctly price[13] risk and financial assets.

The 'efficient markets' logic had humble origins in the world of finance as an elegant refutation of the notion that stock price charts can be used to predict the future and enable their users to make consistently superior returns. Since the stock market already incorporates all available information, rationally-determined share prices will jump around, as if in a 'random walk', in response to the arrival of new pieces of information unrelated to past price movements. Amongst a large enough sample of price charts, some will display a pattern, but this is no more than, at most, a temporary mirage.

Efficient market thinking took on an aura of intellectual superiority across large swathes of academia, but especially economics. In place of a messy reality, it offered elegant mathematics, a convenient morality tale (markets always know best), and powerful, yet simple, policy implications (it is not possible to improve on the market by intervention).

The charm of 'the market knows best' logic was seductive and, over the years, spread way beyond stock market applications, and eagerly embedded itself into all manner of financial and economic models. Happily ensconced, it spawned some startling implications for financial markets and the financial indicators they relied upon, of which the following are just a few. Efficient credit ratings crowd out inefficient credit ratings. Those who diversify and avoid risky financial instruments are safer, and come to populate the market. Price signals incentivize financial players to reconfigure away from those who are dangerously

---

[12] It is difficult to estimate the exact figures. If many countries had been experiencing asset price bubbles and consumption-based bubbles in the years before the crash, a simple extrapolation of that trend would exaggerate upwards the implied losses. Conversely, mismanagement of recovery could add some trillions more.

[13] Conditional on the information available.

interconnected. The market will not misprice the risks in bundled portfolios of subprime mortgages. If risk is repackaged such that it cannot be seen, the repackagers will be punished. Shadow banking will look after itself, and there is no need to give the Federal Reserve or others the legal mandate to bail shadow banks out (incidentally, much of the frantic bank rescue was all about setting such a legal mandate up). The buyers and sellers of CDSs will not settle on a price that is too low. Market forces indicate when economies are more risky, and encourage investors to take actions to make economies less risky. Even more miraculously, a generous sprinkling of the magic dust of the 'efficient market' causes any suspicions that indicators are poor to disappear.

It is easy to counter the more extreme claims of efficient market logic in financial markets. First, investors are not fully rational; they herd and copy each other's behaviour; they panic; they trade on noise (i.e. they are 'noise traders' (Shleifer and Vishny 1997)) extrapolating from a small sample (such as of local house price rises) a story about an upswing. They suffer from disaster myopia, placing less and less probability on extreme outcomes as time fades since experiencing such outcomes. The usual counter-argument to this is that it only takes a few smart investors betting against those who are mispricing risk and using poor indicators, to correct the consequences. This leaves room for, at most, only occasional anomalies from market efficiency.

However, this ignores the fact that rational investors seeking to correct an irrational crowd need to use other peoples' money to do it. This has been modelled as a principal-agent problem (Rees 1985a; Rees 1985b). Because of asymmetric information, those who lend (the 'principals') to 'rational' investors (the 'agents') only see the low return the agents make compared with the rest of the market. In the face of the irrational exuberance of the crowd, the agents may well face margin calls (i.e. demands from the principals for the agents to deposit additional money or securities to give extra protection for the principals against not being fully repaid). If the agents can't post the margin, perhaps by borrowing, they will be forced to pull their positions prematurely, at a loss. Meanwhile, those going along with an inefficient market and using poor indicators find it easier to demonstrate to those who invest in them the value of what they are doing.

Furthermore, even if all agree that a market is inefficient, it may still not be possible to profitably bet against inefficiency if it is difficult to predict the *timing* of correction. Investors have to go liquid a potentially long and indeterminate period and are likely to be killed off long before market correction. Those 'rationally' betting against market inefficiency or trying to use better indicators become insolvent long before the market corrects itself and rewards them. As Keynes put it, 'Markets can remain irrational a lot longer then you and I can remain solvent' (Lowenstein 2000: 123).

Finally, governments tend to take away the rewards of those trying to correct the market or establish 'superior' financial indicators. We saw this repeatedly in the crash. Governments poured liquidity into banks whose strategies had failed, and frequently rescued bank bondholders, and even their shareholders. In so doing, governments took away the rewards of those who might have taken market-correcting acts *ex ante* or tried to establish 'better' indicators.

It is especially difficult to bet against, and set up indicators to counter, tail risks. Those pricing the 'true' (but hidden) tail risk into contracts have to charge higher rates to reflect possible, and not current, high default rates. For their pains, they end up losing market share. This happened to community and regional banks in the United States when they refused to compete on the terms dictated by unregulated mortgage lenders and brokers. A bank will fund itself from a mix of equity and debt. If a bank is taking unduly high risks, and yet the credit ratings are wrong and debt markets are being irrationally exuberant, so long as the stock market is efficient, share prices should fall to reflect the true risks. Instead, bank share prices rose.

In the years before the crash, the huge amounts of short-term funding going through money markets; the intense pressure from bank share-holders on bank managers to raise returns; the emphasis on quantity over quality that pushed credit ratings artificially high; the bulging bank balance sheets; and the growth of shadow banking were all by-products of global imbalances and the underlying forces of secular stagnation. It was failure of market efficiency, under this barrage of forces, that drove the creation of poor indicators, and not the other way around. As the acceptable quality of assets fell, globally, so did the acceptable quality of financial indicators. It was convenient that financial indicators gave the pretence that they shaped the outcome, but it is difficult to see how 'better' financial indicators could have counteracted these forces, and so exist in the first place. Bad models and indicators survived because the masses of investors who constituted the market could not, or did not want to, get rid of them. They benefited too much from bad indicators.

REDISTRIBUTIVE FUNCTION OF
FINANCIAL INDICATORS

We naively presume that poor financial indicators work against the interests of those working in finance, especially price indicators that help them to avoid financial bubbles and crashes. Instead, it is useful to think of financial booms and busts as opportunities for wealth redistribution – with a 'before', 'during' and 'after' phase – and financial indicators as instruments to advance this redistributive agenda. Indicators that help create more upside for large banks (even if in the process creating more downside for taxpayers) are favoured over 'more efficient' indicators that take such highly profitable private opportunities away. Key to the process is that the largess of the boom and the pain of the bust are not equally shared. For large internationally active banks the years running up to the crash and then the crash itself were highly rewarding. The big losers were smaller regional lenders, emerging-market financial institutions, the poor and indeed many of middle income, the unemployed, taxpayers, and anyone relying on savings income. The transnational regulatory space was the battleground for this redistribution.

Before the crash, the returns made by large-bank equity holders were well above that of other industries, and those of smaller rivals and financial institutions in emerging economies. The low price charged for volatility risk boosted the mark-to-market values of financial assets on the balance sheets of financial institutions, and their apparent profits, and enabled vast bonuses to be extracted. Accounting rules and bonus practices allowed the extraction of wealth to be pulled forward, and the losses to be left for others to pay later. The pressures to tolerate this were high, and not just from within banking: some of those in fields as diverse as raw materials extraction and the Internet became mega-rich through financial engineering that converted future imagined profits into multibillion dollar equity stakes up front.

In a world of the survival of the fattest (Haldane and May 2011), gorging on debt was the way to go. Bank holding companies therefore issued huge amounts of debt to investors, and bank executive pay (in the form of shares or options on shares in bank holding companies) became, in effect, a heavily leveraged bet on the value of banks' capital. The greater the risks of getting extremely negative outcomes, the bigger the expected subsidy from a government bail-out, and the greater the wealth redistribution. Big international banks used the risk of their own collective failure (a sort of blackmail) to bias the distribution of the fruits of economic activity towards themselves.

Because of the growing problems of secular stagnation, sufficient returns could not be gotten out of genuine investments. However, a large stock of housing assets already existed and it was easy to pump their prices, such that bank balance sheets could explode without the need for much new investment, or indeed a sustainable boost in GDP. Housing is pretty much the only area in which it is possible to amortise at the start (in the shape of a mortgage) an entire lifetime of payments from a household for a critical life service. With diligent application of the principle of bank leverage, this created a great opportunity to extract wealth. So long as policy-makers kept pumping bubbles in housing market prices (and, in some places, construction), the public was a willing cheerleader. A rise in income and wealth inequality (Farlow 2013: ch. 1) was offset by a massive expansion in credit, so that the financial sector could continue to profit even as many were getting poorer or only just about treading financial water. The point of banking increasingly became not to help the economy grow in the long term, but to shift wealth to those in finance.

After the crash, government policy and central bank actions massively redistributed wealth across the population, but in new ways. First, there were the obvious bank bail-outs. Massive central bank liquidity measures were skewed towards those banks that had been especially reckless. Most large-bank creditors, and nearly all bank shareholders, did not face the losses they were due. Failed banks, with a few inglorious exceptions, emerged at the heart of an even-more oligopolistic banking system, with an even bigger emphasis on the too-big and too-connected to fail, operating afresh under the newly-strengthened signal that they could now take even bigger risks. There were no financial penalties imposed on those who issued poor ratings. Worse, after the crash, the same oligopolistic rating agencies that had failed got on with winning even bigger market shares.

Redistribution did not stop at bank bail-outs. Economic revival was increasingly presaged on the largest manipulation of global financial markets ever, in the shape of super low policy interest rates, Quantitative Easing (QE), freshly-minted moral hazard and new asset-price bubble. The biggest beneficiaries were bankers and the rich (including those who had backed the initial recklessness), because their wealth tended to be dominated by assets that benefited most from this policy response.

Super-low interest rates shifted wealth from those relying on income generated by cash-based savings to those who had amassed debt. In countries such as the United States and the United Kingdom, the housing market was a popular instrument for such redistribution, with wealth shifted from those with savings to those with mortgages; the larger the mortgage, the bigger the wealth redistribution. Super-low interest rates and liquidity pumped housing prices for property hotspots imagined as safe havens for the very rich. Redistributions were further disguised in the form of lower incomes for the masses, and higher taxes imposed on future generations.[14] And so, the harm done by bad financial indicators got shifted onto the poor and those of modest means.

The crash was a by-product of forces pushing towards secular stagnation. Over forty or so years, recovery from successive recessions had involved ever-lower real interest rates. Each time this had triggered a new asset price bubble. Each bubble rescued the last bubble, and was the source of a next round of wealth extraction. It was increasingly difficult to make a good return in any other way in a world of low returns, and those in finance felt compelled to take risks that would later convert into heavy costs for taxpayers. Bankers and the wealthy had the greatest influence on the indicators at the heart of this process, and were not about to plump for indicators that would undermine a wealth redistribution process of which they were the main beneficiaries.

CLOSING THOUGHTS

Having bemoaned the failure of financial indicators, we need to recognize that it is inherently difficult to create financial indicators that capture tail risks – the small probability, disastrous events that create the biggest economic damage – and that asset price bubble, and especially the timing of their collapse, are extremely difficult to model.

There is a danger when writing about the financial crash that the financial system will be made out to be all-important, imparting to financial indicators a greater significance and a more causative role than is justified. The global economy was (and still is) in a very unbalanced state. This fed, and was fed by, financial system imbalances, and was

---

[14] In the United Kingdom, the Institute for Fiscal Studies found that it was the young who had been hurt most by the Great Recession (Institute for Fiscal Studies 2014).

itself a driver of instability and crises (Farlow 2013). Financial indicators, it turns out, were less of a cause and more of a symptom, a distraction even, from these deeper macroeconomic roots of the crash. Yet, financial indicators were also not neutral representations of the world. They shaped understanding of reality, but reality shaped them. Something along these lines has previously been identified in the performativity of financial economics, as not just an analyser of markets, but as a shaper of them, as an engine, 'an active force transforming its environment, not a camera passively recording it' (Mackenzie 2006: 12). A camera still needs someone to point it, and the photographs it produces often hide the subtle framings and manipulations of the hand that holds it. The apparent neutrality of financial indicators allowed them to be used as a veil to disguise the governance, the manipulations, by others, namely, large international financial players themselves.

Financial indicators gave the necessary authority to elites to do what they wanted to do. Financial indicators, especially ratings, made invisible the rise in risk, the massive wealth redistribution and corruption. Because of their authority, they were not questioned, and so neither were the practices they facilitated. Financial firms knew they had the protection of the state; they just needed the pretence that they did not need it. In fulfilling this role, and even in facing the consequences of their own failure, financial indicators, like other indicators, were shielded by their claim to objectivity, rationality and measurement.

Financial indicators are only a part of the structure of the global banking system. This brings us to a fundamental issue. Should we be trying quite so hard to control, via financial indicators, conduct that is the result of the poor incentives caused by the structure of banking? Or should we change the structure of banking to reduce certain kinds of conduct, including the incentives to pervert the role of financial indicators? After the crash, many governments went for containment and not structural reform of banking, which guaranteed that financial indicators would continue to be a source of lively debate and controversy for many years to come.

References

Admati, A.R., P.M. DeMarzo, M. Hellwig and P. Pfleiderer 2013. *Fallacies, Irrelevant Facts, and Myths in the Discussion of Capital Regulation: Why Bank Equity is Not Socially Expensive.* Bonn: Max Planck Institute for Research on Collective Goods

Ashcraft, A.B. and Y. Schuermann 2008. 'The Seven Deadly Frictions of Sub-prime Mortgage Credit Securitization', *Investment Professional* (Fall) 2–11

Basel Committee on Banking Supervision 2009. *Strengthening the Resilience of the Banking Sector*. Basel: Bank for International Settlements

Bernanke, B.S. 2004. 'The Great Moderation', Remarks by Governor Ben S. Bernanke at the meeting of the Eastern Economic Association, Washington, D.C.

Besanko, D. and Kanatas, G. 1996. 'The Regulation of Bank Capital: Do Capital Standards Promote Bank Safety?', *Journal of Financial Intermediation* 5: 160–83

Blommestein, H.J., L.H. Hoogduin and J.J.W. Peeters 2009. 'Uncertainty and Risk Management after the Great Moderation: The Role of Risk (Mis)management by Financial Institutions', paper presented at the Twenty-eighth SUERF Colloquium on 'The Quest for Stability', Utrecht, the Netherlands

Danielson, J., P. Ermbrechts, C. Goodhart, C. Keating, F. Muenich, O. Renault and H. Shin 2001. *An Academic Response to Basel II*, LSE Financial Markets Group Special Report No. 130. London: London School of Economics

Dewatripont, M. and T. Tirole 1994. *The Prudential Regulation of Banks*. Cambridge, Mass.: MIT Press

Farlow, A.W.K. 2013. *Crash and Beyond: Causes and Consequences of the Global Financial Crisis*. Oxford: Oxford University Press

Fender, I. and J. Kiff 2004. *CDO Rating Methodology: Some Thoughts on Model Risk and its Implications*, BIS Working Papers No. 163

Furlong, F.T. and M.C. Keeley 1989. 'Capital Regulation and Bank Risk-Taking: A Note', *Journal of Banking and Finance* 3: 883–91

Gerlach, Stefan and Paul Gruenwald (eds.) 2007. *Procyclicality of Financial Systems in Asia*. London: Palgrave Macmillan

Goodhart, C. and M. Segovino 2004. *Basel and Procyclicality: A Comparison of the Standardised and IRB Approaches to an Improved Credit Risk Method*, Financial Markets Group Discussion Paper No. 524. London School of Economics

Goodhart, C. and A. Taylor 2007. 'Procyclicality and Volatility in the Financial System: The Implementation of Basel II and IAS 39W' in S. Gerlach and P. Gruenwald (eds.), *Procyclicality of Financial Systems in Asia*. London: Palgrave Macmillan

Greenspan, A. 2005. 'Risk Transfer and Financial Stability', Remarks by Chairman Alan Greenspan to the Federal Reserve Bank of Chicago's Forty-First Annual Conference on Bank Structure, Chicago, Illinois (via satellite) 2008. Testimony to the House of Representatives, 23 October

Haldane, A.G. 2010. 'Regulation or Prohibition: The $100bn Question', *Journal of Regulation and Risk North Asia*: 101–19

Haldane, A.G. and R.M. May 2011. 'Systemic Risk in Banking Ecosystems', *Nature* 469: 351–5

Hellwig, M. 2009. 'Systemic Risk in the Financial Sector: An Analysis of the Subprime-Mortgage Financial Crisis', *Economist* 157(2): 129–207

Ho, K. 2009. *Liquidated: An Ethnography of Wall Street*. Durham, N.C.: Duke University Press

Institute for Fiscal Studies 2014. *Living Standards, Poverty and Inequality in the UK, 2014*. London: IFS

Jones, K.D. and R.C. Oshinsky 2009. 'The Effect of Industry Consolidation and Deposit Insurance Reform on the Resiliency of the U.S. Bank Insurance Fund', *Journal of Financial Stability* 5(1): 57–88

Keynes, J.M. 1921. *Treatise on Probability*. London: Macmillan and Co.

Kim, D. and A.M. Santomero 1988. 'Risk in Banking and Capital Regulation', *Journal of Finance* 43(5): 1219–33

Knight, F.H. 1921. *Risk, Uncertainty and Profit*. New York: Harper

Lall, R. 2014. 'Timing as a Source of Regulatory Influence: A Technical Elite Network Analysis of Global Finance', *Regulation and Governance* 1–24

Lowenstein, R. 2000. *When Genius Failed: The Rise and Fall of Long-Term Capital Management*. New York: Random House

Mackenzie, D. 2006. *An Engine, Not a Camera: How Financial Models Shape Markets*. Cambridge, Mass.: MIT Press

Malkiel, G.B. 2003. 'The Efficient Market Hypothesis and Its Critics', *Journal of Economic Perspectives* 17(1): 59–82

Mandelbrot, B.B. 1963. 'The Variation of Certain Speculative Prices', *Journal of Business* 36: 394–419

1966. 'Forecasts of Future Prices, Unbiased Markets, and "Martingale" Models', *Journal of Business* 39: 242–55

Mandelbrot, B.B. and R.L. Hudson 2004. *The Misbehavior of Markets: A Fractal View of Financial Turbulence*. New York: Basic Books

Minsky, H.P. 2008/1986. *Stabilizing an Unstable Economy*. New York: McGraw-Hill Professional

Moody's Investors Services 1999. 'Rating Methodology: The Evolving Meanings of Moody's Bond Ratings' in *Moody's Global Credit Research*. New York

Rees, R. 1985a. 'The Theory of Principal and Agent: Part I', *Bulletin of Economic Research* 37(1): 3–26

1985b. 'The Theory of Principal and Agent: Part II', *Bulletin of Economic Research* 37(2): 75–97

Rochet, J.C. 1992. 'Capital Requirements and the Behavior of Commercial Banks', *European Economic Review* 36: 1137–78

Shiller, R.J. 2000. *Irrational Exuberance*. Princeton, N.J.: Princeton University Press

Shin, H.S. 2009. 'Securitisation and Financial Stability', *Economic Journal* 119: 309–32

Shleifer, A. and R.W. Vishny 1997. 'The Limits of Arbitrage', *Journal of Finance* 52(1): 35–55

Sorkin, A.R. 2009. *Too Big to Fail: Inside the Battle to Save Wall Street*. New York: Viking Press

Standard & Poor's 2001. 'Rating Methodology: Evaluating the Issuer' in *Standard & Poor's Credit Ratings*. New York

Taleb, N.T. 2007. *The Black Swan: The Impact of the Highly Improbable*. London: Penguin

Teulings, C. and R. Baldwin (eds.) 2014. *Secular Stagnation: Facts, Causes, and Cures*. CEPR Press

Tobias, A. and H.S. Shin 2009. *Liquidity and Leverage*, Federal Reserve Bank of New York Staff Report 328

Turner, A. 2008. 'Uncertainty and Risk: Reflections on a Turbulent Year', Cass Business School, Lecture

CHAPTER TEN

NEW GLOBAL VISIONS OF MICROFINANCE: THE CONSTRUCTION OF MARKETS FROM INDICATORS

Barbara Grimpe

INTRODUCTION

Many of the so-called developing and developed countries world-wide have a long history with microfinance, or the provision of small-size financial services to relatively poor people (Seibel 2005: 1). This chapter focuses on a particular set of changes in microfinance that have taken place across both developing and developed countries in the last few years: the formation of global market structures. More specifically, these structures are analysed here to illuminate the ways in which international standard-setting bodies attempt to construct global markets from indicators. If the visions of these groups of actors were to be achieved, the transformation of the microfinance sectors world-wide would be massive: countless small-size financial services to the poor all over the globe would be largely driven by a market that represents these local realities in a new information world that is highly self-contained. The complex and dynamic world of microfinance would be compressed into a few inches of computer screen. Based on these observable efforts of the standard-setters, this chapter makes the following case: a new

I would like to thank the Swiss National Science Foundation for supporting my research on microfinance 'Understanding Trust: Foundations, Forms and Limits of Trust', University of Zurich, 2009–2013. I am also very grateful to Johanna Mugler, Marietta Meier, Mischa Suter and Damian von Stauffenberg who commented on preliminary versions of this chapter. Furthermore, I am very grateful to Larissa Fischer who transcribed many of my recordings (e.g. of interviews). I am also indebted to Amy Field who helped me a great deal in improving my written English and provided very helpful comments on this chapter.

global electronic market for microfinance is in the making and is the product of the long-term cultural and historical formation of 'world society'. The present chapter discusses both the benefits and downsides of this trend.

'World society' is an umbrella term for various theoretical approaches (e.g. Heintz 1982; Meyer, Boli, Thomas and Ramirez 1997; Luhmann 1997; Heintz 2010). For instance, John W. Meyer and others contend that the term denotes a 'culture' that is 'substantially organized on a world-wide basis' and has 'causal significance in its own right', e.g. it cannot be reduced to local forces such as particular national or regional cultures (Meyer, Boli, Thomas and Ramirez 1997: 146–8). In addition to this important basic idea, Bettina Heintz' approach (2010) is particularly apt to interpret the processes of change I wish to discuss here. She argues that globalization and the evolution of global markets largely depend on communication processes with the help of numbers, rather than other media such as spoken language, written text or images. More precisely, global markets would be 'unthinkable' without large-scale quantitative comparisons (Heintz 2010: 162–3, 174–6). To paraphrase Heintz' reasoning further, this transformative power of quantitative comparisons is like a double-edged sword. On the one hand, large-scale quantitative comparisons would allow for the overseeing of widely distributed entities in a completely new way: a new systematic understanding of otherwise fuzzy or unlinked phenomena becomes possible. Consequently, new possibilities to act upon and interact with the world arise. On the other hand, quantitative comparisons would be far from self-evident and thus have the potential to create social conflict: the larger the underlying processes being examined, the more selective is the choice of relevant criteria for comparison of indicators and data collection procedures (Heintz 2010: 166, 169–70).

This chapter supports this thesis of the double-edged transformative power of quantitative comparisons. In order to do so, I use the case of the new global microfinance market and the so-called 'financial' and 'social performance indicators' that are commonly used therein as an empirical example (e.g. SPTF 2012a). Apart from world society theory, the chapter refers to three bodies of literature: first, science and technology studies, particularly the sociology and history of practices of quantification (Porter 1995; Espeland and Stevens 2008); second, the closely related field of the social studies of finance (Knorr Cetina and Preda 2007; Vollmer 2012; cf. Pinch and Swedberg 2008); third, anthropological and related literature on the manufacture and politics of numerical figures and statistics (Kalthoff, Rottenburg, and Wagener 2000; Gupta 2009; Krishna 2012).

This study also contributes to the theoretical dialogue between the social studies of finance and the anthropology of finance. More precisely, it reacts to a criticism made by Annelise Riles (2010). She argues that when the social studies of finance investigate today's financial markets, they focus too heavily on traders and their instruments, 'unwittingly' reifying the 'ideological claim that markets are protoscientific (Riles 2010: 795–6). To understand today's markets, one would have to consider a much broader range of effects and practices (Riles 2010: 798). Moreover, apart from the moments when the 'wondrous' sociotechnical networks function well, Riles argues, the 'breaks in the network, and the points of disconnect and mistranslation' should also be taken into account (Riles 2010: 796). Furthermore, she contends that so far, the 'hidden politics masked as epistemological practice' rather than the equally important 'explicit politics' have been investigated, i.e. the politics of what she calls the 'realm of must, shall, and will' (Riles 2010: 797). The present study aims to shed light on all of these dimensions of sociotechnical networks. The chapter supports therefore 'broadening the frame of the market' and bringing the social studies of finance 'into conversation with a wider set of concerns in the anthropology of gender, politics, exchange, time, and law' (Riles 2010: 796). More precisely, the present study does the following three things: it analyses the 'wondrous' sociotechnical networks, that is, the new possibilities of global knowledge that a particular Internet platform, i.e. a potential market technology, and the related discourse of standard setting open up; it illuminates certain breaks in these global connections by discussing their underlying complexities and uncertainties and by quoting actors who follow distinct knowledge practices apart from these networks; and, finally, it shows in which ways explicit moral politics, namely, the goals of reducing poverty and empowering women, are inextricably linked to these particular forms of knowledge generation.

The next section provides an introduction to the empirical case and develops the central thesis, i.e. the movement towards an electronic global market in microfinance, from a definition of indicators given by Kevin Davis, Benedict Kingsbury and Sally Engle Merry (2010). The third section of the chapter will sketch the history of social and financial performance indicators in the microfinance sector from the 1950s to the present. In the fourth section, the central thesis of the chapter is exemplified by analysing the design features of a particular Internet platform for microfinance institutions (MFIs). To return to the metaphor introduced above, this section explores one of the edges of the sword of quantitative comparisons: their benefits. In the fifth section, the design of this platform and the corresponding managerial discourse are put into perspective with the help of critical voices from sociology, anthropology as well as 'from the field', that is, by quoting three experts from the microfinance fund management and advisory industry. So this section treats the other 'edge' of the 'sword': the downsides of quantitative comparisons. The empirical data in this section also suggests that the world market on computer screens is still mostly a matter of (standard-setting) discourse and technological design: it remains to be analysed in greater detail in how far it is realized in practice, such as everyday fund and investment management. The last section presents preliminary conclusions and an outlook to future research. The outlook points to a recent development that is historically and culturally particularly remarkable: the construction of a potential *second-order* global market of microfinance.

A NEW GLOBAL ELECTRONIC MARKET IN MICROFINANCE: THE EMPIRICAL CASE AND THE CENTRAL THESIS

Within the realm of microfinance, the present study focuses on loans.[1] Microloans are small amounts of money accorded to relatively poor people, a group which did not appear attractive to commercial banks for a long time (cf. CGAP 2012).[2] For decades, the sector was characterized by donations and subsidies from state actors or international aid organizations (cf. Ledgerwood 1999: 2; Robinson 2001: 52–3). While these sources of public and charity money continue to play an important role (cf. CGAP 2008: 2–4; Servet 2011: 303), new major financial sources have also appeared for a few years. For instance, retail as well as institutional investors from abroad put more and more money into the microfinance sector, e.g. by providing loans to so-called 'microfinance institutions' (MFIs) which lend these funds to their local customers in

---

[1] Other financial instruments that are also part of microfinance, such as savings, insurance and payment and transfer services, are not considered.

[2] Many experts define microloans more narrowly. For example, they stress that microloans lack formal collateral, and that consumer loans should be distinguished from microloans because the former would not create any added value.

the form of hundreds or thousands of small loans. Retail and institutional investors have therefore contributed significantly to the quadrupling of foreign investment in MFIs. In 2010, foreign investment in MFIs reached the historically unprecedented amount of US $13 billion, which is around one-fifth of the total assets of all MFIs (CGAP 2011: 1–4). The new finance structures also include completely new legal entities. These are known as 'microfinance investment vehicles' (MIVs). Firms managing MIVs analyse and bundle the financial needs of various microfinance institutions world-wide in order to sell tailored investment opportunities to foreign investors. It is reported that the first MIV was founded in 1993 (LUMINIS 2012a). Consider, for instance, one of the funds managed by responsAbility, a prominent player in the global microfinance industry. According to its fourth quarterly report in 2013, at the end of that year it was invested in 231 MFIs, reaching more than 673,000 micro-entrepreneurs in 70 countries (responsAbility 2013).

If one considers the number of people affected both directly and indirectly, this market transformation has macro-dimensions, which merit closer attention. According to one estimate (the estimation techniques vary), the microfinance sector has served around 94 million credit borrowers world-wide in 2011 (Convergences 2013: 2). If one adds the families often attached to these primary clients, the sector then represents a rather large portion of the world population. Moreover, it is often argued that there is a significant gain in local morale which accompanies this transformation. Like in other areas of 'responsible finance' (e.g. Staub-Bisang 2011), the generation of (moderate) return in microfinance bears the promise that this will happen in a responsible way: nobody would be 'harmed', and some are even expected to benefit from it (cf. SPTF 2012a; Deutsche Bank 2007: 1–2). In a general sense, this view reflects the classic hope that the maximization of individual benefit and the preservation of public welfare can finally be both reconciled and achieved.

In order to reveal the meanings ascribed to microfinance, such as those mentioned above, and also to analyse the structural changes in the sector, I combined different methods. I conducted eleven qualitative interviews with different microfinance experts (e.g. five individuals who work in the fund management and advisory industry), engaged in participant observation at five international microfinance conferences with representatives from standard-setting bodies, industry and academia (altogether around seven days) and did discourse analysis of formal documents and websites of different players. Most of the data was collected between February 2010 and August 2012.[3]

This data shows that one important aspect of the multifaceted transformation of the sector has been the development and spread of so-called 'financial' and 'social performance indicators' (e.g. SPTF 2012a). These two measures are therefore analysed in greater detail in this chapter. The starting point is the definition of indicators provided by Davis, Kingsbury and Merry (2010). They argue that an indicator is:

> a named, rank-ordered representation of past or projected performance by different units that uses numerical data to simplify a more complex social phenomenon ... The representation is capable of being used to *compare* particular units of analysis (such as countries or persons) and to *evaluate* their performance by reference to one or more standards.
> (Davis, Kingsbury and Merry 2010: 2; emphasis added)

The authors add that indicators would be designed to 'reduce the burden of processing information'. Accordingly, they would potentially 'reduce the time, money and other resources required to make decisions' which, when taken together with the reduced time for information processing, are features the authors call the 'cost-benefit attractions of relying on indicators' (Davis, Kingsbury and Merry 2010: 6).

Based on this definition, then, it can be argued that various groups of actors in the field of microfinance strive for the construction of a global information system for the comparative observation of complex social and economic phenomena such as local MFIs and the life-worlds in which they are embedded. This 'system', as it is understood here, consists of discursive practices, standard measures such as social and performance indicators, and concrete technologies that allow for the global visibility of the market, e.g. Internet platforms. This developing system of comparative observation carries potential cost-benefit attractions for its users, such as private investors. Stated briefly, in order to *know* a microfinance institution, users no longer need to travel. More specifically, a new sort of *comparative knowledge* about microfinance institutions emerges which is actually *market* knowledge, in a particular sense. With the help of indicators and advanced technological infrastructures (cf. Davis, Kingsbury and Merry 2010: 6), MFIs that are far away from each other in reality can now be known and understood in close relation to one another, as they are now juxtaposed to one another within a

---

[3] In this chapter all quoted individuals have been made anonymous. Sometimes this includes a change of their actual sex.

few inches on computer screen. A new knowledge pattern can therefore develop: the MFIs can be evaluated in immediate comparison with one another, perceived as if they competed with one another, and understood as if they filled different market niches in relation to one another.

Thus, we can test the following central thesis: the production of compact social and financial performance indicators and their concentration in globally distributed high-power technologies lead to the erection of an entirely electronic microfinance market which is global in scope. Quantitative comparison is the main cognitive operation of the participants in this market. Their world is a self-contained screen world. The screen world is not an arbitrary product, but is rather the result of the multi-stage translation of billions of distant yet embodied borrower-creditor interactions world-wide. Market participants obtain a great deal of new knowledge about microfinance as they track back and forth between the different screens in this world, as well as the information those screens display. The next section sketches the historical trajectories to this new online market.

FROM SUBSIDIES TO PROFESSIONAL MANAGEMENT: A BRIEF HISTORY OF FINANCIAL AND SOCIAL PERFORMANCE INDICATORS

Historically, microfinance has not always meant *finance*, as odd as this might sound. This holds true for 'finance' in the sense of providing loans to relatively poor people in a cost-covering, or even profitable way, which applies to many microfinance institutions today, or in the sense of raising capital from domestic or even international financial markets, which many institutions today do. The microfinance sector underwent a significant transformation throughout the last decades. Roughly, this transformation can be summarized as a shift from the paradigm of subsidized credit delivered by governments or international aid organizations in the period of the 1950s to the 1970s, to the building of more locally anchored microfinance institutions offering commercial financial services in the framework of the so-called 'financial systems approach', a political and economic development trend that started in the 1980s and which still persists. Attaining 'financial sustainability' in microfinance institutions appears to be the guiding principle of this trend (Robinson 2001: 52–4). The need for 'efficiency', 'productivity', 'profitability', 'self-sufficiency' and 'viability' has also been stressed (Ledgerwood 1999: 2, 205; Robinson 2001: 55–8; cf. MicroRate/IADB 2003: 1–3). To find out whether an MFI is actually financially sustainable, a number of different financial performance indicators have been developed. Micro-Rate, a rating agency specializing in microfinance, appears to be one of the driving forces behind this movement. According to its founder, in the mid-1990s his agency started to introduce a number of key ratios such as 'Portfolio at Risk' or the 'Operating Expense Ratio'. 'Return on Equity' and 'Return on Assets' are two other important examples (cf. Meehan 2004: 3). According to MicroRate's guidelines, a high percentage of return on equity and assets indicates that the organization is profitable. The two ratios are calculated the following way: the net income of an institution (after taxes, and without grants or donations) is divided by the average equity, or assets that have been accumulated during a given period (MicroRate/IADB 2003: 34–7). While these ratios, like many others, can be calculated rather easily, their interpretation is not straightforward. The guidelines explain a number of possible misjudgments if the figures are not related to other figures, or to other relevant contextual factors. For example, it is said that a single year's return on equity 'can at times misrepresent the institution's "true" profitability' due to '[e]xtraordinary income or losses, for example in the form of asset sales' (MicroRate/IADB 2003: 34). In the next two sections, the two return indicators will be considered in combination with social performance indicators, and the analysis will mostly focus on the latter. However, an in-depth study of financial performance indicators that explores their global history and their multiple meanings would show great promise for understanding more clearly how 'financialization' takes place in everyday practice (cf. Vollmer 2012).

For many practitioners and authors, this financialization does not categorically exclude the pursuit of welfare. They argue that only those microfinance institutions which operate cost-efficiently and generate profit are attractive to international private investors. International private investors, in turn, would play a necessary role in accommodating the world-wide demand for microloans, which is still reported as tremendous. It has also been argued that public actors (governments, donors, international financial institutions) alone cannot provide all the capital needed. Thus, by filling this financial gap, private capital would contribute to the societal improvements often associated with microfinance, such as poverty alleviation. Among the poor, women are frequently perceived as a particularly disadvantaged group, and their empowerment is frequently understood as an important goal. Altogether, it is often argued that the commercialization of microfinance does not impede the achievement of non-commercial societal goals, such as the empowerment of women, but can actually support it (cf. Robinson 2001: xxxv, 11, 58; Ledgerwood 1999: 2; Meehan 2004: 2, 6; CGAP 2007: 2; Matthäus-Maier 2008: viii–ix; Mayoux 2011: 613, 617, 622).

In the last few years, however, it has been recognized that accommodating demand for microloans does not necessarily imply that the life conditions of people are actually improved once the microloans are disbursed (CGAP 2007: 2; Grameen Foundation 2008: 5). It has also been pointed out that in some cases, commercialization can produce negative consequences, which can snowball. In an interview, for example, a microfinance expert who had worked for an international aid agency for a few years said that she might have been 'naïve' a few years ago when she still believed that 'no one would be in the microfinance market without being committed to a social mission' (translation from German). 'I thought it went without saying! ... The idea that there would be institutions that become like modern lenders was a bit abstruse. That is, it was nearly a fact, almost a given to say: microfinance institutions are oriented socially.'

Recently, for example, the microcredit crisis that took place in the district of Andhra Pradesh in India in October 2010 gave cause for serious concern both among microfinance practitioners and the wider public. Many borrowers became over-indebted, and loan officers were accused of wrongful loan recovery practices. One possible explanation is that investors had emphasized the growth of MFIs at such a rate that 'basic good banking principles' (such as appropriate staff behavior towards clients) were disregarded within the respective MFIs (CGAP 2010: 5).

This and other crises in the microfinance sector (cf. MIX 2011a) have given some authority to already existing standard-setting bodies that had started propagating management ideas for social aspects of microfinance a few years before. These standard-setters are, for example, the Social Performance Task Force (SPTF); the Microfinance Information Exchange (MIX); the Smart Campaign; and a 'knowledge exchange network' called CERISE (SPTF 2012b; MIX 2012a; Smart Campaign 2012; CERISE 2012). Take, for example, the SPTF. It was founded in 2005, and today it consists of over 1,000 individual members representing 550 different organizations worldwide, e.g. MIVs, big commercial banks such as Deutsche Bank, international organizations such as the International Labor Organization (ILO), plus 161 institutions providing microfinance services directly, associated rating agencies, and many other organizations such as Columbia University (SPTF 2012c). The SPTF argues that the 'social performance' of an MFI encompasses 'the entire process by which impact is created' by an MFI: the 'declared objectives' of the organization; the 'internal systems and activities' and their 'effectiveness in furthering the stated objectives'; 'direct outputs' such as 'numbers of very poor households reached'; 'outcomes observed in clients' lives', e.g. 'increased revenue from their business'; and finally 'impact', that is, 'the amount of the observed change in the client's life that can be *directly attributed* to the institution's programs' (SPTF 2012a; emphasis in the original). While the SPTF acknowledges that it is very difficult to prove the precise impact of a microfinance institution, a view shared by many (e.g. Ledgerwood 1999: 3; Robinson 2001: xxxv), the organization believes that 'all other elements' of the process can be 'managed' by the MFI (SPTF 2012a).

This and similar statements of the organization Microfinance Information Exchange (MIX) actually include interesting ambiguities in terms of their reasoning. Whether an MFI *actually* reduces poverty or changes the lives of its clients in other positive ways can barely be claimed because there are so many influencing factors in people's lives. So in practice, there is a fundamental insecurity about whether microfinance is something good or bad for recipients, to put it bluntly. The standard-setters explicitly acknowledge this. However, they *also* claim that an MFI can ensure that it 'does no harm' to its clients, or 'acts in a socially responsible manner', and that the social performance management initiatives can help the microfinance sector meet 'an increasing number of clients' needs' (SPTF 2012a; MIX 2011a). Thus, microfinance is still perceived as a practice that can yield positive societal results, and microfinance institutions as well as their client relationships are portrayed as fundamentally controllable, manageable units, however complex they might be.

The SPTF has the 'vision' to turn social performance management into a 'standard business practice'. Accordingly, its goal is to 'develop, disseminate and promote standards and good practices for social performance management and reporting'. These standards are referred to as 'universal' (SPTF 2012a). The role model for this campaign is actually financial performance management. This is exemplified by the following statement an SPTF representative made during his talk at a microfinance conference: 'We always try to run home the point, that we manage financial performance very well because we realize you have to manage it in order to achieve it, so we are making the same case for social performance, because, what's explicitly defined and measured is what's managed.'

Indeed, social performance management parallels financial performance management in the strong reliance on indicators. In collaboration with MIX, the SPTF developed eleven 'indicator categories' (SPTF 2012d). These 'indicator categories' refer to different kinds of indicators. Only a fraction of them actually 'uses numerical data to simplify a more complex social phenomenon' and includes rankings (Davis, Kingsbury and Merry 2010: 2). For example, in the category, 'social responsibility to clients', there are nine standard statements, composed only of one or two sentences, that an MFI merely has to agree to (or not) by ticking a box labeled 'Yes' or 'No'.[4] The standard-setters call these statements 'process indicators'. By contrast, the so-called 'results indicators' are all numerical representations. For example, the MFI is supposed to declare the current number of 'total active borrowers' and the share of female borrowers (MIX 2012c).

Another part of the definition given by Davis, Kingsbury and Merry clearly applies to the entire 'indicator categories' framework. Davis, Kingsbury and Merry state that indicators are 'authoritative'. In other words, they have high potential to influence others in their decision-making, because they 'claim to be based on scientific expertise' (Davis, Kingsbury and Merry 2010: 7). The official discourse of the SPTF reflects this stance. In his speech, the above-mentioned SPTF representative stressed that '[w]e are all familiar with the nice mission statements and the pictures, but ... there is a real need to actually put data, and evidence, behind the claims that we are making as an industry'. Accordingly, on the SPTF website it is stated that the task force's goal would be 'to establish the true performance of an MFI: get data, not stories' (SPTF 2012a). These expressions signal a fully-fledged, unquestioned trust in numbers as well as trust in all of the data collection processes and bodies needed to produce valid numbers about such complex and dynamic organizations, as many MFIs are (cf. Porter 1995; Mennicken 2000: 39–41; Luhmann 2000: 69).

In fact, for a few years many MFIs have been reporting not only on their financial, but also on their social performance management with

---

[4] For example, an MFI is invited to confirm or negate the following statement: 'Acceptable and unacceptable debt collection practices are clearly spelled out in a code of ethics, book or staff rules or debt collection manual' (MIX 2012c).

the help of indicators propagated by the SPTF, MIX, the Smart Campaign and CERISE. Interestingly, MFIs do this in a way that makes the entire data globally visible: they report to the so-called 'MIX Market', an Internet platform established by MIX in 2002 (MIX 2011b). This mode of global publication of financial and social performance indicators is supported by all four initiatives mentioned previously. It is said that by combining both social and financial performance data, the platform would create 'all-encompassing view[s]' of the participating MFIs (MIX 2011a). Indeed, the degree of global visibility of MFIs, and the degree of immediate access to various performance data as produced by this platform, are most likely historically unprecedented. For example, in 2011 MIX stated that its platform 'has just reached 2000 reporting MFIs...in 110 countries that represent over 92 million borrowers' (MIX 2011c).

The next section analyses this new form of global visibility in greater detail. In particular, it explores the discourse of global visibility, and how the design of the platform echoes it in terms of the perceived relationships between indicators, global visibility, comparability and competition.

A NEW GLOBAL VISION OF MICROFINANCE: THE 'MIX MARKET'

MIX claims that '[m]ore than half (58 per cent)' of all platform visitors 'use MIX to make financial and/or operational decisions' (MIX 2011c). It is not specified, though, how MIX obtained these results. Moreover, it is argued that the platform would ensure 'the highest level of comparability for MFI data on a global scale' (MIX 2012d). CERISE argues more bluntly that social performance indicators would help MFIs 'create distance from the irresponsible practices of [non-reporting] "black sheep" MFIs' (CERISE 2010: 3).

This section picks up this discourse and analyses the design of the MIX platform more closely. The basic argument is this: historically unprecedented, the platform allows for the quick identification of MFIs that perform well, or rather, seem to perform well because they score well in terms of particular performance indicators. The indicators discussed in this section are related to financial return, poverty and gender. The argument I make is, according to the design of and the discourse related to the platform, a potential investor does not need to leave his or her armchair, so to speak, to understand and judge an MFI, but finds a lot of this and other relevant data on his or her computer screen. Thus, potentially with help of the MIX technology, a new tight circle of observation is established between investors, on the one hand, and globally dispersed microfinance institutions on the other. This tight circle of (electronic) observation might develop into a market which is global in scope, but microsocial and microtechnological in terms of its concrete functioning (Knorr Cetina and Preda 2007). More precisely, the platform displays a multitude of financial and social indicators that can be related to one another in various ways. In other words, the platform offers an information world that is experienced as highly self-contained. A potential investor, for example, can move back and forth within this onscreen world to make sense of the day-to-day operations of MFIs (cf. Knorr Cetina and Preda 2007: 131). The more MFIs are reporting, the more a market could actually develop, that is, a multidimensional field in which MFIs hold different positions with regard to different investment criteria.

To see how the MIX platform works, consider one registered institution such as the Bolivian bank 'Banco FIE'. This case has been selected because in 2012, the MIX Market developers themselves used it to explain basic analytical functions in an online tutorial (MIX 2012e). Amongst others, the video showed what Banco FIE reports regarding social performance data. The commentator suggested, 'If we wanted to compare or benchmark these results, we can look at them side by side with another MFI, or with a national average for Bolivia, or the Latin American Region.' The following analysis does precisely what this proposal suggests by juxtaposing Banco FIE's and the Bolivian average data (at the time of my original data enquiry for this analysis in 2012, the latter covering twenty-eight MFIs).

One can begin making this inquiry through the computer screen display (Figure 10.1; MIX 2012f). For example, one could check any of the boxes labeled, 'Indicators', 'Social Performance' and 'Bolivia' in 'Add Countries' with the year 2010 as a reporting period, and then click 'Create Report' – and a few seconds later a report in the form of a table would appear. It shows both Banco FIE and the average of all reporting Bolivian MFIs in terms of more than eighty different fields of data, most of them filled with numbers (percentages or cardinal numbers). A print-out of this table would fill up nearly five pages. As the headings of the reporting sections suggest ('institutional characteristics', 'outreach indicators', 'overall financial performance', to offer a few examples), most of the figures serve as indicators that are supposed to represent

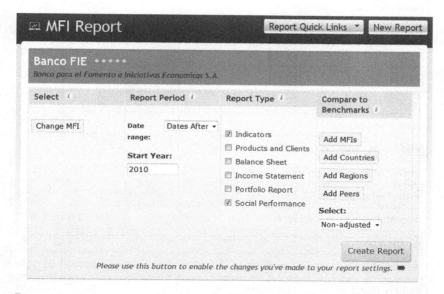

Figure 10.1 How to start enquiries to the 'MIX Market' database
Source: MIX, 31 August 2012.

Return on assets ⓘ		2.02%	1.37%
Return on equity ⓘ		21.90%	7.35%

Figure 10.2 Two financial performance indicators
Source: MIX, 31 August 2012.

organizational states and processes as well as the entire clientele ('out-reach') of an MFI. Figure 10.2 shows a portion of the table (reproduction of the original) displaying the two financial performance indicators 'return on assets' and 'return on equity'.[5] As one can see immediately, Banco FIE (second column) scores well: in both cases it supersedes the Bolivian average (third column).

Moreover, the report includes a paragraph of nearly one page in length titled 'social performance'. Figure 10.3 shows two-thirds of it (reproduction of the original).

Many lines in the table refer either to women or to poverty in one way or another (to highlight these, I have added 'Ws' and 'Ps' to the original

[5] Both indicators were introduced in the last section. The reproduction in Figures 10.2 and 10.3 is as close to the original as possible.

267

▷ Number of active borrowers ⓘ	146.819	13.359
Percent of female borrowers **W**	55.24%	48.13%
Borrower retention rate	86.24%	77.63%
▷ Number of loans outstanding ⓘ	163.946	13.736
▷ Personnel ⓘ	1.941	151
Percent of female staff **W**	50.85%	40.56%
Staff turnover rate	10.90%	21.70%
▷ Number of board members ⓘ	12	7
Percent of female board members **W**	33.33%	27.27%
▷ Number of managers ⓘ	12	4
Percent of female managers **W**	58.33%	8.34%
▷ Loan officers ⓘ	587	72
Percent of female loan officers **W**	48.55%	31.51%
Number of microenterprises financed	120.367	3.934
Number of start-up microenterprises financed	-	0
Percent of financed microenterprises that are start-ups	-	15.72%
Number of jobs created	-	5.445
Number of clients surveyed for microenterprise data	120.367	1.232
Number of microenterprises surveyed for employment data	-	698
Number of clients surveyed for poverty measurement **P**	542	421
Poverty measurement tool used **P**	Grameen PPI	0
Typology of clients surveyed for poverty measurement **P**	mujeres y hombres, clientes nuevos y existentes	0
First poverty line considered **P**	Linea de pobreza nacional	0
Clients below first poverty line **P**	40%-45%	38
Second poverty line considered **P**	-	0

Figure 10.3 The 'social performance' section
Source: MIX, 31 August 2012.

table). Regarding the figures for poverty, for example, the data in terms of 'number of clients surveyed for poverty measurement', 'poverty measurement tool used', 'first poverty line considered' and 'clients below first poverty line' are made available on this screen. The standard-setters put a lot of emphasis on measuring poverty with the help of poverty indexes. The 'Grameen Progress out of Poverty Index' that is listed in Figure 10.1 ('Grameen PPI'; fifth line from below) is one of the officially promoted indexes (cf. SPTF 2012e). The next section discusses some features of this particular tool. 'First poverty line' principally represents a standard that an external party (such as a state or an international institution) has set as an important marker of relatively severe poverty. In this case, it is the Bolivian standard, i.e. the national poverty line, that Banco FIE reports on ('Linea de pobreza nacional'). While it is a bit puzzling to see all of the zeroes in the right-hand column, that is, in the Bolivian average column, the user could interpret all this data regarding poverty in favor of Banco FIE. This institution *does* measure poverty with an acknowledged tool (the Grameen PPI) along with an official poverty benchmark (the national poverty line), and it shows relatively good numerical scores with regard to the two data fields. More precisely, it surveyed more clients than the Bolivian average to determine the poverty of its clients (542 versus 421), and it seems to reach more poor clients than the national average (40–45 per cent versus 38 per cent).

The data related to women seem promising, too. In each category, Banco FIE again scores better than the Bolivian average: it has a comparatively high number of female borrowers (55.24 per cent versus 48.13 per cent), female staff (50.85 per cent versus 40.56 per cent), female board members (33.33 per cent versus 27.27 per cent), especially also female managers (58.33 per cent versus 8.34 per cent), and female loan officers (48.55 per cent versus 31.51 per cent). One might argue that more than other Bolivian MFIs, Banco FIE contributes to one of the classic goals of microfinance, the empowerment of women. Adding therefore the positive qualities regarding the poverty data, as well as the comparatively high scores with regard to financial return, investors aiming at a 'double bottom line', that is, both financial and social gains, might consider investing in this particular MFI (e.g. Deutsche Bank 2007: 1).

In a more theoretical sense, the MIX Market appears to be a remarkable instance of world society (Heintz 2010). It enables its users to oversee large quantities of societal entities such as MFIs, their customers, as well as a number of aspects of the credit-borrower relationship, and to compare these entities relatively quickly. With the help of indicators and related data, these far-ranging entities can be represented in a very concise way in a single, central location. Hence they can be *known* in totally new ways: they can be regarded as parts of a whole (in this case, the Bolivian microfinance sector), and they can also produce new meanings in relation to one another (Heintz 2010: 166). Banco FIE, for example, could now be perceived as a 'pro-poor' organization that supports the empowerment of women, an identity that would not have become so clear if it had not been made visible by quasi-scientific indicators (cf. Davis, Kingsbury and Merry 2010: 7). Moreover, the financial and social dimensions of microfinance have been made *commensurable* throughout the sector to a high degree (Espeland and Stevens 2008: 408). In other words, they have been transformed into quantities that can easily be compared across a few inches of a spreadsheet or table on a computer screen. Due to this imposed commensurability, Banco FIE can easily point to two sorts of figures: its good financial as well as its good social indicators, and its promised double returns. However, it cannot easily claim that it supports start-up enterprises, or that it creates new jobs because it does not show any data related to these categories. Yet, one could argue that in a *market*, this need not be construed as a major problem. Quite the contrary: Banco FIE can now be perceived as filling a particular market *position*, and other MFIs might be able to opt for other market niches.

PUTTING THE NEW VISION INTO PERSPECTIVE: SOME ACADEMIC AND PRACTITIONERS' RESERVATIONS

The 'MIX Market' is a culturally and historically remarkable knowledge system because it is, quite simply, both vast and handy. It includes a tremendous amount of data on the social and financial performance of hundreds of MFIs, which makes it a complex information-world. At the same time, this world is compressed into the size of a computer screen. In this section, some of the downsides of this information-world are discussed.

The MIX Market platform is constantly amended, and the social performance data reporting initiatives started much later than those for financial performance did. For instance, in 2011 only around 440 MFIs had submitted social performance reports, compared to 2,000 reporting MFIs altogether (MIX 2011c). Thus, some of the following sociological, anthropological and practitioners' critical views which put into perspective the vision of the MIX platform as a vehicle for a new global market might become obsolete, or qualified themselves, within a few months or years (as the platform changes and is amplified further). It will be interesting to see, for instance, whether the data providers will keep the following problematic feature observed in 2013: a great deal of the information collected on the platform stems from reports the MFIs deliver *themselves* (MIX 2013). Thus, there is potentially a lot of room for mere lip service.

At first glance, the poverty data that was discussed in the last section seemed to be to Banco FIE's advantage: this MFI uses a recognized poverty measurement tool; it has surveyed more clients than the Bolivian average; and it serves more clients below the first poverty line (which indicates a relatively high degree of poverty). However, a case-by-case investigation of the other twenty-seven Bolivian MFIs (that constituted this average in 2011) reveals that this positive image of Banco FIE is flawed (own MIX Market database enquiry as of 25 August 2012). For example, only one other MFI called 'Emprender' does actually provide data for the categories in question. With regard to other criteria, the inquiry shows that Emprender uses the Grameen PPI, like Banco FIE. And it is indicated that '35–40 per cent' of its clients lie below the first poverty line. In other words, the average that Banco FIE is compared to consists of no one else than Banco FIE itself and this MFI. The seeming positive 'pro-poor' identity of Banco FIE depends on a total absence of data from twenty-six other MFIs in five poverty-related categories.

Moreover, the usage of the 'Grameen Progress out of Poverty Index' as a poverty measurement tool should be questioned. Does it represent poverty in an adequate way? To answer this question, the tool must be described in greater detail. As I have argued, the standard-setters promote this tool. As a user guide of the Grameen Foundation suggests (Grameen Foundation 2008), the production of the index and their corresponding scores is a complex trans-organizational process whereby MFI staff members translate existing country-specific survey data on poverty, e.g. a national survey on household income and expenditures usually including up to 1,000 indicators, into an easily comprehensible sheet of paper that includes only ten questions, or in other words, ten data points for indicators. The questions are all closed ones, 'easy to ask and answer quickly', such as 'How many television sets does the family own' (Grameen Foundation 2008: 13, 17). The questionnaire is a single piece of paper that the MFI staff can rather easily take from the house of one client to the next, concentrating on rather visible dimensions of poverty such as 'flooring material' (Grameen Foundation 2008: 15). Undertaking this survey is said to be 'cost-effective' for MFIs: it would usually take not more than 'five minutes' per household to answer the ten questions, and the staff training is said to take not more than one day (Grameen Foundation 2008: 8, 21). In the end, the scores jotted for each answer are summed up. The aggregate scores are then compared to the data portfolio and poverty line of the original extensive national survey to determine the 'likelihood' that the clients of the MFI in question belong to a particular group of poor (Grameen Foundation 2008: 18–19). The Grameen Foundation claims that an MFI could show in how far its clientele 'move[s] out of poverty' if indicators are chosen that are 'likely to change' through time 'such as the number of radios' (Grameen Foundation 2008: 6, 14).

However, even if the clients of an MFI seem to 'progress out of poverty' as measured by this instrument, this change cannot be accurately *attributed* to the MFI in question. There are numerous factors that can influence the state of poverty in a given group. An acknowledged scientific measure to attribute changes more accurately is to construct a 'control group', for example, a village that has not been submitted to the activities of the MFI in question, and to compare the developments in the two areas. But such a large-scale quantitative field survey cannot be carried out easily either. Its design is complex; it can take years to be completed (which makes it also costly); and the results can still be ambiguous (cf. Banerjee *et al.* 2010: 4, 6–7). Furthermore, the Grameen PPI presupposes a somewhat dubious understanding of poverty. The handful of questions are closed ones posed by the MFI staff, and the procedure favors visible features of the household. All this deliberately excludes any possible alternative views of poverty qualitatively expressed by those interviewed. According to Krishna (2012), however, poverty is embedded in complex 'life-worlds' and depends a great deal on individual and collective (though not universal) perceptions. This does not mean that poverty is not real. As Krishna puts it: 'Poverty is an objective condition that is experienced subjectively' (Krishna 2012). Poverty is therefore 'socially constructed and collectively defined' in different areas in different ways. Poverty measurement tools that are developed for very broad areas such as nation states or the entire world cannot always capture these finer differences. As stated above, the Grameen PPI takes its questions from a national household survey. Thus, Krishna's criticism might apply to this tool. Krishna's other arguments are similarly pessimistic: while measuring poverty in a standard way could increase the comparability of progress across different regions, it would not be 'very helpful for some other purposes', such as 'addressing its causes in diverse domains'. Krishna concludes that 'measuring poverty more precisely (against some common global standard) and dealing with poverty more effectively (in some particular local setting) are not necessarily always the same objective'.[6]

Apart from poverty, figures related to women are also numerous in MIX Market performance reports (e.g. 'per cent of female borrowers', 'female board members' and 'female loan officers'). However, I could not find any explanations on the part of the MIX organization, nor the SPTF as to why it is exactly that so many women-related figures are included in the social performance reporting section. What is clear, though, is that for a long time, microfinance has in a general sense been perceived as a way to empower women (see below). More precisely, with regard to female borrowers, Goetz and Gupta (1996) name some possible reasons why credit programmes in Bangladesh increasingly targeted women instead of men from the 1980s on. Their line of thinking helpfully elucidates the case at hand too. While their analysis relates to female borrowers only, one might ask whether their basic conclusions can also be transferred to the other women-related figures displayed on the MIX platform.

Amongst others, Goetz and Gupta recall the widespread view that a possible increase in women's income with the help of credits could strengthen women's positive roles 'as brokers of the health, nutritional, and educational status of other household members' (Goetz and Gupta 1996: 46; cf. Ledgerwood 1999: 38). They also observe that credit is often regarded as 'a form of economic empowerment which can enhance women's self-confidence and status within the family'. Accordingly, women have frequently been perceived as potential 'independent producers and providers of a valuable cash resource to the household economy' (Goetz and Gupta 1996: 46–7). However, the authors identify a lack of scholarship looking behind the surface of the 'household' as the unit of study, that is, a lack of research about '*intra*household decision making, resource allocation, and empowerment' (Goetz and Gupta 1996: 47; emphasis added). Given this lack of research, the authors try

---

[6] Gupta (2009) developed a similarly critical line of reasoning for global poverty statistics and the global discourse on poverty.

to answer one particular question: To what extent do women actually control the usage of the loans they officially receive? In other words, do women exercise 'managerial control' within the household (Goetz and Gupta 1996: 48)? The authors report a number of interesting and ambiguous results. Two of them are cited here: First, one cannot answer this question clearly, because even in cases where the loans would have supported 'conventionally male activities', such as the purchase of a rickshaw used by the man, it was determined that 'a range of managerial and contractual arrangements can be found through which women retain *some* control over loan use' (emphasis added). Second, female borrowers were 'more likely to retain full control over loan use when they were widowed, separated, or divorced'. But in some cases these single female household heads would have 'given over their loans to male relatives beyond the immediate household...in exchange for a guarantee of a regular food supply'. To paraphrase this, these women paradoxically make decisions that imply a loss of control (over the loan itself), but potentially also a new source of influence (over the men who take the loan). The authors conclude from these and other ambiguous empirical results, amongst others: 'It cannot simply be assumed that individual control over a loan is equivalent to empowerment, nor does the phenomenon of transferring a loan in and of itself signal a loss of power for women' (Goetz and Gupta 1996: 49–50, 52–3).

Regarding the empirical ambiguity of what it actually means to be a 'female borrower', one might question the demonstrativeness of numerical representations of female borrowers, as well as those of the female staff of MFIs on the MIX platform. It is not clear what the 'percentage of female borrowers', a category in which Banco FIE scores well in comparison to the other Bolivian MFIs, represents in reality. What is clear, however, is that the indicator does not always represent empowerment, or (good) 'social performance' of the MFI. Moreover, Goetz and Gupta's analysis of 'managerial control' at the household level raises doubts about the staff figures too. For example, does an officially high percentage of female managers, as Banco FIE reports, represent *effective* managerial control? This is simply something difficult to be certain about. Furthermore, the way the percentages of female borrowers and staff members currently appear on the MIX platform can be challenged in a more basic sense. What would be *appropriate* scores? 100 percent, for example, or 50 percent?[7] Behind these questions lies a more general

---

[7] I thank Damian von Stauffenberg for raising these questions.

one: To what extent can and should gender justice be translated into numbers, standards and benchmarks?

Finally, some practitioners' views put the MIX platform into perspective too. In three interviews, three experts from the fund management and advisory industry were asked different questions about the platform, as well as the decision-making processes they are involved in, to find out to what extent the former influences the latter. In general, their answers revealed that the MIX platform is just one among many information resources or modes of producing knowledge about MFIs and decision-making regarding investment in microfinance. For example, one interviewee spent quite some time explaining how the 'social mission' of an MFI cannot be 'measured' easily by quantitative means such as 'the questionnaire of the SPTF that the MIX Market essentially adopts'. In the interviewee's perspective, there are an 'awful amount of qualitative aspects' and many 'parts of the context' that cannot be grasped by using a solely quantitative approach.

This tendency, i.e. to rely on quantitative measures only to some extent, and to reflect on their shortcomings, supports the observations of Davis, Kingsbury, and Merry (2010: 14–15). In various fields where actors strive for 'global governance', such as the United Nations' efforts to bolster compliance with human rights, indicators are 'only one part of the reporting and monitoring process'. They are 'not meant to replace qualitative reports' or, in other cases, narratives, maps or photographs, but instead, are meant to complement them.

Actually there seems to be a particular complementary mode of knowledge production in microfinance. Two of the interviewees stressed the importance of the so-called 'due diligence process', a thorough inquiry into an MFI including one to three days during which they or their colleagues spend time on-site with the staff of this very institution regarded as a potential investee. While both the work phase before and after this on-site due diligence period seem to be dominated by desk work which is deliberately remote from the life-worlds of the MFIs (i.e. paper work that includes analysing financial and social performance indicators and occasionally also 'MIX Market' data), the local visit apparently follows a contradictory logic. In this period, the existing, rather staged, financial and social reports are systematically confronted with the embodied knowledge gained in personal encounters that the counterpart can control only to a small degree. Thus, one could call this interim work an *express* or *truncated* ethnographic experience on the part of investment personnel. The following quote from one of the interviews exemplifies both the bodily intensity and relevance of this experience (translated from German, emphasis added):

> [During the due diligence visit] we...verify the figures that we had received, *to understand what is behind them.* And actually those due diligences, they are a difficult operation...You must get sufficient information: for your logic, on the one hand, and *for your feeling*, on the other...For me, 'due diligence' is the centerpiece of our decision-making process, right? Because, ...whether something stinks you realize *then*...If you had not used your senses then...[locally] it is over. You could...call them, ask for information via E-mail...but when you *look the people in the eye*, look whether they are now lying or saying the truth or so, these are the most important points.

This on-site production of knowledge stands in sharp contrast to the retrieval of data from the screen world of the MIX Market, as described above. It is an irreplaceable knowledge that is partly tacit, partly dependent on verbal exchange, and gained only in face-to-face encounters ('if you had not used your senses then locally it is over'). One may conclude at this state of research that social and financial performance indicators and other abstract figures do play a role in the everyday work of decision-makers in microfinance, such as experts for fund management and advisory services. But they do not *determine* the final investment decisions. Personal experience and intuitions are indispensable, too.

CONCLUSIONS AND OUTLOOK: TOWARD THE CONSTRUCTION OF A SECOND-ORDER GLOBAL MARKET

This chapter tested the question of whether or not there is a self-contained electronic global market in the making in the microfinance sector, a market that follows the principles of world society. The information platform that was analysed above does exhibit such a market potential. It allows for entirely new forms of knowledge and rapid, low cost decision-making by people (such as potential investors) who otherwise would have never been interested in microfinance. The more microfinance institutions report to this platform along a range of different performance indicators, the more a differentiated field of (market) identities can emerge in the eyes of the platform user. Over time, this field can become increasingly differentiated, and more and more overarching properties of the field can be recognized as well (i.e. the global microfinance sector becomes understandable to many people *as* a specifically shaped sector). The platform thereby bears the potential to attract large sums of international private capital, which many microfinance experts deem indispensable to satisfy what is estimated to be the high demand of poor people world-wide for loans and other financial services.

However, this massive gain in literally *global* microfinancial knowledge comes at a price that is, most likely, equally significant. The last section discussed the actual complexities and ambiguities that lie behind the surface of two groups of performance indicators, which compose this on-screen world. One group of indicators relates to the measurement of poverty, and the other concerns the question of to what extent the empowerment of women is actually achieved. In light of what I have described as underlying complexities and uncertainties, which shape the making of microfinancial knowledge, the on-screen world appears to be only loosely connected to the actual everyday activities of the staff of microfinance institutions and their life-worlds. However, it is important to note that the on-screen world itself is not decoupled; rather, the initiatives that support the information platform strive for ongoing improvements in the translation process from the enumerable local lived realities to the on-screen yet simultaneously decontextualized global reality.

The last section also pointed to the practical limits of the on-screen world. It currently seems that the MIX Market platform is an important source of information for those microfinance experts who make decisions in the investment process in MFIs. But these experts do not deal with such numerical screen knowledge alone. To a great extent they also deal with other forms, such as embodied personal experience acquired during field visits to MFIs.

Thus, the new (electronic, numerical) management of microfinance does not completely dominate other forms of microfinancial knowledge-making. Yet, the movement I have discussed is not the only instance of world society in this field. A more recent initiative of the rating agency MicroRate that started in 2010 even seems to surpass the vision of global knowledge production discussed so far (MicroRate 2010). In concrete terms, 'LUMINIS', a new online rating service, strives to concentrate all relevant information about microfinance investment vehicles (MIVs) into a single Internet platform. As mentioned in the introduction, the MIVs serve as financial intermediaries to enumerable individual and institutional investors world-wide. Since the number of MIVs has increased significantly over the last years to over 100 (LUMINIS 2012a), MicroRate argues that the need arose to create 'widespread transparency in the universe of MIVs' (MicroRate 2010). In other words, the initiative tries to represent properly those institutions that *themselves* bundle numerous data (including social and financial performance data) of up to dozens of microfinance institutions distributed across a number of countries. The information presented in the MIX platform does not reach this high level of global aggregation. However, in a fashion similar to that of MIX, the explicit goal of LUMI-NIS is to produce 'comparative information' with which investors who are considering putting their money in the microfinance sector 'can weigh their own priorities and select funds that best match their [social and financial] preferences' (LUMINIS 2012a). Up to three MIVs can be juxtaposed together on one computer screen (cf. LUMINIS 2012b). As a representative of LUMINIS demonstrated at a microfinance conference, this is made possible by combining a range of pie-charts, bar charts and tables that include different sorts of numerical data. Thus, the basic principle of the MIX Market is pushed even further: it becomes possible to judge in a few minutes, or even a few seconds, the extent to which a financial intermediary, as it is typified in this combination of figures and diagrams, fulfills both financial and social objectives, as well as how it does so as opposed to other MIVs typified in similar ways. It can be assumed that both this mode of second-order knowledge production, and the second-order market differentiation of MIVs it makes possible, require indicators that are even more condensed than those discussed in this chapter. This remains to be investigated in detail in future.

References
Banerjee, Abhijit, Esther Duflo, Rachel Glennerster and Cynthia Kinnan 2010. *The Miracle of Microfinance? Evidence from a Randomized Evaluation*, available at www.povertyactionlab.org/sites/default/files/publications/The%20Miracle%20of%20Microfinance.pdf

CERISE 2010. *Social Audits in Microfinance: What have We Learned about Social Performance?*, available at www.cerise-microfinance.org/IMG/pdf/Analysis-DB-SPI_mis_en_forme.pdf

2012. *CERISE, the Microfinance Knowledge Network*, available at www.cerise-microfinance.org/spip.php?page=sommaire&id_rubrique=2

CGAP 2007. *Beyond Good Intentions: Measuring the Social Performance of Microfinance Institutions*, available at www.cgap.org/gm/document-1.9.2581/FN41.pdf

2008. *Foreign Capital Investment in Microfinance: Balancing Social and Financial Returns*, available at www.cgap.org/gm/document-1.9.50967/FN71.pdf

2010. *Andhra Pradesh 2010: Global Implications of the Crisis in Indian Microfinance*, available at www.cgap.org/gm/document-1.9.48945/FN67.pdf

2011. *Foreign Capital Investment in Microfinance: Reassessing Financial and Social Returns*, available at www.cgap.org/gm/document-1.9.2584/FN44.pdf

2012. *What is Microfinance?*, available at http://cgap.org/p/site/c/template.rc/1.26.1302/

Convergences 2013. *The 2013 Microfinance Barometer*, available at www.convergences2015.org/Content/biblio/BMF_ENG_2013_2205_web.pdf

Davis, Kevin, Benedict Kingsbury and Sally Engle Merry 2010. *Indicators as a Technology of Global Governance*. New York: Institute for International Law and Justice, New York University School of Law

Deutsche Bank 2007. *Microfinance: An Emerging Investment Opportunity*, available at www.dbresearch.com/PROD/DBR_INTERNET_DE-PROD/PROD0000000000219174/Microfinance%3A+An+emerging+investment+opportunity.pdf

Espeland, Wendy and Mitchell Stevens 2008. 'A Sociology of Quantification', *European Journal of Sociology / Archives Européennes De Sociologie* 49(3): 401–36

Goetz, Anne Marie and Rina Sen Gupta 1996. 'Who Takes the Credit? Gender, Power, and Control Over Loan Use in Rural Credit Programs in Bangladesh', *World Development* 24(1): 44–63

Grameen Foundation 2008. *Progress out of Poverty Index: PPI Pilot Training: Participant Guide*, available at www.progressoutofpoverty.org/system/files/PPITrainingGuide.pdf

Gupta, Akhil 2009. 'Nationale Armut, globale Armut und Neoliberalismus: eine anthropologische Kritik' in Hubertus Büschel and Daniel Speich (eds.), *Entwicklungswelten. Globalgeschichte der Entwicklungszusammenarbeit*. Frankfurt: Campus, pp. 113–39

Heintz, Bettina 2010. 'Numerische Differenz. Überlegungen zu einer Soziologie des (quantitativen) Vergleichs', *Zeitschrift für Soziologie* 39(3): 162–81

Heintz, Peter 1982. 'Introduction: A Sociological Code for the Description of World Society and Its Change', *International Social Science Journal* 34(1): 11–21

Kalthoff, Herbert, Richard Rottenburg and Hans-Jürgen Wagener 2000. *Facts and Figures: Economic Representations and Practices*. Marburg: Metropolis

Knorr Cetina, Karin and Alex Preda 2007. 'The Temporalization of Financial Markets: From Network to Flow', *Theory, Culture and Society* 24(7–8): 116–38

Krishna, Anirudh 2012. *Stages of Progress. Disaggregating Poverty for Better Policy Impact*, available at http://sanford.duke.edu/krishna/rationale.htm

Ledgerwood, Joanna 1999. *Microfinance Handbook: An Institutional and Financial Perspective*. Washington, D.C.: World Bank

Luhmann, Niklas 1997. 'Globalization or World Society: How to Conceive of Modern Society?', *International Review of Sociology* 7(1): 67–79

2000. *Vertrauen. Ein Mechanismus der Reduktion sozialer Komplexität*. Stuttgart: Lucius und Lucius

LUMINIS 2012a. *About Microfinance Investment Funds*, available at www.luminismicrofinance.com/MicrofinanceInvestment

2012b. *Tour the LUMINIS Site*, available at www.luminismicrofinance.com/Documents/Luminis_infographic.pdf

Matthäus-Maier, Ingrid 2008. 'Preface: New Partnerships for Innovation in Microfinance' in Ingrid von Matthäus-Maier and J. D. Pischke (eds.), *New Partnerships for Innovation in Microfinance*. Berlin: Springer

Mayoux, Linda 2011. 'Taking Gender Seriously: Towards a Gender Justice Protocol for Financial Services' in Beatriz Armendáriz and Marc Labie (eds.), *The Handbook of Microfinance*. New Jersey: World Scientific Publishing, pp. 613–41

Meehan, Jennifer 2004. *Tapping the Financial Markets for Microfinance: Grameen Foundation USA's Promotion of This Emerging Trend*, available at www.haas.berkeley.edu/HaasGlobal/docs/gfusacapitalmarketswp1004.pdf

Mennicken, Andrea 2000. 'Figuring Trust: The Social Organization of Credit Relations' in Herbert Kalthoff, Richard Rottenburg and Hans-Jürgen Wagener (eds.), *Facts and Figures: Economic Representations and Practices, Ökonomie und Gesellschaft*. Marburg: Metropolis, pp. 35–58

Meyer, John W., John Boli, George M. Thomas and Francisco O. Ramirez 1997. 'World Society and the Nation-State', *American Journal of Sociology* 103(1): 144–81

MicroRate 2010. *MicroRate Launches LUMINIS*, available at www.microrate.com/microrate-launches-luminis-mf-investor-information-platform-may-2010

MicroRate and IADB 2003. Performance Indicators for Microfinance Institutions: Technical Guide, available at www.microrate.com/media/docs/research/technical-guide-3rd-edition-english.pdf.

MIX 2011a. *MIX Brings Social Performance to the Forefront of Microfinance*, available at www.themix.org/press-release/mix-brings-social-performance-forefront-microfinance-0

2011b. *MIX – the Premier Source for Microfinance Data and Analysis*, available at www.themix.org/sites/default/files/MIX%20Brochure.pdf

2011c. *MIX Market Reaches 2000 Reporting Microfinance Institutions!*, available at www.themix.org/press-release/mix-market-reaches-2000-reporting-microfinance-institutions

2012a. *About MIX*, available at www.mixmarket.org/about

2012b. *Social Performance Indicators*, available at www.themix.org/social-performance/Indicators

2012c. *11 Indicators' Categories*, available at www.themix.org/social-performance/Indicators

2012d. *MIX Market Features*, available at www.mixmarket.org/features

2012e. *Videos: How to Analyze Social Performance Data*, available at www .themix.org/social-performance/training-videos

2012f. *MFI Report*, available at www.mixmarket.org/mfi/banco-fie/report

2013. *Social Performance Document Desk Review*, available at www .mixmarket.org/sites/default/files/2013_social_performance_desk_review_ _-seap.pdf

Pinch, Trevor and Richard Swedberg (eds.) 2008. *Living in a Material World: Economic Sociology Meets Science and Technology Studies*. Cambridge, Mass.: MIT Press

Porter, Theodore 1995. *Trust in Numbers: The Pursuit of Objectivity in Science and Public Life*. Princeton, N.J.: Princeton University Press

responsAbility 2013. *responsAbility Global Microfinance Fund: Quarterly Report Q4 2013*, available at www.responsability.com/investing/en/1061/ Product-overview.htm?Product = 19665 and www.responsability.com/ investing/data/docs/en/2745/Quarterly-rAGMF-EN-4Q2013.pdf

Riles, Annelise 2010. 'Collateral Expertise: Legal Knowledge in the Global Financial Markets', *Current Anthropology* 51(6): 795–818

Robinson, Marguerite S. 2001. *The Microfinance Revolution: Sustainable Finance for the Poor*. Washington, D.C.: World Bank, available at http://site.ebrary .com/id/10023658

Seibel, Hans Dieter 2005. *Does History Matter? The Old and the New World of Microfinance in Europe and Asia*, University of Cologne, Development Research Center No. 10

Servet, Jean-Michel 2011. 'Corporate Responsibility Versus Social Performance and Financial Inclusion' in Beatriz Armendáriz and Marc Labie (eds.), *The Handbook of Microfinance*. New Jersey: World Scientific Publishing, pp. 301–22

Smart Campaign 2012. *The Smart Campaign: Keeping Clients First in Microfinance*, available at www.smartcampaign.org/

SPTF 2012a. *Frequently Asked Questions*, available at http://sptf.info/ what-is-social-performance/faqs

2012b. *Home*, available at http://sptf.info/

2012c. *SP Task Force*, available at http://sptf.info/hp-sp-taskforce

2012d. *MIX SP Indicators*, available at http://sptf.info/resources/mix-sp-indicators

2012e. *Client Assessment Tools*, available at http://inthiseconomy.org/SPTF/details-client-assessment.html

Staub-Bisang, Mirjam 2011. *Nachhaltige Anlagen für institutionelle Investoren. Einführung und Überblick mit Fachbeiträgen und Praxisbeispielen*. Zürich: Verl. Neue Zürcher Zeitung

Vollmer, Hendrik 2012. 'Signaturen der Finanzialisierung. Von Finanzmärkten zu Organisationen, zu sozialen Situationen und (von dort) zu allem anderen' in Herbert Kalthoff and Uwe Vormbusch (eds.), *Soziologie der Finanzmärkte*. Bielefeld: Transcript, pp. 87–112

SPIRITS OF NEOLIBERALISM: 'COMPETITIVENESS' AND 'WELLBEING' INDICATORS AS RIVAL ORDERS OF WORTH

William Davies

Market prices are indicators of value or worth. A market is a system of indication, in which quantities of money are viewed as commensurate to the value of goods and services being traded. But is this a *good* system of indication? Why would we select price as our preferred indicator, and not some other indicator? These questions lead towards a 'meta' question, of what is valuable about the price system, and how might *that* be indicated.

An orthodox liberal economic argument is that markets increase efficiency, because both parties in an exchange are better off than they were prior to the exchange, assuming that it was conducted voluntarily. The premise of nineteenth century liberalism was that such exchanges will arise organically and 'naturally', once the state retreats from the economic domain, creating an autonomous space of free trade (Polanyi 1957). But prior to the rise of market society, broader moral arguments had to be mobilized in favour of the price system, which went beyond narrow claims about efficiency (Hirschman 1977). And by the late nineteenth century, with the rise of large corporations, institutionalist ideas and organized socialism, the case for the market was being lost once more. Neoliberalism, as first propagated in the 1930s by Friedrich Hayek, Henry Simons and the ordo-liberals, would necessarily involve restating and reinventing the argument in favour of the market, as a basis for social coordination and valuation (Mirowski and Plehwe 2009).

As Foucault stresses in his lectures on neoliberalism, its proponents never advocated a straightforward reversal of the trends towards bureaucratic, regulated, hierarchical capitalism that had swept Europe and the United States from 1870 onwards (Foucault 2008). Nor did they seek necessarily to shrink the state or the 'social' realm, in the hope that an autonomous free market would emerge once more. Instead, they sought to reinvent society and state in ways that were commensurate with the ethos and logic of the market. What distinguishes neoliberalism is its acutely idealist and constructivist effort to govern, measure and evaluate all domains of society according to principles extracted from the market (Mirowski 2009). Specific behaviours, ideals, characteristics and norms are identified with the free market (most commonly, those associated with 'enterprising' activity), and then employed as a basis on which to criticize and test institutions (Davies 2014). Strange as it may sound, this even includes the criticism and testing of markets and enterprises themselves, which become judged by regulators in terms of how closely they conform to a particular neoliberal ideal. Where liberalism pursued a separation of the economic sphere from the social and political, neoliberalism subjects state, market and society to a uniform economic audit.

On the basis of this understanding of neoliberalism, it becomes easier to see the potential for *multiple varieties of neoliberalism*, resting on multiple accounts of the market's distinguishing moral quality. The normative question of *why* markets are worthwhile is open to a number of different and sometimes conflicting answers. This chapter explores two principles in particular that have been identified with the market, and then used as a basis to criticize and measure market and non-market institutions. The first is the inculcation of an ethos of *competitiveness*, which has long been a driving normative ideal for neoliberals, from Hayek onwards. The second is the facilitation of individual and collective *wellbeing*. This latter principle would not commonly be viewed as 'neoliberal', indeed appeals to 'wellbeing' have often been used to criticize the competitive culture of neoliberal societies. But both competitiveness and wellbeing represent moral values that markets potentially uphold, and can subsequently be used as a moral basis on which to evaluate institutions both inside and outside of the economic sphere. In that specific sense, they each underpin a form of neoliberalism.

To provide a basis for governance and evaluation, these moral values cannot remain purely in the realm of the normative and qualitative. If societies are to be gauged and compared for their competitiveness or wellbeing, certain tests and measures need developing through which to do so. *Indicators* need to be constructed, to reveal how far societies have become imbued with the ethos of the market, however that ethos is defined. The purpose of this chapter is to explore how indicators enable the transition from normative to empirical judgement, in the specific cases of competitiveness and wellbeing. The next section lays out a theoretical and methodological approach, drawing on the pragmatist sociology of the Convention School. I then turn to the examples of competitiveness and wellbeing indicators in turn, before concluding with some speculations regarding transitions in the 'spirit' of neoliberalism.

INDICATORS AS CONVENTIONS OF VALUATION

National statistics display acute Weberian paradoxes of value neutrality. Their authority derives from the sense that they are 'objective', 'neutral' and 'scientific', while also representing something of public concern and political relevance, which is *worth measuring in the first place*. As Innes argues, 'the only way a statistician can keep out of politics is to collect irrelevant data' (Innes 1989: 75). Institutionally, they bridge between the academic social sciences and government policy imperatives, and their authority depends on their capacity to marry scientific and political 'vocations' (Weber 1991a; 1991b). Desrosières has argued that statistics have a dual status in the modern public sphere, whereby they both produce a shared and objective reality which an entire population can inhabit, while also serving as tools and objects of critique (Desrosières 1998: 325). From a pragmatist perspective, any disagreement is only meaningful in the context of an already agreed-upon shared world, including agreed-upon terms on which it is possible to disagree; statistics are involved in both the matters of agreement *and* disagreement. New objects of statistical measurement arise initially as normative, critical and political concerns, against 'objective' statistical backdrops, which they then contribute to renewing. They thereby lose their explicitly normative quality, as they become embedded as expertly and officially constructed realities, which are taken for granted and 'black boxed'. But this then facilitates new critical, public debates, which contribute towards the identification of new objects of statistical measurement.

The term 'indicator' refers to a statistic that successfully combines scientific objectivity with normative authority of some sort, winning agreement from both expert and non-expert publics. Many national

285

statistics emerge initially as indicators, for why else would they be constructed at all? For example, the critique that Gross Domestic Product (GDP) is not a 'good' indicator of national economic performance or doesn't capture activities that are 'worthwhile' ignores the extent to which the measure of aggregate national output initially indicated a great deal about potential military capacity at a time of war (Perlman 1987). The contingent political and moral concerns of statisticians and policy-makers may inadvertently provide the data on which more 'objective' or 'value neutral' analyses and social sciences are based. A convention arises, stating that a particular measurable, objective phenomenon is representative of something of worth, and hence 'a statistical category is the result of an equivalence convention' (Desrosières 2007: 5). In public life, numbers retain a relationship with moral judgement, while at the same time promising to replace moral judgement.

Convention scholars focus on this relationship between moral and empirical evaluations of worth, illuminating the implicit normative presuppositions that underlie apparently neutral and objective statements of social and economic facts (Boltanski and Thévenot 2006). A convention of evaluation ties together a metaphysical claim about *intrinsic* worth with techniques (such as statistics or accounting audits) for demonstrating the presence of that worth, in everyday situations, via *extrinsic* assessment. A principle must also be *testable* in some way, such that it can be used to cast authoritative judgement upon actions and outcomes in real-world situations.

Judged from a pragmatist standpoint, the political purpose of both moral and technical claims is the same, namely, to facilitate agreement amongst a certain group of actors or public. Technical and numerical representations of 'worth' have the rhetorical advantage of appearing neutral and disinterested; they also have the strategic advantage of reducing ambiguity and the scope for deliberation, and providing a clear set of rules (Meyer and Rowan 1977). The shift from the 'political metaphysics' of moral assessment to the 'political physics' of empirical evaluation inevitably robs the social world of much of its qualitative ambiguity, and renders it explicit. Sociologists of commensuration identify this as a 'form of valuing [that] denies the possibility of intrinsic value, pricelessness, or any absolute category of value' (Espeland and Stevens 1998: 324). By this account, the alternative to commensuration and measurement is to defend the *incommensurable* nature of intrinsically valuable goods, activities and relationships. And yet values which are incommensurable with one convention of measurement may them-selves be rendered technical, producing a new and alternative form of commensuration.

Convention scholars talk of situations 'holding together', when there is sufficient agreement on how a situation is to be technically evalu-ated (Desrosières 1998: 9–12; Boltanski and Thévenot 2006: 41). This implies that actors all inhabit the same moral order of worth and asso-ciated socio-economic reality. Consequently, it is also agreed which techniques of objective measurement should be employed as tests of value. Measurement and commensuration therefore stabilize situations, preventing them from becoming matters of excessive dispute. But sit-uations can equally 'fall apart', when actors start to appeal to rival, incommensurable orders of worth, when criticizing and justifying par-ticular actions, and differ over how to test and measure social real-ity. When this occurs, the moral underpinnings of measurement come to light once more, and actors fall back on political skills of rhetoric and compromise in order to negotiate between rival metaphysics of worth.

In applying this analytical approach to neoliberal statistical indica-tors, I make three assumptions, which will steer the line of empirical enquiry in the following sections. First, indicators are devices which facilitate a degree of agreement-reaching in public discourse. Who is to be party to this agreement, and what its terms are, is a separate matter to be investigated. Indicators are designed for different types of audience. Some will specifically seek to reinforce the authority of expert judge-ment, and to close down public debate, aiming for agreement amongst policy-makers, but not necessarily the wider public. The risk of such a strategy is that non-governmental actors, such as non-governmental associations (NGOs), think tanks and the media, might choose not to recognize the moral and/or technical authority of a given indicator or expert. Others will seek to mobilize actors or lobby policy-makers, by raising the profile of an alternative set of normative concerns, which are otherwise outside of the realm of expert evaluation or incommensu-rable with dominant indicators. Numbers then take on a more explicitly rhetorical quality, in seeking to persuade and travel within the public sphere.

Secondly, the political authority of an indicator lies in its capac-ity to mediate between moral and technical modes of evaluation. The ideal of positivist reason is to divorce fully one from the other, but this ideal is never fully realized. Metaphysical philosophies of what is 'ultimately' or intrinsically valuable are converted into scientific techniques for extrinsic valuation, but the former always leave their trace in the latter. The technical expert has merely claimed to identify a particular 'objective' trait, which can be treated as a proxy for intrinsic worth. Following Weber, the sociologist needs to follow this process 'upstream', identifying how normative principles were converted into measures in the first place. Some indicators will be presented with an exaggerated sense of their scientific authority (as if they would remain true, even if nobody agreed with them), while some are presented with an exaggerated sense of their popular authority or political urgency (like opinion polling), but all must have an element of both.

We can therefore speak of indicators possessing a normative 'spirit', in the same way that Weber spoke of the 'spirit of capitalism' (Weber 2002). This 'spirit' is the moral philosophy or ideology which conditions and accompanies a seemingly amoral, technical or utilitarian rationalism. Weber recognized that the pursuit of ever-greater wealth was not alone a sufficient basis on which to engage participants in capitalism. Behind numerical logic, be it economic or statistical, there is the 'spirit' of moral reasoning. The neoliberal justification for markets cannot be predicated purely on arguments about economic efficiency, although appeals to economic objectivity provide considerable rhetorical armoury. Something of *intrinsic* value must be identified in the market to provide a moral basis of critique (including the critique of extant markets), which can then be converted into a technical form of measurement, to evaluate market and non-market institutions, or even entire nations. Boltanski and Chiapello define the 'spirit' of capitalism as '*the ideology that justifies engagement in capitalism*' (Boltanski and Chiapello 2007: 8; emphasis in original). Likewise, the 'spirit' of neoliberalism is the *principle extracted from the market, which is used to justify the transformation of market and non-market institutions*. But in any case, a 'spirit' has to be subject to real-world tests, that is technical processes whereby the worth of a given agent (or institution, nation, process, good, etc.) can be proven, rendered empirical, before a range of actors. Neoliberal indicators put institutions and nations to the test, judging them according to a particular 'spirit' identified in the market.

Finally, the politics of an indicator must also be analysed in terms of its relative position vis-à-vis experts and non-experts, and in terms of its capacity to establish or conform to *standards* that become accepted in public spheres. In studying indicators, we are forced to recognize the extent to which the divisions between expert and non-expert, between technical and moral reason, between state and public, break down. Pressure groups and think tanks use quantitative data for rhetorical, political purposes; expert policy knowledge may rest on charismatic authority, and not scientific authority (Davies 2011a); government statistical agencies increasingly seek public engagement, to find ways of developing statistics that non-experts find credible. Rhetoric, numbers, sovereignty, popular opinion, moral judgement, expertise, governmentality and democratic process do not inhabit separate domains of state and civil society, but are all entangled with one another. The fact that certain statistics become accepted as standards across state, academia and society may be a result of particular monopolies possessed by certain actors (a census, for example, can only be carried out by state actors). But the history of statistics shows that there has never been a monopolist of statistical reasoning, and that amateurs – outside of both state and academy – have always played a crucial role in the innovation and dissemination of new techniques.

INDICATING NATIONAL COMPETITIVENESS

In 1979, the World Economic Forum (WEF) (then the European Management Forum) published its first *Global Competitiveness Report*, measuring and ranking the 'competitiveness' of European nations (European Management Forum 1979). The report noted:

> Traditionally, competitiveness is defined mainly in terms of the cost of production and productivity. However, we know today that many other elements come into play: the internal dynamism of a country, its socio-political consensus, the quality of its human resources, its commercial spirit, the manner in which it prepares for the future, etc.
>
> (European Management Forum 1979)

The task of a national competitiveness evaluation extended well beyond the limits of markets, to examine how successfully non-market institutions were supportive of markets, and imbued with an ethos of competitiveness. Rather than judging markets in terms of how well they served 'society', the evaluation of national competitiveness would judge 'society' in terms of how well it served the needs of entrepreneurs and businesses, in the context of globalizing markets

(Jessop 2002). Competitiveness indicators synthesize multiple social and economic statistics, combining them with survey data, to produce a single 'score' of national competitiveness. The centrepiece of each *Global Competitiveness Report* is the 'Global Competitiveness Index', which ranks nations according to their overall competitiveness levels, with a range of secondary indices ranking nations according to underlying factors in competitiveness. 'Competitiveness' grew to become a dominant organizing narrative for neoliberal policy regimes over the course of the 1980s and 1990s, not only at a national level, but also at the level of local, urban and European policy (Sum 2009). What sort of value or ethos is competitiveness, and how can it be rendered measurable? Let's address these two questions in turn, by focusing first on competitiveness as a moral 'spirit', then on the 'tests' that reveal its quantity.

SPIRIT OF COMPETITIVENESS

It was precisely the competitive dimension of markets that underpinned their normative appeal to the early neoliberals (Foucault 2008). Hayek offered a stark dichotomy, between policy regimes which create economic *plans*, and those which release economic *competition*, where the latter offered the only route to social coordination that did not involve a level of coercion (Hayek 1944). The freedom facilitated by the competitive dynamic of the market was thus its central moral virtue, quite aside from whatever empirical efficiencies might result, which Hayek treated as fortunate side-effects (Hayek 1944: 38). Markets themselves vary in their degree of competitiveness, meaning that an interventionist system of antitrust was initially a central policy demand of neoliberals, with the Freiburg School of 'ordo-liberalism' looking to the state to impose a legal framework upon markets, that would govern them in accordance to an *a priori* idea of competition (Gerber 1994; 1998).

The competitive spirit of neoliberalism extends beyond the limits of markets, thanks to two theoretical traditions. First, Schumpeterian economics greatly expands the 'field' in which competition takes place, to include strategic use of social networks, scientific findings, technology and institutions. Competition that goes on *within* markets assumes that supply and demand will become aligned, thanks to variations in price, but that the rival products being bought and sold are roughly the same. This is known as 'static competition'. By contrast, Schumpeter recognized that the most transformative forms of competition involved entrepreneurs introducing entirely *new* products, creating entirely *new* markets, that could then be monopolized for periods of time (Schumpeter 1976: 67). Entrepreneurs operate on the border of the 'market' and 'social' spheres, acting to usher in new products from outside of the established marketplace, identifying new, previously unmet needs. Hence, the sphere of competition is expanded to include anything that might conceivably serve the interests of entrepreneurs in the future.

Secondly, the Chicago School of economics abandons any *a priori* vision of the ideal competitive market from the 1950s onwards (Van Horn 2011). Instead, via a dogmatic allegiance to the principles of neoclassical economics (that is, to individual rational choice) it evaluates *all* social, political and economic institutions, on the assumption that individuals are constantly strategizing towards their own private advantage (Davies 2010). For Chicago economists such as Becker and Coase, market-type behaviour is present in all situations, and all activity can be assessed 'as if' it were market-based activity.

The significance of competitiveness think tanks (which produce most competitiveness indicators) is in providing a space in which politicians, policy-makers, business leaders and business gurus can network and affirm a shared commitment to the ethos of competitiveness. Studies of competitiveness frequently assert that it is a concern that cuts across all sectors, and all types of organization. The key commissions on national competitiveness, such as the 1985 President's Commission on Industrial Competitiveness in the United States and the European Competitiveness Advisory Group established in 1995, have notably included representatives from business, government and academia. The World Economic Forum's annual Davos conference is notorious as a cross-sectoral meeting point for very senior decision-makers. At least on a rhetorical level, the spirit of competitiveness is pushed into the governmental and political domain, by force of analogy between corporate strategy and national strategy, and by allowing politicians to express patriotism via the language of national competitiveness. The nation, the firm and the individual are all presented as similarly strategic agents, seeking to out-perform their rivals, both inside and outside of markets. Global capitalism becomes the game which all inhabit and all are implored to compete in, even if they also inhabit various other scales of competition (Jessop 2002).

TESTS OF COMPETITIVENESS

Competitiveness indicators are largely produced by think tanks, business schools and 'gurus', operating within what Thrift terms the 'cultural circuit of capital' (Thrift 2005). The most prominent sources of statistical analysis and comparison are the WEF, IMD World Competitiveness Centre, the Council on Competitiveness and Harvard Business School, while a handful of prominent 'gurus' such as Michael Porter and Stefan Garelli sell high profile consultancy alongside many of these institutions, to governments around the world. Pragmatically speaking, the task for those seeking to evaluate national competitiveness is how to produce a shared world, which 'holds' together objectively, inhabited by very senior decision-makers across all sectors of society.[1] Any quantitative data generated on competitiveness has to be relevant to them all, if it is to support the programme of disseminating the spirit of competitiveness. It is not designed to be conclusive or 'black-boxed', but to facilitate discussion and productive disagreement. This places a limit on its scientific sophistication, meaning that if there is one expert community that has been most alienated from this field of analysis, it is academic economists (e.g. Krugman 1994).

How do these think tanks and gurus set about rendering the ethos of competitiveness measurable? How is competitiveness *indicated* empirically? The first thing to note about competitiveness evaluations is that they are essentially comparative. The Hayekian ethos is that freedom consists of the freedom to win and lose, and this permeates the statistical analysis. Much of the data that competitiveness analysts employ and publicize is already in the public domain, but presented so as to benchmark nations against each other. Represented in this way, the exact level of national economic performance might appear less significant than *relative levels*, compared to other nations. The expectation or hope is then that policy-makers will strive to improve their relative position in the rankings, in the same way that entrepreneurs strive to dominate markets, or respond to being 'named and shamed' as low performers, though this is a necessarily weak way to discipline policy-makers (Bruno 2009). Rankings are a particular form of commensuration, which 'reduce distinctiveness to magnitude', focusing the eye upon differences between competitors, and the identity of the

---

[1] The World Economic Forum explains that the purpose of its global competitiveness reports is: 'to provide benchmarking tools for business leaders and policymakers to identify obstacles to improved competitiveness, thus stimulating discussion' (WEF 2011: 3).

'winner' (Espeland and Sauder 2007: 19). A single competitiveness score is awarded to each nation, whose sole significance is to facilitate a final national competitiveness table, which then serves to capture public and media attention.

Commensuration between different competitiveness scoreboards and evaluations is typically impossible, as the methods employed for constructing competitiveness scores differ between institutes and fluctuate over time; there are few methodological standards, which adds to the frustrations of orthodox economists. Longitudinal comparisons are largely made in terms of rank, not absolute performance (i.e. a fall in ranking is what matters, not the decline in the 'score'). In this sense, a national competitiveness 'score' indicates nothing by itself, beyond the confines of a single index. Yet, underlying this score is a series of indicators, each being synthesized out of further indicators, like Russian dolls. For example, one of the WEF's twelve 'pillars' of competitiveness is 'health and primary education', which consists of ten indicators (such as 'malaria incidence' and 'business impact of malaria incidence'), which are independently scored. An overall score for this 'pillar' is given, which will then be weighted and combined with scores for the other 'pillars'. So long as quantitative data exists, and plausible weights can be put on them, heterogeneous social, economic, cultural and political institutions and goods can all be brought into relations of equivalence. The metaphor of the indicator as a 'pillar' suggests an architectural structure, in which a nation's competitiveness is held aloft by a series of supporting structures, each of which needs strengthening by policy.

There is an inescapably normative dimension to the selection of these pillars, and each think tank or consultant will tweak their selection for their own purposes, clients and brand. The authority of 'gurus' in this field of research reflects the impossibility of concealing the normative judgements that are at work, endorsing qualitative judgement with the charismatic authority of a celebrity expert. The various indicators of competitiveness are compiled with a pragmatic awareness that no amount of statistical data can ever quite capture the underlying ethos of competitiveness. Only the use of 'Delphi surveys' comes close to capturing the intangible 'spirit' of competitiveness. This technique, used by WEF and the International Institute for Management Development (IMD) in their scoreboards, is used to quantify those aspects of competitiveness that most resist empirical measurement or for which no data are available. Senior business people are surveyed, and asked to score a given nation, often on tacit and qualitative issues, such as its entrepreneurial 'values'. Where results vary strongly, the divergent scores are sent back to the respondents for a further response. If these subsequent responses vary, the process continues, until some agreement is reached, providing a quantitative evaluation of a nation's ethos, or rather its reputation in the eyes of business leaders. The Delphi technique represents a peculiarly pragmatic example of commensuration, moving gradually between heterogeneous judgements about a given nation's 'spirit', to an empirical, quantitative statement of its worth. The role of the expert in this technique is not so much to supply an 'objective' assessment, as to facilitate agreement-reaching amongst elite non-experts, in a standardized fashion.

INDICATING NATIONAL WELLBEING

In 1974, the economist Frank Easterlin published a paper which would spawn the expression 'Easterlin's paradox' (Easterlin 1974). The paradox in question was that variations in measured levels of human happiness did not correspond to economic growth rates across most developed nations, raising questions regarding the authority of GDP as an indicator of national progress. Easterlin's findings have since been supplemented by a host of economic, psychological and statistical research on happiness, demonstrating the divergences between monetary valuation and measured psychological benefit. The social indicators movement has produced rival measures of societal and national progress, not only measured in money, since the early 1970s, as a challenge to GDP (Innes 1989). In the 2000s, these heterodox methodological approaches acquired growing policy relevance and authority, with a number of national statistical agencies starting to collect data on wellbeing. The high profile Stiglitz Commission was established in 2008 by the French President, to examine how to measure economic and social progress, reporting in 2009 with a report that highlighted wellbeing measurement as a necessary accompaniment to GDP (Stiglitz et al. 2009).

In the previous section, I looked at how neoliberals have focused on competitiveness as the distinguishing moral characteristic of the market, to be valued and measured across society. The proposition I wish to investigate here is that the development of individual wellbeing represents the spirit of a rival form of neoliberalism, which is accompanied by its own set of measures and tests. Markets can be justified in many

ways, not only for their facilitation of exchange, competitiveness or efficiency; they can also be justified for their capacity to satisfy needs and
demands, that is, to produce human happiness and alleviate suffering.
Business has developed various additional techniques and strategies for
delivering this satisfaction, which do not rely on abstract forces of supply and demand, but on market research, marketing and management.
But as with the ethos of competitiveness, this commitment towards psychological satisfaction and pleasure can be extended beyond the limits of the market, and elevated to a generalized moral principle, via
which nations can be evaluated, tested and compared. Here I describe
the ethical 'spirit' of wellbeing, before examining how it is indicated
empirically.

SPIRIT OF WELLBEING

Utilitarianism and market liberalism have intertwined genealogies,
which are synthesized in the British tradition of welfare economics.
Bentham argued in 1780 that 'the business of government is to promote
the happiness of the society, by punishing and rewarding', while classical liberalism presumed that free market exchanges represented a non-
coercive means of maximizing welfare (Bentham 1988: 70). Market liberalism is utilitarian, to the extent that money and psychological utility
are in some stable relationship of equivalence, an equivalence that is
presumed until some form of technical 'market failure' arises. This way,
prices can be assumed as valid indicators of value and of welfare, and
an increase in wealth is an indicator of increased happiness. With the
birth of macroeconomics and Keynesianism in the 1930s, growth of 'the
economy' as a whole became a potential indicator of aggregate wellbeing, though also on the basis that money and utility possessed some form
of equivalence (Mitchell 1998).

But why prioritize happiness at all? What is *intrinsically* good about
this entity or epi-phenomenon that utilitarians and welfare economists
are so keen to measure and maximize? And why should it *grow*, rather
than remain stable? The contemporary happiness economist, Richard
Layard, argues that 'if we are asked why happiness matters, we can give
no further external reason. It just obviously does matter' (Layard 2005:
113). Bentham's own definition of utility was so broad as to make all
human experience (ethical, psychological, economic) commensurable
to a single quantitative scale: 'by utility is meant that property, whereby
it tends to produce benefit, advantage, pleasure, good, or happiness

(all this in the present case comes to the same thing)' (Bentham 1988: 2). Whatever metaphysical or normative presuppositions underpin the Benthamite agenda, they remain carefully concealed at all times, other than a principled hostility towards metaphysical and normative politics. The most extensive system of commensuration (and thus the most complete eradication of intrinsic values from public policy) becomes a political goal in its own right.

But perhaps we can come at this question from another angle. Via what moral critique does the equivalence convention between money and happiness fall apart? Of course, capitalism has always been accompanied by various traditions of anti-capitalism, of both left-wing and right-wing varieties. Markets can be criticized on the basis that some things simply shouldn't be for sale, or shouldn't be commensurable or measured at all (Satz 2010). What is different about critiques made from within the 'spirit' of wellbeing is that they criticize markets and non-market institutions on the basis that *they are not adequately utilitarian*. If the promotion of happiness is to become a broader societal principle, beyond the limits of the market (thereby splitting the equivalence between price and wellbeing), a metaphysics or principle of happiness is required, out of which new indicators can be developed. What form of happiness *should* the market deliver, but doesn't? Three answers suggest themselves, which are relevant to how wellbeing indicators are constructed.

First, the market *should* facilitate rational, self-interested decision-making, but often doesn't. This understands happiness as a form of psychological event – a moment of pleasure or *hedonia*. Through most of the twentieth century, neoclassical economics operated with the 'revealed preference theory of choice', which stated that behaviour was a direct representation of preferences that are held by the individual as stable, knowable epi-phenomena (Hands 2010). Satisfying these preferences could be assumed to produce utility and the individual would know how to achieve this. This methodological presupposition has come under attack from various sources. Market researchers began to study the 'attitudes' of consumers from the 1920s onwards, as phenomena that existed independently of purchasing behaviour, but extended into the social and political realms as well, spawning opinion polling (Baritz 1960; Rose 1996; Osborne and Rose 1999). And experimental economics, focused on choice-making behaviour, grew out of game theory at the University of Michigan in the 1950s, to demonstrate the limited capacity and tendency of individuals to behave in a calculated, self-interested way (Heukelom 2006; 2010). These critiques share a normative commitment to the satisfaction of individual desires, and the creation of mental wellbeing; but they all recognize that consumers are prevented from experiencing this, either by imperfections in markets, or imperfections in their own calculative capacity.

Secondly, the market *should* deliver fulfilling, meaningful lives, but often doesn't. This is happiness as Aristotelian *eudaimonia* (Nussbaum and Sen 1993). The term 'wellbeing' is often used to refer to this form of happiness, having both an 'objective' and a 'subjective' element. 'Objective' wellbeing refers to various substantive goods that are necessary preconditions of a good and happy life for all human beings, such as health and democratic government. 'Subjective' wellbeing refers to the individual's own sense of life satisfaction, and the sense of meaning or purpose that they find in their life. If there is one market which most impacts upon eudaimonic happiness, it is the labour market, seeing as how a meaningful, coherent life has increasingly become associated with 'job security' and a 'career' in modern times. Thus, one area where the equivalence convention of the market has been disrupted by eudaimonic critique since the early twentieth century is in the psychological studies of workplaces, which bred the Human Resources industry (Baritz 1960; Rose 1996). The recognition that alienated workers and meaningless work could impact negatively on employers *and* employees was a recognition that the equivalence convention between wages and labour did not hold together fully. An additional means of valuing and rewarding work was required, beyond what the labour market alone could facilitate.

Finally, the market *should* facilitate a form of progress towards societal wellbeing, in some quasi-Enlightenment sense, but often doesn't. The assumption here is an implicitly Kantian one, that the future must be somehow better, more fulfilled, greater than the past, and that the present is a moment of critique between the two (Kant 1970a). This is the Aristotelian teleology of the individual pursuing a good life, aggregated up to a national teleology towards 'a perfectly constituted state as the only condition in which the capacities of mankind can be fully developed' (Kant 1970b: 50). The historical telos of nations took on an increasingly technical and statistical dimension over the course of the nineteenth century, and macroeconomics made the aggregate national flow of goods and services a potential indicator of a nation's progress. But the question of where a nation is heading, what its wealth is *for* and how it should evaluate itself remain open ones, which cannot be resolved using economics. Identifying aspects of life that are valuable, but which can't be bought or sold, and adding these to indicators of national 'progress' is central to development economics and the social indicators movement.

TESTS OF WELLBEING

As much as Benthamites and economists might wish for a single theory of wellbeing, to be indicated in a single measure of wellbeing, once we look behind the primary existing measure (namely, the price system) we discover that there are heterogeneous forms of happiness that require measuring in heterogeneous ways. Many such measures have been constructed since the 1960s, meaning that the utilitarian critique of the price system is no longer merely negative or 'anti-capitalist', but can now offer alternative conventions via which wellbeing is to be indicated, but which do not rest on monetary valuation (Diener and Seligman 2004; Diener and Ryan 2008). This includes forms of national wellbeing indicators, as are now being compiled by various national statistical agencies around the world.

Of the three ethical philosophies of happiness outlined in the previous section, the first (individual rational choice) is least suitable to indication at a national level. Behavioural and wellbeing economists have developed extensive bodies of evidence, to distinguish the circumstances under which individuals *do* calculate in a rational, self-interested fashion, from those in which they don't, and the circumstances in which their decisions *do* lead to the experienced utility which they predict, from those in which they don't (Kahneman and Sugden 2005). The critical empirical-normative question is which circumstances do we *adapt to*, and hence when do our experienced happiness levels cease to correspond to our objective conditions, including our economic conditions. This has various policy uses, for instance, attaching quantitative values to health outcomes and public goods, and some high profile policy prescriptions for 'nudging' individuals towards better choices (Dolan and Kahneman 2008; Thaler and Sunstein 2008). Hence, it is possible to produce quantitative indications of a given individual's happiness at precise moments, using techniques such as the Day Reconstruction Method or even brain scans. But few people would argue that this notion of happiness should be used as a basis on which to evaluate or compare nations.

Statistical interest in happiness has largely focused on *self-reported* happiness (or 'life satisfaction'), rather than on experienced happiness. The crucial technical characteristic of self-reported happiness is what Cantril originally termed the 'self-anchoring technique' (Cantril 1966). This involves surveying individuals on their quality of life, but without offering them an objective basis or measure via which to assess it. Instead, questions such as 'overall, how satisfied are you with your life nowadays' are asked with a range of possible answers, but the individual assesses their life according to values and aspirations that are private to them. This is in contrast to the 'attitudinal' research of the marketing and polling industry, in which individuals are asked to express an opinion of a specific institution or product. The resulting data indicates 'subjective wellbeing', and forms a central part of the social indicators movement and development economics. Variations in aggregate levels of subjective wellbeing, both over time and between nations, have been used as part of a critique of GDP as an indicator of 'progress'.

Self-reported happiness data are scarcely indicative of either individual *eudaimonia* or of societal progress on their own. They suffer from a range of technical and normative problems, such as the possibility that some cultures have a greater propensity to report happiness than others. However, when combined with *objective* wellbeing data (that is, data on a nation's level of material, political and human development), a richer notion of national wellbeing can be built up, which is more indicative of a nation's socio-economic fulfilment or progress than purely monetary measures. Selecting indicators of objective wellbeing is an inevitably somewhat arbitrary process, that (as with identification of 'pillars' of competitiveness) reflects something of the normative presuppositions of the statistician or social scientist. The 'spirit' of these indicators is not hidden, but instead makes certain teleological assumptions explicit. Combining measures of subjective wellbeing (i.e. happiness) with measures of objective wellbeing produces an indicator of a nation's quality of life, which ought normatively to grow over time, diverting the Kantian Enlightenment spirit away from a fixation on GDP, towards more carefully designed indicators.

In the early twenty-first century, a number of national statistical agencies began to collect data on subjective wellbeing (life satisfaction) and objective wellbeing, including those of Australia, Canada, the United States and Britain. The case of the British Office for National Statistics (ONS) highlights how various technical-normative equivalence conventions need to be established, before a nation's wellbeing can be measured. Initially, authority for the ONS's study of national wellbeing came directly from the Prime Minister, who announced that he was commissioning national wellbeing indicators in 2010. The ONS established a number of expert groups (containing economists, psychologists and statisticians), to advise on how to construct life satisfaction surveys, in ways that would elicit meaningful answers, identify regional variations and also be potentially commensurable with national surveys being run in other countries (Office for National Statistics 2010; 2011). The technical intricacies of subjective wellbeing measurement were left to experts, who published the questions for assessing subjective wellbeing in 2011.

However, the ONS also ran a 'national debate' on the meaning of 'national wellbeing', consisting of 150 public events around the country, enabling statisticians and economists to take questions from audiences. This was accompanied by a consultation exercise, which asked individuals to identify those aspects of life which 'matter most to you', then which of these should also be included in a measure of national wellbeing (Office for National Statistics 2010). The ONS consultation notes stated that:

> Before ONS can start to measure national well-being we need to find out what national well-being means to those with an interest in it and how the new measures would be used…ONS is seeking views on what well-being means to you and what affects well-being, both for you as an individual and for the nation overall.
>
> (Office for National Statistics 2010)

This emphasis on the intuitive or vernacular meaning of 'national wellbeing' was echoed by the Chief Statistician, who explained the purpose of the 'national debate' as seeking 'good ways of showing figures which people recognise as telling a story which reflects their experiences' (Matheson 2011). The method or procedure for integrating public interpretations of 'wellbeing' is not revealed by the ONS, but what is interesting about this case is the work that is put into consolidating wellbeing as a relevant, meaningful and robust indicator, that is both technically strong and publicly relevant. The technique of indication is the responsibility of the ONS and its various advisory groups, but the ethos to be indicated is (at least rhetorically) presented as a matter of public opinion or preference. The teleology of individuals and nations is not amenable to expert specification, though experts are tasked with framing questions and designing measures.

CONCLUSION: RIVAL NEOLIBERALISMS?

The financial crisis which began in 2007 has led many to question whether neoliberalism is alive or dead (Peck *et al.* 2010). David Harvey's reply is that this depends on what you mean by neoliberalism (Harvey 2009). In this chapter, I've offered a particular definition of neoliberalism as an effort to govern both economy and society, according to normative principles that have been extracted or deduced from an idea of the liberal market. And where such a principle is identified, the question then arises of how that is to be employed as a tool to criticize, judge and evaluate in everyday, concrete situations. A neoliberal moral principle, or 'spirit', must also be converted into an empirical test, if it is to succeed in facilitating an agreed-upon reality for decision-makers. One way of understanding the constitution and fate of neoliberalism is in terms of *which* moral-empirical indicator is used as the dominant basis for evaluation and comparison, and how successfully that indicator 'holds together' as a form of publicly agreed-upon objective reality. As this chapter has explored, competitiveness and wellbeing growth are rival principles that are, from a neoliberal perspective, ideally present in markets, but which can be used to criticize, measure and compare market and non-market institutions and whole nations.

The construction of wellbeing indicators may not appear like an example of neoliberalism. Certainly in its more developmental or Aristotelian forms, national wellbeing measurement may not necessarily privilege a neoclassical or consumerist vision of happiness as preference satisfaction or pleasure. Yet the project of subjecting market and non-market institutions to an integrated performance evaluation is in keeping with applied neoliberal policy-making. Moreover, an idealized vision of a 'good' market (including a good job, rational consumers, healthy lifestyles) provides a norm against which empirical evaluation of actual markets and individual behaviour is conducted.

The more speculative reason for looking at competitiveness indicators and wellbeing indicators side by side is that the current crisis of neoliberalism *could possibly* involve a shift from a privileging of competitiveness to a privileging of wellbeing, both morally and technically (Davies 2011b; 2012). Instead of individuals, communities and nations being invited to mimic the entrepreneurial properties of markets, which are decisive in splitting 'winners' from 'losers', they may increasingly be invited to mimic the therapeutic properties of markets, which facilitate gradual organic growth of relationships and selves. Technical apparatuses of measurement and comparison accompany both these rival 'worlds' of moral evaluation. Neoliberalism may not be disappearing, but it may be experiencing a shift in its dominant spirit and measure.

Boltanski and Thévenot draw our attention to the various compromises and rhetorical battles that go on between rival orders of worth. If competitiveness and wellbeing are the spirits of rival neoliberalisms then we can already see emerging conflicts and compromises between them. Competitiveness and inequality have already been roundly criticized, by drawing attention to their impact on measured levels of wellbeing (Wilkinson and Pickett 2009; Layard 2005). The WEF, which remains closely associated with the measurement of national competitiveness, has sought compromise by publishing evidence on the importance of wellbeing to long-term competitiveness (WEF 2011). Reports from its 2014 Davos meeting suggested that concern with wellbeing (mental and bodily) may now even have trumped competitiveness (Greenhill 2014). But ultimately, these rival neoliberalisms operate with rival notions of the intrinsic value of markets. Both claim to be in touch with the original 'spirit' of liberalism – and with Adam Smith in particular – but interpret that spirit in incommensurable ways, producing incommensurable neoliberalisms.

In terms of the tests of neoliberalism, two final discrepancies in the *styles* of indication are worth noting. The first is in the principal manner of comparison: competitiveness indicators are designed chiefly to facilitate synchronic commensuration (that is, over space), while wellbeing indicators are designed to facilitate both synchronic and diachronic commensuration (over space and time), with a particular emphasis on the latter. Everything about competitiveness indicators is geared towards inculcating a sense of rivalry between nations. The absolute values or 'scores' attached to various national goods and outcomes are only meaningful inasmuch as they result in a ranking for the nation concerned, relative to other nations at the same time. National wellbeing, on the other hand, places a strong emphasis on the notion of national *progress*, that is, its development over time. 'Easterlin's paradox' is a specifically diachronic phenomenon, the fact that GNP *growth* does not correlate to happiness *growth*. These rival spirits of neoliberalism pose the question: is it more important to compare with rivals in the present, or with the same nation in the past?

Secondly, they both include measures for ensuring that subjective, normative valuations are factored into indicators, and not entirely suspended in favour of expert, objective measurement. But these differ markedly in style. The Delphi Survey mediates between the opinions of senior business people, in order to put quantitative values on the aspects of a national culture which most resist quantification. Competitiveness indicators therefore offer a form of objective reality which is guaranteed to chime with the instinct of a particular audience, and which other audiences (especially policy-makers) are then invited to recognize and inhabit. Wellbeing indicators are more populist and relativist than this, inviting members of the public to place a value on their lives, relative to their own goals and aspirations. The consultation and 'national debate' run by the ONS in the United Kingdom demonstrate an additional form of populism, in the way that the 'objective' indicators of wellbeing are selected, though with little transparency surrounding the procedure for factoring in public opinion.

Each in its own way demonstrates an uneasy tension which an indicator has to manage, between expertly-endorsed objectivity and the attitudes, preferences and values of broader publics. These indicators are both somewhat heterodox and controversial; the dilemma of their protagonists (many of whom operate in the grey areas between state, academia and civil society) is whether to claim expert authority, and fall back on largely technical claims regarding the efficiency of markets, or some form of moral authority, which also articulates why markets are an intrinsically good thing in the first place, regardless of measured outcomes. This latter strategy is the distinctly neoliberal one.

References

Baritz, Loren 1960. *The Servants of Power*. Middletown, Conn.: Wesleyan University Press

Bentham, Jeremy 1988. *The Principles of Morals and Legislation*. Buffalo, N.Y.: Prometheus Books

Boltanski, Luc and Eve Chiapello 2007. *The New Spirit of Capitalism*. London: Verso

Boltanski, Luc and Laurent Thévenot 2006. *On Justification: Economies of Worth*. Princeton, N.J.: Princeton University Press

Bruno, Isabelle 2009. 'The "Indefinite Discipline" of Competitiveness Benchmarking as a Neoliberal Technology of Government', *Minerva* 47(3): 261–80

Cantril, Hadley 1966. *The Pattern of Human Concerns*. New Brunswick, N.J.: Rutgers University Press

Davies, Will 2010. 'Economics and the "Nonsense" of Law: The Case of the Chicago Antitrust Revolution', *Economy and Society* 39(1): 64

2011a. 'Knowing the Unknowable: The Epistemological Authority of Innovation Policy Experts', *Social Epistemology* 25(4): 401–21

2011b. 'The Political Economy of Unhappiness', *New Left Review* 71 (September–October)

2012. 'The Emerging Neocommunitarianism', *Political Quarterly* 83(4): 767–76 (October–December)

2014. *The Limits of Neoliberalism: Authority, Sovereignty and the Logic of Competition*. London: Sage

Desrosières, Alain 1998. *The Politics of Large Numbers: A History of Statistical Reasoning*. Cambridge, Mass.: Harvard University Press

2007. 'Comparing the Incomparable: The Sociology of Statistics' in J. Touffet (ed.), *Augustin Cournot: Modelling Economics*. Cheltenham: Edward Elgar

Diener, Ed and Katherine Ryan 2008. 'Subjective Well-being: A General Overview', *South African Journal of Psychology* 39(4): 391–406

Diener, Ed and Martin E.P. Seligman 2004. 'Beyond Money: Toward an Economy of Well-Being', *Psychological Science in the Public Interest* 5(1) 1–31

Dolan, Paul and Daniel Kahneman 2008. 'Interpretations of Utility and Their Implications for the Valuation of Health', *Economic Journal* 118(525): 215–34

Easterlin, Richard 1974. 'Does Economic Growth Improve the Human Lot?: Some Empirical Evidence' in P. David and M. Reder (eds.), *Nations and Households in Economic Growth: Essays in Honor of Moses Abramovitz*, New York: Academic Press, Inc.

Espeland, Wendy and Michael Sauder 2007. 'Rankings and Reactivity: How Public Measures Recreate Social Worlds', *American Journal of Sociology* 113(1): 1–40

Espeland, Wendy and Mitchell Stevens 1998. 'Commensuration as a Social Process', *Annual Review of Sociology* 24(1): 313–43

European Management Forum 1979. *Global Competitiveness Report*

Foucault, Michel 2008. *The Birth of Biopolitics: Lectures at the Collège De France, 1978–79*. Basingstoke: Palgrave Macmillan

Gerber, David J. 1994. 'Constitutionalizing the Economy: German Neo-Liberalism, Competition Law and the "New" Europe', *American Journal of Comparative Law* 42(1): 25–84

1998. *Law and Competition in Twentieth Century Europe: Protecting Prometheus*. Oxford: Clarendon Press

Greenhill, Robert 2014. 'Davos 2014: Beware – a Healthy Economy Puts High Value on Wellbeing', *Guardian*, 19 January 2014

Hands, D. Wade 2010. 'Economics, Psychology and the History of Consumer Choice Theory', *Cambridge Journal of Economics* 34(4): 633–48

Harvey, David 2009. 'Their Crisis, Our Challenge', *Red Pepper* (March)

Hayek, Friedrich August von 1944. *The Road to Serfdom*. London: Routledge & Sons

Heukelom, Floris 2006. *Kahneman and Tversky and the Origin of Behavioural Economics*, Tinbergen Institute Discussion Paper

2010. 'Measurement and Decision Making at the University of Michigan in the 1950s and 1960s', *Journal of the History of the Behavioral Sciences* 46(2): 189–207

Hirschman, Albert 1977. *The Passions and the Interests: Political Arguments for Capitalism Before Its Triumph*. Princeton, N.J.: Princeton University Press

Innes, Judith Eleanor 1989. *Knowledge and Public Policy: The Search for Meaningful Indicators*. New Brunswick, N.J.: Transaction Publishers

Jessop, Bob 2002. *The Future of Capitalist State*. Oxford: Polity

Kahneman, Daniel and R. Sugden 2005. 'Experienced Utility as a Standard of Policy Evaluation', *Environmental and Resource Economics* 32(1): 161–81

Kant, Immanuel 1970a. 'An Answer to the Question "What is Enlightenment"' in Kant's Political Writings, edited with an Introduction and Notes by Hans Reiss, translated by H. B. Nisbet. London: Cambridge University Press

1970b. 'Idea for a Universal History with a Cosmopolitan Purpose' in *Kant's Political Writings*, edited with an Introduction and Notes by Hans Reiss, translated by H. B. Nisbet. London: Cambridge University Press

Krugman, Paul 1994. 'Competitiveness: A Dangerous Obsession', *Foreign Affairs* (March/April)

Layard, Richard 2005. *Happiness: Lessons from a New Science*. London: Allen Lane

Matheson, Jil 2011. Transcript of Jil Matheson's speech on 'Measuring National Well-being', 25 November

Meyer, John W. and Brian Rowan 1977. 'Institutionalized Organizations: Formal Structure as Myth and Ceremony', *American Journal of Sociology* 83(2): 340–63

Mirowski, Philip 2009. 'Postface: Defining Neoliberalism' in P. Mirowski and D. Plehwe, (eds.), *The Road from Mont Pèlerin: The Making of the Neoliberal Thought Collective*. Cambridge, Mass.: Harvard University Press

Mirowski, Philip and Dieter Plehwe (eds.) 2009. *The Road from Mont Pèlerin: The Making of the Neoliberal Thought Collective*. Cambridge, Mass.: Harvard University Press

Mitchell, Timothy 1998. 'Fixing the Economy', *Cultural Studies* 12: 82–101

Nussbaum, Martha and Amartya Sen 1993. *Quality of Life*. Oxford: Oxford University Press

Office for National Statistics 2010. *Consultation: Measuring National Well-Being*

2011. *Measuring National Wellbeing Technical Advisory Group: Terms of Reference*

Osborne, Thomas and Nikolas Rose 1999. 'Do the Social Sciences Create Phenomena?: The Example of Public Opinion Research', *British Journal of Sociology* 50(3): 367–96

Peck, Jamie, Nik Theodore and Neil Brenner 2010. 'Postneoliberalism and its Malcontents', *Antipode*, 41: 94–116

Perlman, Mark 1987. 'Political Purpose and the National Accounts' in W. Alonso and P. Starr (eds.), *The Politics of Numbers*. New York: Russell Sage Foundation

Polanyi, Karl 1957. *The Great Transformation: The Political and Economic Origins of Our Time*. Boston, N.J.: Beacon Press

Rose, Nikolas 1996. *Inventing Our Selves: Psychology, Power, and Personhood*. Cambridge: Cambridge University Press

Satz, Debra 2010. *Why Some Things Should Not be For Sale: The Moral Limits of Markets*. Oxford: Oxford University Press

Schumpeter, Joseph 1976. *Capitalism, Socialism and Democracy*. London: Allen & Unwin

Stiglitz, Joseph, Amartya Sen and Jean-Paul Fitoussi 2009. *Report by the Commission on the Measurement of Economic Performance and Social Progress*

Sum, Ngai-Ling 2009. 'The Production of Hegemonic Policy Discourses: "Competitiveness" as a Knowledge Brand and Its (Re-)Contextualizations', *Critical Policy Studies* 3(2): 184

Thaler, Richard H. and Cass R. Sunstein 2008. *Nudge: Improving Decisions about Health, Wealth, and Happiness*. New Haven, Conn.: Yale University Press

Thrift, Nigel J. 2005. *Knowing Capitalism*. London: SAGE Publications

Van Horn, Robert 2011. 'Chicago's Shifting Attitude Toward Concentrations of Business Power (1934–1962)', *Seattle University Law Review* 34: 4

Weber, Max 1991a. 'Science as a Vocation' in *From Max Weber: Essays in Sociology*. New edn, London: Routledge
    1991b. 'Politics as a Vocation' in *From Max Weber: Essays in Sociology*. New edn, London: Routledge
    2002. *The Protestant Ethic and the "Spirit" of Capitalism and Other Writings*. London: Penguin

Wilkinson, Richard G. and Kate Pickett 2009. *The Spirit Level: Why More Equal Societies Almost Always Do Better*. London: Allen Lane

World Economic Forum 2011. *Global Competitiveness Report, 2011*. WEF

CHAPTER TWELVE

CLIMATE CHANGE VULNERABILITY INDICATORS: FROM NOISE TO SIGNAL

Till Sterzel, Boris Orlowsky, Hannah Förster,
Anja Weber and Dennis Eucker

INTRODUCTION

Using several examples, this chapter explores the application, advantages, limitations and academic debate with respect to climate change vulnerability indicators (CCVIs) as complexity-reducing representations of societal vulnerability to climate change. In recent years, the need has increased for understanding the factors which determine the vulnerability of societies around the world to climate change. Decision- and policy-makers are in need of useful and usable information on this matter to reduce climate change vulnerability, and require it in a way that permits the development of appropriate policies in a given context. CCVIs appear to be an example of how such information is provided: they are a means of quantifying societal vulnerabilities to climate change into a single number, and of communicating to policy-making how vulnerable particular entities are to specific aspects of climate change.

The following example illustrates the need and provision of such indicator-driven information on climate change vulnerability. In November 2008, the sub-committee for the Pilot Program for Climate Resilience (PPCR) of the Climate Investment Funds (CIF), initiated by the World Bank, appointed an expert group to produce a list of ten countries or regions that are the most vulnerable to anthropogenic climate change. These countries were to benefit from the funding of the PPCR programme for actions toward improved climate change resilience. By September 2010, the PPCR fund had grown to roughly

US$1 billion, receiving aid from several different donor countries (Climate Investment Funds 2010). In the face of this substantial sum, transparency and replicability in selecting the receiving countries were of key importance. The expert group therefore decided on an approach based on the use of vulnerability indicators (Brooks *et al.* 2009).

The identification of the most vulnerable countries with regard to climate change is a task of large complexity, one that begins with the very notion of vulnerability. The aspects of vulnerability investigated often included health, food security, access to water, or the capacity to adapt and develop different combinations of these. If it is difficult to quantify the current status of any of these aspects (let alone if available data is scarce, which is often the case), it is even more difficult to derive their dependence on climate and to estimate how they evolve under a future, changing climate.

In light of these difficulties, a wide range of rather loose climate change vulnerability definitions have emerged, which have one common ground: they, ideally, provide a 'measure of possible future harm' (Hinkel 2011) caused by climate change.

The task of the PPCR expert group was to operationalize such definitions, as well as to translate them into numbers. This would finally yield a ranking of country vulnerability. Vulnerability indicators are a means of determining such numbers. They usually capture individual aspects of climate change and relate them to their consequences for society. For example, they give estimates of the proportion of a population living below sea-level which would be particularly affected by sea-level rise, or the fraction of people above sixty-five years of age who would suffer the most from increasing frequency and severity of heat-waves.

Considering a multitude of such indicators together potentially provides a comprehensive view of the challenges a given population will face under climate change. However, even the most comprehensive set of indicators can never be complete since the concept of vulnerability, referring to future harm, necessarily contains un-measurable dimensions, for example, when the societal harm caused by a projected future climate trend is assessed. Subjective interpretations and value judgments are integral parts of any climate change vulnerability assessment; they accompany those aspects that are, by means of indicators, measurable.

With these difficulties in mind, the PPCR expert group decided to adopt a pragmatic approach: they identified continent-scale regions *particularly affected* by climate change (based on future climate simulations using climate models). The vulnerability ranking of countries within such hot spots was based on a set of ten commonly available standard indicators, including access to water, sea level rise exposure, climate disaster risk, food security, adaptive and managing capacity, and environmental vulnerability. Instead of a numeric aggregation, the PPCR expert group then analysed the context-dependent relevance of each indicator and derived their final ranking through collective discussion and expert judgment. The obtained ranking led to the distribution of large sums of money, while it was not produced in an entirely objective fashion due to the difficulty of grasping the precise nature of vulnerability to climate change.

As research advances, the view on CCVIs has undergone revision as the limitations of the practicality of their use have become clearer: CCVIs have been, and still need to be, constituted in multiple ways and for different purposes. There are a wide range of temporal and spatial scales, as well as diverse social realities which need to be considered when determining vulnerability to climate change. We discuss the use of such indicators as a means to quantify vulnerability to climate change, highlighting their strengths and weaknesses within the scientific debate.

Our chapter now turns toward the notion of vulnerability itself, followed by a discussion of the usage and properties of climate change vulnerability indicators, as well as the criticism they have received in the scientific debate, which is still ongoing. In the light of the uses, properties and criticisms thus identified, the following section reflects on a case study of a recent climate vulnerability assessment of livelihoods in two districts of Mozambique, which we consider a useful example for a diligent application of vulnerability indicators in a specific, practical context. The final section concludes this chapter.

CONCEPT OF 'VULNERABILITY'

'Vulnerability' is a widely used concept in understanding and assessing the negative impacts of climate change. The term has gained increasing importance in climate-related research over time (Tompkins and Adger 2005). Researchers have argued that because vulnerability and its causes play essential roles in determining the consequences of climate change, understanding the dynamics of vulnerability is as important as understanding climate itself (Smit and Pilifosova 2001).

Overall, the limitations of climate system models for capturing the dynamic nature of vulnerability to climate change[1] have created an increasing interest in social science, social theory and their potential contributions to a more nuanced understanding of the existing relations between climate and society.

Most of the definitions of vulnerability to climate change and related terms used in current research originate from the Intergovernmental Panel on Climate Change (IPCC), as it represents the widest consensus on climate change terminology available (Nelson *et al.* 2008). Based on the work undertaken by the IPCC, its Third Assessment Report contains the most consequential definition of vulnerability. The report defines vulnerability as:

> [t]he degree to which a system is susceptible to, or unable to cope with, adverse effects of climate change, including climate variability and extremes. Vulnerability is a function of the character, magnitude, and rate of climate variation to which a system is exposed, its sensitivity, and its adaptive capacity. (IPCC 2001: 995)

Based on the IPCC definition, it is, in particular, the above three factors of exposure, sensitivity and adaptive capacity that determine vulnerability. It is also important to understand that the IPCC conceptualizes vulnerability within a *systems* perspective. It therefore judges an entire system as being vulnerable if it is exposed to climate change impacts, if it is sensitive to those impacts, and if it has a low capacity to cope with those impacts (Adger and Vincent 2005).

Essentially, vulnerability can be understood as a *process* variable, or a variable determined by the internal properties of a system. This is, for example, in line with Kelly and Adger (2000), who argue that the vulnerability of any individual or social group to some particular form of natural hazard is determined primarily by their presently existing state. This state is characterized by their capacity to respond to that hazard, rather than by what may or may not happen in the future. Vulnerability therefore is the *susceptibility* of people to the harmful consequences of climate variability and extremes (Richards 2003).

In this context, the notion of adaptive capacity has attracted much interest from researchers and practitioners in the field of development cooperation, and both governmental and non-governmental organizations (NGOs). While exposure and sensitivity determine the potential

---

[1] Hinkel 2011, for example, refers to problems of measuring future harm which includes making normative decisions.

consequences of climate-induced change based on their physical and bio-physical consequences,[2] adaptive capacity can have a major influence on what consequences actually arise, and is therefore the component of vulnerability most amenable to influence by social systems (Marshall *et al.* 2010).

Some of the main considerations refer to the concept of 'social vulnerability' (Adger 1999; Brooks 2003; Brooks *et al.* 2005), which can be defined as 'the exposure of groups or individuals to stress as a result of social and environmental change, where stress refers to unexpected changes and disruption to livelihoods' (Adger 1999: 249). This is in contrast to those views which concentrate on the physical dimensions of the issue because of the greater emphasis placed on the dynamic interaction between climate change and the social, political, institutional and economic structures which shape individuals' lives (Adger 2006; O'Brien *et al.* 2007). This approach also brings into relief the dividing line between social science and physical climate science: the former mainly strives to extend knowledge on adaptive capacity inherent *to* a system (and from a starting-point perspective), while the latter focuses on the physical exposure given to it (an end-point approach).

Vulnerability is principally impacted by the negative consequences of the external dimension of climate change-related threats; but it also embodies the internal constraints of a system to respond to these. Hence climate change does not itself provide the central determinant of vulnerability, but rather, its context does (Dietz 2006; O'Brien *et al.* 2007). In addition, vulnerability to climate change can be aggravated by the presence of other societal stressors, the particular combination of which are the very core of understanding vulnerability to climate change as a contextual condition for a given system.

In an attempt to reconcile both understandings, Füssel (2007) identifies four main contextual features of vulnerability: (1) the system of analysis; (2) the valued attributes of concern; (3) the external hazard; and (4) a temporal reference. Based upon this specification, the challenge is to understand the interactions between and relative importance

---

[2] It must be stressed here that 'vulnerability' is no longer a new concept in the mainstreaming development literature (Georg 2009). The emerging interest and conceptualization of vulnerability clearly draws on insights that are firmly rooted in disaster management (Watts and Bohle 1993). This older paradigm in the study of risks and hazards mainly perceived vulnerability as a combined function of hazard, exposure and sensitivity, and therefore may be referred to as purely physical or bio-physical vulnerability, with the latter being more commonly used since it also includes certain aspects of the living environment (Brooks 2003).

of factors within social systems that contribute to social vulnerability (Warner 2007).

However, due to the interdependence of the several scales and characteristics with which the concept operates, vulnerability can only remain a vague concept used to express a complex idea. Vulnerability research related to climate change is still a relatively new development. It demonstrates the complexity we are faced with in the light of the variety of climate impacts, systems, spatial and temporal scales, as well as the people they affect. We now turn to a more detailed discussion of these aspects and their quantification through vulnerability indicators.

CLIMATE CHANGE VULNERABILITY INDICATORS

This section begins with addressing properties, functions and applications of climate change vulnerability indicators. Subsequently, it provides an overview and review of criticism and suggested room for improvement from parts of the academic community regarding the current practice of these indicators.

In a rapidly evolving field, climate change vulnerability research has experienced a proliferation in the use of indicators. They have become a widely used approach for making the complex concept of vulnerability to climate change operational through what are called *vulnerability assessments*. In the past two decades, many vulnerability indicators have emerged from such climate change vulnerability assessments, which determine and quantify vulnerability to climate change in different systems and at different spatial and temporal scales. The wide range of resulting publications illustrates how vulnerability is conceptualized, operationalized and understood in many different ways.

Climate change vulnerability indicators (CCVIs) principally simplify complexity by quantifying the interdependence of many circumstances into a single number, which should then be usable and comprehensible for policy-makers. But just like there is no general framework on how to quantify an area's vulnerability to climate change, no general framework exists for generating or selecting the appropriate indicators in climate change vulnerability research.

What distinguishes vulnerability indicators from well-known indicators such as the Human Development Index (see UNDP 2011; 2012), is the indication of a possible *future* development (in this case possible future harm) rather than the indication of a situation in a current state (Ionescu *et al.* 2008; Hinkel 2011). The vast majority of climate

312

change vulnerability indicators are of quantitative character and they explicitly address vulnerability to projected future climate change.

The following five examples of the use of CCVIs illustrate the wide-ranging applications and implications vulnerability indicators can have across a variety of spatial scales.

As described in the introduction, the Climate Investment Fund (CIF) utilised CCVIs as a pragmatic approach for identifying among a set of countries those that seem to be most vulnerable to climate change impacts. Based on the results of this assessment, several countries were selected for the allocation of funds to manage the negative impacts of climate change. In another programme, the World Bank sought to identify climate-relevant input, output and outcome indicators to track how climate action could best support key development goals (IBRD and World Bank 2008). On the district level, Hahn *et al.* (2009) developed a 'Livelihood Vulnerability Index' to evaluate climate and climate change vulnerability for two districts in Mozambique, and compared the results in an example that will be further discussed below. On the highly aggregated, (largely) national level, Diffenbaugh *et al.* (2007) indicate what they call 'Twenty-first century socio-climatic exposure' to global climate change through a combination of regional climate change projections and population, poverty and wealth metrics. In calculating their regional vulnerability indicator for heat-waves in the German state of North Rhine-Westphalia, in another example, Kropp *et al.* (2009) combine sub-components using fuzzy logic in order to quantify 'fuzziness' in assigning variable values to classes. Fuzzy logic is a mathematical system that uses degrees of truth rather than binary logic in order to describe the vagueness of the real world.

The function CCVIs performed in the CIF study exemplifies a commonly stated purpose for using them: CCVIs are used to identify entities (e.g. regions, people or sectors) particularly vulnerable to adverse effects of climate change. In the CIF case, they were used to identify highly vulnerable regions. On the basis of this identification they had to fulfil their secondary purpose of allocating climate change adaptation funds to these regions.

In addition to the purpose of identifying vulnerable entities, there are a number of other applications identified in the literature which CCVIs are used for. These applications are both scientific and political, and address different sets of questions pertinent to different spatial scales (Eakin and Luers 2006; Patt *et al.* 2008; Füssel 2009; Hinkel

2011). Such purposes include identifying entry points for vulnerability reduction and monitoring. Based on the proposition that the study of vulnerability (and hence, vulnerability indicators) to global environmental change should currently fall into the domain of policy instead of the domain of science (Patt *et al.* 2008; Klein 2009), in the following we focus on the purposes that broadly inform decision-making in order to reduce vulnerability to adverse effects of climate change through pointing out ways for a society to intervene or adapt. Arguably, the most successful and intuitive way of achieving these goals through CCVIs is by using a robust methodology to reduce the complexity of the aspect of climate change vulnerability in question, and providing users with communicable, usable answers to policy-relevant questions. Often, the purposes CCVIs are designed to fulfil and what they finally fulfil are not identical (Hinkel 2011). This mismatch will be further discussed below.

Assessing climate change vulnerability implies normative judgments and decisions at a variety of stages. In developing, interpreting and using CCVIs, it is necessary to define what is a good or bad state, and which kinds of outcomes should be thought of as better or worse (Ionescu 2008; Klein 2009). In determining what constitutes vulnerability in a certain study, decisions on which factors to include and which to exclude need to be made. In aggregating these components into a CCVI, then, the assignment of relative weights is necessary and entails varying degrees of judgments on the influence of each indicator, and depends particularly on the methodology used (Eakin and Bojórquez-Tapia 2008).

These steps can be consequential: the normative choices made in developing national-level vulnerability indices can largely determine the resulting vulnerability ranking (Eriksen and Kelly 2006; Füssel 2009). In identifying which countries are to be considered particularly vulnerable to the negative effects of climate change based on CCVIs, the CIF needed to establish definitions that would clarify what the term 'particularly affected' means, where it begins and where it ends. The basis upon which such comparisons are made inherently necessitates the use of normative input.

There are a number of reasons for the increased use of CCVIs. In the previous section, we discussed vulnerability as an equivocal, complex concept. CCVIs attempt to reduce complexity, thereby representing a means of simplification. Moreover, the simplification of an issue which is as complex as climate change vulnerability appears to be an intuitive approach for communicating to policy-making or the general public how vulnerable which entities are, and to which specific climatic changes (Hinkel 2011). In addition, CCVIs can make the results of climate change vulnerability assessments more tangible for the public and for policy-makers.

Next, the ambiguous definition of vulnerability in the Third Assessment Report of the IPCC (McCarthy *et al.* 2001) theoretically makes indicators advantageous for operationalizing the concept of climate change vulnerability by indicating each of the aspects – (changing) exposure, vulnerability and adaptive capacity – with either single or composite indicators. It has been argued that vulnerability *per se* cannot be measured because it is not an observable phenomenon, such as temperature (Patt *et al.* 2008). The most common way to overcome this constraint and to make the concept of vulnerability operational is to use indicators (Schauser *et al.* 2010). The changing focus of climate change research over time provides another reason for using indicators. The increasing incorporation of indicating social conditions is clearly reflected in the different generations of vulnerability assessments: while first-generation vulnerability assessments were based on climate impact assessments relative to baseline conditions, second-generation assessments increasingly incorporated adaptive capacity (Füssel and Klein 2006).

The pragmatic use of such aggregated indices (Brooks *et al.* 2009) in the process of allocating CIF funds is understandable for different reasons: often only coarse data-sets allow for global comparability on a national scale, while more detailed data with larger coverage which accounts for regional differences are often unavailable. In addition, a predetermined allocation of funding on a national scale arguably requires a national-scale approach with global coverage.

Thus, using vulnerability indicators for broad comparability comes with certain trade-offs. For example, local circumstances and differences may not be taken into account as thoroughly as they could if one specifically dealt with determining vulnerability on a local scale. In addition, different social vulnerability rankings at the national level produce different rankings, depending on the methodology and data used and the degree of rigour in the definitions and terminology deployed (Füssel 2009). This makes it difficult to devise a strategy for prioritizing vulnerability-reducing measures. In turn, this does not provide an ideal basis upon which to make objective judgments about where to nationally allocate funds (Eriksen and Kelly 2006).

CHALLENGES AND ROOM FOR IMPROVEMENT

A global approach to determining vulnerability to climate change at the national level, such as the study ranking particularly vulnerable countries for the CIF, inevitably faced criticism from parts of the academic community (e.g. Eriksen and Kelly 2006; Füssel 2009; Klein 2009). National level indicators or indices inherently oversimplify the diversity and complexity of interactions between scales, stakeholders and socio-ecological systems relevant to vulnerability by masking the wealth of circumstances which co-determine it at subnational levels in a single number or class for an entire country.

This brings us squarely to how the growing demand for climate change vulnerability indicators has also been contrasted with criticism from the academic community: substantial conceptual and methodological weaknesses of CCVIs and other indices have been pointed out, and the utility and purposefulness of such indicators have been subject to much debate (e.g. Eriksen and Kelly 2006; Patt *et al.* 2008; Eakin *et al.* 2008; Füssel 2009; Hinkel 2011). The main reasons for this criticism can be traced back to vagueness and oversimplification. As we have shown above, the umbrella term 'vulnerability' suffers from these very symptoms in its definitions, terminology and operationalization. They persist in those vulnerability assessments that use CCVIs with vague concepts, methodologies and purposes.

In theory, CCVIs with similar labels, e.g. 'social vulnerability to climate change', and the same area of interest, e.g. a global overview with countries as a unit of analysis, should derive a similar picture of climate change vulnerability. And in theory, a comprehensive view of a specific climate change vulnerability, e.g. of coastal zones, should successively emerge from a variety of different CCVIs addressing a multiple number of external stressors and systems. But that this is not necessarily the case is best illustrated through those indicators operating on the national level in general, and through comparing the rankings of the results these yield.

Comparing the rankings of five different national level indices of social vulnerability to climate change comprising 38 up to 167 countries, Eriksen and Kelly (2006) found relatively little agreement as to which countries are most vulnerable. In a study outlining the appropriateness of existing vulnerability indicators for co-determining the prioritization of money for adaptation, Füssel (2009) found similar disagreements between two studies on national coastal zone vulnerability to sea-level rise regarding the 'hot spots' of vulnerability, as well as the overall picture. This is explained by the fact that developing national-level vulnerability indices requires substantial normative choices in selecting and aggregating information, which in turn determines the resulting ranking (Füssel 2009).

The subsequent interpretation of CCVIs can add another degree of subjectivity and value judgment, which, upon closer inspection, can blur the objectivity of the indicators. The dilemma remains, at least for applications that aim for vulnerability of larger, sometimes even global scales, such as the Pilot Program for Climate Resilience outlined in the introduction to this chapter.

In the light of this criticism, the following questions regarding the use and usability of climate change vulnerability indicators for policy-makers are relevant, and have been implicitly or explicitly raised in the literature: When are CCVIs appropriate for informing policy-makers on how to reduce vulnerability? If they can be appropriate, what constitutes an appropriate CCVI? In the subsequent paragraphs we will elaborate on each of these questions.

(1) When are CCVIs appropriate for informing policy-makers on how to reduce vulnerability?

The discussion of national-level CCVIs show a clear preference for disaggregated information in the building of CCVIs. They are best developed with a clear, delineable context and spatial scale in mind because vulnerability is highly context-specific, as pointed out above (Vincent 2004; O'Brien et al. 2007).

Data requirements depend, inter alia, on these features. This also clearly demonstrates the limitations of applying these kinds of indicators to other scales and contexts: a community-level vulnerability indicator devised for a sub-Saharan African context may be largely irrelevant in a German context, and entirely irrelevant at the national scale (Vincent 2007). Barnett et al. (2008) and Hinkel (2011) emphasize that the use of CCVIs is only appropriate for local scales, where systems can be clearly defined such that the number of variables remains manageable. This is in line with arguing that determinants of vulnerability are place- and system-specific (Smit and Wandel 2006).

Ideally, CCVIs contribute to fulfilling a formulated, specific purpose in that they reduce the complexity of vulnerability policy-making. Such a purpose can aid decision-makers in reducing vulnerability by identifying regions that are most vulnerable to climate change as well as other external stressors (Patt *et al.* 2008).

Füssel (2009) argues that the clarity of purpose needs to be a crucial element in the guiding of any development of a CCVI itself or set of indicators, noting the lack of clarification regarding the purpose and application of indicators in many studies. With respect to its development and application, a CCVI theoretically is a means to an end, i.e. fulfilling a specific purpose. In practice, however, there are examples in which a CCVI has been used without a clear statement of purpose accompanying it, or without having a clear purpose in mind how the results could, in the broadest sense, aid in reducing vulnerability. In this case a CCVI becomes an end itself. A possible explanation for this is echoed in similar critiques of policy documents showing the recurrent absence of the specific purposes vulnerability indicators are meant to be used for (Hinkel 2011). Indeed, stating the purpose clearly would also help in determining its ultimate use and utility, regardless of its scientific or policy-related nature.

As a result, there is often room for improvement as to whether or how the purpose of using CCVIs is communicated. From a scientific point of view, the use of CCVIs requires great care and should be largely restricted to local, well-constrained situations, which is a more modest approach than what many studies and climate change adaptation programmes actually expect CCVIs to deliver.

(2) What, then, constitutes an appropriate CCVI?

Reducing complexity through the use of CCVIs requires a rigorous scientific approach in order to make a concept as complex as vulnerability operational. There is risk in oversimplifying or distorting this complexity through a number of possible conceptual, methodological or empirical shortcomings, and in failing to establish and explicitly communicate what the vulnerable situation of reference is. This requires being unequivocal regarding the actual attribute of concern, the system of interest, the external stressor and the temporal reference (Füssel 2007). When rigorously applying these four dimensions, it becomes evident that many studies professing to assess climate change vulnerability in fact indicate current rather than potential future harm.

Studies have identified insufficiently rigorous scientific methodologies (Eriksen and Kelly 2006); lack of transparency in methodologies (Klein 2009); failures to convey the unavoidable uncertainty they contain (Patt, Klein and de-la-Vega-Leinert 2005); and vague links between indicator data-sets and what should actually be encapsulated by the indicators (Brooks *et al.* 2009). Such conceptual, methodological and empirical shortcomings of aggregated indices of vulnerability to climate change have been pointed out as one major reason why there is little agreement on which countries are most vulnerable to it (Füssel 2009). As a result, applying indicators for informing decision-making processes would greatly benefit from more explicit research design and description (Eakin *et al.* 2008; Nicholls *et al.* 2008; Hinkel 2011). This applies to the framing, terminology, methodology and limits of CCVI applicability.

This section demonstrated that the difficulties encountered when defining vulnerability to climate change are re-encountered when designing indicators to measure vulnerability. Different regions and societies experience varying exposures to climate change, and their ability to cope with this exposure also varies significantly. Policy-makers who are aware of this complexity still need a way of gaining information upon which to base adaptation strategies. In principle, CCVIs appear to suit this need: they quantify and aggregate complex processes into simple numbers and thereby allow, for example, for a ranking of the regions most vulnerable and, therefore, most entitled to financial support first. Such a designation, however, must go hand in hand with explicitly stating the research design; metrics used; the purpose, utility and normative judgements involved; and, crucially, the limitations. Although methods of quantifying complex climate change vulnerabilities are markedly needed, CCVIs often cannot entirely comply with the requirements for such quantification, especially on larger, e.g. national, scales. However, as we have shown, CCVIs are better applied in local, specific situations, where the boundaries and characteristics of the studied population and their interaction with climate impacts are better known.

The following section introduces a case study which, in our view, serves as an example of a pragmatic, good practice approach toward a more successful application of climate change vulnerability indicators.

TOWARDS BEST PRACTICE

While the previous section, *inter alia*, provided an overview of the existing criticism and suggested room for improvement regarding the application of CCVIs, this section looks at a recent case study, a climate and climate change vulnerability assessment of livelihoods in two rural districts of Mozambique (Hahn *et al.* 2009). We will first summarize the approach and main outcomes of the case study as outlined in Hahn *et al.* (2009). Second, we demonstrate (on the basis of some criteria specified by Hinkel 2011) why we consider the case study to be a suitable example of the application of vulnerability indicators, despite some limitations, which we will point out. The example of Hahn *et al.* (2009) illuminates one way by which vulnerability indicators can be developed and applied to empirical work, leading to results that can be particularly useful for decision-making and for identifying goal-oriented development policies and initiatives.

The case study was carried out through a collaboration between Emory University (Atlanta, Georgia, United States) and CARE-Mozambique. Based on existing methods, the Livelihood Vulnerability Index (LVI) was devised to serve two purposes: first, that it provide the target users with an understanding of the influences that demographic, social and health factors have on climate change vulnerability at the district or community level and of potential areas for intervention. Second, it should provide them with a practical tool to be used for assessing the different impacts of climate change on livelihood vulnerability in the two districts. In and of itself, the design turned out to be flexible and adjustable to the specific needs and goals of the analysis of these two different target regions.

In addition to the use of secondary data derived from a systematic literature search, primary household data on each of the seven main indicators (socio-demographics; livelihoods; social networks; health; food and water security; natural disasters; and climate variability) were collected from a survey of 200 households in both districts. For each main indicator, several sub-indicators were defined. For example, for the indicator 'livelihood', the sub-indicators 'per cent of households with family member working in a different community', 'per cent of households dependent solely on agriculture as a source of income', and 'average Agricultural Livelihood Diversification Index (range: 0.20–1.00)' were selected. To assemble the indicators into a composite index, the data were then aggregated with the use of two approaches: the Livelihood Vulnerability Index (LVI) and the Livelihood Vulnerability Index-Intergovernmental Panel on Climate Change (LVI-IPCC), the latter with an aggregation to three sub-indices – exposure, sensitivity and adaptive capacity – in step with the commonly used IPCC vulnerability definition. The resulting differential vulnerabilities were then compared.

The first approach, the LVI, comprises the seven major indicators listed above and categorizes the results on a scale from 0 = least vulnerable to 0.5 = most vulnerable. The second approach, the LVI-IPCC, aggregates the seven main indicators into three factors contributing to vulnerability as defined by the IPCC: exposure (combining the components of natural disasters and climate variability); sensitivity (combining the components of health, food and water); and adaptive capacity (combining the components of socio-demographic profile, livelihood strategies and social network), on a scale from −1 as the least vulnerable to +1 as the most vulnerable (Hahn et al. 2009). The aggregation was conducted by weighting all sub-indicators equally, explicitly stating that this weighting could be adjusted and handled differently by future users.

The results of the two approaches showed a similar level of vulnerability for each district; more specifically, Moma, located in the northern Nampula province, was more vulnerable with regard to water resources and Mabote, located in southern Inhambane, was more vulnerable with regard to its socio-demographic structure. While the current vulnerability level to climate impacts is indicated in a first step, the approach included climate change vulnerability, albeit under a simplified climate change scenario, in a second step.

The results derived by using climate projections (in this case, the implications of an average annual temperature rise of 1°C in each district within the next twelve years) showed opposite effects in the two districts: an increasing LVI in Mabote and a decreasing LVI in Moma.

The case study discussed here provides an example of what an appropriate and well-targeted application of vulnerability indicators could look like, inter alia, by taking some of the academic criticism into account in order to improve the use of vulnerability indicators. Hahn et al. focused on a comparative study between two districts only, highlighting the vulnerability aspects of livelihoods at a clearly defined local level rather than at national level. This is in line with Hinkel (2011), who identified six purposes for which vulnerability assessments have already been used, but out of which he determines one to be appropriate, namely, for identifying particularly vulnerable people, regions or sectors at a local scale.

With the purpose of providing the targeted users with an understanding of the different factors that generate vulnerability, the assessment from Hahn et al. (2009) provides insights into the processes that shape vulnerability. This goes beyond the narrow focus of indicating the state of vulnerability alone, and is in line with criticism suggesting that too little attention is being paid to the processes that shape vulnerability, and too much to the state of vulnerability itself (Eriksen and Kelly 2006).

Furthermore, the use of primary data from household surveys was included to construct the index in order to align it with the local context conditions. Known biases in using secondary data from different spatial and temporal scales were thereby reduced. As regional climate model outputs were considered too coarse, and thus not accurate enough to project the effects of climate change at the local level, the project also tried to avoid depending on the models by quantifying the strength of actual livelihood and health systems, as well as the capacity of the communities to modify their strategies when responding to climate exposures (see Hahn *et al.* 2009: 16).

The need for transparency and, moreover, the need for preventing misinterpretation (see Schröter *et al.* 2005: 583; Hinkel 2011; Costa and Kropp 2012) were addressed by in-depth explanations of the chosen LVI-indicators and their sub-indicators (Hahn *et al.* 2009). This included their sources, and importantly, the explicit outlining of the existing or potential limitations of the study itself and of certain methodological aspects (e.g. the role played by normative judgments in the selection of the sub-indicators, and the limitations of the duration of temperature and precipitation analysis data due to lack of further data, see Hahn *et al.* 2009: 12–13). The results were then contextualized, and the quantitative results were contrasted with qualitative perceptions. In other words, the results were embedded within an explanation of local characteristics for which a specifically local knowledge set is needed.

Hahn *et al.* (2009) also explicitly discuss for whom their approach could be of use (development organizations, policy-makers and public health practitioners, to name a few), and how this could be done. They also demonstrate how certain aspects can or should be adapted to the user's need (e.g. by way of subcomponents and weightings). The results, furthermore, allow for the construction of a simple, complexity-reducing metric and accompanying set of charts and diagrams, which facilitate communication between indicator users; in this example, by comparing the districts with respect to the individual indicators. Put another way, visualizing the data with the help of diagrams may also offer intuitive access to the results for potential use by policy-makers and development organizations in development and adaptation planning.

Weaknesses and room for improvement are also delineable in the approach we have presented. As pointed out earlier, the observed temperature and precipitation data were limited by the short time series available (six years in this case). Furthermore, the indicators generally represent the current situation as opposed to future climate change vulnerability, despite projecting vulnerability to climate change into the future by another six years – too short a timespan to speak of changing climate (Hahn *et al.* 2009). The assessment of 'climate change' vulnerability under this simple scenario made the connection to climate change less robust than in other climate change vulnerability assessments. But considering the avoidance of known biases and problems deriving from the usage of regional climate models for their local scale of choice, this approach at least offers the possibility of addressing and including the issue of climate change in vulnerability assessments.

To conclude, as Hinkel (2011) points out, vulnerability indicators can only act as a 'high-level entry point', which, in a second step, need to be followed by further and more detailed stages of information development. Finally, the data analysis and calculations still remain complex and time-consuming and, in any case, expert input is needed. However, as a German Federal Ministry of Transport, Building and Urban Development (BMVBS) report argues: 'Ultimately, purely scientific studies cannot show which ideas and concepts are in fact compatible to fit the practice. This is only possible through the testing and application in practice' (BMVBS 2011: 7). Therefore, '[g]iven the novelty of the issues there is a need to experiment and learn' (Hinkel 2011: 207).

CONCLUSIONS

Over the last two decades, a growing awareness of the societal impacts of climate change resulted in the proliferation of climate change vulnerability research. Since the very beginning, its complexity has challenged science and policy alike. Due to the vast diversity of involved factors and players, a clear definition of the term remains an unresolved issue.

Consequently, attempts to quantify climate change vulnerability in order to inform decisions and policies regarding climate change adaptation have been most useful when coming from well-defined and limited applications where the interplay between society and climate change is favourably clear and understood, and where the available data allows for a robust quantification of this interdependency. However, applications to larger aggregated scales such as the national level, or generalizations of approaches derived for specific regional contexts have often failed to yield such robust results and interpretation.

Nevertheless, it is common sense that climate change will impact with region-dependent severity. At the same time, the resulting societal harm will strongly depend on the coping and adaptation ability of the affected population, which is also regionally diverse. The fact that this disparity exists is rarely denied; however, its quantification is not straightforward. The crucial need for climate change adaptation is increasingly recognized by policy-making, which in turn is, *inter alia*, increasingly interested in simple and yet robust quantifications of climate change vulnerability. CCVIs offer an avenue by which to resolve the difficulty of over-complexity. Their main characteristic, namely, that they aggregate complex processes into one or few numbers, makes them extremely attractive to all involved stakeholders. The scientific community, on the other hand, which is the player expected to facilitate this quantification, has limited methods and data to produce such simple and robust quantifications, and is increasingly aware of current limitations of CCVIs as the complexity of the subject unfolds more strongly as research proceeds. So at times there is dissatisfaction with current CCVIs in parts of the scientific community and heightened demand from policy-makers to produce and use them.

Usually, the common assumption is that numbers are neutral, allow for more- versus less- in need comparisons, represent a perfect means for decision-making, and appear to be objective. This chapter has inquired into the characteristics and the design of such indicators, pointing out that they inevitably involve subjective and normative choices: for example, when determining which effects of vulnerability to climate change are considered 'bad' for society and to be avoided; when identifying variables as proxies thereof; when combining several such variables; and when deciding which of them are more important than others. The curtailed objectivity that follows from such choices is inherent to the subject, however, and will remain an issue for future climate change vulnerability assessments. Therefore, it can be considered important for studies using CCVIs to explicitly state the normative judgments applied in their design and use, and to make the overall research design of the studies explicit.

From a scientific perspective, great care is advised when utilizing vulnerability indicators. As a rule of thumb, the larger the spatial scale, the less meaningful the information condensed into such indicators can be. If the limitations of a CCVI are appropriately taken into account and explicitly stated in the study, CCVIs can prove useful. At smaller spatial scales, such as individual households, carefully designed vulnerability indicators can successfully describe both current and future linkages between societal harm and climate impacts and, therefore, point out their vulnerability, as the above discussion on the Mozambique case study shows.

Thus, climate change vulnerability indicators, if applied properly, can be useful tools that successfully support climate change adaptation policies. However, they should be seen as what they are: non-universal tools, which do not, and cannot, account fully for the complex reality of climate change vulnerability – which is what they may be mistaken for.

References

Adger, W. Neil 1999. 'Social Vulnerability to Climate Change and Extremes in Coastal Vietnam', *World Development* 27(2): 249–69

2006. 'Vulnerability', *Global Environmental Change* 16(3): 268–81

Adger, W. Neil and K. Vincent 2005. 'Uncertainty in Adaptive Capacity', *Comptes Rendus Geoscience* 337: 399–410

Barnett, Jon, Simon Lambert and Ian Fry 2008. 'The Hazards of Indicators: Insights from the Environmental Vulnerability Index', *Annals of the Association of American Geographer* 98(1): 102–19

BMVBS 2011. *Vulnerabilitätsanalyse in der Praxis. Inhaltliche und methodische Ansatzpunkte für die Ermittlung regionaler Betroffenheiten.* BMVBS

Brooks, Nick 2003. *Vulnerability, Risk and Adaptation: A Conceptual Framework.* Tyndall: Tyndall Centre for Climate Change Research

Brooks, Nick, Neil W. Adger and Mick P. Kelly 2005. 'The Determinants of Vulnerability and Adaptive Capacity at the National Level and the Implications for Adaptation', *Global Environmental Change* 15(2): 151–63

Brooks, Nick *et al.* 2009. *The Selection of Countries to Participate in the Pilot Program for Climate Resilience (PPCR).* Climate Investment Funds

Climate Investment Funds 2010. *Creating a Climate-Smart World.* Washington, D.C.: World Bank Group

Costa, Luís and Jürgen P. Kropp 2012. 'Linking Components of Vulnerability in Theoretic Frameworks and Case Studies', *Sustainability Science* 8: 1–9

Dietz, Kristina 2006. *Vulnerabilität und Anpassung gegenüber Klimawandel aus sozial-ökologischer Perspektive*, Diskussionspapier 5, BMBF Förderschwerpunkt Global Governance und Klimawandel. Berlin: Free University Berlin

Diffenbaugh, Noah S. *et al.* 2007. 'Indicators of 21st Century Socioclimatic Exposure', *Proceedings of the National Academy of Sciences of the United States of America* 104(51): 20195–8

Eakin, C. Mark, Joan Kleypas and Ove Hoegh-Guldberg 2008. 'Global Climate Change and Coral Reefs: Rising Temperatures, Acidification and the Need for Resilient Reefs', *Science* 318: 1737–42

Eakin, Hallie and Luis A. Bojórquez-Tapia 2008. 'Insights into the Composition of Household Vulnerability from Multicriteria Decision Analysis', *Global Environmental Change* 18(1): 112–27

Eakin, Hallie and Amy Lynd Luers 2006. 'Assessing the Vulnerability of Social-Environmental Systems', *Annual Review of Environment and Resources* 31(1): 365–94

Eriksen, S.H. and P.M. Kelly 2006. 'Developing Credible Vulnerability Indicators for Climate Adaptation Policy Assessment', *Mitigation and Adaptation Strategies for Global Change* 12(4): 495–524

Füssel, Hans-Martin 2007. 'Vulnerability: A Generally Applicable Conceptual Framework for Climate Change Research', *Global Environmental Change* 17(2): 155–67

2009. *Review and Quantitative Analysis of Indices of Climate Change Exposure, Adaptive Capacity, Sensitivity, and Impacts*, Background note to the World Development Report 2010. Potsdam: Potsdam Institute for Climate Impact Research

Füssel, Hans-Martin and Richard J.T. Klein 2006. 'Climate Change Vulnerability Assessments: An Evolution of Conceptual Thinking', *Climatic Change* 75(3): 301–29

Georg, C. (Rapporteur) 2009. *Climate Change and Social Vulnerability, Conference Report from the IHDP Open Meeting, April 26–30, 2009*. Bonn: World Conference Center

Hahn, Micah B., Anne M. Riederer and Stanley O. Foster 2009. 'The Livelihood Vulnerability Index: A Pragmatic Approach to Assessing Risks from Climate Variability and Change – A Case Study in Mozambique', *Global Environmental Change* 19(1): 74–88

Hinkel, Jochen 2011. '"Indicators of Vulnerability and Adaptive Capacity": Towards a Clarification of the Science–Policy Interface', *Global Environmental Change* 1: 198–208

IBRD and World Bank 2008. *Development and Climate Change: A Strategic Framework for the World Bank Group*, Technical Report. Washington, D.C.

Ionescu, Cezar et al. 2008. 'Towards a Formal Framework of Vulnerability to Climate Change', *Environmental Modeling and Assessment* 14(1): 1–16

IPCC 2001. *Impacts, Adaptation, and Vulnerability: Summary for Policymakers and Technical Summary of the Working Group II Report*. Cambridge: Cambridge University Press

Kelly, P.M. and W.N. Adger 2000. 'Theory and Practice in Assessing Vulnerability to Climate Change and Facilitating Adaptation', *Climatic Change* 47: 325–52

Klein, Richard J.T. 2009. 'Identifying Countries that are Particularly Vulnerable to the Adverse Effects of Climate Change: An Academic or a Political Challenge?', *Carbon and Climate Law* 10–11

Kropp, Jürgen *et al.* 2009. *Klimawandel in Nordrhein-Westfalen. Regionale Abschätzung der Anfälligkeit ausgewählter Sektoren.* Potsdam Institute for Climate Impact Research

Marshall, N.A. *et al.* 2010. *A Framework for Social Adaptation to Climate Change: Sustaining Tropical Coastal Communities and Industries.* Gland

McCarthy, J.J. *et al.* 2001. 'Glossary of Terms' in K.S. White (ed.) *Climate Change 2001: Impacts, Adaptation, and Vulnerability: Contribution of Working Group II to the Third Assessment Report of the Intergovernmental Panel on Climate Change.* Cambridge: Cambridge University Press

Nelson, Valerie, Richard Lamboll and Adele Arendse 2008. *Climate Change Adaptation*, Adaptive Capacity and Development Discussion Paper

Nicholls, Robert J. *et al.* 2008. 'Climate Change and Coastal Vulnerability Assessment: Scenarios for Integrated Assessment', *Sustainability Science* 3(1): 89–102

O'Brien, Karen, Siri Eriksen, Lynn P. Nygaard and Ane Schjolden 2007. 'Why Different Interpretations of Vulnerability Matter in Climate Change Discourses', *Climate Policy* 7(1): 37–41

Patt, Anthony G., Anne de-la-Vega-Leinert and Richard J.T. Klein 2008. 'Vulnerability Research and Assessment to Support Adaptation and Mitigation: Common Themes from the Diversity of Approaches' in A.G. de-la-Vega-Leinert, D. Patt, D. Schröter and R.J.T. Klein (eds.), *Assessing Vulnerability to Global Environmental Change: Making Research Useful for Adaptation Decision Making and Policy.* London

Patt, Anthony G., Richard J.T. Klein and Anne de-la-Vega-Leinert 2005. 'Taking the Uncertainties in Climate Change Vulnerability Assessment Seriously', *Comptes Rendus Geosciences* 337: 411–24

Richards, Michael 2003. *'Poverty Reduction, Equity and Climate Change: Global Governance Synergies or Contradictions?'.* London: Overseas Development Institute

Schauser, Inke *et al.* 2010. *Urban Regions: Vulnerabilities, Vulnerability Assessments by Indicators and Adaptation Options for Climate Change Impacts, Scoping Study.* Bilthoven

Schröter, Dagmar, Colin Polsky and Anthony G. Patt 2005. 'Assessing Vulnerabilities to the Effects of Global Change: An Eight Step Approach', *Mitigation and Adaptation Strategies for Global Change* 10: 573–96

Smit, Barry and Olga Pilifosova 2001. 'Adaptation to Climate Change in the Context of Sustainable Development and Equity' in *Climate Change 2001: Impacts, Adaptation and Vulnerability.* Cambridge: Cambridge University Press, pp. 877–912

Smit, Barry and Johanna Wandel 2006. 'Adaptation, Adaptive Capacity and Vulnerability', *Global Environmental Change* 16(3): 282–92

Tompkins, Emma L. and W. Neil Adger 2005. 'Defining Response to Enhance Climate Change Policy', *Environmental Science and Policy* 8(6): 562–71

UNDP 2011. 'Human Development Index and its Components' in *Human Development Report 2011*, pp. 127–30

2012. *Human Development Index (HDI)*, available at http://hdr.undp.org/en/statistics/hdi/

Vincent, Katherine 2004. *Creating an Index of Social Vulnerability to Climate Change for Africa*. Tyndall: Tyndall Centre for Climate Change Research

2007. 'Uncertainty in Adaptive Capacity and the Importance of Scale', *Global Environmental Change* 17(1): 12–24

Warner, Koko 2007. 'Perspectives on Social Vulnerability: Introduction' in K. Warner (ed.), *Perspectives on Social Vulnerability*. Bonn: Studies of the University: Research, Counsel, Education (SOURCE), pp. 14–22

Watts, Michael J. and Hans G. Bohle 1993. 'The Space of Vulnerability: The Causal Structure of Hunger and Famine', *Progress in Human Geography* 17(1): 43–67

CHAPTER THIRTEEN

RETROACTION: HOW INDICATORS FEED BACK ONTO QUANTIFIED ACTORS

Alain Desrosières (1940–2013)

INTRODUCTION

Are quantitative indicators an instrument of emancipation or an instrument of oppression? In line with the philosophy of Enlightenment, they were generally perceived as a means of giving society a mirror-image of itself so that it could move towards greater justice. Today, in the world of neoliberal economics, they are mostly seen as an excuse to fuel individualism and competition between individuals, particularly through the performance indicators involved in management techniques, such as benchmarking. They can have *direct effects*, repercussions, qualified here as *feedback*, on those in charge of the statistical monitoring of unemployment. For example, the director of the French national statistics bureau, INSEE, was suspended for having 'badly managed' the conflict over unemployment figures. Deep budget cuts to the statistics bureau were announced. In spite of that, public statistics in France still enjoyed a good reputation among their users: economic actors, journalists, trade unionists, teachers and researchers. The media published numerous opinion pieces deploring what was perceived as a threat to dismantle the system. A commonly used metaphor was 'breaking the thermometer in order to treat the fever'.

A similar version of this chapter was published in French by Emmanuel Didier together with other manuscripts left behind by Alain Desrosières. See Alain Desrosières, *Prouver et gouverner: une analyse politique des statistiques publiques*, texte établi et introduit par Emmanuel Didier (Paris: La Découverte, 2014).

Shortly thereafter, a young INSEE researcher was struck by a revealing incident. While marching in a trade union demonstration against government policy to dismantle public services, she was soliciting demonstrators to show their support by signing a petition. To her surprise she was told: 'Your statistics are only used to control us, police us, and make our working conditions worse.' Again in 2009, academics, researchers and health workers were up in arms against the 'reforms' being applied to their activities, which involved quantified evaluations of their 'performance'. This would lead, as they saw it, to the dispossession of their specific skills for the benefit of 'New Public Management', which relies heavily on the use of quantitative indicators. A culture of dissent emerged against the generalization of quantification among academic physicians. Resistance against quantitative evaluation was one of its keywords.

Spring 2009 was also a season for other demands of a completely different kind. The French government asked the eminent economists Amartya Sen, Joseph Stiglitz and Jean-Paul Fitoussi to propose revisions for the calculation of Gross Domestic Product (GDP). They suspected that GDP was a poor measure of the 'wealth' generated by a nation within a year. Activist researchers had already anticipated this request, which was given a great deal of media coverage. They joined in to demand other statistics, called 'new wealth indicators', which could evaluate, for instance, environmental damages, the unpaid work of women or the social effects of inequality (Gadrey and Jany-Catrice 2006). The movement called for yet *another* form of quantification, arguing that 'what is not counted does not count'.

How should we account for this emerging critique of the use of statistics? Statistics thus far were seen as a means to help democracy, a way for the underprivileged to denounce privileges and inequalities, to criticize unfair policies, and to fight for the maintenance of purchasing power. The aspect of statistics enabling it to function as an 'instrument for the weak to combat the powerful' is analysed by the historian Theodore Porter (1995) in his study *Trust in Numbers: The Pursuit of Objectivity in Science and Public Life*. The idea of 'progressive' statistics is still widely shared, in particular among French public (i.e. government) statisticians, who are highly attached to the qualifier 'public', synonymous with 'public service', the custodian of general interest. This is quite distinct from the 'official' statistics of the English language.

RETROACTION OF QUANTITATIVE INDICATORS ON QUANTIFIED ACTORS

This crisis of confidence is a symptom of the longer historical evolution of the relations between types of government and ways of using quantification. Quantitative tools are not only tools of *proof* used by scientists to substantiate their argument, but they are also tools of *coordination*, or of *government*. This had already been suggested as early as 1978 by Michel Foucault (2007; 2008) with his idea of *governmentality*; then by Porter, as well as by Pierre Lascoumes and Patrick Le Gales through the title of the book they edited, *Gouverner par les instruments*, or Governing Through Instruments (2007). From this point of view, the theme of quantification encompasses not only statistics proper, but also accounting, performance indicators, ranking and all the New Public Management (NPM) quantitative tools. Porter's analysis of the causes and effects of trust in the numbers is convincing, but the recent extension of the use of such indicators by New Public Management raises new questions and introduces a discontinuity in the long-standing traditional usage of statistics by governments, which dates back to the eighteenth century.

Public statisticians claim that their activity is objective and independent, regardless of the fact that objectivity and independence can be sociologically disputed; indeed, they are a constant source of questioning and conflict. Yet NPM indicators, which induce feedback effects on the situations and behaviour of the actors involved, involve very different cognitive, political and sociological rationales. This had already been analysed in accounting by English researchers (Hopwood and Miller 1994; Hood 1995). It does not mean that official statistics have no effect on the actors, but (1) the ethos of professional statisticians rules out, in principle, taking these effects into account; and (2) if they exist, these effects are more macro-social than directly individual. We are not suggesting that public statisticians are more 'neutral' and 'objective' than accountants, but rather that it is sociologically relevant to distinguish among various understandings of 'objectivity' and of 'reality' involved in these different cases, as Lorraine Daston (1992) has done in her analysis of the history of the concept of 'scientific objectivity'.

The evolution of the role of quantitative indicators in government reflects the evolution of the state since the eighteenth century according to the following typology: (1) conceptualizations of society and of the economy; (2) methods of public action; and (3) forms of quantification and modelling. After introducing a distinction of method between *quantifying* and *measuring*, I will review the logics of five forms of state governmentality, then show how NPM indicators appear in the fifth, the neoliberal state (in the 1980s in Great Britain, and in the 2000s in France).[1] This has some bearing on the status of official statistics, in particular on the claim that statistics are an objective representation of reality. By acknowledging that quantitative indicators *feed back* into the behaviour of actors, we are moving away from the realist epistemology underpinning the metrics of official statistics. Our intention in doing this is not to denounce any form of deceit, manipulation, misuse or fraud, even though of course this all happens. It is, rather, to clarify the role of quantification in the public debates and political contexts in which it occurs.[2]

This applies to new indicators used in the monitoring of public policies and in the management of certain European Union policies, as well as in the debates on the flexibility and changes in company accounting standards. Although the idea of feedback is absent from the culture and ethos of statisticians, it is ubiquitous in the practices of managers and accountants and has for this reason been the subject of much theoretical and applied research. This raises the issue of whether feedback is intrinsic to indicators and the outcome of the historically contingent division of labour between professions and disciplines?

CONVENTION, MEASUREMENT, QUANTIFICATION

Our approach is sociological, not epistemological. It requires giving a non-normative definition of the verb 'to quantify'. The quantitative indicators used by New Public Management are often criticized. What does 'measuring a performance' actually mean? The feedback of indicators induces paradoxical effects: the actors focus on the indicator instead of on the action itself. Just using the verb 'measure', however, implicitly refers to the realist metrics of natural sciences. It is vital to

---

[1] The typology of the five forms of governmentality, and of their corresponding statistics, is presented in greater detail in Desrosières 2003.

[2] Economists using statistics have long been describing (to deplore them) the 'biases' resulting, in their view, from retroactive effects (Morgenstern 1944/1963), but here the notion of *bias*, part of a realist metrology, is merely an inconvenient obstacle to 'real measures'. It bars studying, sociologically, the play per se on quantification.

distinguish two ideas that are often confused, that of *quantification*, and that of *measurement*. The verb 'to quantify' is used here broadly as a neutral term: to convert into numerical existence what was previously expressed in words and not in numbers (this is a descriptive, not a normative statement). On the other hand, the idea of *measurement*, inspired from the natural sciences, implies that something exists already in a form that is physically measurable.

In the case of social sciences or in policy studies, the word 'measure' is misleading and leaves conventions of quantification unexamined. The verb 'to quantify', in its active form (to make into a number), supposes that a series of hypothetical equivalences has been developed and made explicit, involving comparisons, negotiations, compromises, translations, registrations, encoding, codified and replicable procedures, and calculations leading to numericization.[3] Measurement itself comes after that, as the rule-based implementation of these conventions. From this point of view, quantification breaks down into two successive parts: *convention* and *measurement*. The first, often unknown to the users (notably economists), is at least as important as the second.

The verb 'to quantify' draws attention to the socially and cognitively creative dimension of this activity. Indeed, this activity not only provides a reflection of the world (as it is usually understood to do), it also transforms and reconstitutes it. The distinction between quantifying and measuring is not a relativist one in the sometimes negative sense attributed to relativism. It aims to separate, for the purpose of analysis, two historically and socially distinct moments, a modification like that for 'intelligence' when the idea of an 'intelligence quotient' was brought in, for 'opinion' when Gallup-type polling began, and for the more recent debates on the quantification of the effects of public action. The seventeenth-century invention of the notion of *probability* to quantify what was uncertain in a number between zero and one provides a famous precedent.

Those who believe that the measurement itself brings the object into being are often accused of relativism. For such persons, 'intelligence' would be 'what is measured by IQ tests' and 'opinion' would be 'what is measured by opinion polls'. Quantification, seen as a set

[3] The social and logical concept of *equivalence convention* owes a lot in particular to Bruno Latour (1988) in the supplement *Irréductions* to his book on Pasteur, and to Laurent Thévenot (1984).

of socially recognized conventions and measurement operations, brings about a new way of thinking, representing and expressing the world, and of acting upon it. The recurring question about whether a statistic gives a more-or-less accurate reflection of reality is a deceptive shorthand, and assumes the metrological realism of natural sciences. Statistics, and all forms of quantification in general (probabilistic or accounting quantification, for instance), change the world through their very existence, their circulation and their rhetorical usage in science, politics or journalism. Once quantification procedures are encoded and become routine, their products are objectified. They tend to become 'reality' in an apparently irreversible way. The initial conventions are forgotten, the quantified object is naturalized and the use of the verb 'to measure' comes to mind or is written with no further thought.

This remains true until these 'black boxes' are opened when controversies arise, as for instance those on 'measuring' unemployment or on the economy's growth rate, or when the 'measurement' of price increase is criticized because product 'quality' has risen (as for computers). In this case, measurement of the GDP growth rate in volume (in constant euros), which is the relationship between growth in value (in current euros) and the inflation rate, is directly affected by this criticism. In a report to the US Senate in 1996, Michael Boskin developed this critique in relation to the consumer price index and to the growth rate of the economy. The report caused a lot of commotion (a fine example of feedback) because many economic decisions regarding retirement pensions, wages and balancing budgets are automatically pegged to these two rates (Boskin *et al.* 1996).

Quantification offers a specific language to enable the transfers, comparisons, aggregations and manipulations standardized by calculations, and routine interpretations (Desrosières 2008a and 2008b). It makes 'objects that hold together' available to social actors or researchers because they are robust (resistant to criticism), standardized (and therefore interchangeable), and can 'hold people together' by constraining them to a standard set of linguistic terms. This critical approach to quantification differs from the usual one in quantitative social sciences and, more generally, in the uses of statistics and accounting tools. Conventions of quantification are themselves products of the history of the state and of forms of government. Neoliberal governmentality may be contrasted to its predecessor notably through its massive use of performance indicators and benchmarking.

FEEDBACK OF INDICATORS DIFFERS ACCORDING TO THE FORM OF STATE

The five forms of governmentality, which I introduce in the following, are not an absolute succession in time. They are not merely successive strata preserving and encompassing previous strata. Rather, they transform the previous strata. There is some feedback in all of them, but it does not play the same role as it does in the case of neoliberalism.

Direct intervention in the *engineering state* encompasses a variety of perspectives ranging from mercantilism and Colbertism (seventeenth century) to the 'major projects' of Gaullist France and of Socialist planned economies. Its statistics are comparable to those of a large company planning its workshops, or to those of an army managing its logistics. Population censuses, product flows in physical quantities, input-output tables (or Leontief matrixes) and accounting are essential here.[4] The engineering state has expanded particularly during times of war, which entail centralization of production (Dahan and Pestre 2004). For a long time, French engineers from the École Polytechnique (a military school) were worthy representatives of this technical and political culture, a culture that is distinct from the market-based culture of the Anglo-Saxon world.[5]

In the case of planning in the Soviet Union, two very different forms of quantification succeeded one another (Blum and Mespoulet 2003). In the 1920s, random sample surveys of households maintained the tradition of mathematical statistics that were already vibrant before the Revolution. Their aim was to quantify the population's needs. Then, after 1930, accounting practices introduced by Stalinist planning replaced this advanced statistical technique. Several statisticians were shot. Stakhanovism was in fact a brutal precursor of NPM performance indicators. After the 1960s, Soviet statistics were, in the West, reputed to be of poor quality because they were associated with planning forecasts and goals and therefore subject to manipulation. This criticism is very much like the one now levelled at NPM indicators, where English researchers (Hood 2002) talk of 'gaming and cheating'.

---

[4] The 1930s debate on 'Socialist Calculation' and on the possibility of planning without market-determined prices can be understood as part of the dream of the engineering state (Caldwell 1997).

[5] A comment by Jacques Lesourne, an alumnus of this school, mining engineer and founder of the Société d'Étude et de Mathématiques Appliquée (SEMA) who worked for the state in the 1960s, reflects this surprisingly close connection between France of that time and the USSR: 'Basically, Gaullist France may be qualified a Soviet Union that succeeded'.

What these two otherwise very different situations have in common is constituted by the perverse effects of the feedback of the indicators on the actors whose actions have been quantified.

In contrast, the classic nineteenth-century *liberal state* reduces state intervention to a minimum. It advocates the liberation of market forces. The dream of a stateless 'liberal-libertarian' society founded exclusively on market mechanisms, where prices factor in all the necessary information, is the diametric opposite of the preceding dream of the purely engineered state. If it uses statistics at all, they are used to bring real markets closer to theoretical markets (full information, identical for all the actors), in particular for prices. Farm surveys conducted in the United States for more than a century show that this stateless market society is a Utopia. The aim of these surveys is to ensure that all farmers have the same information on crop forecasts and to prevent speculation by big buyers. Their administrative organization is complex and they require a well-organized federal state (Didier 2009). In this case, feedback is all-inclusive: its target is to guarantee a market in which the relations between suppliers and buyers are based on justice.

The *welfare state* seeks to protect wage earners from the consequences of having extended market-based principles even to labour (Polanyi 1944). It organizes protection systems against unemployment, accidents at work and illness, and for the family. It was set up in the wake of the major social and economic crisis of the late nineteenth century. Its statistical instruments are focused on wage labour, and they are mostly sample surveys on labour, needs, employees' income and family budgets, and on the price indices of their consumption. These are the subjects covered by the official statistics of this time. This is the context in which sample surveys on the living conditions of working-class families appear (Desrosières 1998). To conduct them, the Norwegian Anders Kiaer introduced the method of 'purposive selection' in 1895 (Lie 2002), also used in 1921 by the Italian Corrado Gini (Prévost 2009). In 1905, the Englishman Arthur Bowley developed the 'random selection' method and defined the probabilistic 'confidence interval'. Here again, feedback is all-inclusive in that it involves the entire working class, for instance in the case of the consumer price index used to index wages in negotiations between unions and employers. This index, however, only covers the consumption of salaried workers.

The *Keynesian state*, for its part, has some responsibility in the macroeconomic management of a society otherwise unquestionably based on a market economy. It appeared against the background of the 1930s crisis and prevailed between 1945 and 1975. National accounting is its core instrument (Fourquet 1980; Vanoli 2005), and official statistics systems were reorganized to meet its needs. The consumption and price indices quantifying inflation were then extended from just salaried workers to the entire population. Policy-making was based on macroeconomic models comparing overall supply and demand (Armatte 1995; Armatte and Dahan Dalmedico 2004). Overall feedback then applied to the macroeconomic policies, not the actors at the microeconomic level. In both the welfare state and the Keynesian state, feedback often comes from *indexing*, and affects in particular the price index or the gross domestic product. Thus, the European Maastricht Treaty criteria specify that country deficits and debts must be less than 3 per cent and 60 per cent, respectively, of their GDP.

Finally, the *neoliberal state* is grounded in microeconomic market dynamics, attempting to direct these via incentive systems, and accepts the main assumptions of the rational-expectations theory. Its rapid development kicked in after the major crisis of the 1970s. Under the neoliberal state, feedback notably took the form of *benchmarking*, that is, the assessment, categorizing and ranking of performance (Bruno 2008). Microeconomic models make it possible to separate and isolate the 'specific effects' of variables or public-action tools on their performance with a view to improve the 'target variables' of policies that incentivize behaviour, notably through tax policy. The emulation generated among public-action tools makes it possible to define 'best practices'.

Incentive procedures are evaluated by studying individual data or data provided by quasi-experimentation (or microsimulation) intended to model the behaviour of actors, *including that of public authorities*. This is an important difference between the neoliberal state and the preceding forms of state. It comes from the rational-expectations theory, which contends that public policies fail whenever the actors tactically integrate the expected effects of public decisions into the information guiding their behaviour. In this perspective, all actors, and definitely the state, are part of the game. The state multiplies into several more-or-less autonomous command centres or 'agencies' managed almost like companies. These are actors among other actors, falling under the same forms of modelling as any other microeconomic actor.

QUALIFICATION, COMPARISON, EVALUATION, CATEGORIZATION: THE POLICY OF STATISTICAL INDICATORS

Unlike market activities, public policies do not have accounting criteria such as 'market share' or profitability to judge their capacity to meet users' needs, or their effectiveness. Traditionally, the concept of public service pre-supposes members to be strongly committed and managed under top-down authority systems. The French state was long an example of this. Since the 1980s, however, this civic sense of public service has been seen as insufficient for effective monitoring of publicly financed activities. Public authorities sought quantifiable indicators that could play a role comparable to that performed by cost accounting, operating accounts and balance sheets in profit-making companies. National accounting did not fulfil this role because it was located at the macroeconomic level in a Keynesian or indicative-planning perspective and therefore did not delve into the details of public actions. In this new perspective, indicators could not be strictly monetary, as the effects of these actions (school, public health, diplomacy, defence, etc.) cannot usually be expressed in the familiar equivalence framework provided by money.

Efforts to develop effective measures of public policies are vast experiments in building and negotiating *new equivalence frameworks* by drawing up *conventions* on the procedures for quantifying the ends and the means of action using a variety of units that can include money, but not exclusively. We shall mention two examples here: the Constitutional Bylaw on Budget Acts (Loi organique relative aux lois de finances (LOLF)) adopted almost unanimously by the French Parliament in 2001, and the Open Method of Coordination (OMC) used by the European Union.[6] Although the historical and political contexts of these two instruments (one French, the other European) for managing public policies are different, they have in common that they give a central role to *statistical indicators*, in other words to tools that are hardly ever mentioned in public discussions when in fact they constitute the very framework and language that define and structure these debates.

---

[6] There are historical precedents that could be studied in this perspective: the economic-planning experiences of Socialist countries, or the Planning, Programming and Budgeting System (PPBS, or Rationalisation des Choix Budgétaires (RCB) in French) applied in France in the 1970s, inspired from the system of the same name in the United States, which was subsequently pursued under the name '*évaluation des politiques publiques*' (evaluation of public policies). In all these cases, non-monetary quantified indicators were implemented.

The LOLF reorganizes the state budget in terms of goals to be reached, rather than just in terms of the resources allocated to them. These goals need to be made explicit and *quantified* so Parliament can, beyond just approving expenditure, also check that the goals have been reached and review how effectively public services have been delivered. Quantifying the goals and means of public action is a matter of course if Parliament wishes to play its constitutional role of shaping and monitoring budget implementation. It involves, however, serious work to produce objective data and to make dissimilar activities comparable. These activities must be expressed, discussed, named, qualified, compared, categorized and evaluated. Choosing the proper indicator is always problematic. An old, institutional, social, and most often implicit order is then suddenly described in terms of objective data. In principle, this can only be done by involving the interested parties. Yet the very idea of a quantitative indicator often provokes resistance. Such procedures mean 'comparing the incomparable' and can appear absurd, particularly when they are carried out by those who are personally involved in the actions that are to be made commensurable. Just the fact of setting up categories, in principle to simplify the world and make it readable, also modifies it and turns it into a different world. The actors in this new reference framework are no longer the same actors, since their actions are now guided by these indicators and categorizations that have become the criteria for action, and the means for evaluating it.

From the perspective of a healthy balance of powers between the legislative and executive branches, the LOLF is meant to provide Parliament with better knowledge of how public policy is implemented by furnishing the means to evaluate public action. That this involved developing and operationalizing a variety of quantified indicators did not draw much attention between 2001 and 2004. It seemed a technical issue, better left to technicians. And yet the discussions, which became increasingly sharp as of 2005, have shown that this moment of quantification was critical for the events that were to follow. The effects of *feedback* are at times visible as 'paradoxical effects', appearing case by case, and are often dismissed without further examination. They may be denounced or joked about. An example: the police and gendarmerie forces, in charge of road safety, both chose an indicator that would measure the share of positive alcohol-level tests in the overall alcohol testing of drivers. The former, however, hoped that through the quantification, their action would show this share to be growing, while the latter hoped on the contrary that it would be seen as declining. Each choice responds to its own rationale. This case shows what a political sociology of quantification could cover to study the implicit effects of the LOLF 'indicator policy', or at the European level, the effects of the Open Method of Coordination.

These effects have already been observed in other contexts. Centralized planning in Socialist countries failed because it was impossible to set reliable indicators to measure whether planning goals had been achieved, due to the paradoxical, retroactive effects of the indicators on the actors' behaviour. In the United States, when hospital professions were categorized and previously implicit activities were made explicit and formalized, this produced changes in the different professions and activities (Bowker and Star 1999). Indicators and categorizations are both limitations and resources that change the world simply by existing.

The Open Method of Coordination is used by the European Union to harmonize social policies (employment, education, aid, etc.) that are not part of the economic and monetary fields actually under its jurisdiction. An example of this was the European Employment Strategy (EES) proposed in 1997. Its principle is that states will set goals intergovernmentally, and these goals will be expressed as quantified indicators, in reference to which the states will then be evaluated and ranked. The results of this benchmarking process are simply meant as indications, but just the fact that they are published turns them into a stimulant to guide national policies in the directions indicated during European summits (Dehousse 2003; Salais 2004). A 70 per cent employment rate was thus set as a goal. The LOLF and the OMC give statistical indicators a key role, the former to monitor the state budget, the latter as indirect guidance for European social policies.

How the EU Member States reached an agreement on this quantification is poorly understood, despite its obvious broader political, social and economic significance. Technically, this work is divided into two parts. The political authorities decide on the choice of indicators and define them briefly with words. Then they farm out the quantification to the statisticians working at Eurostat (the statistical office of the European Union) and at the national statistics institutes (NSIs). The 'convention' phase itself is therefore shared since policy-makers leave statisticians to work out the 'details', such as, for instance, to reach specific definitions of the notions of employment rate (Salais 2004), disposable household income (Nivière 2005) and homeless persons (Brousse 2005). These studies show that, given the institutional differences among the countries, statisticians cannot avoid leaving certain measurement procedures, sometimes important ones, fuzzy; nor can they harmonize them completely. This method is called 'open' because it is not mandatory and leaves states free to adapt it to their institutional idiosyncrasies, notably by choosing direct surveys or administrative records as their sources.

These indicators then are, in other words, not exhaustively defined. They can therefore be used in several fields, some of which were previously disconnected and can now be compared, as with a lingua franca. Natural language has analogous properties: communication is possible because speakers do not spend their time making the meaning and content of the words they use explicit. Official statistics (unemployment rate, price index and GDP for instance) work in the same way. Making the bases for their development and their content explicit might weaken their argumentative effectiveness, not only because this would reveal conventions and approximations unsuspected by users, but simply because clarifying these conventions would require time-consuming discussions, debates and demonstrations. All of this generally remains implicit unless there is a controversy. This does not prevent the fuzziness from being deplored by professionals who are keen on defining and standardizing their objects. They are caught between two contradictory requirements. On the one hand, as good engineers, they would like to specify their procedures. On the other hand, the negotiations urge them to tolerate compromises without which the requested indicators would be impossible to provide. Meeting these two contradictory imperatives requires that they strive to achieve a delicate balance that is always fluid and implicit.[7]

> When a measure becomes a target, it ceases to be a good measure.
> ('Goodhart's law', cited by Bird 2004)

TOWARD A SOCIOLOGY OF FEEDBACK: THE CASE OF ACCOUNTING

The feedback issue may be unfamiliar to statisticians, but in contrast, it is important in the thinking of accountants and now, by

---

[7] This ambiguity can nevertheless be perceived in the metadata (the data on the data). It is requested and provided, but giving too many details can introduce insidious, unwanted doubts. The statistical argument is more effective if it is called upon stark and naked, with no footnotes to qualify it.

extension, in the debates on the use of quantified management indicators. I will mention a few examples from different theoretical traditions ranging from neoclassical microeconomics to sociology and
political science as inspired from Michel Foucault. 'Goodhart's law'
is one of its iconic expressions. Charles Goodhart was an advisor to
the Bank of England. His 'law', stated in 1975, gained popularity when
Margaret Thatcher's government undertook to conduct her monetary
policy on the basis of 'targets' for money supply. It was already implicit
in the idea of 'rational expectations' and in Lucas's critique of Keynesian policies (Chrystal and Mizen 2001). It was first expressed as
follows: 'Any observed statistical regularity will tend to collapse once
pressure is placed upon it for control purposes.' It was later extended
to all indicators used as targets. The formulation quoted above was
mentioned in 2004 in an editorial of the *Journal of the Royal Statistical
Society* entitled: 'Performance Monitoring in the Public Services'. This
led to the idea of 'perverse incentive', a classic in the management literature. The existential question remains: 'Can a measurement of human
affairs be completely independent from the way it is used?' The ethos
of the statistician's metrological neutrality makes this an uncomfortable
question. This is why the neoliberal state, based on performance indicators, has trouble with statistics, the same as Soviet statistics had before
that.

Corporate accounting is a rich source for the sociology of feedback,
given the diversity of its uses and the malleable nature of its standards,
particularly in the Anglo-Saxon world, which entertains such ironic
expressions as 'creative accounting', 'window dressing' and 'cooking the
books'. Thus for instance, to 'value' the assets in the balance sheet, three
possible conventions may be used, each based on a different rationale.
(1) The original cost (or historical cost) will be used by a manager seeking to spread annual amortization instalments. (2) The resale value will
be of concern to a company's creditor, wondering what his assets are still
worth. Finally, (3) the discounted sum of the expected future income
will be of interest to an investor spreading out his existing financial
resources.[8] The third convention (called fair value) was adopted by the
European Union to the detriment of the first, and by the new International Financial Reporting Standards (IFRS) (Chiapello and Medjad

---

[8] According to the so-called neoclassical 'efficient market' hypothesis, conventions 2 (resale
value) and 3 (discounted sum of the expected future income) are equivalent.

2009).[9] There is a comparable diversity in the different ways of calculating company profits, depending on what the purpose of the calculation is. The active form of the verb 'to value' used by accountants reflects an approach that is implicitly more constructivist than realist. Where economists discuss the 'value bases', accountants 'value', in other words, they manufacture a value according to conventions. The rules and legal conventions for accounting give companies a certain amount of leeway, allowing them to show greater or lesser profit, depending on the message they wish to convey to their shareholders, potential investors, the government or other economic actors.

Flexibility in accounting standards was at the source of the strange but influential Positive Accounting Theory (PAT) (Watts and Zimmerman 1978).[10] This branch of academic research in accounting seeks to explain and predict the actual accounting practices. It is opposed to normative accounting, which aims to define and prescribe optimal theoretical standards as 'reflections of reality' by answering questions such as 'What is income?' or 'What is an asset?' through deductive reasoning, with no reference to what accountants actually do. In contrast, 'positivists', inspired in particular by 'agency theory', state that the actual practices and choices of accountants need to be analysed before telling them what they should do. They are not interested so much in what accountants say in metrological terms, but they are interested in the strategic behaviour revealed by their practices. What they do is mobilize statistical correlations and state-of-the-art econometric tools to develop models of accounting practices associated with strategic goals. Thus, the metrological goal of accounting quantification seems to disappear to the benefit of a sophisticated analysis of the feedback effect. Therein lies the paradox: a 'positive' method is made to serve a relativist conception of the quantification of the economy, a far cry from the 'fundamental value' idea. The 2008 financial meltdown provided some examples of the consequences of this kind of theory, notably with the use of the now famous fair value.

A completely different sociology of feedback is at work in the efforts of English researchers grouped around Anthony Hopwood at the journal *Accounting, Organizations and Society* (AOS) or around

[9] The fair value convention makes the value of assets very volatile and uncertain when there is a crisis. This was one of the causes of the escalation of the 2008 crisis.

[10] This paragraph on Positive Accounting Theory owes a lot to work conducted jointly with Eve Chiapello (Chiapello and Desrosières 2006).

Christopher Hood at Oxford. Neoliberalism swept through Great Britain long before it reached France, starting in the 1980s after Margaret Thatcher's election (Le Gales 2004). This explains why the questions regarding feedback and, more generally, neoliberal governmentality, were raised there at that moment (see Miller and O'Leary 1987; Miller 1992; Hopwood and Miller 1994; Hood 1995; 2002; Power 1999; 2004). AOS raised questions about feedback that were analogous to those raised about the Positive Accounting Theory (PAT), but dealt with them in a radically different way. It put accounting back in its historical, sociological and political context, whereas the PAT only used the tools of microeconomics, agency theory and econometrics. AOS called upon a wide assortment of social sciences.[11] By 1991, these researchers were already referring to Michel Foucault's work on governmentality to analyse neoliberal management (Burchell, Gordon and Miller 1991), long before his lectures on the subject had been published in French (in 2004) and before they were being widely read by management researchers (Pezet 2007) and sociologists (Dardot and Laval 2009). This reveals the impact of the New Public Management school, which became increasingly popular in Great Britain starting in the 1980s.[12]

These English researchers drew on Foucault's ideas of *action at a distance, conduct of conduct* and *entrepreneurship of the self*. The theme of accountability is central here. This word reflects both responsibility and the obligation to account for and to evaluate results and performance. Eric Pezet (2007) provides a good description of this technical and moral combination: individuals' entrance into accounting does not only make them responsible, they become accountable for their behaviour on the basis of measurement scales that are given by Human Resources Management departments and managers. Management through direct command is replaced by indirect management based on the conduct of the conduct of others, and on the internalization of constraints by the subject, who is thus turned into a

---

[11] The history of the editorial line of the journal AOS since 1975 has been analysed through the editorials of its founder, Anthony Hopwood, by Stéphane Lefrancq (2004).

[12] With other analytical categories and a different vocabulary (they spoke of *capitalism* and not of *neoliberalism*), Boltanski and Chiapello (2005) were already dealing with the question of the radical changes in management methods brought about by NPM. They were analysing a different type of feedback, i.e. the feedback of the various forms of *critique* of capitalism as a whole. From this point of view, the work on the controversies and critiques surrounding the IFRSs and their roles in financial capitalism, are highly valuable for our project of the sociology of feedback (Capron (ed.) 2005).

'self-entrepreneur'.[13] From then on, the feedback of quantitative indicators affects the individual at every moment of his or her life.[14] This form of management can have, as we know, serious repercussions on the mental balance of individuals, leading them sometimes to commit suicide.

In 1992, Peter Miller introduced two ideas that are closely connected with our idea of feedback: *calculating selves* and *calculable spaces*. Quantification and calculation thus move in and out of the individual, who evaluates and calculates him- or her*self*, and the individual's environment (*space*), which imposes ways of calculating on him or her and encloses him or her in a straitjacket adorned with the robes of freedom. Miller designates five specific features of this way of using quantified performance indicators:

(1) *Calculating selves* and *calculable spaces* make it possible to act upon others' actions. These indicators are, however, 'loosely linked to each other'. (This feature is characteristic of how NPM deploys statistics as a collection of indicators which does not necessarily have any coherence, in contrast to national accounting aggregates, strongly linked to each other by the constraints of balanced accounting and of economic models.)

(2) *Calculative expertise* replaces professional authority. The political and the moral become factual and calculable. Social adversarial debate is weakened to the benefit of this engineering claimed to be objective and neutral.

(3) *It doesn't work, but that doesn't matter.* Quantitative indicators are criticized, but this does not in any way discredit the system, which is always ready to change. They are supposed to 'be constantly improved, in the light of experience' (for example the Shanghai rankings).

(4) *Resistances* occur, and come from professionals who are dispossessed of their specificities and of their own territories by this calculative expertise coming from the outside which is unrelated to the fields in which it is applied. (The protest movements of the winter of 2009 in France, in the universities,

---

[13] The new French legal status of *auto-entrepreneur* (self-entrepreneur) is a striking illustration of this.

[14] The New York police department was completely reorganized in the 1990s and police officers were submitted to close monitoring of their activities and their results. This textbook case is presented by Didier (2012).

schools, hospitals and in psychiatry were an example of precisely this type of resistance.)

(5) The *future* becomes knowable, calculable and amenable to control through the choice and use of a *discount* rate, a convention of equivalence between the present and the future.

FELICITY CONDITIONS OF THE STATISTICAL ARGUMENT

These analyses seem, at least for the moment, to be removed from the questions raised by statisticians, whose practice and professional ethos are different from those of accountants. The abundant literature on accounting and management, in French and in English, is largely ignored by statisticians and economists, even though the raw material of their statistics often originates in the fields of accounting and management. Or rather, when they suspect that accounting does not reflect 'reality' as adequately as they would like it to, it is something they will deplore, as shown in Oskar Morgenstern's book published long ago (1944/1963).[15] Supposing that the ethos of statisticians is different than that of accountants does not imply that statisticians are more honest, but that their social and administrative integration, and their reasons for acting, are not the same. This can lead to the establishment of 'codes of ethics' and 'charters of best practices', but, more deeply, this ethos implies a specific professional culture which ideally combines, in an original way, a scientific stance with respect to statesmanship.[16]

It is difficult to characterize the official statistics specific to the neoliberal state, as we were able to for the previous forms of state. Several recent developments do show, however, that they are not free of feedback phenomena. Statisticians were thus called upon to define and quantify the indicators of the European Union's Open Method of Coordination, based on benchmarking state performance, a typical tool of this new governmentality. Application of the criteria of the

---

[15] The 1950 translation into French of the title of the book pointedly used the word 'illusion', not part of the original title in English: *L'illusion statistique. Précision et incertitude des données économiques* (*The Statistical Illusion: Accuracy and Uncertainty of Economic Data*).

[16] It also implies a recurring claim for independence from the political authorities. This independence is now written into the European Statistics Code of Practice, adopted in 2005 in the wake of the first 'Greek crisis', which aims to curb, if not to prohibit, feedback (see www.cnis.fr/agenda/DPR/Dpr_0291.pdf).

Maastricht Treaty (government debt and deficit) raised problems due to the feedback of quantitative indicators, leading to what accountants call 'window dressing', as in the case of Greece.

Another example: in 2007, there was a bitter conflict on unemployment statistics in France. The files at the national employment bureau were being blatantly manipulated. This undermined the regular statistical series on unemployment so keenly expected by policy-makers and the press. Statisticians attacked political interventions as deeply adverse to their professional ethos.[17] Statisticians may eventually consider that the analyses on feedback produced by accounting and management sociologists are relevant, even though their institutions today still proclaim the independence from political or sociological interference of statistical measurement. In this case, the battles (mentioned above: Peter Miller's point 4) over the loss of professional specificity and independence would involve the quantifiers themselves. In some countries statisticians are already in this situation.

Why should this strange notion of feedback be brought to the fore? After all, isn't quantification always ultimately about usage and effects? Otherwise, why bother with the always costly development of conventions and measurements? The only reason this idea came about was the social division, in the production and use of knowledge, among professions or among academic disciplines having different professional cultures. Having made the profession of statistician independent, warranted by the importance of the use of statistics as the specific common language of a form of government, has had contradictory consequences. On the one hand, the efficiency of the statistical argument implies that the possible effects of feedback must be ignored, if not denied, when they are stated. Paraphrasing linguists, we can speak here of the *felicity condition* of the statistical argument. On the other hand, given that these effects actually happen, how can the statistician become aware of them and deal with them? Speech-act theory introduced the distinction between so-called constative and performative utterances long ago in *How to Do Things with Words* (Austin 1962). We can transpose this distinction here as *How to Do Things with Numbers*. The constative/performative distinction and the very notion of performativity have been discussed and criticized abundantly in the literature, first

---

[17] A good illustration of the claim for independence is given by a trade union symposium in 2007, '*États généraux des chiffres du chômage et de la précarité* (General Assembly on Unemployment and Precariousness of Numbers)' (see http://cgtinsee.free.fr/dossiers/chomage/Etat-actes.pdf).

in the field of linguistics, then in those of sociology and economics (Callon 2007). Our notion of feedback, although different, can be associated to these discussions. The critiques of quantification mentioned in the introduction to this chapter can be reviewed under this angle by underscoring the causes and effects of the division of labour in the production and circulation of quantified statements.

Two critiques of quantification, levelled by different actors, have arisen since the 1990s. On the one hand, the equivalence conventions implied by NPM to 'evaluate performance' have been hotly contested by many professionals, as we have already noted. On the other hand, at a more macroeconomic level, the 'measure of wealth' of a nation via the GDP is challenged, a substitute demanded, yet with no specification of the new equivalence conventions that would be needed to do so. These two critiques seem unrelated, stated within very distant contexts. Why bring them closer together? The intelligibility of each of them depends, in each case, on a trio consisting of: (1) a way of thinking about society; (2) ways of acting upon it; and (3) an appropriate mode of quantification (Desrosières 2007). The clarification and specification of this trio sheds light, not only on a form of governmentality, but also on the procedures for criticizing it.

Criticism of NPM performance indicators relies on the fact that *actually incommensurable* actors and actions are equated (or made to be commensurate), evaluated and categorized, then acted upon through incentive mechanisms. The indicators are designed as *benchmarking* tools (Bruno, Jacquot and Mandin 2006). Commensuration is a social act that transforms the world, in particular by making it calculable and categorizable in terms of rankings.[18] This critique of commensuration deals in particular with the perverse effects of feedback. It does not rely on any other form of quantification. On the contrary, it advocates respecting the uniqueness and specificity of each and every actor and each and every action. This gesture of resistance is completely warranted in the debates on the social role of numbers.

The other critique, symbolized by the debate on the 'imperative need to move beyond the GDP', is at the other extreme from the first, since the desired indicator would aggregate, or at least 'take into account'

---

[18] These two aspects have been analysed in two articles by Wendy Espeland, the telling titles of which are: 'Commensuration as a Social Process' (Espeland and Stevens 1998) and 'Rankings and Reactivity: How Public Measures Recreate Social Worlds' (Espeland and Sauder 2007). Alain Supiot (2010) provides an analogous critique on the disappearance of the 'Spirit of Philadelphia' characterizing the progressive philosophy of the thirty years that followed 1945.

every possible element supposedly left aside by the traditional GDP: the environment (climate, biodiversity), unpaid work, inequalities, etc., according to the principle 'beyond GDP: reconciling what counts and what is counted' (Thiry and Cassiers 2010). This project is then implicitly placed in the perspective (barely formalized as yet) of a sort of 'post-welfare' and 'post-Keynesian' state giving significant importance to a new, yet to be imagined type of statistics.[19] This state would focus more in particular on the conservation of nature and on moving beyond predatory and inegalitarian capitalism. The effects of feedback here could be of the macro-social type, as in the Keynesian state, or of the incentive type, as in the European OMC.

The apparent tension between these two critiques, one hostile to any form of commensuration, and the second calling for a form of commensuration appropriate for another form of governmentality, can be interpreted, in terms of moral philosophy, as an opposition between a *core ethical* principle and a *teleological* principle as stated in relation to issues about the allocation of scarce resources in health economics (Fagot-Largeault 1991). One (the core ethical one) posits that every person has a unique value, incommensurable with any other. The life of an old man cannot be balanced against the life of a young man. According to the other one (the teleological, or utilitarian), there is a common good that is superior to individuals, warranting decisions from the community, notably regarding the allocation of limited economic resources to potentially unlimited public health needs. The economism of neoliberalism may well push irrevocably toward the obviously justified second principle, but the first must ceaselessly be restated in its full legitimacy.

How can we resolve the contradiction between the statisticians' ethos and taking feedback into account, even when the latter seems to be no more than regrettable impediments to the mission of the former, which is supposed to 'provide unbiased reflections of reality'? It is impossible to isolate a moment in measurement that might be independent of its usages, and particularly of the conventions that are the first stage of quantification. The training of statisticians should be opened up to include elements of history, political science and the sociology of statistics, econometrics, probabilities, accounting and management. Such a programme, inspired by what has been learned from Science

---

[19] Gadrey and Jany-Catrice (2006) explicitly compare the current period with the 1950s, which in France gave birth to national accounting and the Keynesian and plan-based political project that went with it, vividly described by Fourquet (1980).

Studies (Pestre 2006), could make it easier to take quantitative tools into account in the social debates and avoid both their outright rejection and the unconditional and naive acceptance of 'facts that are incontestable because they are quantified'.

References

Armatte, Michel 1995. *Histoire du Modèle linéaire. Formes et usages en statistique et en économétrie jusqu'en 1945*, thèse. Paris: EHESS

Armatte, Michel and Amy Dahan Dalmedico 2004. 'Modèles et Modélisations (1950–2000): nouvelles pratiques, nouveaux enjeux', *Revue d'Histoire des Sciences* 57(2): 243–303

Austin, John L. 1962. *How to Do Things with Words*. Oxford: Clarendon

Bird, Sheila M. 2004. 'Editorial: Performance Monitoring in the Public Services', *Journal of the Royal Statistical Society* 167(3): 381–3

Blum, Alain and Martine Mespoulet 2003. *L'anarchie bureaucratique. Statistique et pouvoir sous Staline*. Paris: La Découverte

Boltanski, Luc and Eve Chiapello 2005. *The New Spirit of Capitalism*. London: Verso

Boskin, Michael J. *et al.* 1996. *Toward a More Accurate Measure of the Cost of Living, Final Report to the Senate Finance Committee*. Washington, D.C.: US Government Printing Office

Bowker, Geoffrey and Susan Leigh Star 1999. *Sorting Things Out: Classification and its Consequences*. Cambridge, Mass.: MIT Press

Brousse, Cécil 2005. 'Définir et compter les sans-abri en Europe: enjeux et controverses', *Genèses* 58: 48–71

Bruno, Isabelle 2008. 'La Recherche scientifique au crible du benchmarking. Petite histoire d'une technologie de gouvernement', *Revue d'histoire moderne et contemporaine* 5(55-4bis): 28–45

Bruno, Isabelle, Sophie Jacquot and Lou Mandin 2006. 'Europeanization through Its Instrumentation: Benchmarking, Mainstreaming and the Open Method of Coordination: Toolbox or Pandora's Box?', *Journal of European Public Policy* 13(4): 519–36

Burchell, Graham, Colin Gordon and Peter Miller 1991. *The Foucault Effect: Studies in Governmentality*. Chicago, Ill.: University of Chicago Press

Caldwell, Bruce 1997. 'Hayek and Socialism', *Journal of Economic Literature* 35(4): 1856–90

Callon, Michel 2007. 'What Does It Mean to Say that Economics is Performative?' in D. MacKenzie, F. Muniesa and L. Siu (eds.), *Do Economists Make Markets? On the Performativity of Economics*. Princeton, N.J.: Princeton University Press, pp. 311–57

Capron, Michel (ed.) 2005. *Les normes comptables internationales, instruments du capitalisme financier*. Paris: La Découverte

Cassiers, Isabelle and Geraldine Thiry 2014. *A High-Stakes Shift: Turning the Tide from GDP to New Prosperity Indicators*, IRES Discussion Paper 2014002. Louvain: Institut de Recherches Economiques et Sociales, Université catholique de Louvain

Chiapello, Eve and Alain Desrosières 2006. 'La quantification de l'économie et la recherche en sciences sociales: paradoxes, contradictions et omissions. Le cas exemplaire de la "Positive Accounting Theory"' in F. Eymard-Duvernay (ed.), *L'économie des conventions. Méthodes et résultats*, vol. 1, *Débats*. Paris: La Découverte, pp. 297–310

Chiapello, Eve and Karim Medjad 2009. 'An Unprecedented Privatisation of Mandatory Standard-setting: The Case of European Accounting Policy', *Critical Perspectives on Accounting* 20(4): 448–68

Chrystal K. Alex and Paul D. Mizen 2001. *Goodhart's Law: Its Origin, Meaning and Implications for Monetary Policy, Festschrift in Honour of Charles Goodhart*, 15–16 November, Bank of England

Dahan, Amy and Dominique Pestre 2004. *Les sciences pour la guerre. 1940–1960*. Paris: Éditions de l'EHESS

Dardot, Pierre and Christian Laval 2009. *La nouvelle raison du monde. Essai sur la société néolibérale*. Paris: La Découverte

Daston, Lorraine 1992. 'Objectivity and the Escape from Perspective', *Social Studies of Science* 22(4): 597–618

Dehousse, Renaud 2003. *The Open Method of Coordination: A New Policy Paradigm?*, Les Cahiers européens de Sciences Po 3

Desrosières, Alain 1998. *The Politics of Large Numbers: A History of Statistical Reasoning*. Cambridge, Mass.: Harvard University Press

2003. 'Managing the Economy' in T. Porter and D. Ross (eds.), *The Cambridge History of Science*, vol. 7, *The Modern Social Sciences*. Cambridge: Cambridge University Press, pp. 553–64

2007. 'Surveys Versus Administrative Records: Reflections on the Duality of Statistical Sources', *Courrier des statistiques* 13: 7–19

2008a. *Pour une sociologie historique de la quantification*. Paris: Presses de l'École des mines

2008b. *Gouverner par les nombres*. Paris: Presses de l'École des mines

Didier, Emmanuel 2009. *En quoi consiste l'Amérique? Les statistiques, le New Deal et la démocratie*. Paris: La Découverte

2012. 'Public Safety and Wall Street', *Limn* 2, http://limn.it/public-safety-and-wall-street/

Espeland, Wendy N. and Michael Sauder 2007. 'Rankings and Reactivity: How Public Measures Recreate Social Worlds', *American Journal of Sociology* 113(1): 1–40

Espeland, Wendy N. and Mitchell L. Stevens 1998. 'Commensuration as a Social Process', *Annual Review of Sociology* 24: 313–43

Fagot-Largeault, Ane 1991. 'Réflexions sur la notion de qualité de la vie', *Archives de philosophie du droit, Droit et Science* 36: 135–53

Foucault, Michel 2007. *Security, Territory, Population: Lectures at the Collége de France, 1977–78.* Basingstoke/New York: Palgrave Macmillan
2008. *The Birth of Biopolitics: Lectures at the Collège de France, 1978–1979.* New York: Palgrave Macmillan

Fourquet, François 1980. *Les comptes de la puissance. Histoire de la comptabilité nationale et du Plan.* Paris: Encres-Recherches

Gadrey, Jean J. and Florence Jany-Catrice 2006. *The New Indicators of Well-being and Development.* London: Palgrave Macmillan

Hood, Christopher 1995. 'Contemporary Public Management: A New Paradigm?', *Public Policy and Administration* 10(2): 104–17
2002. 'Control, Bargains, and Cheating: The Politics of Public-service Reform', *Journal of Public Administration Research and Theory* 12(3): 309–32

Hopwood, Anthony G. and Peter Miller (eds.) 1994. *Accounting as Social and Institutional Practice.* Cambridge: Cambridge University Press

Lascoumes, Pierre and Patrick Le Gales 2007. 'Understanding Public Policy through Its Instruments: From the Nature of Instruments to the Sociology of Public Policy Instrumentation', *Governance* 201: 1–21

Latour, Bruno 1988. *The Pasteurization of France.* Cambridge, Mass.: Harvard University Press

Le Gales, Patrick 2004. 'Contrôle et surveillance. La restructuration de l'État en Grande-Bretagne' in P. Lascoumes and P. Le Gales (eds.), *Gouverner par les instruments.* Paris: Presse de Sciences-Po, pp. 237–71

Lefrancq, Stéphane 2004. 'Recherche et action: la comptabilité dans son contexte. Une étude de la politique éditoriale d'Accounting Organizations dans Society', *Comptabilité Contrôle Audit* 10: 297–315

Lie, Einar 2002. 'The Rise and Fall of Sampling Methods in Norway 1875–1906', *Science in Context* 15(3): 385–409

Miller, Peter 1992. 'Accounting and Objectivity: The Invention of Calculating Selves and Calculable Spaces', *Annals of Scholarship* 9(1/2): 61–86

Miller, Peter and Ted O'Leary 1987. 'Accounting and the Construction of the Governable Person', *Accounting, Organizations and Society* 12(3): 235–65

Morgenstern, Oskar 1944/1963. *On the Accuracy of Economic Observations.* Princeton, N.J.: Princeton University Press

Nivière, Delphine 2005. 'Négocier une statistique européenne: le cas de la pauvreté', *Genèses* 58: 28–47

Pestre, Dominique 2006. *Introduction aux Science Studies.* Paris: La Découverte/Repères

Pezet, Eric (ed.) 2007. *Management et conduite de soi. Enquête sur les ascèses de la performance.* Paris: Vuibert

Polanyi, Karl 1944. *The Great Transformation: The Political and Economic Origins of Our Time*. Boston, N.J.: Beacon Hill

Porter, Theodore M. 1995. *Trust in Numbers: The Pursuit of Objectivity in Science and Public Life*. Princeton, N.J.: Princeton University Press

Power, Michael 1999. *The Audit Society: Rituals of Verification*. Oxford: Oxford University Press

2004. 'Counting, Control and Calculation: Reflections on Measuring and Management', *Human Relations* 57(6): 765–83

Prevost, Jean-Guy 2009. *A Total Science: Statistics in Liberal and Fascist Italy*. Quebec/Ontario: McGill Queens University Press

Salais, Robert 2004. 'La Politique des indicateurs. Du taux de chômage au taux d'emploi dans la stratégie européenne pour l'emploi (SEE)' in B. Zimmermann (ed.), *Action publique et sciences sociales*. Paris: MSH, pp. 287–331

Supiot, Alain 2010. *L'esprit de Philadelphie: la justice sociale face au marché total*. Paris: Seuil

Thévenot, Laurent 1984. 'Rules and Implements: Investments in Forms', *Social Science Information* 23(1): 1–45

Vanoli, André 2005. *A History of National Accounting*. Amsterdam: IOS Press

Watts, Ross L. and Jerold L. Zimmerman 1978. 'Towards a Positive Theory of the Determination of Accounting Standards', *Accounting Review* 53(1): 112–34

INDEX

CAMBRIDGE STUDIES IN LAW AND SOCIETY

The New World Trade Organization Knowledge Agreements:
2nd Edition
Christopher Arup

Justice and Reconciliation in Post-Apartheid South Africa
Edited by François du Bois and Antje du Bois-Pedain

Militarization and Violence against Women in Conflict Zones in the
Middle East:
A Palestinian Case-Study
Nadera Shalhoub-Kevorkian

Child Pornography and Sexual Grooming:
Legal and Societal Responses
Suzanne Ost

Darfur and the Crime of Genocide
John Hagan and Wenona Rymond-Richmond

Fictions of Justice:
*The International Criminal Court and the Challenge of Legal Pluralism in
Sub-Saharan Africa*
Kamari Maxine Clarke

Conducting Law and Society Research:
Reflections on Methods and Practices
Simon Halliday and Patrick Schmidt

Planted Flags:
Trees, Land, and Law in Israel/Palestine
Irus Braverman

Culture under Cross-Examination:
International Justice and the Special Court for Sierra Leone
Tim Kelsall

Cultures of Legality:
Judicialization and Political Activism in Latin America
Javier Couso, Alexandra Huneeus, Rachel Sieder

Courting Democracy in Bosnia and Herzegovina:
The Hague Tribunal's Impact in a Postwar State
Lara J. Nettelfield

The Gacaca Courts and Post-Genocide Justice and Reconciliation in
Rwanda:
Justice without Lawyers
Phil Clark

Law, Society, and History:
Themes in the Legal Sociology and Legal History of Lawrence M. Friedman
Robert W. Gordon and Morton J. Horwitz

After Abu Ghraib:
Exploring Human Rights in America and the Middle East
Shadi Mokhtari

Adjudication in Religious Family Laws:
Cultural Accommodation:
Legal Pluralism, and Gender Equality in India
Gopika Solanki

Water On Tap:
Rights and Regulation in the Transnational Governance of Urban Water Services
Bronwen Morgan

Elements of Moral Cognition:
Rawls' Linguistic Analogy and the Cognitive Science of Moral and Legal Judgment
John Mikhail

A Sociology of Constitutions:
Constitutions and State Legitimacy in Historical-Sociological Perspective
Chris Thornhill

Mitigation and Aggravation at Sentencing
Edited by Julian Roberts

Institutional Inequality and the Mobilization of the Family and Medical Leave Act:
Rights on Leave
Catherine R. Albiston

Authoritarian Rule of Law:
Legislation, Discourse and Legitimacy in Singapore
Jothie Rajah

Law and Development and the Global Discourses of Legal Transfers
Edited by John Gillespie and Pip Nicholson

Law against the State:
Ethnographic Forays into Law's Transformations
Edited by Julia Eckert, Brian Donahoe, Christian Strümpell and Zerrin Özlem Biner